World Philosophy

A Text with Readings

World Philosophy

A Text with Readings

EDITED BY

Robert C. Solomon
University of Texas at Austin

Kathleen M. Higgins
University of Texas at Austin

Boston, Massachusetts   Burr Ridge, Illinois   Dubuque, Iowa
Madison, Wisconsin   New York, New York   San Francisco, California
St. Louis, Missouri

McGraw-Hill

*A Division of The **McGraw·Hill** Companies*

This book was set in Palatino by ComCom, Inc.
The editors were Judith R. Cornwell and Tom Holton;
the production supervisor was Denise L. Puryear.
The cover was designed by Wanda Siedlecka.
R. R. Donnelley & Sons Company was printer and binder.

Cover Art
The Babylonian Map of the World,
probably composed in about 700 B.C.
Source: The Bridgeman Art Library, London

WORLD PHILOSOPHY
A Text with Readings

This book is printed on acid-free paper.

7 8 9 0   DOC/DOC   9 0 9 8 7 6 5 4 3 2 1

ISBN 0-07-059674-3

Library of Congress Cataloging-in-Publication Data

World philosophy: a text with readings / edited by Robert C. Solomon
and Kathleen M. Higgins.
p.   cm.
Includes bibliographical references and index.
ISBN 0-07-059674-3
1. Philosophy—Introductions.   I. Solomon, Robert C.
II. Higgins, Kathleen Marie.
BD21.W67   1995
109—dc20   94-31513

http://www.mhhe.com

Instead of a dedication, a vision:
the philosophers of the world,
listening and appreciating their differences

Contents in Brief

Contents

Timeline

Zoroaster (660–583 B.C.E.)
Thales (ca. 640–546 B.C.E.)
Pythagoras (ca. 581–507 B.C.E.)
Heraclitus (ca. 535–470 B.C.E.)
Lao-tzu (570–510 B.C.E.)
Pythagoras (571–497 B.C.E.)
Confucius (551–479 B.C.E.)
Siddhartha Gautama (Buddha) (566–486 B.C.E.)
Heraclitus (536–470 B.C.E.)
Parmenides (fl. 500–450 B.C.E.)
Zeno of Elea (fl. 475 B.C.E.)
Socrates (469–399 B.C.E.)
Plato (427–347 B.C.E.)
Chuang-tzu (4th century B.C.E.)
Aristotle (384–322 B.C.E.)
Mencius (372?–289? B.C.E.)
Epicurus (341–277 B.C.E.)
Hsün Tzu (ca. 298–230 B.C.E.)
Huai-nan Tzu (f. 140 B.C.E.)
Philo (fl. 20 B.C.–50 C.E.)
Jesus Christ (ca. 5 B.C.E.–30 C.E.)
St. Paul (ca. 10–65)
Galen (ca. 130–200)
Nāgārjuna (ca. 2nd century)
Plotinus (ca. 205–270)
Wang Pi (226–249)
Mani (3d century)
St. Augustine (354–430)
Mohammed (ca. 570–632)

al-Kindī (ca. 800–866)
Jalaluddin Rumi (d. 922)
al-Rāzī (Rhazes) (865–c. 925)
al-Fārābī (ca. 870–950)
Sei Shōnagon (b. 966)
Yahya ibn ʿAdi (d. 972)
Ibn Sīnā, or Avicenna (980–1037)
St. Anselm (ca. 1033–1109)
al-Suhrawardi (d. ca. 1191)
Ibn Rushd, or Averroës (1126–1198)
Moses Maimonides (1135–1204)
Dōgen (1200–1253)
Thomas Aquinas (1224–1274)
Martin Luther (1483–1546)
John Calvin (1509–1564)
Mulla Sadra (Sadra al-Din Shirazi) (ca. 1571–1641)
Takuan Sōhō (1573–1645)
Thomas Hobbes (1588–1679)
René Descartes (1596–1650)
Baruch Spinoza (1632–1677)
John Locke (1632–1704)
Hakuin Ekaku (1685–1768)
David Hume (1711–1776)
Jean-Jacques Rousseau (1712–1778)
Immanuel Kant (1724–1804)
Moses Mendelssohn (1729–1786)
Georg Wilhelm Friedrich Hegel (1770–1831)
Søren Kierkegaard (1813–1855)
Karl Marx (1818–1883)
Friedrich Engels (1820–1895)
William James (1842–1910)
Friedrich Nietzsche (1844–1900)
John Dewey (1859–1952)
Black Elk (1863–1950)
Kitaro Nishida (1870–1945)
Ghose Aurobindo (1872–1950)
Martin Buber (1878–1965)
Martin Heidegger (1889–1976)
Mao Tse-tung (1893–1976)
Keiji Nishitani (b. 1900)

Lame Deer (1903–1984)
Jean-Paul Sartre (1905–1980)
Léopold Sédar Senghor (b. 1906)
Simone de Beauvoir (1908–1986)
Kwame Nkrumah (1909–1972)
Octavio Paz (b. 1914)
Frantz Fanon (1925–1961)

Syllabus for a World Civilization Course

I. Mythic Time and Everyday Life

AFRICA (CHAPTER 8)

Ethnophilosophy

 Placide Franz Tempels, from Bantu Philosophy
 Léopold Sédar Senghor, from "On Negrohood"

INDIA (CHAPTER 3)

 From the Ṛg Veda (1200–900 B.C.E., excluding tenth book)
 From the *Upanishads* (early: 800–300 B.C.E.; middle and late: ca. 300 B.C.E.–1500 C.E.)

NORTH AMERICA (CHAPTER 6)

 "The Woman Who Married a Beaver" (Traditional Ojibwa Tale)
 "The Moose and His Offspring" (Traditional Ojibwa Tale)

LATIN AMERICA (CHAPTER 7)

 Miguel León-Portilla, from *Aztec Thought and Culture*

CHINA (CHAPTER 2)

 From the *I Ching (The Book of Changes)* (perhaps from fifth to sixth and third to fourth centuries B.C.E.)
 Wang Pi (226–249) *Commentary on the Book of Changes*

II. The Axial Period

III. Religious Innovations

AFRICA AND THE MIDDLE EAST (CHAPTER 9)

Christianity

Jesus Christ (ca. 5 B.C.E.–30 C.E.)
St. Augustine (345–430), from *Confessions*

PERSIA (CHAPTER 5)

Manichaeism

From *Fihrist-al-Nadim* (tenth-century Muslim chronicle)

Mazdakism (fifth to sixth century)

Islam

Mohammed (ca. 570–632)
The Shi'ites
Nasir-i Khusraw, from "Speech"
Nasir-i Khusraw, from "Free Will and Determination"

IV. Philosophical Reconstructions of Tradition

INDIA (CHAPTER 3)

Nāgārjuna (150 C.E.), from "Averting the Arguments"
Nyāya-sūtra (ca. 200 C.E.)
From Mādhava's Philosophic Compendium: Cārvāka
(ca. 750 C.E.)

EUROPE (CHAPTER 9)

Scholasticism

St. Anselm (ca. 1033–1109), from *Proslogion*
St. Thomas Aquinas (1224–1274), from *Summa Theologica*

Rationalism

René Descartes (1596–1650), from *Meditations on First Philosophy*
René Descartes, from *Discourse on Method*

British Social Philosophy and Empiricism

Thomas Hobbes (1588–1679), from *Leviathan*

John Locke (1632–1704)
David Hume (1711–1776), from *Treatise of Human Nature*

Reformation

Martin Luther (1483–1546)
John Calvin (1509–1564)

Enlightenment

Jean-Jacques Rousseau (1712–1778), from *On the Social Contract*
Immanuel Kant (1724–1804), from *Prolegomena to Any Future Metaphysics That Will Be Able to Come Forward as Science*
Immanuel Kant, from *Grounding for the Metaphysics of Morals*

Religious Existentialism

Søren Kierkegaard (1813–1855)

ARABIC WORLD (CHAPTER 4)

al-Kindī (ca. 800–866), "On God"
al-Rāzī (865–ca. 925), "On Reason"
al-Fārābī (870–950), "On Hierarchies of Existence"
al-Fārābī, "On Aristotle's *De Interpretatione*"
Yuhyā ibn ʿAdī (d. 972), "On Cultivation of Character"
from Ibn Sīnā (980–1037), from *Autobiography*
Ibn Sīnā, "On the Soul"
Moses Maimonides (1135–1204), from *Guide for the Perplexed*
Ibn Rushd (Averroës) (1126–1198), "On Creation"

PERSIA (CHAPTER 5)

The Shi'ites

Nasir-i Khusraw, from "Speech"
Nasir-i Khusraw, from "Free Will and Determination"

SUFI POETRY (LATE MIDDLE AGES)

Jalaluddin Rumi (d. 922), *Divan a Shamsi-Tabriz*
from 'Attar (d. ca. 1230), "The Dullard Sage"

from Forughi's "Lover's Craft"
from Savaji's, "The Drunken Universe"
from Hashemi's, "The Tale of the Uniquely Beautiful
Mirror Maker"
from Rumi's *The Mathnawi*
Rhazes (eighth century), "Rhazes on the Philosophic
Life"
Jalaluddin Rumi (d. 922), from *Discourses*
Yahya Suhrawardi (d. 1191), from "The Sound of
Gabriel's Wing"
Yahya Suhrawardi, from "A Tale of Occidental Exile"
Mulla Sadra (1571–1641), from *The Wisdom of the Throne*

JAPAN (CHAPTER 1)

Sei Shōnagon (b. 966), from *The Pillow Book of Sei
Shōnagon*
Dōgen Kigen (1200–1253) (Sōtō School of Zen), from
Shōbōgenzō-Zuimonki
Rinzai Zen (beginning 1101)
Hakuin Ekaku (1685–1768) (Rinzai revival), from *The
Zen Master Hakuin*
The Unfettered Mind: Takuan Sōhō (1573–1645) (Rinzai
Zen), from *The Unfettered Mind*
Dōgen (1200–1253)

V. Secular Revolutions

EUROPE (CHAPTER 9)

G. W. F. Hegel (1770–1831), from *The Phenomenology of
Spirit*
Karl Marx (1818–1883)
Friedrich Nietzsche (1844–1900), from *Thus Spoke
Zarathustra*
Simone de Beauvoir (1908–1986)

JAPAN (CHAPTER 1)

*Kyoto school
Nishitani Keiji (b. 1900), from "The Japanese Art of
Arranged Flowers"*

CHINA (CHAPTER 2)

Mao Tse-tung (1893–1976), "On Contradiction"

INDIA (CHAPTER 3)

Sri Aurobindo (1872–1950), from The Life Divine

AFRICA (CHAPTER 8)

Professional Philosophy

Paulin J. Hountondji, "African Philosophy: Myth and Reality"
Theophilus Okere, *African Philosophy: A Historico-Hermeneutical Investigation of the Conditions of Its Possibility*

Philosophic Sagacity

Henry Odera Oruka, "Sagacity in African Philosophy"
J. O. Sopido and Barry Hallen, *Knowledge, Belief, and Witchcraft*

Nationalistic-Ideological Philosophy

Frantz Fanon (1925–1961), "Concerning Violence"
Kwame Nkrumah (1909–1972), *Consciencism*

NORTH AMERICA (CHAPTER 6)

Black Elk (1863–1950), from John G. Neihardt, *Black Elk Speaks: Being the Life Story of a Holy Man of the Oglala Sioux*
John (Fire) Lame Deer (1903–1984), from Lame Deer and Richard Erdoes, *Lame Deer: Seeker of Visions*
N. Scott Momaday, "A First American Views His Land"

LATIN AMERICA (CHAPTER 7)

Octavio Paz (b. 1914), from *The Labyrinth of Solitude*
Augusto Salazar Bondy, from *The Meaning and Problem of Hispanic American Thought*
Gustavo Gutierrez, from *The Power of the Poor in History*

Preface

World Philosophy: A Text with Readings is an introduction to some of the great philosophical traditions of the world, both Western and non-Western. In every culture, philosophy is an intellectual adventure, an exploration, a distinctively human attempt to understand and deal with the world in one's own terms, to discern some meaning and order in the contingencies and mysteries of life. Looked at collectively, the various philosophies of the world provide a fascinating perspective on the very different ways that people do and have done this, most of them believing, sometimes belligerently, that their way is the best or the only way. In this book, we want to encourage an open-minded appreciation of the rich variety of philosophical traditions.

Until very recently, however, most introductory philosophy courses focused exclusively on that more or less singular Western tradition that begins in ancient Greece with Socrates, Plato, and Aristotle, proceeds through medieval Europe, the Enlightenment, and then modern times, mainly in England, France, and Germany. The philosophical legacies of Asia and the Middle East, which have been powerful influences on the development of Western thinking and without which many of the classics of the Western tradition would not have survived, have been all but ignored. So, too, the complex oral traditions of Africa and the Americas are all but totally ignored by the standard studies of philosophy, in part because these have been devastated by European colonialism but also because they seem so different in kind from mainstream philosophical discourse in Europe.

"World philosophy" is a conception of philosophy that takes into account the great variety of philosophies and philosophical types and styles around the globe without trying to give special sta-

80°N

KALAALLIT NUNAAT
(DEN.)

ICELAND

ALASKA
(U.S.)

60°N

CANADA

UNITED
KINGDOM

IRELAND

FR

40°N

UNITED STATES

PORTUGAL

AZORES
(PORT.)

ATLANTIC

MADEIRA IS.
(PORT.)

Tropic of Cancer

MEXICO

CANARY IS.
(SP.)

WESTERN SAHARA
(MOR.)

HAWAII (U.S.)

BAHAMAS

20°N

CUBA

DOMINICAN
REPUBLIC

27

29

MAURITANIA

HAITI

BELIZE
GUATEMALA HONDURAS
EL SALVADOR NICARAGUA
COSTA RICA

JAMAICA

28

30
31
32
33
34

CAPE
VERDE SENEGAL
GAMBIA
GUINEA BISSAU GUINEA

PACIFIC

GRENADA

SIERRA
LEONE LIBERIA

PANAMA

VENEZUELA

GUYANA
SURINAME
FRENCH GUIANA (FR.)

CÔTE
D'IVOI

COLOMBIA

OCEAN

EQUATOR

GALÁPAGOS IS.
(EC.)

ECUADOR

OCEAN

KIRIBATI

PERU

BRAZIL

WESTERN
SAMOA AMERICAN
SAMOA (U.S.)

BOLIVIA

OCEAN

TONGA

FRENCH POLYNESIA
(FR.)

20°S

PARAGUAY

Tropic of Capricorn

CHILE

40°S

ARGENTINA URUGUAY

60°S

FALKLAND IS. (U.K.)

80°S

160°W 140°W 120°W 100°W 80°W 60°W 40°W 20°W

0   1000   2000 Miles

0   1000   2000 Kilometers

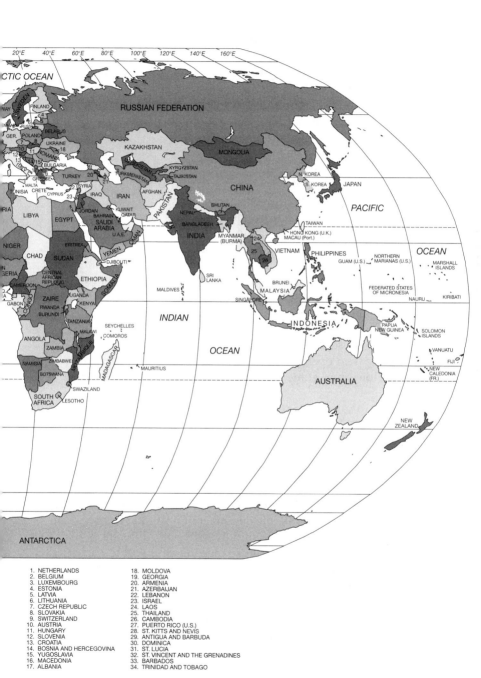

20°E 40°E 60°E 80°E 100°E 120°E 140°E 160°E

CTIC OCEAN

RUSSIAN FEDERATION

NAY FINLAND

GER. POLAND BELARUS

UKRAINE KAZAKHSTAN

ROMANIA MONGOLIA

13 BULGARIA KYRGYZSTAN

14 15 TURKEY 20 TURKMENISTAN TAJIKISTAN

MALTA CRETE CYPRUS 23 IRAQ IRAN AFGHAN. CHINA

TUNISIA SYRIA

RIA LIBYA EGYPT JORDAN BAHRAIN KUWAIT QATAR NEPAL BHUTAN N. KOREA JAPAN

SAUDI ARABIA U.A.E. OMAN BANGLADESH S. KOREA

NIGER CHAD SUDAN ERITREA YEMEN INDIA MYANMAR (BURMA) TAIWAN PACIFIC

ERIA DJIBOUTI HONG KONG (U.K.) MACAU (Port.)

CENTRAL AFRICAN REPUBLIC ETHIOPIA SRI VIETNAM PHILIPPINES OCEAN

CAMEROON MALDIVES LANKA GUAM (U.S.) NORTHERN MARIANAS (U.S.) MARSHALL ISLANDS

ZAIRE UGANDA KENYA BRUNEI

GABON RWANDA BURUNDI SOMALIA MALAYSIA FEDERATED STATES OF MICRONESIA NAURU KIRIBATI

TANZANIA SINGAPORE

SEYCHELLES INDIAN INDONESIA PAPUA NEW GUINEA SOLOMON ISLANDS

MALAWI COMOROS

ANGOLA ZAMBIA OCEAN VANUATU

ZIMBABWE NEW CALEDONIA (Fr.) FIJI

NAMIBIA MADAGASCAR MAURITIUS AUSTRALIA

BOTSWANA

SWAZILAND

SOUTH AFRICA LESOTHO NEW ZEALAND

ANTARCTICA

1. NETHERLANDS
2. BELGIUM
3. LUXEMBOURG
4. ESTONIA
5. LATVIA
6. LITHUANIA
7. CZECH REPUBLIC
8. SLOVAKIA
9. SWITZERLAND
10. AUSTRIA
11. HUNGARY
12. SLOVENIA
13. CROATIA
14. BOSNIA AND HERCEGOVINA
15. YUGOSLAVIA
16. MACEDONIA
17. ALBANIA

18. MOLDOVA
19. GEORGIA
20. ARMENIA
21. AZERBAIJAN
22. LEBANON
23. ISRAEL
24. LAOS
25. THAILAND
26. CAMBODIA
27. PUERTO RICO (U.S.)
28. ST. KITTS AND NEVIS
29. ANTIGUA AND BARBUDA
30. DOMINICA
31. ST. LUCIA
32. ST. VINCENT AND THE GRENADINES
33. BARBADOS
34. TRINIDAD AND TOBAGO

tus to any one of them. This book attempts to exemplify such a conception and thus expand the idea of introductory philosophy. In a world (and a country) defined by multiculturalism, it is more important than ever to appreciate the rich legacies of many traditions. *World Philosophy: A Text with Readings* is intended to provide an introduction with readings from original sources to nine of the world's philosophical traditions, including Western philosophy, viewed here as a single tradition.

There are, of course, many more traditions, both within the so-called Western tradition and in cultures of the world not covered or given their own chapter in this book. We considered including chapters on Jewish and Russian philosophy, for example, but we ultimately incorporated them only briefly in the Western philosophy chapter. Chinese and Indian philosophy are in fact both mixtures of dozens of different philosophies, and African and Native American philosophies, of course, number in the hundreds if not the thousands. There is much room for debate about what we have included, what we have not included, and what we ought to have included, but our intention has been to open the field, not to cover it. Thus we have tried to provide a substantial if brief introduction to world philosophy, but we do not for a moment pretend to have done more than open doors and offer the reader a peek at some fascinating ideas and some encouragement to explore these traditions further.

Inevitably, a student entering into one of these traditions for the first time will be tempted to assimilate new ideas and unfamiliar thinkers with Western ideas and authors with whom he or she is already comfortable, and this is unavoidable. At the same time, however, it is essential to pay attention to the differences, in style as well as in substance, and while it might be desirable to be able to encompass all of the philosophies in the world under some single umbrella or to fit them all into a number of neat little categories, it is more valuable to appreciate the diversity and differences than to force foreign ideas into domestic pigeonholes. Within each tradition, it is important to take what has been called a "holistic" or "systems" approach, that is, to not pull this or that interesting idea out of context but to appreciate the shape and direction of a whole set of ideas together with the overall contours of the culture.

Each chapter has been prepared by a leading scholar in the area.

The book does not presuppose either prior study of philosophy or of the cultures in question. The chapters are self-contained, so that they can be used in any order or can be used selectively, as a supplemental text. Technical jargon has been kept to a minimum, and exotic language has been introduced only where it is informative and helpful in understanding a particular culture. Each chapter has a glossary, as well as suggestions for further reading. The chapters will vary in organization and emphasis. We would not want to present an oral, folk-philosophical tradition in the same form and under the same categories ("epistemology," "ethics," etc.) that one might present a self-consciously historical, written tradition. There are chapters on philosophy in Africa, China, Japan, Native America, Latin America, Arabia, Persia, and India as well as an introduction to Western philosophy. Again, this list is not meant to be all-inclusive, we must emphasize, and there are many other traditions that may be equally worth studying. And, again, what we have presented as a single tradition is often, as the chapters make clear, a variety of different traditions. There are many African, Latin American, and Native American Indian tribes, and they are by no means all the same. India, China, Persia, and Japan are rich amalgams of many different philosophical traditions, and even Western philosophy is by no means so uniform as the standard introductory textbooks make it out to be. But by providing a taste of the profound richess of world philosophy, we hope to stimulate both students and their teachers to look further again, to seek out those many voices which have much to say but have been neglected or denied an adequate hearing. What we have tried to do is to provide a "taste" of the traditions and classics of world philosophy with the hope that many students (and their instructors) will be encouraged to seek out much more.

For their help and advice, we would like to thank Linda A. Bell, Georgia State University; Inga Clendinnen, LaTrobe University, Australia; Mary Ann Cutter, University of Colorado; Robert Gooding-Williams, Amherst College; Burton G. Hurdle, Virginia State University; Laura Lyn Inglis, Buena Vista College; Robert McDermott, Institute for Integral Studies; Ann Mahoney, Mesa Community College; Fedwa Malti-Douglas, University of Indiana; Lucius Outlaw, Haverford College; Douglas W. Shrader, SUNY–Oneonta; Jay M. Van Hook, Northwestern College; Paul Woodruff,

University of Texas; and Cynthia Ward at McGraw-Hill. We would also like to thank all of the contributors to the book for their special patience and dedication to the project.

Robert C. Solomon

Kathleen M. Higgins

Introduction

It is the presupposition of this book that virtually every society, every civilization, has its philosophy or philosophies. These philosophies differ from culture to culture, needless to say, but perhaps just as profound is the fact that the expressions of philosophy vary as well. In the pages that follow, the reader will find all sorts of arguments, allegories, metaphors, folk tales, religious appeals, questions and quandries, declarations and warnings, expressions of devotion and indignation, descriptions of atrocities and ecstasies. Some traditions, notably in Europe, in the Middle East, and in India and China, have long written histories and classic as well as sacred texts. These philosophical traditions consist, accordingly, of a great deal of commentary and interpretation. It has been said that all of Western philosophy is a footnote to Plato, and the long philosophical traditions of Confucianism, Buddhism, and Islam consist largely of reflection and debate concerning the original texts or pronouncements of Confucius, the Buddha, and the Qur'an, respectively. Other traditions, including much of early Greek philosophy, are expressed in poetry, folktales, and in oral traditions passed along from generation to generation by sages and wise men and women.

WHAT IS PHILOSOPHY?

The word "philosophy" means, literally, "the love of wisdom," but what this involves is itself open to debate and interpretation. For the purpose of this book, it is essential that we keep in mind that philosophy has been conceived and practiced in many different ways, under a variety of names as well, in many different languages, cultures, and societies. All philosophies, one might suggest, are thoughtful and creative responses to the exigencies of life, the limits of our knowledge of the world, and our mutual necessity of living together. At the very least, philosophy would seem to involve thought and reflection, but philosophy as such does not always require or even allow the rigorous criticism and extensive argumentation and proof that now forms the core of so much of the philosophy in the Anglo-American tradition. Perhaps it is enough that one has a sense of wonder—as Aristotle once defined philosophy—that one asks certain kinds of questions, questions about the ultimate nature of the world and about what might be beyond the world, questions about the purpose and value of human life and what it means for one's life to come to an end, questions about the nature of society and one's place within it.

Philosophy has as its immediate neighbors science, religion, mythology, and politics. Philosophy and its questions have been embedded in all sorts of different creative human activities, not only in myth and religion but in certain rituals, in art, and science. In all of these creative activities, we can come to appreciate the excitement of the human adventure. What is distinctive about philosophy is that it involves articulation, an attempt to understand not only the details but the "big picture," the nature and origins of the universe, the nature of "human nature" and the proper workings of society. But philosophy is not (usually) just a sequence of insights; it is an attempt to work out a coherent picture, a scheme, a system of insights about the world and ourselves. Such a scheme would likely include some sense of personal identity, of proper relations between people, of the nature of society, of the nature of ultimate reality, of the existence and nature of God or gods or spirits. A philosophy would tell us something about who we are, what we can know about the world, and what we can hope for. Ideally, people who have a philosophy also manage to live by it, doing what they say as well as making pronouncements. Thus practices and rituals may not only be the expressions of a philosophy but an essential part of it.

There are many meanings of the word "philosophy." From our brief description above, it is only to be expected that in some societies, philosophy will overlap with science; in others, religion or politics. In some, it will include and at times conflict with all of the above. Thus it is understandable, if misguided, that some philosophers in the Western academic context attempt to define philosophy in some narrow and specific way. Some philosophers would insist that philosophy is logic and argument, while others would say that philosophy is imaginative vision, or religion articulated. Some philosophers insist that philosophy is social and political criticism or the articulation of a personal outlook or worldview. Still others, less committal, insist that philosophy is nothing but, in Michael Oakshott's memorable phrase, "the conversation of mankind." But it is not at all clear that humanity has been having a single conversation. Once we step outside of the university, the conversation starts to sound very different, and the word "philosophy" takes on all sorts of broader meanings. Definitions of philosophy that would limit its practice to a few thousand professors and students in Europe and North America are inappropriate.

Turning to other cultures, the question, What is philosophy? takes on new meaning and produces new dangers. It is sometimes said that philosophy is a uniquely Western invention, although with some qualification the word may be extended to the cultures of India, which did in fact produce theories of knowledge and display a concern with formal logic that is readily recognized even if still foreign to Western professional philosophers. But this narrow, ethnocentric view is demeaning as well as stultifying. Conceived of as a general outlook on the world, a worldview that is motivated by a number of basic questions about the human condition, it is quite evident that every culture has its philosophy or philosophies. Not all philosophies are fully articulated, much less so literal-minded and argumentative as many American philosophy professors would require. In Japan, for instance, the word for philosophy, *tetsugaku*, refers to Western philosophy, while their own discursive practices do not get a special name or get taught in a specially designated set of courses. Japan is a thoughtful society, steeped in wisdom, but this wisdom may be more evident in their daily activities than in any particular philosophical books. So, too, some philosophies celebrate wordless intuition, while others produce their philosophies in song, poetry, or riddles. Indeed, the greatest philosophies of the West (the philosophies of Plato and Kant, for example) often turn on metaphors that are extremely difficult to render in literal terms.

Since ancient times, philosophers have suggested, when they have not asserted outright, that philosophy is an activity which is both peculiar and essential to "man." But just as that masculine noun suggests a slight to one sex, it no less subtly implies a slight to other cultures, those whom the Greeks called "barbarians," who

Explain

Are there
Any women philosophers?

were not interested in the rigors of dialectical thought and argument practiced by a small number of eccentrics in Athens and Asia Minor. The Chinese, by way of contrast, experienced a brief period of such philosophical "disputation" but found it disharmonious and most unpleasant, and it disappeared from view some 2,000 years ago. Socrates famously insisted that "the unexamined life is not worth living." That is to say, you are inferior if not worthless if you do not hold your life and your opinions open to criticism, if you do not challenge the views with which you have been raised, including the politics and the religion of your tradition. But do we really want to insist that this sort of challenge to authority is an essential part of philosophy, much less an essential part of what it means to be human? In many cultures, the authority of the Scriptures, or of one's ancestors, or of the chief is such that a challenge or any request for further proof is considered wholly inappropriate. Indeed, even in the West, criticism has its limits. For several centuries, biblical criticism frequently ended with excommunication or even death. And in the modern university, philosophers who raise the wrong questions often do not get tenure.

The question, What is philosophy? has become particularly pressing in the context of world philosophy, where the dispute over what counts as philosophy and what does not has moved far beyond the localized battles between one sort of European philosophy and another to the question of philosophy as such. In African philosophy, for example, there is vigorous debate whether the predominantly oral and mythological folk traditions of many African peoples should count as philosophy at all. The view that philosophy proper should be limited to the sorts of inquiry found in the Western university is by no means limited just to those American and European philosophers who view such folk traditions as foreign to their own. Yet why should what is "universalistic"—which often refers to a philosophy's pretensions rather than its actual scope—be considered as the test of a true philosophy? Indeed, as certain African philosophers argue, isn't the fact that philosophy tends to be so much the same all over the globe due to the long presence of colonialism, which established philosophy in the universities explicitly along the lines of what was being studied in Europe. The professors who taught in these colonial universities were trained at Oxford and Cambridge, at the Sorbonne and at Heidelberg. This doesn't seem to say very much about the nature of philosophy as such, except to say that the dominant culture typically determines the acceptable conception of philosophy, along with so much else. That makes it all the more important to try to recapture other traditions, which have not found their way or have been ignored in the established philosophy curriculum.

PHILOSOPHY, SCIENCE, MYTH, AND RELIGION

From the Western standpoint, it is important to draw some distinction between philosophy and myth, for it is out of myth that the philosophy of Greece, in particular, is said to emerge and it is the difference between them that marks the end of one era and the beginning of another. That difference, as it is usually stated, has to do with the mythological emphasis on anthropomorphism—the projection of human form and personality onto nonhuman natural forces—as opposed to the hard-headed literalness of philosophy. Thus the ancient Greeks, and before them the Egyptians, explained the universe in terms of the actions and emotions of gods and goddesses and other spirits; but beginning with Thales and the first Greek philosophers, the explanations became more scientific, more materialistic, with an emphasis on matter and causes rather than spirits behind the scenes.

This view does not, however, hold up to scrutiny. The first Greek philosophers were often steeped in mythology as well as the new philosophy, and some of the greatest breakthroughs in philosophy—in Pythagoras and Plato, for example—involved the rejection of materialist explanations of the world. To be sure, the origins of philosophy in Greece were also the origins of Western science, but philosophy is not science (at least not exclusively), and mythology—the endowing of the cosmos with personality as well as rational explicability—continues in philosophy to this day.

So what is the distinction between philosophy and myth if it is not the distinction between science and superstition, between the figurative and the literal, between the material and the spiritual? It is probably a mistake to put too much weight on these distinctions, but there is a difference between the populated narratives of myth which "explain" a particular phenomenon and the close attention to the systematic nature of the concepts that make up a philosophy. A narrative can turn on a whim of the gods, but a philosophy appeals to

If Greece can start philosophy with mythology then why can't africa.

durable if not eternal principles. A good narrative may obey the laws of (human) psychology, but philosophy has a "logic." A narrative can embrace contradictions and even absurdities, and these add charm rather than subtract credibility. A philosophy, however, incorporates contradictions and incoherence at its considerable peril, and most philosophers of every culture are anxious to avoid them, even when (like the German philosopher Nietzsche and some great philosophers of the Zen tradition) they court and even encourage contradiction and incoherence as an essential part of both life and any philosophy that describes life comprehensively. When we read or listen to the telling of a myth, our suspenseful reaction is, What then? When we read or talk philosophy, our reaction is rather, How does that fit in? Myth leads to edification and philosophy to understanding, although the best myths, like the best philosophy, do both.

So, too, one should carefully consider the relationship between religion and philosophy. Some of the ancient Greeks cautiously separated religion and philosophy, but for most of the past 2,000 years Western philosophy has been inseparable from the Judeo-Christian tradition, even in the case of those philosophers who spend their lives attacking that tradition. It is only in the past 200 years that many American and some European philosophers have separated the two, and in many other cultures, the identity of religion and philosophy remains entirely intact. In many societies, including most tribal cultures, the religion defines the philosophy. In others, the philosophy defines the religion, notably in Confucianism and Buddhism, which are both nontheistic religions, religions without a God. One might try to distinguish religion and philosophy according to the fuzzy demarcation between myth and philosophy, but this often means misunderstanding religion. To be sure, philosophy can play a considerable role beyond the bounds of religion, but it is a mistake to conclude that religion, theology, and religious philosophy—as opposed to the more secular and critical philosophy of religion—lies outside the bounds of philosophy.

One should also carefully consider the relation between science and philosophy and take care that in trying to distinguish philosophy from religion one does not hastily conclude that if philosophy is not religion then it must be science or, at least, scientific. There is much to think about in life—one's personal and social identity, our relationships with others, and even the wonders of nature—which are not necessarily either science or religion. Indeed, the modern idea that philosophy ought to be scientific is only a few hundred

How has the western world seperated from religion + philosophy it all leads back to religion?

years old, mainly a product of the European Enlightenment. It has been fought tooth and nail every inch of the way, and most other cultures are not particularly concerned with this idea—which is emphatically not to say that they are unenlightened. What about ritual and philosophy? Do nonverbal actions and practices count as reflection, as thought, as philosophy? The obvious answer seems to be yes, when they are reflective and thoughtful. But even that requires some qualification. Many modes of meditation eschew thought and do not encourage reflection as such. Yet they do provide experiences that are themselves insightful and thought-provoking, and to that extent, at least, they are clearly philosophical. Indian yoga is an excellent example, and the dances of many peoples have a profound philosophical significance. In Chinese philosophy, ritual is an essential part of philosophy. We in the West usually think of philosophy as an extremely argumentative, critical, "dialectical" enterprise, in which disagreement is essential. But a philosophy may also be an established tradition of agreed-upon ideas, an outlook that is shared, a way of living. Philosophy can be authoritarian as well as argumentative, devout as well as dialectical, and while we might agree and argue vigorously for the importance of freedom of thought and freedom of speech (which do not always go together), these are not necessary for a culture to be philosophical.

It is tempting to make a distinction between philosophy and anthropology in these matters, insisting, for example, that metaphysics is philosophy but folktales and myths are more properly the subject of anthropology. It is important, however, to beware of the prejudice that resides in that distinction. Philosophy is a people's own expression of their values and beliefs. Anthropology is the description of those values and beliefs by others, typically in the name of "science." It relegates the people described to the status of objects of study, and sometimes as mere curiosities. The difference between taking ideas seriously *as ideas* and simply entertaining them as folk products, like masks, pots, and strange superstitions, is enormous. Granting them the word "philosophy" may mean the difference between taking people's ideas seriously and just looking at their different ideas as mere oddities without the need to debate or evaluate them.

Laurence Thomas has written of the importance of what he calls "group autonomy" to the self-esteem of a culture. He suggests that one of the reasons why the Jewish people have survived over 5,000 years of persecution and pogroms is the fact that they had such autonomy—the autonomy to describe and define themselves in their own terms and from their own perspective. African Americans, by contrast, have long been described and defined by others, first as slaves, more recently in terms of sociology and the "problem of race." Thus African and African American philosophy is important, not just as another "point of view" but as a vehicle of self-definition. Having been defined almost wholly by others, the loss in terms of a shared sense of self is incalculable. Having a philosophy and being fully recognized as having one is not only one of the earmarks of the intellectual health of a people but an essential ingredient in their conception of themselves. Being denied a philosophy and being merely described by others, as part of anthropology rather than philosophy, is another backhanded way of being denied group autonomy. Denying that another culture's ideas are a "philosophy" is rejecting the legitimacy of others' beliefs and values, their ideas about life and how to live, about nature and its ways. Just because these ideas are not "scientific" in form does not mean that they are not philosophy.

So, what is philosophy? It has not been our intention to provide a rigorous definition or to suggest lines of demarcation between philosophy and myth, religion, science, or nonverbal practices. Indeed, it has been our whole intention here in this introduction to soften those distinctions and reject those narrowly Western definitions of philosophy that celebrate logic and argument to the exclusion of more sociable and spiritual beliefs and concerns. To understand the breadth and scope of philosophy in the world, it is essential that we open up our expectations, loosen our demands for logic and literalness, and lighten up on our sometimes too demanding insistence on "the truth and nothing but the truth." We will find philosophy wherever we find human beings living thoughtfully, and to understand the many traditions of thought that they have evolved means, first of all, not assuming that all of those thoughts and the systems of which they are an integral part are the same.

"WESTERN" AND "NON-WESTERN" PHILOSOPHY

What is the "West"? In our discussion of the nature of philosophy, we have referred rather casually to "Western" philosophy and philosophers. Nevertheless, it is important to ask exactly what this familiar designation refers to. At the same time, we want to know what is meant by the designation "non-Western," apart from the potentially racist idea that it is "Other." When many philosophers refer to "the East," furthermore, they are often making a mere gesture toward India and China, usually in the context of a noncommital reference to Buddhism (which began in India and migrated to China more than 1,000 years ago), as if all of the philosophies of Asia were more or less the same, combinations of mysticism, meditation, and various rituals of self-denial.

The idea of "the West" is as old as the human sense of geography. The early Greeks, looking east, promptly declared themselves superior to the "barbarians" of what they would call the "Orient." Later on, the adjective "Western" came to refer to the western portions of Europe, mainly England and France, and the "East"—especially the scattered medieval states of Germany and the monstrosity that was Russia—was again viewed as inferior. The notion of the West later expanded to include Germany as well as North America but excluded Asia. In the past several decades, however, Japan and several other Asian countries have adopted many aspects of Western thought in order to forge both powerful democracies and some of the most successful economies in the world. Obviously this geographical division is, and always was, a simple-minded and often unfair way of carving up the world.

Today, the term refers generally to the ideas and concepts that are best known in Europe and North America, but immediately all sorts of counterexamples come to mind. Native American ideas and culture are not "Western." Australia and New Zealand are said to be "Western" even though they are geographically as far as possible on this planet from Britain, from whence their majority populations arrived, and, more telling, even though they have substantial indigenous populations which are not "Western" at all. Both Australia and New Zealand were settled by the British only at the considerable expense of their native populations, the Aborigines and the Maori, respectively, and these peoples had established impressive philosophies and cultures of their own. By the mid-nineteenth century, the various countries of Europe had colonized most of the globe, and with their merchants and armies came their religions and their philosophies. European ideas confronted established precolonial cultures, and where the native philosophies were not all but wiped out, they were nevertheless put on the defensive and often altered, sometimes drastically. Whether or not the European ideas had anything to offer these peoples—and that is by no means a simple question nor one to be dismissed with the simple-minded argument that every culture's ideas are as good as those of any other—they often became the ruling ideas. "Non-Western" philosophy was forced to translate itself into Western terms and prove itself in Western eyes.

Even Western philosophy is not what it seems to be. For example, it is not by any means inclusive. Italian, Spanish, Portuguese, and Russian philosophy, for example, are generally excluded, except in those rare instances in which a figure allies himself to the British, French, or the Germans. Scandanavian philosophy (including that of the Finns) is now typically included as "Western" because of its strong "analytic" tendencies. Spanish religious and political philosophy gets barely a mention in the history of philosophy books, and the Italians are occasionally included only insofar as they were kindred to British or German philosophers. To make matters more complicated, extensive systems of colonial universities have set the curriculum in such far-flung places as Singapore, Hong Kong, New Delhi, Mozambique, Beirut, Sierra Leone, Mexico City, and Buenos Aires without much regard to the indigenous philosophy. And so one can fly to Singapore and Hong Kong to study British philosophy or to Argentina to study the analytic philosophy of science. Japan is a good place to study the German idealists and their successors, if one can manage the discussions in Japanese.

To make matters even more complicated and interesting, what is glibly called "the Western tradition" largely originates and is continuously influenced by much of what is called "the East." It has been suggested that some of the primary sources of Greek philosophy were first developed in Asia, Egypt, and perhaps other parts of Africa.* In any case, we know that the first known philosophers of the Western tradition were from Asia Minor, and the various religions that define this tradition were all from the Middle East. Moreover, just as the pre-Socratics were digested through Aristotle,

---

*Martin, Bernal, Black Athena. New Brunswick: Rutgers University Press, 1987. Bernal effectively demonstrates the outrageous bias and editing of ancient texts that denied their African heritage and argues that the Egyptians were black Africans, making African philosophy the center of the Western tradition, rather than marginal to it.

both Plato and Aristotle were kept alive and often interpreted through Arab and other Eastern medieval scholars. Indian philosophy was a part of Western philosophy perhaps from the very beginning, but in any case indirectly, as it influenced the late medievals through the Arabs and directly entered into European thinking through Schopenhauer in the nineteenth century. All of this has been filtered through and edited by the sometimes straightforwardly racist scholars of the nineteenth century, and both the similarities and differences to be found in world ideas have often been distorted or denied.†

When we and the other authors in this book talk of Western philosophy, accordingly, we should understand that this designation refers to a very selective history of British, German, and French philosophy preceded a long time before by certain (also selective) philosophies of Greece and Rome. Certain aliens are counted as well, for example, the African Saint Augustine who settled in Rome. "Non-Western" philosophy, by contrast, may designate almost anything that does not fit neatly into that small European theater, especially if it is far away or unfamiliar. China, Japan, India, Africa, Latin America, and those cultures of the Middle East that converted to Islam are typically considered non-Western, whatever their geography. Colonialism may have affected those cultures (and by no means just European colonialism), but traditional philosophies nevertheless remain more or less intact. (Their survival in writing, perhaps, is the single most important ingredient in their continued existence.) Elsewhere, native philosophy is almost always a problem, for where it has not been decimated or drastically altered by colonialism, the defensiveness of the surviving tradition is already a serious distortion of the once-thriving culture. (Africa and Latin America provide many examples.) This is especially true where the only "texts" of the culture have been handed down through generations according to various oral traditions.

Ultimately, like most distinctions, that between Western and non-Western philosophy is largely arbitrary and misleading. Nevertheless, it provides us with a starting point. When students study philosophy in the university today, they almost always (until very recently) studied the "Western tradition," and that in turn was

†Bernal, op. cit.

essentially defined as the lineage of a dozen or so "great" philosophers, along with their lesser-known colleagues, students, and predecessors. World philosophy, by contrast, is the attempt to break beyond that limited list of a dozen or so and appreciate ideas and cultures and traditions that may be just as old, just as well-developed, and just as interesting. They may be very different in their style, their mode of presentation, and their history, but that doesn't mean that they are not philosophers, and worthy of being studied as such.

QUESTIONS IN AND OF WORLD PHILOSOPHY

In reading the chapters that follow, the student would do well to keep two sets of questions in mind, some straightforward philosophical and others *about* philosophy (or "meta-philosophical" questions). Among the former are certain basic questions of metaphysics—how the world began (or "cosmogony") and the essential composition of the world (or "ontology"). Was the world created, and if so by whom and how? Is the world and all the things of the world viewed as living beings ("animism")? Are there pervasive gods or God or spirits? Is there a sharp distinction or distance between the secular and the divine, between people and their God or gods? What do these gods or God expect or demand of us? What is the nature of time? Does the philosophy include a conception of eternity? And then there will be certain basic ethical questions—what are the origins and sources of good and evil? How important are the commands of God or the gods in determining right and wrong? How important is the concept of social harmony? Is the philosophy more or less egalitarian, or does it defend some sort of hierarchy or elitism? How important is tradition in this philosophy? How does it see itself in relation to other philosophies; for example, does it see them as alternative but equally valid perspectives, or does it simply reject them? Are some people in a privileged position to gain philosophical knowledge or wisdom, or can anyone who puts his or her mind to it become philosophically wise?

Among the latter ("meta-philosophical") questions would be the various relationships between philosophy and science, religion and the everyday practices of life, the extent to which a philosophy is ethnocentric and the extent to which it reaches out to or includes other cultures. And then there is the question of "philosophy" itself: Does this tradition see itself as "philosophical"? What is the accepted style or styles of philosophy? What are the status of philosophers in the culture in question?

THE READINGS

In the opening chapter on Japanese philosophy, Graham Parkes suggests that philosophy might be understood as "clear thinking about the fundamental elements, structure, and meaning of human existence in the world." Since some features of human experience— human dependence on nature, the inevitability of death, the use of tools and technologies, and interrelationships among individuals— are relatively similar for everyone, we can expect that these themes will be significant in most philosophies, even those of radically different cultures.

Parkes's chapter on Japanese philosophy stresses especially the Japanese emphasis on the practical character of human experience. While "practical" in the context of Western philosophical discussions usually refers to relatively abstract questions about ethics and politics, the practical concerns of Japanese philosophy are much broader. Thus Sei Shōnagon, a lady in waiting at the Heian court of the tenth century, is in keeping with the tenor of Japanese philosophical discussion when she discusses etiquette. Similarly, swordsmanship is considered a philosophical practice, as Takuan Sōhō indicates in the excerpt from his writing, some seven centuries later.

Takuan Sōhō, like most of the other authors in this chapter, is part of the Zen tradition of Buddhism, the dominant strain of Buddhism in Japan. A major theme of the chapter, therefore, is the way in which Zen thought emphasizes the body's role in gaining enlightenment. Physical postures in meditation, along with practices ranging from martial arts to flower arranging, are all conceived as expressions of a body-mind continuum, as is evident in the reading of Dōgen Kigen. One central goal of Zen practice is to see everything in relationship to its whole environment, including oneself. The texture of relationships is thus more emphasized than individual self-consciousness. Indeed, Buddhists believe that individual egos are illusory, and that the ultimate goal for the human being is nirvana, a desireless state in which even one's attachment to one's own ego is eliminated. Yet for some Zen thinkers, like Hakuin Ekaku, even these ultimate realizations can be achieved through practice, in the midst of one's everyday activities.

Despite the differences in emphasis between Japanese thought and that of the West, some recent thinkers have addressed the recent burgeoning of practical encounters between the two cultures through philosophical efforts at syntheses of the two traditions. The chapter closes with a reading by Nishitani Keiji, one of the leading figures in the Kyoto school, which has sought to address thought from the Western, Christian tradition from a Buddhist perspective. Parkes observes that this school has been pioneering in its efforts to create a genuine cross-cultural dialogue.

Roger T. Ames and David L. Hall's chapter on Chinese philosophy stresses some of the differences between Chinese thinkers and their Western counterparts in approaching such basic problems as how one should behave toward other people and how one can organize one's understanding of things. In particular, Hall and Ames stress that Chinese thought approaches both sorts of issues by stressing relationships. This relational principle of ordering, which they label "aesthetic," contrasts with the more atomistic and hierarchical "logical" ordering that is more dominant in the Western tradition. Because relationships are of primary concern for the Chinese, coordination is more important than rigid distinctions, and social roles are understood contextually.

The importance of relationships is obvious in the teachings of the most influential thinker of the Chinese tradition, Confucius. Largely concerned with ethics and political philosophy, the selections from the Confucian *Analects* focus on interpersonal relations, the organization of the community, the ideal government, and the place of human beings in the cosmic order, as well as on personal propriety and development. The *Book of Mencius*, written about a century after Confucius, similarly stresses that personal growth itself is dependent on interaction with others and with one's environment. Mencius was convinced that human beings are basically good, and that human nature intuitively directed individuals toward Confucian social ideals. By contrast, Hsün Tzu, another influential Confucian thinker, believed that human beings are naturally evil. Accordingly, he stressed the importance of law and governmental control over the members of society. The selection from Hsün Tzu nevertheless reveals that he, like Mencius, linked individual virtue to social relationships and that he expected such virtue to inspire others. The Taoist tradition is focused on attuning "the way" (the *tao*) of one's life with that of one's world. Hall and Ames observe that Confucianism and Taoism often mutually reinforce one another, especially in their concern for human relationships. Nevertheless, Taoism is distinctive in its focus on the natural as well as the social environment. The readings from the *Lao-tzu* and the *Huai-nan Tzu* use many images from nature in offering their account of how one comes to know "the way." The reading from the *Chuang-tzu* emphasizes another naturalistic Taoist theme, the idea that we are always situated in a particular perspective, never able to take a complete, "objective" view of the world around us.

Nature imagery is not unique to the Taoist tradition in Chinese philosophy. The *Book of Changes* (the *I Ching*), an ancient Chinese classic, employs images of change within nature which are metaphorically interpreted to reveal the processes of change within human life. The selection from Wang Pi's "Commentary on the *Book of Changes*" suggests the ways in which the images of the *I Ching* are used to gain insight into one's situation and to direct one's course of action.

The final reading in Chapter 2 is an excerpt from a recent work, Mao Tse-tung's *On Contradiction*. Drawing on the Western tradition of Marxism, Mao nevertheless incorporates traditional Confucian and Taoist themes into his analysis of social and political development.

Like China, the Indian subcontinent has a rich historical philosophical literature that spans several millenia. The chapter by Stephen H. Phillips on South Asian philosophy begins with selections from some of the earliest and most religiously significant Indian works, the Vedas and the Upanishads. The nature of Brahman (or God) and the human being's relation to God are central philosophical themes in these works. The *Bhagavadgītā*, an epic work of approximately 200 B.C.E., is, in Phillips' words "culturally clearly the most important" of India's many sacred texts. The passage excerpted from the Gita depicts a famous discussion regarding war and ethics that takes place between the god Krishna and warrior Arjuna as a battle is about to begin.

Phillips emphasizes the diversity of Indian philosophy, and the next several readings suggest something of the range. The nature of yoga, the practices of self-discipline that figure so prominently in the Indian tradition, is the topic of the reading from the Yoga-sūtra, which touches on philosophical issues regarding the relationship of the self to reality. The next reading is from the Buddhist philosopher Nāgārjuna, who stressed intellectual justification of belief, considers the basic epistemological issue of how we can be confident that we know what we believe we know. He draws skeptical conclusions. The Cārvāka school, featured in the next reading, contrasts with most Western impressions of Indian thought, for it is materialistic, antireligious, and skeptical of any conclusions that extrapolate beyond the direct testimony of the senses. The excerpt from the *Nyāya-sūtra*, which follows, reveals another logical perspective, this time a realistic one, that directly counters the skeptical orientations of Nāgārjuna and the Cārvāka school.

Phillips' chapter ends with an excerpt from Sri Aurobindo's *The Life Divine*. Educated at Cambridge University and a political activist in his youth, Aurobindo eventually developed a philosophy that synthesizes the traditional Indian themes of devotion to Brahman and yogic practice with ideas current in Western thought. Like Nishitani in Japan, Aurobindo is a pioneer in developing a creative synthesis of insights from different cultural traditions.

We have already suggested that the term "Western" has been more metaphoric than regional, and that the purview of the "West" is arguable. Generally, the Islamic world is not considered part of the Western philosophical tradition except to the extent that its medieval scholars influenced their Christian philosophical contemporaries. Yet the development of Islamic thought is intimately connected with Western thought. Indeed, it shares certain philosophical forefathers. Eric L. Ormsby's chapter on Arabic philosophy reveals the extent to which Neo-Platonic writings and Aristotelean thought were central influences on such medieval Islamic thinkers as al-Kindī, al-Rāzī (Rhazes) and al-Fārābī. Their writings are also concerned with philosophical issues that were of equal importance to Christian theologians.

Chapter 4 begins with selections from al-Kindī on the nature of God and on the relationship of reason to revelation. One of the readings from al-Fārābī considers the nature of human dependence on God, and whether human existence should be considered a less complete existence than that of God. The second reading by al-Fārābī, from his commentary on Aristotle's *De Interpretatione*, considers the relationship between speech and writing.

Muslim expansion at one point extended through Spain to southern France. Arabic was the language of philosophical discussion through the Middle Ages, and even Maimonides, one of the most significant figures in Jewish philosophy, wrote his major works in Arabic. The selection from his classic *The Guide of the Perplexed* offers an analysis of evil and the nature of providence. The Christian Aristotelean Yahyā ibn ʿAdī also wrote in Arabic. The reading from Yahya ibn Adi is from one of his writings on ethics, this one having to do with the development of character.

Ibn Sīnā is arguably the most influential Islamic philosopher. His work had an impact throughout the Islamic world as well as medieval Christian Europe (where he is known as Avicenna). The selections from Ibn Sīnā are taken from his *Autobiography*, which indicates his philosophical background and influences, and a defense of the immortality of the soul. The final reading in the chapter is an account of God's relationship to creation by Ibn Rushd. By contrast with the theological views of Ibn Sīnā, who considered God transcendent and remote, Ibn Rushd considers God as directly involved with the world He created.

The extensive range of Persian philosophy is the topic of Chapter 5, by Janet McCracken and Homayoon Sepasi-Tehrani. The chapter begins with Mary Boyce's account of Zoroaster, or Zarathustra, and the religion he founded. The readings that follow are taken from the Zoroastrian scriptures, the *Gathas* and the larger *Avesta*. The impact of Zoroastrianism on later Persian thought is pronounced. It also extended beyond Persia in the form of Manichaeism, the variant (or heresy) formulated by the third-century figure Manes. The reading from the *Fihrist-al-Nadim*, a tenth-century Muslim chronical, offers an account of Manes's teachings.

The second half of Chapter 5 considers post-Islamic Persian thought. The passages from Nasir-i Khusraw's poetry give moral advice on the path to perfection and defends the doctrine of free will. The readings from Yahya Suhrawardi represent the Illuminationist school of Persian thought, which he founded. Suhrawardi contended that knowledge of truth came through "illumination," an inner experience of light. The passage from the Sufi poets Rumi, 'Attar, Forughi, Savaji, and Hashemi are concerned with love, a central theme in Sufism (or Islamic mysticism). Their often erotic images represent the soul's relationship to God.

Mulla Sadra was the great synthesizer of Islamic mysticism and Western philosophical categories. The selections from his *Wisdom of the Throne* approach philosophical questions about knowing from the presupposition that mystical union with God is possible. Mulla Sadra draws upon Illuminationist thought, characterizing knowledge in terms of light.

Chapter 5 closes with an indication that Persian philosophy, like Arabic philosophy, developed certain lines of ancient Greek thought. The final reading is a characterization of the philosophical life by Rhazes. A Platonist, Rhazes describes the philosophical life in terms reminiscent of Socrates' requirements.

Chapter 6 is devoted to American Indian philosophy. J. Baird Callicott and Thomas W. Overholt propose that our current worries about the condition of our environment offer a timely approach to American Indian philosophy. The readings that they present span traditional stories from the Ojibwa tribe and autobiographical accounts of two members of the Lakota tribe (Black Elk and Lame Deer) after the arrival of Europeans through recent writings of Pulitzer Prize winner N. Scott Momaday, a member of the Kiowa tribe. Despite the distances of time and space separating these accounts, they are linked by a common concern with how human beings should relate to the natural world that they inhabit.

In certain cases, comparable historical situations provoke radically different societies to similar philosophical reflection. Latin America and Africa share a background of European colonialism followed by nationalism and independence. In both cases, the devastating impact of colonialism on indigenous culture is a central topic of philosophical reflection. Contemporary philosophers in both cultures confront the difficulty of characterizing their own philosophical traditions, for on both continents, European domination of cultural institutions has tended to eliminate or marginalize indigenous philosophies.

Jorge Valadez addresses these concerns in his chapter on Latin American philosophy. The first two readings consider the philosophy of the Aztecs and its continuing legacy in Mexican culture. The chapter opens with a selection by Octavio Paz. Paz observes that contemporary Mexican thought reveals continuities with Aztec thinking, particularly ideas about death. The second reading introduces the doctrines of Aztec wise men called *tlamatinime*, who advocated an aesthetic approach to questions about the nature of reality.

The latter two readings in Chapter 7, however, consider the situation of Latin America as a postcolonial culture. Philosophy in Latin America must recuperate from the domination of European thought, according to Augusto Salazar Bondy, and become more authentically engaged in the historical realities of its situation. The chapter closes with a reading from Gustavo Gutierrez, a member of the "liberation theology" movement, which attempts to deal with the poverty and political disenfranchisement of the people in Latin America by interpreting the Christian Gospel in a political light, as advocating that the poor should be given preferential treatment.

Jacqueline Trimier's chapter on African philosophy, similarly, considers the range of approaches recent and contemporary African thinkers have taken toward philosophy in a postcolonial situation. Trimier draws upon Henry Odera Oruka's classification of approaches to philosophy. The readings from Tempels and Senghor represent the approach of "ethnophilosophy," which characterizes the traditions, myths, and folklore of traditional African tribes as indigenous African philosophy. The readings from Hountondji and Okere take the approach that Oruka calls "professional philosophy." This approach is concerned with making universalistic claims, which allegedly have the same meaning in all cultures. The readings from Oruka himself and from Sopido and Hallen reflect the "philosophical sagacity" approach in Oruka's taxonomy. This approach emphasizes individual sages, who engaged in critical reflection but did not write books of philosophy. The readings from Fanon and Nkrumah, finally, represent the category of "national-ideological philosophy." This approach, on Oruka's scheme, is not necessarily theoretical. Its concerns are primarily practical; national-ideological seeks the development of political and cultural identity and the definition of a social order.

We close with a chapter on "Western philosophy." While virtually everyone in the field of philosophy would tell this story somewhat differently, we have chosen those brief selections that would probably be most commonly included in any comprehensive narrative. These include passages from Plato, Aristotle, St. Anselm, St. Thomas Aquinas, Descartes, Hume, Kant, Hobbes, Rousseau, Hegel, and Nietzsche. We have not attempted to include or summarize contemporary (twentieth century) work in philosophy, the significance (and story) of which is now a matter of lively debate.

CHAPTER 1

Japanese Philosophy

GRAHAM PARKES

When professional philosophers hear the term "Japanese philosophy," their frequent response is still, after all these years, "Oh? Is there really such a thing as Japanese philosophy?" There is—though it tends to look sufficiently different from what we in the West regard as philosophy that doubts as to its existence are understandable. It is true that until a little more than a century ago there was no equivalent in the Japanese language to our word "philosophy," and that when the country was reopened to the West toward the end of the nineteenth century a new word had to be coined for the discipline that was imported in the form of texts (and philosophy professors to explain them) from Europe and the United States. Nevertheless, if we understand philosophy broadly as something like "clear thinking about the fundamental elements, structures, and meaning of human existence in the world," then the Japanese must be considered as having practiced it for well over 1,000 years.

A distinctive feature of the history of Japanese culture is the relatively late acquisition of a system of writing. It was not until the sixth century of the Common Era, during a phase of massive importation of Chinese culture, that the Japanese first began to develop a writing system for their spoken language. When the ideographic system of written Chinese was introduced, there came with it several philosophies that were embodied in that writing—Confucianism, Buddhism, and Taoism—and these have continued to this day to exert an influence on Japanese thinking. In comparison with Indian and European worldviews, East Asian thought is generally quite concrete and disinclined to engage in abstraction and speculation. The relatively down-to-earth nature of Chinese philosophy thus reinforced the tendency of the Japanese to focus their thinking on particular, concrete issues rather than to indulge in flights of metaphysical fancy.

A few more pointers—deliberate generalizations—may help to orient the reader to the cast of mind embodied in the excerpts that follow. Rather than constructing systems of theories, Japanese philosophy tends to stay very close to praxis, or *practice*, in its thinking. This is in part because the major dualisms on which so much of Western philosophy is predicated—the intelligible as opposed to the sensible realm, mind (or spirit) in opposition to the body (or matter), the divine in contrast to the human, the logical and rational versus the aesthetic and intuitive—are not prominent in East Asian thinking. And since Japanese philosophy tends to be so firmly embodied in practice, there are many other ways to engage it than by reading explicitly philosophical texts: for example, by going to performances of Japanese theater, practicing Japanese arts (whether martial or fine), watching Japanese movies, or eating in Japanese restaurants—where the meal should be as much a feast for the eyes as for the mouth and stomach, and the table setting and service important parts of the overall experience. (For a more detailed account of the "practical" embodiments of Japanese philosophy, see Graham Parkes, "Ways of Japanese Thinking," listed under "Further Readings.")

Modern Japanese thinkers are fond of pointing out two other general differences between Western and East Asian thinking. Whereas the European tradition has tended to produce philosophies that deal primarily with *being*, the Asian traditions (under influences from Buddhism and Taoism) have been more inclined to make nonbeing, or *nothingness*, a central concern. More concretely, whereas the emphasis in the West has been on philosophies of *life*, Asian thought has focused equally on the issue of *death*, giving rise to philosophies of life-*and*-death. An exception to this generalization is provided by the more existential aspects of the philosophies of such Western thinkers as Schopenhauer, Kierkegaard, Nietzsche, and Heidegger—all of which have considerable affinities with Asian thought. (The comparative approach is often a helpful way of gaining access to alien philosophical traditions. Readers familiar with Nietzsche or Heidegger may find useful some of the contributions to Graham Parkes, ed., *Heidegger and Asian Thought*, Honolulu,

University of Hawaii Press, 1987, and *Nietzsche and Asian Thought,* Chicago, University of Chicago Press, 1991.)

There is some truth to the generalization that whereas Western cultures are individualistic, East Asian cultures give precedence to the social group (whether family, community, or nation) over the individual. In the case of Japan, this tendency is reinforced by the structure of the language, which, in contrast to the subject-predicate structure of Indo-European languages, puts the major emphasis on the predicate and often dispenses with the grammatical subject altogether. This means, among other things, that personal pronouns—and especially the self-referential first-person singular (the equivalent of "I")—are used relatively seldom. If in the course of a conversation I want to say that I have understood something, I simply say something like "Understanding has taken place," letting the context suggest on whose part the understanding has been. Japanese sentences often fade out into indeterminacy, since the writer-speaker wants to avoid insulting the intelligence of the reader-hearer by stating the obvious. Japanese society discourages self-assertiveness at the same time that it encourages indirectness and allusiveness in communication.

All this poses a problem when it comes to reading Japanese philosophical texts. For one thing, given the vast differences that separate Japanese from European languages, they are very difficult to translate well. And if the reader approaches them with preconceptions from the Western tradition concerning the proper nature and form of philosophical writing—that it should take the form of logical argument, for example—he or she will be disappointed. More important, however, the point will be missed altogether. The Aristotelian logic so beloved of Western philosophers is, after all, only one kind of logic; several different logics have been developed over the centuries by extremely acute thinkers from the Indian, Chinese, and Japanese philosophical traditions. Whereas much of Western philosophy depends upon the exactness of concepts, in Japan the precision and clarity of the imagery may be more important. Whereas thinkers in the Western tradition often strive to eliminate ambiguity, the ambiguous and multivocal tend to be cultivated in Japan as fertile ground for broader understanding. And whereas most Western philosophers regard self-contradiction as something to be avoided, Japanese thinkers see the extreme form of self-contradiction that is paradox as a unique source of philosophical insight.

Some Japanese philosophy has been criticized for being ethnocentric, for being concerned with the nature of the Japanese rather than with human existence in general. Some of these criticisms may be valid—but similar criticisms can be made with equal justification of some Western philosophy too. Nevertheless, much of Japanese philosophical thinking successfully addresses the human condition in general—and yet, even so, it may not be possible to understand it without having a sense of its cultural context. This means that two virtues are especially to be desired in the reader who approaches Japanese philosophy for the first time: on the one hand *openness,* and on the other *perseverance.*

One thing that will immediately strike anyone already familiar with Japanese philosophy about the following selections is their bias toward Zen Buddhism. It is probably true that more of the significant philosophical texts in Japanese have been influenced by the Zen outlook than by any other single worldview. But there are several major thinkers whose basic stance was conditioned by other influences: for example, the philosophies developed by Kūkai (774–835), who represents the esoteric Shingon school of Buddhism; by Shinran (1173–1262), who was a Shin (Pure Land) Buddhist; by Itō Jinsai (1627–1705) and Ogyū Sorai (1666–1728), who were neo-Confucians; and by Tanabe Hajime (1885–1962), who was influenced by Pure Land Buddhism as well as by Christianity and modern European philosophy. (Note that Japanese names are given in the East Asian order, which is the reverse of the English: surname first, followed by the given name. For a brief account of the ideas of Kūkai and Tanabe, as well as of neo-Confucianism and several other prominent Japanese thinkers, see the relevant entries in Ted Honderich, ed., *The Oxford Companion to Philosophy.*) The reason for the bias toward Zen is a purely practical one: most Japanese philosophical texts are pretty difficult to understand, and especially so in the form of a short excerpt. Zen texts, however, are more readily excerpted in brief passages and—if not ultimately easier to explain—can be elucidated more satisfactorily in the scope of a short introduction. Also, since more people are familiar with Zen than with other Japanese cultural traditions, providing the philosophical background to Zen may be a worthwhile way to begin.

A LIFE OF AESTHETIC REFINEMENT: SEI SHŌNAGON

If it threatens to stretch the definition of philosophy too far to make it include the work of Sei Shōnagon (b. 966), the risk is worth taking for two reasons. The inclusion of excerpts from her *Pillow Book* serves to remind us that the earliest flowering of Japanese literature in the Heian period was dominated by women, who wrote in *kana*—the phonetic script developed for the native Japanese language—rather than in Chinese characters. (Sei Shōnagon's most famous contemporary was another woman, Murasaki Shikubu, author of *The Tale of Genji*, a monumental work that lays claim to being the world's first psychological novel.) It also serves to remind us that the line between philosophy and literature—or poetry or religion—is not so clearly definable in the Japanese tradition as it has been in the West.

Shōnagon was a lady at the Heian court during the tenth century, which was the pinnacle of one of the most refined aesthetic cultures that has ever existed. (An excellent account of life in the Heian period can be found in Ivan Morris's *The World of the Shining Prince*.) It was above all an intensely literary culture, where calligraphy, the cultivation of beautiful handwriting, was the measure of a person's virtue. Because of Japan's geographical isolation from the Asian mainland, Heian civilization had developed into such a uniform and homogeneous entity that its members were able to understand one another with a minimum of overt communication (a feature that continues to some extent to distinguish Japanese society to this day). To borrow a wonderful image from Arthur Waley: "A phrase, a clouded hint, an allusion half-expressed, a gesture imperceptible to common eyes, moved this courtly herd with a facility as magic as those silent messages that in the prairie ripple from beast to beast."

The Pillow Book of Sei Shōnagon is a kind of diary in which the author records her impressions and reactions to a wide variety of events in daily life at the court. She comes across as a complex character, consummately concerned with etiquette and good taste, but graced with a sense of humor and keen psychological insight. The language of *The Pillow Book* is widely praised for its incomparable clarity and beauty. On occasion it lifts the narrative to the heights of

poetry and penetrates to the core of our universal humanity in a
way that may well be regarded as philosophical.

The following extract is typical of the way in which the text
mixes first- and third-person narrative.

The Pillow Book of Sei Shōnagon

SEI SHŌNAGON

Among "embarrassing things," Shōnagon mentions "An unpleasant- 1
looking child being praised and petted by parents who see it not as it
is but as they would like it to be. Having to listen while its parents
repeat to one the things the child has said, imitating its voice."

And again, "Sometimes when in the course of conversation I have 2
expressed an opinion about someone and perhaps spoken rather
severely, a small child has overheard me and repeated the whole
thing to the person in question. This may get one into a terrible
fix. . . ."

I have the same feeling if someone is telling me a sad story. I see 3
the tears in his eyes and do indeed agree that what he says is very sad;
but somehow or other my own tears will not flow. It is no use trying to
contort one's face into an expression of woe; in fact, nothing is any good.

Of the gentlewomen's apartments attached to the Empress's own 4
quarters, those along the Narrow Gallery are the most agreeable.
When the wooden blinds at the top are rolled up, the wind blows in
very hard, and it is cool even in summer. In winter, indeed, snow and
hail often come along with the wind; but even so, I find it very agreeable. As the rooms have very little depth and boys, even when so near
to the Imperial apartments, do not always mind their manners, we
generally ensconce ourselves behind screens, where the quiet is
delightful, for there is none of the loud talk and laughter that disturb
one in other quarters of the Palace.

I like the feeling that one must always be on the alert. And if this 5
is true during the day, how much more so at night, when one must be

Sei Shōnagon. *The Pillow Book of Sei Shōnagon.* Translated by Arthur Waley. New
York: Grove Press, 1960. Reprinted with the permission of the publisher.

prepared for something to happen at any moment. All night long one hears the noise of footsteps in the corridor outside. Every now and then the sound will cease in front of some particular door, and there will be a gentle tapping, just with one finger; but one knows that the lady inside will have instantly recognized the knock. Sometimes, this soft tapping lasts a long while; the lady is no doubt pretending to be asleep. But at last comes the rustle of a dress or the sound of someone cautiously turning on her couch, and one knows that she has taken pity on him.

In summer she can hear every movement of his fan, as he stands   6
chafing outside; while in winter, stealthily though it be done, he will hear the sound of someone gently stirring the ashes in the brazier, and will at once begin knocking more resolutely, or even asking out loud for admittance. And while he does so, one can hear him squeezing up closer and closer against the door.

In the fifth month I love driving out to some mountain village. The   7
pools that lie across the road look like patches of green grass; but while the carriage slowly pushes its way right through them, one sees that there is only a scum of some strange, thin weed, with clear, bright water underneath. Though it is quite shallow, great spurts fly up as our horsemen gallop across, making a lovely sight. Then, where the road runs between hedges, a leafy bough will sometimes dart in at the carriage window; but however quickly one snatches at it, one is always too late.

Sometimes a spray of *yomogi* will get caught in the wheel, and for   8
a moment, as the wheel brings it level, a delicious scent hovers at our window.

I love to cross a river in very bright moonlight and see the tram-   9
pled water fly up in chips of crystal under the oxen's feet.

In the second month something happens in the Hall of the Grand   10
Council. I really don't know exactly what it is, but they call it the Tests. About the same time there is a thing they call the Shakuden. I believe it is then that they hang up Kuji* and the rest. They also present something called the Sōmei to the Emperor and Empress. It comes in a stone pot and includes some very queer stuff.

People value sympathy more than anything in the world. This is   11
particularly true of men; but I do not exclude women. One always

---

* Confucius. This is a ceremony in honor of Confucius and his disciples.—*ed.*

regrets an unkind remark, even if it was obviously quite unintention-
al; and it is easy, without entering very deeply into someone else's
sorrow, to say "How unfortunate!" if the situation is indeed unfortunate, or "I can imagine what he is going through," if the person in
question is likely to be much perturbed. And this works even better if
one's remark is made to someone else and repeated than if it is heard
at first hand.

One ought always to find some way of letting people know that   12
one has sympathized. With one's relations and so on, who expect
fond inquiries, it is difficult to get any special credit. But a friendly
remark to someone who sees no reason to expect it is always certain
to give pleasure. This all sounds very easy and obvious; but surprisingly few people put it into practice. It seems as though people with
nice feelings must necessarily be silly, and clever people must always
be ill-natured, men and women too. But I suppose really there must
be lots of nice, clever people, if only one knew them.

Features that one particularly likes continue to give one the same   13
thrill of pleasure every time one looks at a face. With pictures it is different; once we have seen them a certain number of times, they cease
to interest us; indeed, the pictures on a screen that stands close to
your usual seat, however beautiful they may be, you will never so
much as glance at!

Again, an object (such as a fan, mirror, vase) may be ugly in gen-   14
eral, but have some particular part which we can look at with pleasure. Faces do not work like this; they affect us disagreeably unless
they can be admired as a whole.

IMPERMANENCE AS BUDDHA-NATURE: DŌGEN KIGEN

The Zen master Dōgen (1200–1253), whom the Japanese Sōtō school
regards as its founder, was not only a deeply religious spiritual figure but also a profound and insightful thinker and an accomplished
poet of nature. His most explicitly philosophical work, the monumental *Shōbōgenzō* ("Treasury of the True Dharma Eye"), is the first
major Buddhist text to be written in Japanese rather than classical
Chinese as well as the first comprehensive work of philosophy in
Japanese. It is an extremely dense and difficult text, over which
philosophers in Japan (and, more recently, in the West) have pon-
dered long and hard. As such, it does not lend itself to being

excerpted and easily explained, so the passages from Dōgen that follow have been drawn from a more accessible work, *Shōbōgenzō-Zuimonki*, a collection of stories and sayings from Dōgen's life compiled by his disciple Ejō. (An excellent account of Dōgen's life and thought can be found in Dumoulin's *Zen Buddhism: Japan.*)

The word "Zen" is ultimately derived from a Sanskrit term connoting meditation, and while techniques of contemplation had been practiced for some time in Japan, Dōgen revitalized the practice with his emphasis on *zazen* ("seated meditation"). Seated in a firm but relaxed cross-legged posture, with the eyes open, one breathes through the nose and opens oneself to a prereflective, nonconceptual awareness that Dōgen characterizes as "without-thinking." (See Chapter 6 of Kasulis's *Zen Action / Zen Person* for an explanation of Dōgen's notion of "without-thinking.") It is important that one sit simply as an expression of one's true nature, rather than *in order to* gain enlightenment. Proper practice will, however, result in what Dōgen calls "the molting of body-mind."

This last term, which could also be translated "body-heart," is intended to emphasize the unity of the physical and the psychical, to remind us that these are simply two aspects of our person rather than two separate components of the human being. As one of the passages excerpted below shows, Dōgen tends to view Zen practice as having even more to do with the body than the mind, and to see following "the Buddha Way" as a physical rather than simply mental activity. The Japanese term for "way" here is the same as the Chinese *tao* and is often used in Zen writings to stress that Zen practice is a matter of finding how to live one's own, unique life in harmony with the rest of the cosmos.

It will be helpful to mention two other ideas emphasized by Dōgen: impermanence and Buddha-nature. It is a central tenet of Buddhism that the world is basically impermanent, in the sense that all elements of existence are continually "arising and passing away." Buddhism suggests that the inherent "unsatisfactoriness" of existence is a result of the deep-rooted desire to grasp and hang on to the ephemerality of life. It sees the idea that there are enduring, self-identical things—including human egos or selves—as a pervasive illusion fabricated in an attempt to deny the radically ephemeral nature of existence. The full acknowledgment and experiential appreciation of impermanence takes one quite some distance along the Buddha Way.

The idea of Buddha-nature is more difficult, having to do with the fundamentally "enlightened" nature of everything in the world. Dōgen associates Buddha-nature with the central notion of later, Mahayana Buddhism, which is *sunyatā*: "nothingness" or "emptiness." The realization of the essential emptiness of all things has to do with seeing that nothing is what it is "in itself," that everything is what it is only in relation to other things. Thus Dōgen writes, "Buddha-nature is vast emptiness, open, clear, and bright." He extends the idea of Buddha-nature beyond all sentient beings to everything in the universe and claims that it is thus not different from impermanence. (This idea is the theme of a recent book by a Western philosopher, Joan Stambaugh: *Impermanence Is Buddha-Nature.*) Everything is, just as it is, perfectly enlightened; but this basic condition is obscured from us by layers of conceptualization and by discriminating consciousness which divides things into good and bad, beautiful and ugly, pleasurable and painful.

In one of the passages that follow, Dōgen admonishes his students: "Remember that you are alive only today in this moment." In other writings Dōgen develops some highly sophisticated ideas about time, which make it clear that there is more to enlightenment than simply "living in the moment"—which is something, after all, that animals manage effortlessly and without any trouble. Thanks to the complex temporal structure of human existence, when one manages to enter fully into the flow of impermanence, one finds that the past and future are somehow gathered up into every moment of the present. (Dōgen's ideas about time bear remarkable similarities to the thinking of some modern Western philosophers—namely, Kierkegaard, Nietzsche, and Heidegger—about the "moment.")

Shōbōgenzo-Zuimonki

DŌGEN

Next, to arouse such an aspiration, think deeply in your heart of the   1
impermanence of the world. It is not a matter of meditating using

Dōgen. *Shōbōgenzō-Zuimonki*. Translated by Okumura Shohaku. Kyoto: Soto Zen Center, 1987. Reprinted with the permission of the publisher.

some provisional method of contemplation. It is not a matter of fabricating in our heads that which does not really exist. Impermanence is truly the reality right in front of our eyes. We need not wait for some teaching from others, proof from some passage of scripture, or some principle. Born in the morning, dead in the evening, a person we saw yesterday is no longer here today—these are the facts we see with our eyes and hear with our ears. This is what we see and hear about others. Applying this to our own bodies, and thinking of the reality (of all things), though we expect to live for seventy or eighty years, we die when we must die.

During our lifetime, though we may see the reality of sorrow, pleasure, love of our families, and hatred of our enemies, these are not worthy matters. We could spend our time letting go of them. We should just believe in the Buddha-Way and seek the true joy of Nirvana. Much more so for the aged whose lives are already more than half over. How many years still remain? How can we let up studying the Way? This is still not close enough to reality. In reality, it is only today or even this moment that we can thus think of worldly affairs or of the Buddha-Way. Tonight or tomorrow we may contract some serious disease, or may have to endure such terrible pain as to be unable to distinguish east from west. Or, we may be killed suddenly by some demon, encounter trouble with brigands, or be killed by some enemy. Everything is truly uncertain.

Therefore, in such an unpredictable world, it is extremely foolish to waste time worrying about various ways of earning a living in order to postpone one's death—uncertain as it is—to say nothing of plotting evil against others.

Precisely because this is reality, the Buddha preached it to all living beings, the patriarchs taught only this truth in their sermons and writings. In my formal speeches or lectures too, I emphasize that impermanence is swift; life-and-death is the great matter. Reflect on this reality again and again in your heart without forgetting it, and without wasting a moment. Put your whole mind into the practice of the Way. Remember that you are alive only today in this moment. Other than that, [practice of the Way] is truly easy. You needn't discuss whether you are superior or inferior, brilliant or dull.

Dōgen also said,

Is the Way attained through mind or body? In the teaching-schools, it is said that since body and mind are not separate, the Way is attained through the body. Yet, it is not clear that we attain the Way through the body, because they say "since" body and mind are not separate. In Zen, the Way is attained through both body and mind.

As long as we only think about the buddha-dharma with our 7 minds, the Way will never be grasped, even in a thousand lifetimes or a myriad of eons. When we let go of our minds and cast aside our views and understandings, the Way will be actualized. One sage clarified True Mind (Reality) when he saw peach blossoms, and another realized the Way when he heard the sound of tile hitting a bamboo. They attained the Way through their bodies. Therefore, when we completely cast aside our thoughts and views and practice *shikantaza,* we will become intimate with the Way. For this reason, the Way is doubtlessly attained through the body. This is why I encourage you to practice zazen wholeheartedly.

Dōgen instructed, 8

Students of the Way, the reason you do not attain enlightenment 9 is because you hold onto your old views. Without knowing who taught you, you think that "mind" is the function of your brain— thought and discrimination. When I tell you that "mind" is grass and trees, you do not believe it. When you talk about the Buddha you think the Buddha must have various physical characteristics and a radiant halo. If I say that the Buddha is broken tiles and pebbles, you show astonishment. The views you cling to are neither what has been transmitted to you from your father nor what you were taught by your mother. You have believed them for no particular reason; they are the result of having listened for a long time to what people have said. Therefore, since it is the definite word of the buddhas, and patriarchs, when it is said that "mind" is grass and trees, you should understand that grass and trees are "mind," and if you are told that "Buddha" is tiles and pebbles, you should believe that tiles and pebbles are the "Buddha." Thus, if you reform your attachment, you will be able to attain the Way.

THE *UBIQUITOUSLY MOBILE MIND:* TAKUAN SŌHŌ

The Zen master Takuan Sōhō (1573–1645) is the major representative at the beginning of the Edo period of the second main school of Japanese Zen, the Rinzai school. As well as being a Zen monk, Takuan was a talented scholar, poet, calligrapher, and adept of the tea ceremony. Since the medieval period in Japan, a number of schools of archery and swordsmanship, while informed primarily by Confucian virtues, had also been inspired by the spirit of Zen, so their members became well-versed in Zen practice. Through his friendship with the famous sword master Yagyū Munemori, Takuan was prompted to express a number of Zen teachings in the context of the art of swordsmanship. (A comprehensive account of the relation of Zen to swordsmanship can be found in D. T. Suzuki, *Zen and Japanese Culture;* see also the more nuanced treatment of Takuan by Dumoulin in *Zen Buddhism: Japan.*)

While the Rinzai school of Zen accords with Dōgen in understanding the mind and body as an inseparable unity, Takuan's ideas about the Zen sword are in many respects exemplifications of Dōgen's idea that "the attainment of the Way is truly accomplished with the body." Takuan remarks an important analogy between Zen practice and the kind of physical discipline necessary for becoming a master of the sword. When the student first begins to learn, he tends to respond instinctively and without thinking (even if not very effectively) to an attack by an opponent. After a good amount of training in how to hold the sword and wield it, where to place the mind, and so on, he tends to be somewhat hampered by all the information and technique gained through the practice. But finally, after many more years of work, when the body's responses have been honed to the finest of edges, the student is able once again to respond and take action without thinking—but by now the technique has become flawless to the point of being almost superhuman. As Takuan says: "When the highest perfection is attained, hands, feet, and all bodily members move by themselves, without any intervention from the mind."

In speaking about the heart-mind, Takuan uses two terms from the Chinese Zen tradition: "no mind" and "original mind" (translated as "right mind" in the excerpt that follows). The condition of "no mind" is attained through the elimination of all attachment to the world through conceptualization or representation, feelings and desires, prejudices and preconceptions. With the body's reflexes disciplined to perfection, and the mind thus emptied, one is able to respond appropriately to the new life situation of every moment with utter spontaneity. In an actual sword fight, the greatest obstacle to success may be the desire to beat the opponent or preserve one's life. Since the instinct for self-preservation is one of the deepest in all animals, the aim of the Zen art of the sword is shot through with paradox: by overcoming the desire to preserve himself, the sword master is free to act in totally open spontaneity—such that his life in fact is preserved after all. This is one of the major ideas behind the famous motto of Bushido, the way of the warrior: "The way of the samurai is the way of death." (Excerpts from the classic text of Bushido can be found in *Hagakure: The Book of the Samurai;* some reflections on the contemporary relevance of the book are contained in *Yukio Mishima on Hagakure: The Samurai Ethic and Modern Japan.*)

Takuan employs an image drawn from Taoism to describe the workings—or, better, the play—of what he calls "original mind": it must be like water (and not frozen like ice) so that it may flow immediately to whatever part of the body or the environment is appropriate at the moment. This is the image behind his emphasis in the excerpt that follows: one must never let the mind *stop* at anything, or disaster will ensue. The passage that follows is an extract from a letter to Yagyū Munemori, containing Zen reflections on the art in which his friend was so accomplished.

The Unfettered Mind

TAKUAN SŌHŌ

WHERE ONE PUTS THE MIND

We say that: 1

If one puts his mind in the action of his opponent's body, his   2
mind will be taken by the action of his opponent's body.

If he puts his mind in his opponent's sword, his mind will be   3
taken by that sword.

If he puts his mind in thoughts of his opponent's intention to strike   4
him, his mind will be taken by thoughts of his opponent's intention to
strike him.

If he puts his mind in his own sword, his mind will be taken by his   5
own sword.

If he puts his mind in his own intention of not being struck, his   6
mind will be taken by his intention of not being struck.

Takuan Sōhō. *The Unfettered Mind.* Translated by William Scott Wilson. Tokyo and New York: Kodansha International, 1986. Reprinted with the permission of the publisher.

If he puts his mind in the other man's stance, his mind will be   7
taken by the other man's stance.
What this means is that there is no place to put the mind.   8
A certain person once said, "No matter where I put my mind, my   9
intentions are held in check in the place where my mind goes, and I
lose to my opponent. Because of that, I place my mind just below my
navel and do not let it wander. Thus am I able to change according to
the actions of my opponent."
This is reasonable. But viewed from the highest standpoint of   10
Buddhism, putting the mind just below the navel and not allowing it
to wander is a low level of understanding, not a high one. It is at the
level of discipline and training. It is at the level of seriousness.

When a person does not think, "Where shall I put it?" the mind will   11
extend throughout the entire body and move about to any place at all.
Not putting the mind anywhere, can't one use the mind, having it   12
go from place to place, responding to the opponent's movements?
If the mind moves about the entire body, when the hand is called   13
into action, one should use the mind that is in the hand. When the
foot is called for, one should use the mind that is in the foot. But if you
determine one place in which to put it, when you try to draw it out of
that place, there it will stay. It will be without function.
Keeping the mind like a tied-up cat and not allowing it to wander,   14
when you keep it in check within yourself, within yourself will it be
detained. Forsaking it within your body, it will go nowhere.
The effort not to stop the mind in just one place—this is disci-   15
pline. Not stopping the mind is object and essence. Put nowhere, it
will be everywhere. Even in moving the mind outside the body, if it is
sent in one direction, it will be lacking in nine others. If the mind is
not restricted to just one direction, it will be in all ten.

In not remaining in one place, the Right Mind is like water. The   16
Confused Mind is like ice, and ice is unable to wash hands or head.
When ice is melted, it becomes water and flows everywhere, and it
can wash the hands, the feet or anything else.
If the mind congeals in one place and remains with one thing, it   17
is like frozen water and is unable to be used freely: ice that can wash
neither hands nor feet. When the mind is melted and is used like
water, extending throughout the body, it can be sent wherever one
wants to send it.
This is the Right Mind.   18

The No-Mind is the same as the Right Mind. It neither congeals nor   19
fixes itself in one place. It is called No-Mind when the mind has neither discrimination nor thought but wanders about the entire body
and extends throughout the entire self.

The No-Mind is placed nowhere. Yet it is not like wood or stone.   20
Where there is no stopping place, it is called No-Mind. When it stops,
there is something in the mind. When there is nothing in the mind,
it is called the mind of No-Mind. It is also called No-Mind-No-
Thought.

When this No-Mind has been well developed, the mind does not   21
stop with one thing nor does it lack any one thing. It is like water over-
flowing and exists within itself. It appears appropriately when facing a
time of need.

The mind that becomes fixed and stops in one place does not   22
function freely. Similarly, the wheels of a cart go around because they
are not rigidly in place. If they were to stick tight, they would not go
around. The mind is also something that does not function if it
becomes attached to a single situation.

If there is some thought within the mind, though you listen to the   23
words spoken by another, you will not really be able to hear him. This
is because your mind has stopped with your own thoughts.

If your mind leans in the directions of these thoughts, though you   24
listen, you will not hear; and though you look, you will not see. This
is because there is something in your mind. What is there is thought.
If you are able to remove this thing that is there, your mind will
become No-Mind, it will function when needed, and it will be appropriate to its use.

The mind that thinks about removing what is within it will by the   25
very act be occupied. If one will not think about it, the mind will
remove these thoughts by itself and of itself become No-Mind.

SEEING INTO ONE'S TRUE NATURE: HAKUIN EKAKU

The Zen master Hakuin (1685–1768) is responsible for a major
revival of the Rinzai school in the eighteenth century and is one of
the outstanding figures in Japanese Buddhism. Like Takuan before
him, Hakuin was a man of many talents; he was highly regarded as
a poet, a painter, and calligrapher, as well as a thinker of the first

rank who produced an enormous body of writings. As an artist, he was no mere amateur: his brush-and-ink paintings rank among the highest achievements of the genre in Japan. (An excellent account of Hakuin's life and ideas can be found in Dumoulin's *Zen Buddhism: Japan*. See also Kasulis, "Hakuin: The Psychodynamics of Zen Training," *Zen Action / Zen Person*, which highlights the philosophical implications of Hakuin's aims and methods.)

Some schools of Buddhism have tended toward quietism, holding that enlightenment is to be attained by realizing the essential nullity of the world and by withdrawing from life. The later, Mahayana schools of Buddhism that developed in India and China went against this tendency in order to promote a more life-affirming stance, maintaining that *nirvana* (a condition of enlightenment in which all desire and attachment to self are extinguished) is in fact not different from *samsara* (the endless cycle of death and rebirth).

It is by no means easy to withdraw from the world and engage in meditation in a mountain-top monastery with sufficient diligence that one realizes the ultimate nothingness, or emptiness, of all things. More difficult, however, is to embody that realization in such a way that it allows one to engage in all aspects of daily life with deepened insight and enhanced vitality. (A good criterion of enlightenment would be provided by one's degree of composure after a few hours of being stuck in rush-hour traffic on the freeway.) One of the ways Hakuin promotes meditation in the midst of activity is through the extreme vitality of his language and the striking imagery it employs, the dynamism of which dispels all notions of Zen as quietistic.

On the premise that, deep down, the human being is already enlightened, but that this enlightenment is obscured by layers of conceptualization and distorted by inappropriate desires and emotions, the Rinzai school understands the aim of Zen practice as "seeing into one's own (true) nature." For Hakuin this consists in "true meditation and uninterrupted sitting [in the midst of all activities]" rather than the "dead sitting and silent illumination" advocated by the quietistic schools. He also advocates the use of the traditional *koan* method, in which the student takes as the object of his meditation a koan assigned to him by the teacher. A koan—of which there are hundreds in the Zen tradition—may consist of a single word, such as *mu* ("nothing"), or a baffling question, such as "What is the sound of one hand clapping?"—this latter being one developed by

Hakuin himself. (A good source on the koan is *Zen Dust: The History of the Kōan and Kōan Study in Rinzai Zen*.) But ultimately everything in life—including even "coughing and swallowing"—is to be incorporated into one's koan.

Disciplined practice will eventually lead to what Hakuin calls "the great doubt" and "the great death." In this experience one comes upon the yawning abyss of utter meaninglessness, the arid desert of nihilism where nothingness is a realm of death. But if one has the courage to endure, and let one's hands be "released over the abyss," terror will turn into joy and one will "return to life" reborn. The experience of the "great death" as described by Hakuin bears a striking resemblance to the revelation of "the abyss" in Nietzsche and the encounter with the nothingness disclosed by *Angst* described by Heidegger. (For a comparative treatment of some of the ideas of Rinzai Zen, see Graham Parkes, "Nietzsche and Zen Master Hakuin on the Roles of Emotion and Passion," in Joel Marks and Roger T. Ames, eds., *Emotions in Asian Thought: A Dialogue in Comparative Philosophy*, Albany, SUNY Press, 1994.)

The following passages from Hakuin begin with an extract from a letter he wrote to the governor of a neighboring province. Hakuin laments the fact that modern practitioners of Zen appear to have lost the art of "meditation in the midst of daily activity." He praises the achievements of a variety of poets and statesmen from the earlier Zen tradition who were capable of sustaining their Zen practice while fully engaged in the affairs of the world.

The Zen Master Hakuin

Hakuin

All of these men were possessed of insight far surpassing that of ordi-   1
nary monks. Yet they assisted constantly in countless governmental affairs, rubbed shoulders with the elite of many lands, associated with nobles of the highest rank, participated in music, the rituals, and military affairs, engaged in ceremonial competitions, but never for a

Hakuin. *The Zen Master Hakuin*. Translated by Philip Yampolsky. New York: Columbia University Press, 1971. Reprinted with the permission of the publisher.

moment did they lose their affinity for the Way, and in the end awakened to the essentials of the Zen teaching. Isn't this the miracle of true meditation and uninterrupted sitting? Was this not the deep repayment of their obligations to the Buddha Way? Isn't this the awesome dignity of Zen? Indeed they are as different from those fools who starve to death on mountains, thinking that dead sitting and silent illumination suffice and that Zen consists of the source of the mind being in tranquility, as heaven is from earth. Aren't men of this sort like people who not only fail to catch the hare before their eyes, but lose the falcon as well?

Why? It is because not only do they fail to see into their own   2
natures, but they neglect their obligations to their lord as well. What a regrettable thing this is! It must be understood that the quality of the accomplishment depends upon the degree of the perseverance. If in your meditation you have the vitality of a single man fighting ten thousand, what is there to choose between being a monk and being a layman? If you say that seeing the Way can only be accomplished by monks, does this mean that all hope is lost for parents among the commoners, for those in service to others, for children? Even if you are a monk, if your practice of the Way is not intense, if your aspiration is not pure, how are you any different from a layman? Again, even if you are a layman, if your aspiration is intense and your conduct wise, why is this any different from being a monk? Therefore it has been said:

> If the Way lies deep within the mind,
> It is just as well not to go off to the mountains of Yoshino.

At any rate, there is no kind of sitting more suited to military lead-   3
ers than this uninterrupted true meditation. This is an ancient truth that for the past two hundred years has been discarded.

What is this true meditation? It is to make everything: coughing,   4
swallowing, waving the arms, motion, stillness, words, action, the evil and the good, prosperity and shame, gain and loss, right and wrong, into one single koan.

You must become aware that meditation is the thing that points out   5
your own innate appearance. To carry on the real practice of seeing into your own nature by transcending the great matter of birth and death and by closing the True Eye of the Buddhas and the Patriarchs, is by no means an easy thing to do. Placing the essential between the

two states, the active and the passive, and being in a position to be able to move in any direction, with the true principle of pure, undiluted, undistracted meditation before your eyes, attain a state of mind in which, even though surrounded by crowds of people, it is as if you were alone in a field extending tens of thousands of miles. You must from time to time reach that state of understanding described by old P'ang, in which you are "with both your ears deaf; with both your eyes blind." This is known as the time when the true great doubt stands before your very eyes. And if at this time you struggle forward without losing any ground, it will be as though a sheet of ice has cracked, as though a tower of jade has fallen, and you will experience a great feeling of joy that for forty years you have never seen or felt before.

What is this root of life? It is that instant of ignorance that has come   6
down through endless kalpas of time. Evolving through heaven and hell, this evil world and the Pure Land, that the three evil realms and the six evil paths are made to appear is all because of the power of this root of life. Although it is nothing but dreamlike, illusory fancied thoughts, it can block the Great Matter of seeing into one's own nature more effectively than an army of a hundred thousand demons. Sometimes it is called illusory thoughts, sometimes the root of birth and death, sometimes the passions, sometimes a demon. It is one thing with many names, but if you examine it closely you will find that what it comes down to is one concept: that the self is real. Because of this view that the self exists, we have birth and death, Nirvana, the passions, enlightenment.

If you are not a hero who has truly seen into his own nature, don't   7
think it is something that can be known so easily. If you wish accordance with the true, pure non-ego, you must be prepared to let go your hold when hanging from a sheer precipice, to die and return again to life. Only then can you attain to the true ego of the four Nirvana virtues.

What is "to let go your hold when hanging from a sheer   8
precipice"? Supposing a man should find himself in some desolate area where no man has ever walked before. Below him are the perpendicular walls of a bottomless chasm. His feet rest precariously on a patch of slippery moss, and there is no spot of earth on which he can steady himself. He can neither advance nor retreat; he faces only

death. The only things he has on which to depend are a vine that he grasps by the left hand and a creeper that he holds with his right. His life hangs as if from a dangling thread. If he were suddenly to let go his dried bones would not even be left. So it is with the study of the Way. If you take up one koan and investigate it unceasingly your mind will die and your will will be destroyed. It is as though a vast, empty abyss lay before you, with no place to set your hands and feet. You face death and your bosom feels as though it were afire. Then suddenly you are one with the koan, and both body and mind are cast off. This is known as the time when the hands are released over the abyss. Then when suddenly you return to life, there is the great joy of one who drinks the water and knows for himself whether it is hot or cold. This is known as rebirth in the Pure Land. This is known as seeing into one's own nature. You must push forward relentlessly and with the help of this complete concentration you will penetrate without fail to the basic source of your own nature. Never doubt that without seeing into your own nature you cannot become a Buddha; without seeing into your own nature there is no Pure Land.

9

CUT FLOWERS SUSPENDED IN EMPTINESS: NISHITANI KEIJI

When in the 1870s Japan was opened up to the rest of the world again after several centuries of isolation, the country set about the business of modernization by importing a wide range of ideas from the West: not only scientific and technical ideas, but also—a testimony to the thoroughness of the Japanese practice of appropriation—philosophical ones. Many of the philosophies that have subsequently been developed in Japan take the form of a unique blend of traditional thinking (based on the Chinese classical canon and Buddhist thought) and Western philosophy. The major figure in modern Japanese philosophy is Nishida Kitarō (1870–1945), who in his pathbreaking work of 1911, *An Inquiry into the Good*, articulated a philosophy based on the Zen Buddhist experience in terms drawn from French, German, and Anglo-American philosophy. (See Kitarō Nishida, *An Inquiry into the Good*, trans. Abe Masao and Christopher Ives, New Haven, Yale University Press, 1990. Some of Nishida's later works are also available in English translation: *Last*

Writings: Nothingness and the Religious Worldview, trans. David Dilworth, Honolulu, University of Hawaii Press, 1987.)

Several of Nishida's students became outstanding philosophers in their own right, and they came to be known collectively as the Kyoto school of philosophy. (Available in English are the following representative works: Nishitani Keiji, *Religion and Nothingness,* trans. Jan Van Bragt, Berkeley, University of California Press, 1985; Takeuchi Yoshinori, *The Heart of Buddhism,* trans. James Heisig, New York, Crossroad, 1983; Tanabe Hajime, *Philosophy as Metanoetics,* trans. Takeuchi Yoshinori et al., Berkeley, University of California Press, 1987.) A primary feature of Kyoto school philosophy is that it engages ideas and figures from the Western philosophical tradition from a basis in Buddhist thought. Insofar as it is in large part a religious philosophy, its representatives have been instrumental in promoting the "Buddhist-Christian dialogue" that has developed over the past few decades. Because he studied the history of Western philosophy in its own right, rather than as simply a source of conceptual tools with which to articulate Buddhist thought, Nishitani Keiji (1900–1990) ranks as a major pioneer in the field of East-West comparative philosophy whose work has helped to initiate a truly cross-cultural philosophical dialogue. (Two other works of Nishitani's have been translated into English: *Nishida Kitarō* and *The Self-Overcoming of Nihilism.*)

On the one hand Nishitani was deeply influenced by such Western figures as Meister Eckhart, Dostoevsky, Nietzsche, and Heidegger. But he was firmly rooted in the Chinese and Japanese Zen traditions—being a special admirer of both Dōgen and Hakuin. Like his teacher Nishida and several other senior members of the Kyoto school, Nishitani is greatly concerned with the Zen notion of "absolute nothingness" as the field or place from which all our actions must flow if we are to realize ourselves as fully human beings-in-the-world. But since this idea defies explication within the compass of a brief excerpt, it is intimated obliquely in what follows, through some reflections of Nishitani's on the Japanese art of flower arrangement.

It is worth noting that the idea of "cutting off the root of life," which we encountered in the passage from Hakuin, occurs again here—though this time in connection with the life of flowers rather than human life. But perhaps part of the point is to prompt us to question the difference between those two forms of life.

The Japanese Art of Arranged Flowers

NISHITANI KEIJI

I once read a newspaper article to the effect that the existentialist   1
philosopher Sartre was interested in the Japanese art of ikebana,
"arranged flowers." The article was a brief one and it did not give the
reason for his interest in it, but I felt I had some idea why. I recalled
the impression I myself had upon seeing ikebana with new eyes when
I returned to Japan from study in Europe ten or so years ago.

My study abroad lasted only two-and-a-half years, but by the time   2
I had to return home I had become accustomed to life in Europe. And
so, upon my return I saw many things with something of a foreigner's
eye. Being in such a state of mind, I was particularly struck by the
beauty of ikebana in houses I visited. No matter how accustomed we
may be to seeing something, after not seeing it for awhile our curiosity is reawakened and we are made to see it anew. This is a common
enough occurrence, but on occasion one's eyes might even be struck
open in amazement. Seeing ikebana again was one such experience
for me.

While in Europe, I had gone to see as many works of art as I   3
could, not only in the large cities but in small towns and villages as
well. There I found art which had been made by techniques handed
down for many generations, and it possessed a real refinement and
sense of composure. But I realized in ikebana something entirely different from the whole ethos of European art.

First of all, the beauty expressed in ikebana is created to last only   4
for a short time. Such art changes with the season and reveals its
beauty only for the few days after the flowers and branches have been
cut. It is, by its very nature, something temporary and improvised. The
essential beauty lies precisely in its being transitory and timely. It is a
beauty which embraces time, a beauty which appears out of the
impermanency of time itself. People who arrange flowers understand
this. The pleasure found in creating such beauty might even be in proportion to its temporal character.

Of course it is true that all art has some kind of life expectancy.   5

Nishitani Keiji. "The Japanese Art of Arranged Flowers." Translated by Jeff Shore.
Chanoyu Quarterly 60 (1989). Reprinted with the permission of the publisher.

Even the great cathedral at Cologne, and Saint Peter's—all things in the world eventually perish. And yet buildings, sculpture, paintings, and so forth, are all made to withstand this thing called time. Ignoring the change wrought by time and desiring to remain no matter what, these works of art manifest a will to endure. Perhaps this desire or will to endure is present in the artist's urge to produce, and so we find it reflected in the work of art.

Ikebana and the mind of the artist reflected in it are of a com-   6
pletely different character. Instead of trying to deny time while in the midst of it, ikebana moves along in time without the slightest gap. It is like the legend of Senjo sick in bed and at the same time gone away, or like breathing naturally during zazen so that the inhalation and exhalation become as one and the person thoroughly identifies with his existence in time.

The art of ikebana is wholly encompassed in the cutting and   7
arranging of the flowers and branches. The difference between ike- bana and the other plastic arts is not simply that with ikebana the artist works with material just as it is found in nature; that is merely a super- ficial difference. The essential difference lies in the cutting of the flow- ers and branches.

A tree or blade of grass growing naturally out of the ground also   8
shows a mode of being which tries to deny time while in the midst of it. It resists the pull within itself working to bring about its own cessa- tion, as if it were trying to get ahead of time, continually going beyond itself, forging ahead of itself. But it cannot transcend time in this way because its existence is in time to begin with. In trying to deny time or get ahead of it, the tree or grass is itself a temporal existence continu- ally changing. In trying to deny time, it is alive and can exist (albeit in time). Its existential possibility is realized in the gravitational field. It is fighting a losing battle within itself. The tree or grass is giving itself to the sunlight, rain and wind, to the nutrients and insects in the soil. This giving is also a part of its struggle to live. All of this is nothing but a way of trying to deny time. Trees and grass naturally growing out of the earth are like this.

And not only trees and grass, but people as well—all natural life   9
is so. Plato said that all living things seek eternity in this changing world through procreation, but even here we can find the same attempt to deny time while in the midst of it. The life of the artist and his urge to produce mentioned above is the same as the life of natur- al things. Art belongs to the world of man and his culture, and is dif- ferent from simple nature. But life in art has its fundamental source in

the life of nature. It was Goethe who realized that artistic creativity is based on natural productivity, that it is alive and is the same as all life, and that its essence is the will or desire to deny time while in the midst of it.

Ikebana is a severing of this very life of nature. Flowers in the field   10
or garden pollinate in order to procreate. This is part of the natural will or desire of life. The arranged flower has had this will or desire cut off. It is rather in the world of death, poised in death. It has become severed from the life which denies time, and has itself entered time and become momentary.

While the life of nature has temporality as part of its essence, it   11
goes against and conceals that essence. Nature exists as if it were trying to slip away from time. On the other hand, the flower with its roots cut off has, in one stroke, returned to its original, essential fate in time. This is not the life of a flower in nature. The flower cannot do this by itself. It is merely man's caprice to force the flower against its natural will or desire. The flower is thus made to stand poised in its hidden essence, to reveal that essence.

From the perspective of their fundamental nature, all things in the   12
world are rootless blades of grass. Such grass, however, having put roots down into the ground, itself hides its fundamental rootlessness. Through having been cut from their roots, they are, for the first time, made to thoroughly manifest their fundamental nature—their rootlessness. To be shifted from the world of life into the world of death is, for the flower, a kind of transcendence. The flower made to stand upon death has been cut off from the constructs of time that occur in life, and it is just as though it stands in the timeless present; its evanescent existence of several days becomes a momentary point in which there is no arising or perishing. The flower is shifted to this transcendent moment and fixed there. It becomes a temporary manifestation of eternity that has emerged in time.

Death in which life has been severed, or nothingness *(mu)* in   13
which the possibilities of existence have been cut off—this is not a mere natural death. The natural death of flowers lies in withering and decaying, and arranged flowers must be thrown out before they wither. The death of flowers that have been severed while living transcends the life of nature, transcends the constructs of time, and signifies a movement into new life as a moment. This nothingness is the attainment of new possibilities of existence as a temporary manifestation of eternity within time. Probably the person who arranges the flowers senses these things, either consciously or unconsciously—for

example, when he or she places them in the tokonoma and gives them the space they are to dominate. Within that space, the flowers exist with solemnity, floating in emptiness, just as though they have emerged from nothingness. The space about them, the space of the entire room, is drawn taut by the existence of the flowers, just as if it had received a charge of electricity, and the air takes on a tension and gravity. The flowers, through the certainty with which they occupy the space, sweep clear the atmosphere. The flowers themselves, however, have no awareness or intention of doing this. The sweeping clear of the air about them is the response of the space of nothingness (it is for this reason that arranged flowers, by their fundamental nature, require a setting like the tokonoma). The flowers are simply there, in their correctness. While sending forth a faint coolness from within a fathomless composure—like a person who has eradicated all attachments to life and abandoned all the expectations fundamental to our mundane existence—through a complete silence they communicate that which is eternal.

I have been talking about the character of beauty in ikebana. 14 Being completely momentary, it is an improvisational art. The beauty of ikebana changes with the seasons and with the temporal existence of the plants. The beauty of ikebana is one that vanishes after only a few days, and yet it can be created easily. Such beauty is momentary and yet it is as if that momentariness is transformed into a beauty of a higher order. The essence of the plant being turned into art lies in the aforementioned activity of cutting the plant. With this activity, the emptiness (*kū*) which lies hidden in the depths of the plant is unveiled. It can even be said that the plant itself, in being empty, is the appearance of eternity in time. This momentariness of a higher order expresses eternity. Finitude itself, in being thoroughly finite, becomes a symbol of eternity. Time itself, in being completely temporal, becomes an eternal moment. With the activity of cutting, emptiness is unveiled in the depths of existence, and the eternal moment is realized.

With this realization, one enters a completely different dimension 15 in which art is of two possible kinds. One is an art directly in life, and the other is an art alive in death. In other words, one kind of art seeks eternity by denying temporality, and the other tries to unveil eternity by being thoroughly temporal. The former arises out of the natural will or desire of life, and the latter arises out of emptiness which has severed that natural will or desire.

Many Japanese arts, particularly those influenced by Zen, belong   16
to the latter—for example haiku, waka poems, the noh theater, the
Way of Tea, and perhaps ikebana as well.

One of the great strengths of many pure Japanese arts is that their cre-   17
ative activity is not limited to the professional but is taken up by the
common people. Therefore, this creative activity is connected to the
daily life of the people. [T. S.] Eliot said that culture is not just the
thought and art of so-called chosen people of culture; it is life and
even includes daily life and its activity. I agree completely, but in the
case of the Japanese arts of which I speak here, it is not even limited
to that. The activity of everyday life is itself connected with art and is
equal to the arts of the chosen people of culture. And it is this that is
found in the Way of Tea and ikebana. There are no other arts like
these. If this can be elucidated, the unique character of Japanese art
can be seen from a new and different angle.

PRONUNCIATION GUIDE

In Japanese the consonants are pronounced more or less as in
English, and the vowels as in Italian. In Romanized transliteration,
there are no silent letters: all letters are pronounced. Long vowels—
written, for example, as *aa*, *ā*, or sometimes as *ah*—are twice as long
as ordinary vowels; while double consonants, such as *pp*, are also
double (often signified by a pause or "lingering" on the pronunciation of the consonant). Japanese does have pitch accents (the usage
of which is too complex to go into here), but the important thing to
remember is that stress is generally *evenly* distributed throughout
the syllables of a word—unlike English, which tends to stress one
syllable more than the others.

GLOSSARY

Bushido: "The way of the warrior," the code of ethics of the samurai
class.
haiku: Traditional poem of seventeen syllables.
Heian period: In Japan, 794–1185 C.E.
ikebana: "Arranged flowers."

koan: Riddle or puzzle used in Zen training.

Kyoto school: Twentieth-century school of philosophy, synthesizing Buddhist and Western ideas.

Noh (Nō): Classical theater that developed during the late fourteenth century.

Rinzai school: School of Zen Buddhism predicated upon the idea of "sudden enlightenment."

Shin Buddhism: Pure Land Buddhism, based on the worship of the transcendent Buddha Amida.

Shingon Buddhism: "True Word" school of esoteric Buddhism, based on belief in the cosmic Buddha Vairochana.

Sōtō school: The other major school of Japanese Zen (along with Rinzai) predicated upon the idea of "gradual enlightenment."

waka: Traditional poem of thirty-one syllables.

FURTHER READINGS

General

GRAHAM PARKES. "Ways of Japanese Thinking," in Robert Solomon and Kathleen Higgins, eds., *From Africa to Zen: An Introduction to World Philosophy*. Savage, Md.: Rowman & Littlefield, 1992, pp. 25–53.

GRAHAM PARKES. Entries on "Japanese Philosophy," "Absolute Nothingness," "Neo-Confucianism," "Dōgen," "Kūkai," "Nishida Kitarō," "Nishitani Keiji," and "Tanabe Hajime," in Ted Honderich, ed., *The Oxford Companion to Philosophy*. Oxford: Oxford University Press, 1994.

RYUSAKU TSUNODA, ed. *Sources of Japanese Tradition*. New York: Columbia University Press, 1958.

H. PAUL VARLEY. *Japanese Culture*. Honolulu: University of Hawaii Press, 1973.

Dōgen

MASAO ABE. *Study of Dōgen: His Philosophy and Religion*. Albany, N.Y.: State University of New York Press, 1992.

JOAN STAMBAUGH. *Impermanence Is Buddha-Nature*. Honolulu: University of Hawaii Press, 1990.

Nishitani

NISHITANI KEIJI. *Nishida Kitarō*. Translated by Yamamoto Seisaku and James W. Heisig. Berkeley: University of California Press, 1991.

NISHITANI KEIJI. *Religion and Nothingness*. Translated by Jan Van Bragt. Berkeley: University of California Press, 1985.

NISHITANI KEIJI. *The Self-Overcoming of Nihilism.* Translated by Graham Parkes with Setsuko Aihara. Albany, N.Y.: State University of New York Press, 1990.

Sei Shōnagon

IVAN MORRIS. *The World of the Shining Prince.* New York: Knopf, 1964.
The Pillow Book of Sei Shōnagon. Translated and edited by Ivan Morris. New York: Columbia University Press, 1967.

Takuan (and Bushido)

MISHIMA YUKIO. *Yukio Mishima on Hagakure: The Samurai Ethic and Modern Japan.* Translated by Kathryn Sparling. Tokyo and Rutland: Tuttle, 1978.
YAMAMOTO TSUNETOMO. *Hagakure: The Book of the Samurai.* Translated by William Scott Wilson. Tokyo and New York: Kodansha International, 1979.

Zen

HEINRICH DUMOULIN. *Zen Buddhism: A History,* 2 vols. Translated by James W. Heisig and Paul Knitter. New York: Macmillan, 1989/90.
T. P. KASULIS. *Zen Action / Zen Person.* Honolulu: University of Hawaii Press, 1981.
ISSHŪ MIURA AND RUTH FULLER SASAKI. *Zen Dust: The History of the Kōan and Kōan Study in Rinzai Zen.* New York: Harcourt, Brace & World, 1967.
DAISETZ T. SUZUKI. *Zen and Japanese Culture.* Princeton: Princeton University Press, 1959.
ALAN WATTS. *The Way of Zen.* New York: Vintage, 1957.

STUDY QUESTIONS

1. In what general ways do Japanese philosophies differ from Western modes of thinking? What implications do these differences have for the ways we approach Japanese thought?
2. What features distinguish the Zen view of human beings and the world from what might be called the modern Western worldview?
3. Compare and contrast any of the thinkers presented in this chapter with an appropriate figure from the Western philosophical tradition.

CHAPTER 2

Chinese Philosophy

DAVID L. HALL AND ROGER T. AMES

AN AMBIGUITY OF ORDER:
CHINA AND THE WEST

Cultures are like people—complex and diverse. And generalizations made about their persisting character tend to simplify them. However, if we are to be sensitive to the importance of identifying and acknowledging the underlying and often unannounced assumptions which give cultures their distinct personalities and make them profoundly different from one another, we cannot do without generalizations. If we don't begin by appreciating general differences, we are inclined to impose our own values on the other culture, and to thus assume that it is largely the same as our own. Hence, in seeking to understand another culture, perhaps the only thing more dangerous than making generalizations is failing to make them.

As a starting point for understanding the development of Chinese culture, we are going to use a sampling of philosophical literature primarily taken from classical sources to try to demonstrate the viability of one such generalization. We will focus mainly on texts from classical times because this is the formative period for Chinese philosophy. But to demonstrate the relevance of classical culture to contemporary issues, we will conclude by considering to what extent classical assumptions are still evident in selections from the writings of Mao Tse-tung.

The philosopher Wilfrid Sellars defined philosophy as the study of how things in the most general sense hang together in the most general sense. Philosophers worry about the order of things— how our natural, social, and cultural worlds hang together. The following passages, taken from both classical and contemporary

30

sources, should illustrate that when the Chinese philosophers address the issue of how things hang together, they express a rather different sense of order than do their Western counterparts. Coming to an understanding of the contrasting senses of order illustrated by China and Western cultures will constitute a strong first step in the direction of understanding Chinese ways of thinking and living. In the contrast, we also learn a great deal about ourselves. As Goethe observed, we only come to understand home when we have left it.

It should not be surprising that Chinese and Western cultures are fundamentally different. The Indo-European and Chinese civilizations developed almost entirely independently of one another. A fundamental contrast can be established by distinguishing between the dominance of a "scientific" and of an "aesthetic" sense of order in the West and in China, respectively: the way in which the scientist might think about discovering the natural laws which underlie and regulate the universe and the way in which the artist might think about creating a pleasing composition. The difference is between discovering an order already there and helping to invent one.

Personal, social, political, and cosmic order in Western systematic philosophy tends to begin from "metaphysical" assumptions, where metaphysics is defined as "the science of first principles." This classical Western commitment stands in rather stark contrast to the nonsystematic "life-is-art" attitude that has been the signature of the Chinese tradition. It is our claim that the ambiguity resulting from confusing these two rather distinct senses of order has been a long-standing obstacle in Western attempts to understand Chinese culture, and vice versa.

Before we can know another, we must know ourselves. The signal and recurring feature of what we have called the "scientific" sense of order, which had a dominant effect in the development of Western philosophical and religious orthodoxy, is the presumption that there is something permanent, perfect, objective, and universal that disciplines the changing world and guarantees natural and moral order—whether we identify it as the One True God of the Judeo-Christian universe, as some originative and determinative yet impersonal natural principle, as Plato's Form of the Good, as the Principle of Sufficient Reason, as Natural Law, or as scientific method. The model of a single-ordered world where the unchanging source of order stands independent of, sustains, and ultimately provides explanation for the sensible world is a familiar assumption in the Western tradition.

The Western sense of order, then, stretching back in time to its Greek roots, tends to be cosmogonic and teleological. These terms, "cosmogony" and "teleology," mean simply that classical Western philosophy has assumed some initial beginning, some notion of creation, and has assumed that there is a "given" cosmic design which gives meaning and purpose to human life. Because Western philosophers have tended to believe that life in the universe begins somewhere and is going somewhere, this tradition is characterized by a predominance of linear, cause-and-effect explanations for why things are what they are and the way they are. It has frequently been thought that such explanations are available to human beings through their shared and defining faculty of reason, which authorizes argumentation as evidence for justified beliefs. Reasoned arguments make things clear. There is implicit in this worldview a primacy given to some principle which stands independent of the world it orders, like the axioms of geometry or the basic rules of logic that govern the operation of these sciences. Its most familiar presence in Western culture emerges from the combination of Hebraic religion and Greco-Roman philosophy in the personal and universalistic Judeo-Christian conception of God. It is a top-down, disciplining principle of order which is responsible for unity, intelligibility, and meaning in the world, existing external to us as Deity or internal to us as the hard-wiring of our essential natures, or both. It is a given—a standard of order independent of our own actions and experience as human beings which we can appeal to in distinguishing good from evil, right from wrong, and the beautiful from the ugly.

There is a fundamental contrast between this externally existing order assumed in the Western tradition and the Chinese assumption that order is simply the patterned regularity we find in the world both as we discover it and as we add to it. Order is the way things happen and the way we make things happen; in Chinese, *tao*.

In the world of nature, *tao* is the always unique graining in any piece of wood, the DNA which resides as the genetic map in every cell, the veins in each blade of grass, the complex structure of any particular snowflake, the cadence of the surf as each set of waves rolls up on the beach, the striations that line each piece of jade, and so on. In the world of the human being, *tao* is the pattern of roles and rituals, laws and institutions, music and dance, language and letters, which combine to function as a communal grammar, defining each person and the various relationships among people that make life in community meaningful. *Tao* is an always changing pattern of order which inheres in and is inseparable from the world that is ordered. *Tao* is both *how* the world is and *what* the world is.

For the Chinese philosophers generally, we live in a spontaneously self-originating and self-ordering world which has no beginning or end and no independently assigned purpose. The Chinese worldview is an "aestheticism," which means that shaping a life is a process of education and refinement, comparable in many ways to learning to draw a bamboo ink painting or to write well-formed characters in the art of calligraphy. In fact, the art of cooking is frequently used as an example of harmonious order in Chinese philosophical literature, where the specific goal is to take full advantage of all of the ingredients by blending them together in combination and proportion so that the maximum diversity of taste, texture, and color can be achieved. Each ingredient retains its integrity while being enhanced by its relationship with every other compatible ingredient. The successful Chinese menu is long, diverse, and efficient—the garbage pail stands empty. The "Basic Flavors" chapter of the *Spring and Autumn of Mr. Lu* (ca. 250 B.C.) describes this attitude:

> In the business of proper flavoring and seasoning, there must be sweet, sour, bitter, acrid and salty, and there must be an order in the mixing and proper proportion. Blending these together is extremely subtle, and they all must be self-expressive. The variations within the cooking pot are so delicate and subtle that they defy words and conceptualization.

The cooking metaphor can be extended to all other dimensions of human life: shaping one's own character, harmonizing family relationships, building a successful community, governing a country, or leading an army to victory on the battlefield. The underlying strategy is to take account of all of one's resources, to get the most out of them.

Given that maximum benefit lies in developing productive relationships among ingredients, whether they are vegetables in a wok or people in a community, the focus in the Chinese tradition is on the interdependence and complementarity of opposites. There is no dualistic opposition, such as we find in Western philosophy, that separates mind from body as a different order of being, no dualism that separates reality from appearance as being behind what changes and only seems to be, no dualism that separates God from the world as an independent and self-sufficient entity. On the model of *yin* and *yang*, mind and body are a continuum where each can only be explained by reference to the other; time and being are continuous as abstractions from the ongoing process of existence; divinity and humanity are continuous where gods are ancestors and dead cultural heroes that still exist as they are remembered and celebrated by the human community.

While a commitment to the notion of a single-ordered world defined by overarching metaphysical principles emerged early in classical Greek philosophy to give dominant figures and movements within Western philosophy a basis for making universalizable conceptual and theoretical claims, the same was not so in classical China. It can be argued that the sense of order which has persisted in the Chinese tradition from historical times is the regularity and pattern discerned within the process of change itself as it appears in each participant. To "know" the world is not a "scientific" discovery of the laws which govern the world, but the "artful" realization (in the sense of "making real") of the world around oneself by doing whatever it takes to have fruitful and productive relationships in all of one's dealings.

CLASSICAL CONFUCIANISM

The Analects of Confucius

One cannot speak of "Chineseness," past or present, without reference to perhaps the most influential human being who ever lived: Confucius (Kung Fuzi) (551–479 B.C.E.). In the teachings of Confucius there is an emphasis on uniqueness, concreteness, and particularity and a deep suspicion of any metaphysical, universalistic claims. There is an emphasis on the interdependence between persons and their natural, social, and cultural environments and a deep suspicion of notions such as individuality, independence, and autonomy. There is an emphasis on the radical malleability of the human being through enculturation and a deep suspicion of claims to a given "human nature." There is an emphasis on effectiveness in practice and a deep suspicion of ambitious theoretical programs. There is an emphasis on being responsive to changing historical conditions and a deep suspicion of the status quo. There is an emphasis on ritually constituted community and rule by man and a deep suspicion of objective laws and institutions.

Because Confucius begins from the concrete here and now, the realization of a Confucian world begins from one's own personal growth. It is because of the immanence and hence uniqueness of order that Confucius can describe the process of learning in terms of "starting from what is most basic and immediate, and penetrating through to what is most elevated" (*Analects* 14/35). Order begins here and extends there. Personal realization entails at once the preservation and development of one's own integrity and full integration in one's community. The goal is to become "authoritative" as a person (*jen*)—to become a model that influences one's friends, relatives, and community through patterns of deference rather than coercion. The authority that makes one an example for others derives from the embodiment of a shared tradition that all respect. It is one's participation in traditional roles, rituals, and institutions that reinforces a sense of community. At the same time, these ritual practices require creativity: one must "author" the tradition by appropriating it and making it one's own. As a wise person, one actively interprets the world and makes it what it is; as an authoritative person, one stands as a human beacon, lighting the way for others.

THE ANALECTS

CONFUCIUS

ON PERSONAL GROWTH

Confucius said, "At 15 my heart-and-mind were set upon learning; at   1 30 I took my stance; at 40 I was no longer of two minds; at 50 I real-

Translated by Roger T. Ames.

ized the order prevailing in the world; at 60 my ear was attuned; at 70 I could give my heart-and-mind free rein without overstepping the mark." (2/4)

Kung-sun Ch'ao of Wei asked Tzu-kung, "Who did Confucius learn   2
from?" Tzu-kung replied, "The culture [*tao*] of King Wen and Wu has not yet fallen to the ground. It resides in people. While none remain unaffected by it, those who are worthy have got it in great measure, while those who are not still have a modicum of it. Who then did Confucius not learn from? Again, how could there be a single, constant teacher for him?" (19/22)

Learn broadly yet be determined in your own dispositions; enquire   3
with urgency yet reflect closely on the question at hand: becoming authoritative in your person lies in this. (19/6)

If someone can recite the three hundred *Songs* but yet when you give   4
him official responsibility, he fails you, or when you send him to distant quarters he is not able to act on his own initiative, then although he knows so much, what good is it to him? (13/5)

To realize that you know something when you do, and to realize that   5
you do not when you do not—this then is knowing. (2/17)

The wise—those who realize the world—enjoy water; the authorita-   6
tively human enjoy mountains. The wise are active; the authoritatively human are still. Those wise find enjoyment; the authoritatively human are long-lived. (6/23)

Having a sense of propriety as one's raw stuff, to practice it in ritual   7
relations, to express it with humility, and to complete it in living up to one's word: this, then, is the exemplary person. (15/18)

Since the exemplary person will be deemed wise or not because of   8
one word, how could one be but careful about what one has to say?
(19/25)

The Master said, "My, but I am in a state of decline. How long has it   9
been since I have visited with the Duke of Chou in my dreams!" (7/5)

ON INTERPERSONAL RELATIONS

The exemplary person seeks harmony rather than agreement; the small person does the opposite. (13/23)   10

Tzu-kung asked, "Is there one expression that one can act on to the end of one's days?"   11
The Master replied, "There is deference: do not impose on other people what you yourself do not desire." (15/24)   12

Confucius said, "Having three kinds of friends will bring personal improvement; three kinds will bring injury. To have friends who are   13 straight, who are true to their word, and who are well-informed is to be improved; to have friends who are ingratiating, foppish, and superficial is to be injured." (16/4)

The disciples of Tzu-hsia asked Tzu-chang about friendship. Tzu-chang queried, "What has Tzu-hsia told you?" They replied, "Join   14 together with those from whom you can learn; spurn those from whom you can't." Tzu-chang says, "This is different from what I have heard. The exemplary person exalts the worthy and is tolerant of the common, praises those who are capable and is sympathetic to those who are not. If in comparison with others I am truly worthy, who am I unable to tolerate? If I am not worthy in the comparison, and people are going to spurn me, on what basis do I spurn them?" (19/3)

ON RITUALLY CONSTITUTED COMMUNITY

Confucius said, "To discipline oneself through ritual practice is to   15 become authoritatively human. If for the space of one day one were able to accomplish this, the world would turn to one as a model of humanity. However, becoming truly human emerges out of oneself; how could it emerge out of others?" (12/1)

What does one who is not authoritatively human have to do with ritual practice or with music? (3/3)   16

ON GOVERNMENT

Lead the people with administrative injunctions and organize them   17
with penal law, and they will avoid punishments but will be without
a sense of shame. Lead them with excellence and organize them
through roles and ritual practices, and they will develop a sense of
shame, and moreover, will order themselves harmoniously. (2/3)

Someone asked Confucius, "Why are you not in government?"   18
Confucius replied, "The *Book of Documents* says: 'Filiality! Simply
extend filiality and fraternity into government.' This 'filiality' then, is
also taking part in government. Why must one take part in formal government?" (2/21)

Fan Ch'ih asked about becoming authoritatively human, and the   19
Master replied, "Love others." He asked about realization, and the
Master said, "Realize others." Fan Ch'ih did not understand and so the
Master explained, "If you promote the straight over the crooked you
can make the crooked straight." (12/22)

ON COSMIC ORDER

It is the human being who broadens natural and moral order [*tao*], not   20
natural and moral order that broadens the human being. (15/29)

The Master did not converse on strange omens, the use of force, the   21
problem of disorder, or the gods. (7/21)

Chi-lu asked about serving the gods and the spirits of the dead, but the   22
Master replied, "If you are not yet able to serve other people, how can
you serve the spirits of the dead?" Chi-lu then asked about death, but
the Master replied, "If you do not yet understand life, how can you
understand death?" (11/12)

Confucius was the sun and moon which no one can climb beyond.   23
Even if someone wanted to cut himself off from the sun and moon,
what damage could one do to him? (19/24)

The exemplary person holds three things in awe: the natural order of   24
things, the distinguished person, and the words of the sage. (16/8)

The Mencius

The foremost promoter of Confucius in the tradition was Mencius (372?–?289 B.C.E.), who lived more than a century later. Like Confucius, Mencius saw the human being as a historical and cultural achievement. Being human is not what one is; it is what one does. Both Confucius and Mencius saw the realization of the human being as emerging through the development of interpersonal relationships. Thus, personal cultivation leads simultaneously to a strong family, a harmonious community, a viable country, and a stable world. It is because human culture enhances the world so dramatically that, for the classical Confucian, the truly cultured human being has a divine aspect. Human spirituality leads directly to divinity; human beings become gods.

Human community is constructed through lines of interpersonal communication. This communication certainly entails, but is not limited to, what we have to say. People use many languages to communicate: body, ritual, speech, music, dance. The "Great Preface" to the Confucian classic, the *Book of Songs*, reflects on the increasingly personal nature of communication as one moves from speech to dance:

> Poetry is the consequence of dispositions and is articulated in language as song. One's feelings stir within one's breast and take the form of words. When words are inadequate, they are voiced as sighs. When sighs are inadequate, they are chanted. When chants are inadequate to express these feelings, unconsciously, the hands and feet begin to dance them.

Personal cultivation is pursued through the harmonizing effect of communicating effectively. Lines of communication like lines of a painting define the quality of the composition. It is this life-is-art aspect of classical Confucianism that makes the dissemblance of the "village worthy"—seeming to be what he is not—the greatest threat to community.

The Book of Mencius

For a person to realize fully one's heart-and-mind is to realize fully   1
one's nature and character, and in so doing, one realizes Nature.
(7A/1)

Translated by Roger T. Ames.

Nature's mandate is not immutable. (4A/7, citing the *Book of Songs*   2
235)

When enjoyment arises, it cannot be stopped. And when it cannot be   3
stopped, one unconsciously taps it with his feet and dances it with his
arms. (4A/27)

The mouth's propensity for tastes, the eye's for colors, the ear's for   4
sounds, the nose's for smells, and the four limbs' for comfort—these
are a matter of nature, yet basic conditions also have a part in it. That
is why the exemplary person does not refer to these as one's nature.
The relevance of authoritativeness to the father-son relationship, of
appropriateness to the ruler-subject relationship, of ritual action to the
guest-host relationship, of wisdom to the good and wise person, and
of sages to the way of Nature, are basic conditions, yet one's nature
also has a part in it. That is why the exemplary person does not refer
to these as basic conditions. (7B/24)

Yao and Shun made it human nature; Tang and Wu embodied it in   5
their persons; the Five Hegemons imitated it. Where one imitates
something resolutely over an extended period, who is to say that it is
not one's own? (7A/30)

What the exemplary person cultivates as nature and character is   6
authoritative personhood, appropriateness, ritual propriety, and wisdom. These components are rooted in one's heart-and-mind, and the
complexion that develops in the process is disclosed radiantly in
one's face, manifested in one's posture, and extended throughout
one's four limbs. One's four limbs thus communicate effectively without speaking. (7A/21)

Sage-kings have failed to arise. The feudal lords do whatever they   7
want, scholars who are not employed in government are quite ready
to pronounce on affairs, and the words of Yang Chu and Mo Ti fill the
empire. . . . I am deeply troubled by this. I protect the way of the former sages by taking a stand against Yang and Mo and by driving out
their depraved views, so that those who would advocate heretical theories will not get the opportunity to do so. (3B/9)

The admirable person is called "good." The one who has integrity is   8
called "true." To be totally genuine is called "beautiful," and to radiate

this genuineness is called "greatness." Being great, to be transformed and transforming is called "sageliness." And being sagely, to be unfathomable is called "human spirituality and divinity." (7B/25)

Mencius said to Wan Chang, "The best people in one village will   9
make friends with the best people in another village; the best people in one state will make friends with the best people in another state; the best people in the empire will make friends with other people in the empire like them. And not content with making friends with the best people in the empire, they go back in time and commune with the ancients. When one reads the poems and writings of the ancients, can it be right not to know something about them as persons? Hence one tries to understand the age in which they lived. This can be described as 'looking for friends in history.'" (5B/8)

Mencius recalled Confucius who had said, "The only person who   10
gives me no regret in passing by my gate without coming in is the village worthy. The village worthy is the thief of virtue. . . ."

Mencius said, "If you want to condemn the village worthy, you   11
have nothing on him; if you want to criticize him, there is nothing to criticize. He chimes in with the practices of the day and blends in with the common world. Where he lives he seems to be conscientious and to live up to his word, and in what he does, he seems to have integrity. His community all like him, and he sees himself as being right. Yet one cannot pursue the way of Yao or Shun with such a person. Thus Confucius said he is 'the thief of virtue.' Confucius further said, 'As for my dislike and condemnation of what is specious, I dislike weeds lest they be confused with grain; I dislike flattery lest it be confused with what is proper for one to say; I dislike a glib tongue lest it be confused with integrity; I dislike the tunes of Cheng lest they be confused with music; I dislike purple lest it be confused with vermillion; I dislike the village worthy lest he be confused with the virtuous. The exemplary person simply reverts to the standard. Where the standard is upheld, the common people will flourish, and where they flourish, there will be no perversity or aberration.' " (7B/37)

The Hsün Tzu

Although Mencius came to be heir to teachings of Confucius, another important disciple who was influential in the establishment of

Confucianism as the state ideology was Hsün Tzu (ca. 298–230 B.C.E.). One point on which all of the representatives of classical Confucianism agreed is that the human being is irreducibly social. This means that personal realization is neither selfish (causing others to love oneself) nor selfless (loving others). Rather, self-esteem, "loving oneself," is nurturing all of the interpersonal relationships that constitute a Confucian self. Self-esteem is a necessary condition for the development of one's sense of shame—a concern for how one is regarded by the other members of one's community.

Hsün Tzu

Tzu-lu came in and Confucius asked him, "What is the authoritative   1
person like?" He replied, "The authoritative person causes others to love
him." Confucius remarked, "Such can be called a refined person."

Tzu-kung came in and Confucius asked him the same question. He   2
replied, "An authoritative person loves others." Confucius remarked,
"Such can be called a consummately refined person."

Yen Yüan came in and again Confucius asked him the same question.   3
He replied, "An authoritative person loves himself." Confucius remarked,
"Such can be called the truly enlightened person." (Chapter 29)

CLASSICAL TAOISM

The *Lao-tzu, Chuang-tzu,* and *Huai-nan Tzu* are three Taoist classics dating from the third and second centuries B.C. Although Taoism served as a counterpoint to Confucianism in the tradition, at the most fundamental level, Taoist assumptions tend to reinforce rather than contradict the worldview of Confucius. Taoism, like Confucianism, is relational rather than dualistic, advocating the pursuit of self-sufficiency in one's circumstances by taking full advantage of all of those possibilities made available to one by one's various relationships in the world. Like Confucianism, it suggests that the most productive relationships are inclusive and noncoer-

Translated by Roger T. Ames.

cive. Hence, rather than dividing human possibilities into gender traits that distinguish male and female, and then privileging the former, it is better to be androgynous—both male and female—and have access to the full range of possibilities. Likewise, hard and soft is better than just hard; hot and cold is better than just hot. We impoverish our world by dividing it up into positive and negative conditions, and then desiring only what we take to be the good things. Respecting the interdependence that is characteristic of all relationships, Taoism insists that we avoid divisive value discriminations and keep our world intact.

One area in which Taoism does depart from classical Confucianism is in its ecological sensibilities: the emphasis it places on the human being's relationship to the natural as well as to the social and cultural environments. Classical Confucianism asserts that one can only find realization in community with other people. Taoism contends that this is drawing the circle too small, extending the locus of personal realization to include all of our natural conditions as well—trees, dogs, and rainbows. Not only do these natural conditions have a bearing on the quality of human life; further, they provide a model of how to take best advantage of our resources.

A second major concern of the Taoists is the limitations of language. There is a real worry that the fixed structures of language tend to persuade us, often unconsciously, that there is something permanent and enduring in our experience. The fact that a person has the same name across an entire lifetime belies the enormous process of change one undergoes, both physically and mentally.

A third point that is particularly important in the *Chuang-tzu* is "perspectivism"—a recognition that we are always looking at a situation from one perspective or another, from this or that point of view. And there is no such thing as "a view from nowhere." The implications of this assertion are profound. The *Chuang-tzu*'s perspectivism challenges notions such as objective fact, universal truth, dispassionate knowledge, a single-ordered universe, moral absolutes, and so on. At the same time, since everything is continuous with everything else, Taoism is not a relativism which claims that there is no basis for making judgments. Hitler is an abomination because far from getting the most out of his circumstances, he diminished them with coercion and destruction.

There is a mystical side to Taoism, but it is not the kind of mysticism that claims knowledge of the supernatural. Rather, it is a mysticism that celebrates the bottomless richness and uniqueness of each particular thing. Each thing is defined by its particular relationships and, in some degree, is related to every other thing. Hence, even the most simple thing with all of its relationships is extraordinarily complex.

In the Chinese tradition, "knowing" is not a correspondence between mental ideas and some external reality. Rather, it means mapping out the relationships which define a situation and make it the way it is. Knowing means "to penetrate," "to get through without obstruction." Hence, in modern Chinese, "I know" is *chih tao*, "I know the way." The metaphor frequently used to express this sense of knowing is the expert charioteer, coursing freely through the cosmos without encountering any obstacles to his progress. The *Huainan Tzu* (ca. 140 B.C.E.) passage is a good example.

The Lao-tzu

You carry the spiritual and sentient souls and unite them as one,
But can you keep them together? *yes*
You concentrate your vital forces and attain pliancy, *three treasures*
But can you assume the bearing of a child?
You cleanse the dark mirror of your mind, *3 meditation*   5
But can you be free of imperfection?
You love the people and order the country properly,
But can you be anarchic? *government*
Your senses are open to the world, *yang harmony*
But can you act the female? *yin*   10
You are clear and penetrating in all things,
But can you be ignorant? (10) *willingness to let go of scientific knowledge*

The most excellent ruler—the people do not know he's around; *invisible*
The second most excellent—they love and praise him;
The next—they fear him;   15
And the worst—they look on him with contempt.
When his integrity is inadequate,
There will be those who do not trust him.
Relaxed, he is economical with his words.

Translated by Roger T. Ames.   *three treasures (essence, vitality, spirit)*

When his accomplishments are full and the affairs of state are 20
    in proper order,
The common people all say, "We are naturally like this." (17)

You have to be bent to be made whole;
You have to be warped to be straightened;
You have to be hollow to be filled up; 25
You have to be broken to be renewed;
You have to have little to get a lot;
You have to have much to become confused;
Thus the Sage embraces One to be the model of the world.
It is because he does not show himself that he is brilliant; 30
It is because he does not assert himself that he is distinguished;
It is because he does not boast that he is accomplished;
It is because he is not conceited that he is enduring.
It is only because he does not compete that no one in the world
    is able to compete with him. 35
As the ancients said, "You have to be bent to be made whole."
How can this be empty talk?
This is really returning to it whole. (22)

One who understands masculinity and preserves femininity
Is the river gorge of the world. 40
As the river gorge of the world,
One's constant potency does not quit one, *Virtues*
And one returns to a state of infancy.
One who understands white and preserves black *Harmony*
Is the model of the world. *Potency* *three treasures* 45
As the model of the world,
One's constant potency does not err,
And one returns to a state of boundlessness.
    tao
One who understands glory and preserves disgrace
Becomes the valley of the world. 50
As the valley of the world,
One's constant potency is thus sufficient,
And one returns to a state of unworked wood.
When unworked wood is splintered,
It becomes vessels. 55
The Sage uses it,
Only to become the chief of the officials.
Therefore, the best organization does not divide things up. (28)
    (whole) *tao*

Tao engenders one,
One engenders two, 60

Two engenders three,
And three engenders the myriad things.
The myriad things shoulder the *yin* and embrace the *yang,*
And in blending their psychophysical vapors, they achieve
    harmony. (42) *three treasures*   65

The Chuang-tzu

Hui Tzu said to Chuang-tzu, "The King of Wei presented me with   1
some seeds of a large calabash. I planted them and brought them to
fruit, at which time they produced a gourd that had a volume of five
bushels. I used it as a water container, but its skin was not sufficiently
resilient to hold the water. So I split one in two to make a dipper, but
it was so enormous that no water crock would take it. It was not that
these gourds were wanting in size, but rather because they were of no
use that I smashed them up."

"You certainly are inept when it comes to using large things,"   2
Chuang-tzu replied. "There were some people of Sung who were
skilled at making a salve which prevented chaffed hands. Generation
after generation they took washing and bleaching silk as their trade.
Some stranger heard about them and asked to buy their prescription
for a hundred measures of gold. Assembling the family, they talked it
over and said, 'Generation after generation we engage in washing and
bleaching silk and have earned only a fraction of what he offers us.
Now in one morning we have a chance to sell our technique for a
hundred measures of gold. Let's give it to him!' The stranger got the
technique and used it to gain access to the King of Wu. There being
some conflict with Yüeh, the King of Wu dispatched the stranger in
command. That winter they engaged the Yüeh forces in a naval battle
and vanquished them. Dividing up the conquered territory, the King
of Wu gave him a fiefdom. The salve that could prevent chaffing of
the hands was one and the same in both cases. The fact that one of
them was able to get a fief out of it while the other was stuck washing
and bleaching silk was simply because of a difference in application.
Now you have a five-bushel calabash. Why don't you consider mak-

Translated by Roger T. Ames.

ing it into a buoy to go floating in the rivers and lakes instead of fretting over the fact that no water crock will take it. You still suffer from a wooly and unpenetrating mind." (Chapter 1)

Now, speaking is not simply discharging air. Speaking has that which   3
it says, only that about which is spoken is never fixed. In effect, do we say something or have we never said anything? It is considered to be different from the chirping of young birds, yet is there really any distinction or not? How is the dynamic pattern of things [tao] so obscured that there is such a thing as "genuine" and "counterfeit"? And how is what is said about this pattern so obscured that there is such a thing as right and wrong? Where can the pattern of things go to that it does not exist? And how can what is said about it exist and yet be unacceptable? The dynamic pattern of things [tao] is obscured by small contrivances, and what is said about it is obscured by embellishments on them. Thus we have the right and wrong of the Confucians and Mohists who contradict each other. If we really want to contradict them both, nothing can compare with enlightenment. (Chapter 2)

There is nothing which is not a "that" and nothing which is not a   4
"this." Because we cannot see from a "that" perspective but can only know from our own perspective, it is said that "that" arises out of "this" and "this" further accommodates "that." This is the notion that "this" and "that" are born simultaneously. But being born entails dying, and vice versa; being acceptable entails being unacceptable, and vice versa; accommodating right is accommodating wrong, and vice versa. It is for this reason that the sage, illuminating this situation with the way things really are rather than going along with discriminations among them, is also a further case of accommodating what is right and what is "this." But "this" is also "that," and vice versa. And a "this's" "that" further has one set of right and wrong, while "this" has another. In truth, is there really such a thing as "this" and "that" or not? (Chapter 2)

Acceptable arises out of what is identified as acceptable; unaccept-   5
able arises out of what is identified as unacceptable. A path becomes a path by walking along it; a thing is made a thing by being so-called. Why are things so? They are so because they are so. Why are they not something other than what they are? They are not something else

because they are not. Things certainly have their so-ness and certainly are acceptable on their own terms. There is nothing which is not so and should not be the way it is. Because of this, while we distinguish between a stalk and a beam, a leper and the classic beauty, Hsi Shih, the dynamic pattern of things [*tao*] pervades every weird and wonderful, strange and extraordinary thing. The discrimination of a thing is its actualization, and its actualization is its destruction. Now where things as they are, are free of actualization and destruction, they are continuous as one. Only the enlightened person understands that they are continuous as one. Because of this, rather than seek the specific utility in things, he lodges in their commonality. Their commonality is their utility, their utility is their continuity, and their continuity is what they have. And to get what they have is to be almost there. Simply accommodating "this" and not knowing why it is so is called *tao*. (Chapter 2)

Suchness of the North Sea said, "If we view a particular thing from the perspective of the dynamic pattern of things [*tao*], we find that nobility and baseness do not apply. If we view a particular thing from its own perspective, we find that the thing will take itself as noble and other things as base; if we view a particular thing from the perspective of popular opinion, we find that nobility and baseness do not lie in the thing itself. If we view a particular thing from the perspective of distinctness and consider it big on the basis of a context relative to which it is big, then everything is big; if we consider it small on the basis of a context relative to which it is small, then everything is small. Where we can understand how the cosmos is a single shoot of grain and the tip of an autumn hair is a hill or mountain, the nature of a particular's degree of distinctiveness has been apprehended. If we view a particular thing from the perspective of utility and consider it useful on the basis of a context in which it has utility, then everything has utility; if we consider it useless on the basis of a context in which it has no utility, then everything is useless. Where we can understand how east and west are opposite directions yet cannot exist without each other, the nature of a particular's share of utility has been ascertained. If we view a particular thing from the perspective of its own inclinations and grant it approval on the basis of a context in which it warrants our approval, then everything will be approved; if we condemn it on the basis of a context in which it warrants our condemnation, then everything will be condemned. Where we can understand how both Yao and Chieh would approve of themselves and yet condemn each other, the nature of one's commitment to its own inclinations will be seen.

"In ancient times when Yao abdicated the throne in favor of Shun the imperial succession continued, yet when King K'uai of Yen did the same in favor of Tzu Chih the succession was cut off. When T'ang and Wu contested the throne they became kings, yet when Duke Po did the same thing he was destroyed. Viewing it from this perspective, in evaluating the propriety of contest or abdication and the conduct of men like Yao and Chieh, nobility and baseness are a function of the times and can in no way be construed as constants. That a large beam can be used to batter down a city wall but can't be used to plug up a small hole speaks of a difference in function. That noble steeds like Ch'i-chi and Hua-liu could gallop 400 miles a day yet are not equal to the badger and weasel in catching rats speaks of a difference in skills. That an owl at night can catch a flea with his claws and spy the tip of a hair yet in the light of day regardless of how wide he opens his eyes still cannot see a hill or mountain speaks of a difference in natural capacities. Therefore, one who would say, 'Why not model ourselves on right and dispense with wrong, model ourselves on proper order and dispense with disorder?' understands neither the pattern implicit in the cosmos nor the conditions governing particular things. This would be like trying to model ourselves on Heaven while dispensing with earth or trying to model ourselves on *yin* while dispensing with *yang*. That this cannot be done is clear. Such being the case, those who go on talking this way and won't give it up must be either stupid or up to no good! Among emperors and kings there have been differences in their abdications and for the Three Dynasties there have been differences in their continuance.

> "Where one is out of step with the times and at odds with convention
>   he is called an usurper;
> Where he is in step with the times and apropos of convention he is
>   called an adherent of rightness.
> Silence! Lord of the Yellow River.
> How would you know the gate of nobility and baseness or the
>   residence of big and small."

The Lord of the Yellow River asked Suchness, "If this is the case, what should I do and what should I refrain from doing? In the final analysis, on what basis do I go about accepting and refusing, pursuing and rejecting?"

Suchness of the North Sea replied,   9

"If we view things from the perspective of the dynamic pattern of things
     (tao):
What is nobility and what is baseness?
This is called drifting with the tide.
You don't want to be obdurate of will—
This would be a great handicap with respect to *tao*.
What is many and what is few?
This is called taking things as they come.
You don't want to be inflexible in what you do—
This would put you on a different plane from *tao*.
Dignified like the ruler of a state
He has no private bounty;
Broad and munificent like the god of the soil at its sacrifice
He has no private fortune;
Vast and all-pervading like the boundlessness of the four directions,
He has nothing which confines or delimits him.
Embracing all things without exception
Which of them receives his special protection?
This is called being boundless.
With the myriad things equal
Which of them is short and which is long?
The dynamic pattern of things *(tao)* is without beginning or end.
Since things partake of both life and death,
You cannot depend upon some realized condition;
Since they are at one point empty and another full,
You cannot locate them in a given form.
The passage of the years cannot be forestalled,
Time cannot be halted.
Fading, growing, full, empty,
Ending and then again beginning.
This is why we talk about the great meaning
And discuss the pattern of the myriad things, treasures
The life of a thing is like a sprint or gallop,
In every action there is change and in every moment there is
     movement.
What should you do?
What shouldn't you do?
You are certain to transform of your own accord. (Chapter 17)

The ruler of the North Sea was "Swift," the ruler of the South Sea was   10
"Sudden," and the ruler of the Central Sea was "Chaos." Swift and
Sudden had on several occasions encountered each other in the terri-
tory of Chaos, and Chaos had treated them with great hospitality.

Swift and Sudden, devising a way to repay Chaos's generosity, said: "Human beings all have seven orifices through which they see, hear, eat, and breathe. Chaos alone is without them." They then attempted to bore holes in Chaos, each day boring one hole. On the seventh day, Chaos died. (Chapter 7)

Chuang-tzu and Hui Tzu were strolling across the bridge over the Hao 11
River. Chuang-tzu observed, "The minnows swim out and about as they please—this is the way they enjoy themselves."

Hui Tzu replied, "You are not a fish—how do you know what 12
they enjoy?"

Chuang-tzu returned, "You are not me—how do you know that I 13
don't know what is enjoyable for the fish?"

Hui Tzu said, "I am not you, so I certainly don't know what you 14
know; but it follows that, since you are certainly not the fish, you don't know what is enjoyment for the fish either."

Chuang-tzu said, "Let's get back to your basic question. When 15
you asked *'From where* do you know what the fish enjoy?' you already knew that I know what the fish enjoy, or you wouldn't have asked me. I know it from here above the Hao River." (Chapter 17)

Yen Hui said, "I have made progress." 16
"How so?" inquired Confucius. 17
Yen Hui said, "I have sat and forgotten." 18
Confucius, noticeably flustered, inquired: "What do you mean by 19
'sitting and forgetting'?"

"I have demolished my appendages and body, gotten rid of my 20
keenness of sight and hearing, abandoned my physical form and cast off knowledge to find identity with the Great Continuity," said Yen Hui. "This is what I call 'sitting and forgetting.' " (Chapter 6).

The Huai-nan Tzu

Hence, the person of great stature:
Being placidly free of all reflection
And serenely without thoughts for the morrow,
Has the heavens as his canopy,
The earth as his box, 5
The four seasons as his horses,

Translated by Roger T. Ames and D. C. Lau.

And the *yin* and *yang* as his charioteer.
He mounts the clouds and climbs beyond the skies,
To be with the demiurge of change.
Doing as he pleases and following a freer rhythm   10
He gallops the great abode.
He walks his horses when he should walk them,
He runs them hard when he should run them.
He gets the god of rain to sprinkle the roads
And the god of wind to sweep away the dust.   15
With lightning as his whip
And thunder as his wheels,
Above he rambles in the free and roaming vastness
Below he goes out of the gates of boundlessness.
Having scanned all round and left nothing out,   20
Remaining whole he returns to guard what is within.
He manages the four corners of the earth
Yet always returns to the pivot.

Thus, since the heavens are his canopy,
There is nothing unsheltered;   25
Since the earth is his box,
There is nothing unconveyed;
Since the four seasons are his horses,
There is nothing unemployed;
Since the *yin* and *yang* are his charioteers,   30
There is nothing lacking.
Hence, he travels fast without pitching
And travels far without fatigue.
Without taxing his four limbs
And without draining the keenness of his hearing and sight,   35
    He knows the lay and the boundaries of the
    various divisions and quadrants of the
    cosmos. How is this so?

It is because he has his hands on the control handles of the *tao* and rambles in the land of the inexhaustible. (Chapter 1)

The way of the ruler is said to be round because revolving and turn-   1
ing, it is without a starting point. He transforms and nurtures like a
god, is vacuous and vacant, and follows the natural course of things.
Always keeping to the rear, he never takes the lead.

    The way of the minister is said to be square because he finds out   2
what is appropriate and dwells in what he is best fitted for. It is by taking the lead in carrying out affairs and by clearly keeping to his
defined duties that he realizes his accomplishments.

Where the ruler and minister have different ways, there is proper order; but where they are the same, there is disorder. If each gets what is appropriate to him and dwells in what is right for him, the one above and those below will know how to deal with each other. (Chapter 9)   3

The ruler sees with the eyes of the empire, hears with the ears of the empire, deliberates with the intelligence of the empire, and contends with the strength of the empire behind him. His edicts and commands are able to penetrate to the lowest level and the real condition of his subjects can be known by him above. His bureaucracy has open access to the throne, and his various ministers are like spokes converging at the hub. He does not reward on account of pleasure or punish on account of anger. His awesomeness being established will not be put aside, his intelligence shining forth will not be obscured, his laws and edicts being circumspect will not be unduly harsh, his sight and hearing being penetrating will not be beclouded, and what is actually good and bad being set out before him daily, he will not indulge in conjecture. (Chapter 9)   4

BOOK OF CHANGES (I CHING)

The first of the Confucian classics and undoubtedly one of the most influential texts in the entire imperial tradition is the *Book of Changes*. Its sixty-four hexagrams, or "images," served the tradition as a concrete vocabulary for reflecting on existing circumstances and for anticipating the future. In using the *Book of Changes* to interpret a future, the adherent is not a passive enquirer into what was preordained by some supernatural power, but an active participant in recommending and shaping events to come. One uses the *Book of Changes* like a cookbook, teasing the most productive future out of available circumstances. Using the images of the text as a heuristic to articulate possible futures, one then had the language and the distinctions necessary to refine the situation, and to configure a place and posture most conducive to meaningful personal and communal relationships.

Wang Pi's commentary on the *Book of Changes* points out the circular interdependence of language, image, and meaning. His point is to reject the notion of literal language which supposedly corresponds to some external reality. Word and image in themselves are not containers of meaning; in fact, if they are so interpreted, they can obstruct it.

In the *Book of Changes,* the meaning of a general situation is captured in an image, and the image is explained in words. The words are an entrée. They are the most abstract level of discourse, and as such, have the least degree of "meaning" for one's particular situation. Words, however, have the power to evoke an image, which in stirring one's "imagination," enables one to focus the situation for oneself. What was general becomes increasingly particular. By virtue of its relative explicitness, the image displaces the words, and as the image is explored as having significance for one's own circumstances, the lines of the image itself begin to fade. The image gives way to meaning. In being deepened and made more specific, more "meaningful" for oneself, the image loses its more general character and becomes increasingly indistinct. The image retreats as the particular situation is defined.

This process entails both clarity and ambiguity. Words and images as literal abstractions are clear, and yet are equivocal in their application to particular situations. The meaning of a particular event, on the other hand, is clear as a concrete experience, and yet in its particular detail, is resistant to conceptual clarity and generalization. Hence, in moving from words to meaning, the vagueness of generality gives way to the vagueness of particularity.

The I Ching

The Sages, having the wherewithal to contemplate the complexity and   1
diversity of the world and to fathom in it shapes and appearances, captured in "images" what is appropriate to things. For this reason, we call them "images." (Commentary on the Judgments 6)

The Master said: "The written word cannot do justice to speech, and   2
speech cannot do justice to meaning."

"If this is the case, then is the meaning of the Sages beyond our   3
grasp?"

The Master replied: "The Sages constructed 'images' to give a full   4
account of their meaning, set up the hexagrams to give a full account

Translated by Roger T. Ames.

of what is natural and what is contrived, wrote their judgments on the images and hexagrams in order to say completely what they had to say, introduced the presumption of change and continuity as a way to take full advantage of any situation, and elaborated upon and embellished all this to do justice to its profundity." (Commentary on the Appended Judgments 12)

Commentary on the *I Ching*
WANG PI

An image expresses meaning; words clarify the image. To do full justice to meaning, nothing is as good as an image; to do full justice to an image, nothing is as good as words. Because words arise from images, we can explore the words as a window on the image. And because the image arises from meaning, we can explore the image as a window on meaning. Meaning is given full account with an image, and the image is articulated in words. Hence, words are whereby we clarify the image. In getting the image, we forget the words. The image is whereby we hold onto meaning. In getting the meaning, we forget the image. It is like the snare serving to capture the rabbit; in snaring the rabbit, we forget the snare. Or like the fishtrap serving to catch the fish; in catching the fish, we forget the trap. As such, words are the "snare" for the image. And the image is the "trap" for meaning. For this reason, holding onto the words is not getting the image; holding onto the image is not getting the meaning.

Given that an image arises from the meaning, in holding onto the image, what you are holding on to is not really the image. Given that words arise from the image, in holding onto the words, what you are holding on to is not really the words. As such, to forget the image is to get the meaning; to forget the words is to get the image. Getting the meaning lies in forgetting the image; getting the image lies in forgetting the words.

CHINESE MARXISM

Mao Tse-tung (1893–1976) was both a Chinese philosopher and a Marxist. Marxism was a "Western heresy" appropriated by Mao and other Chinese reformers earlier in this century as a means to deal with the West. As a doctrine it appealed to them because many of its characteristics are consistent with Confucianism. Where Maoism departs from more orthodox and ideological Marxism, it is generally the degree of emphasis that Mao places on particularity and concreteness—his use of specific cases. Even when Mao appeals to language translated as "universal" and "absolute," he is not using it in any technical philosophical sense, and means by it "general" and "unequaled."

For example, the explanation of creative processes in terms of the interaction of complementary elements like *yin* and *yang* is fundamental to and pervasive in the Chinese tradition. In defining the relationship between economic principle and superstructure, Mao translates it into a kind of *yin-yang* dialectic in which these factors are mutually influencing and determining. For Marx, economic principle is far more deterministic. In fact, on most readings, Marx is teleological, anticipating the evolution of a utopian society. For Mao, because the future is completely open, society must pursue a continuing revolution to counter reactionary tendencies.

Again reflecting the *yin-yang* kind of opposition, Mao argues that contradictions must always be dealt with as resolutely hierarchical in nature, with a primary and a secondary aspect. The vocabulary that Mao uses to describe the relationship between these aspects—interconnected, interpenetrating, interpermeating, interdependent, collaborative—recalls the *yin-yang* complementarity.

In the education of the people, Marx regards class origins as determinant and for the most part similar for all class members. Mao goes to great pains to insist that all of a person's life experiences must be factored into the evaluation of a person and of human needs in general. Further, while for Marx certain universal human needs set constraints on the malleability of the human being, Mao, in subscribing to a far more radical malleability, sets no constraints at all. Notions such as "the unconscious," which were popular in the first half of this century and which might introduce some determinative force beyond the control of the human being, are given little attention in Mao.

Standard readings of Marx tend to interpret the practical Marx as functionally theoretical, allowing that his analyses can be abstracted and applied to other geographical sites of human development with little qualification. Mao has an unwavering commitment to practice, regarding theoretical abstractions with great distrust, and insisting that specific historical and cultural circumstances must be factored into any explanation. It was for this reason that Mao led the way in revising an ambitious and universalistic Marxism into a peculiarly Chinese style of socialism.

On Contradiction

Mao Tse-tung

Contradictions exist in all developmental processes. Contradictions 1
run through things from beginning to end in the process in which each of them develops. As discussed above, this is the universal and absolute nature of contradictions. Now let's talk about the particularity and the relativity of contradictions. This issue should be studied from various different situations. . . .

With respect to the order in the process of human knowledge, 2
there is the gradual extension from the knowledge of individual and particular things to the knowledge of things in general. It is only once a person knows the particular character of many different things that he can take the additional step of making generalizations about them, and come to know the shared character of various kinds of things. Once a person has acquired this knowledge of the shared character of things, he can use it as a guide, and can then proceed to investigate a given concrete thing that has not yet been investigated, or which has only been superficially investigated, and discern its particular character. In this way, he is able to supplement, enrich, and develop his knowledge of the shared character of things, and to prevent this knowledge from becoming withered and ossified. These are the two processes of gaining knowledge: first, moving from the particular to the general, and second, moving from the general to the particular. Human knowledge accrues through this cyclical movement, and with each cycle (as long as scientific method is strictly adhered to) human knowledge can advance a notch, making it increasingly profound. Where our dogmatists go wrong on this issue is, on the one hand, not understanding that one must investigate the particular nature of contradictions and recognize the particular character of each thing before

Mao Tse-tung. "On Contradiction." Adapted from the *Selected Works of Mao Tse-tung*, vol 1. Peking: Foreign Languages Press, 1965.

he can adequately know the universal nature of contradictions and adequately know the shared character of various different things, and on the other hand, not understanding that once one has come to know the shared character of things, he must still continue to investigate those concrete things which have not as yet been thoroughly investigated or have only just appeared. Our dogmatists are lazy; they refuse to do any painstaking investigation of concrete things, they believe that general truths are things that appear from nowhere, and they change these truths into purely abstract formulas which none are able to fathom, denying utterly, and moreover, inverting the proper order whereby the human being comes to know truth. They do not understand the interconnectedness of the two processes in human knowledge—from the particular to the general, and again from the general to the particular. They understand nothing of the Marxist theory of knowledge.

It is necessary not only to investigate the particular contradictions   3
and the character they determine in every great system of the forms of matter in motion, but also to investigate the particular contradiction and the character of each process in the long development of each form of matter in motion. In every form of matter in motion, each actual and unimagined process of development is qualitatively different in character. Our investigation must stress this point, and must begin from it.

Contradictions qualitatively different in character can only be   4
resolved by the application of methods that are qualitatively different in character. . . . Processes change, old processes and old contradictions dissolve, and new processes and new contradictions emerge, and the methods for resolving these contradictions must accordingly be different. . . .

The relationship between the universal and the particular nature   5
of contradictions is the relationship between the common character and the individual character of contradictions. Its shared nature lies in the fact that contradictions exist in all processes, and that they run through all processes from beginning to end. Contradictions, then, are movement, are things and events, are processes, are thought. To deny contradictions in things is to deny everything. . . .

On the issue of the particular nature of contradictions, there are   6
still two circumstances which must especially undergo analysis: namely, the primary contradiction, and the primary aspect of a particular contradiction. In the process of the development of a complex

thing, there exist many contradictions, but among them there is only one which is the primary contradiction, the existence and development of which determines or influences the existence and development of all the others. . . . In the two aspects of any contradiction, there must be one that is primary, and the other, secondary. The primary aspect is the aspect which has the dominant function in the contradiction. The nature of a thing is determined mainly by the primary aspect of the contradiction, the aspect which has taken the dominant role. . . .

Certainly, the forces of production, practice, and the economic foundation generally play the primary and determinative role. Whoever denies this is not a materialist. However, under certain circumstances, aspects such as the relations of production, theory, and the superstructure can in turn manifest themselves in the primary and determinative role. This must also be recognized. . . . Are we going against materialism in saying this? No. Because we acknowledge that in the broad sweep of historical development material things determine mental things, and social existents determine social consciousness. But at the same time, we also acknowledge, and must acknowledge, the reaction of mental things on the material, the reaction of social consciousness on social existents, and the reaction of the superstructure on the economic foundation. This is not to go against materialism. In fact, it avoids mechanical materialism, and upholds dialectical materialism. . . .

Identity, integration, coherence, interpenetration, interpermeation, interdependence (or mutuality in existing), interconnectedness or collaboration—all of these different expressions mean one thing and refer to the following two situations: first, the two aspects of each kind of contradiction in the process of the development of a thing each have the other aspect as a precondition of their own existence, and both aspects coexist in the single entity; second, under certain conditions, each of the two aspects of a contradiction transforms into its opposite. . . . If there were no life, there would be no death, and vice versa; if there were no above, there would be no below, and vice versa; if there were no calamity, there would be no good fortune, and vice versa. . . . All opposing factors are like this. Under certain conditions, in one aspect they are opposed to each other, and in the other they are interconnected, interpenetrating, interpermeating, interdependent. . . . All contradictory things are interconnected; not only under certain circumstances do they coexist in a single entity, they also under certain circumstances transform into each other. This is the full meaning of the identity of opposites.

GLOSSARY

androgyny: Having both male and female gender traits.

authoritative: The quality of being a model and inspiring admiration in others for a particular talent or trait.

autonomy: Independence and self-sufficiency; governance over one's own conditions—a central value in the liberal democratic conception of self.

axiom: A self-evident proposition, principle, or rule that has received general acceptance.

Being: In classical Greek philosophy, the assertion that there is something real behind appearance, something essential and necessary behind changing phenomena.

Book of Documents: A collection of political documents and speeches that is traditionally thought to have been assembled by Confucius, and which ultimately became one of the classics.

Book of Songs: An anthology of just over 300 songs reflecting daily life in the early Chou dynasty both among the people and in the court that is reputed to have been edited by Confucius, and that became one of the classics.

calligraphy: The writing of Chinese characters (or any script) as an art form.

coercion: Yielding because of the imposition of some external force.

complementary opposites: Correlative paired opposites, where they are interdependent and must reference each other for explanation; for example, *yin* and *yang*, up and down, left and right; to be distinguished from dualistic opposites.

Confucius: A fifth-century B.C. Chinese philosopher whose ideas in the Han dynasty (206 B.C.–220 A.D.) became the state ideology which lasted down to the twentieth century. By the fourth century A.D., temples were erected to celebrate Confucius in every county in the country. Followers of Confucius shaped the development of Chinese civilization and gave it its distinctive character.

contradictions: In a dialectical process, the direct opposition of competing factors which must be resolved in order to move the process ahead.

cosmogony: An account of the origination—the coming-into-being—of the cosmos.

deference: Yielding to the judgment or opinion of someone else.

dialectic: The art of moving a discussion ahead through some rational process applied in investigating the truth of a particular theory or opinion.

dualistic opposites: Paired opposites, where the former member of the pair is independent of the latter, and the latter is derived from the former; for example, God and world, knowledge and opinion, reality and appearance; to be distinguished from complementary opposites.

Duke of Chou: Brother of King Wu, founder of the Chou dynasty (ca. 1111 B.C.), who is so renown in the tradition for his wise advice that he came to be a symbol of Chou institutions and statecraft.

enculturation: The process of living in and being shaped by a given culture.

exemplary person: A person who, by virtue of a cultivated moral excellence, has become an example to other members of the community.

filiality: Filial piety—the observance of respectful conduct in dealing with one's elders—parents and grandparents—while they are living, and sacrifice to them after they have died.

Goethe: Johann Wolfgang von Goethe (pronounced "Gu-te") (1749–1832) was a poet and author at the center of German romanticism in the eighteenth and nineteenth centuries.

heart-and-mind: In the Chinese tradition, the heart is the seat of both emotion and intellect; hence, in English it must be translated to include both heart and mind.

hexagram: A pattern of six complete or broken lines which expresses a particular meaning, and which in the sum of 64 different patterns constitutes the language of the Chinese classic, the *Book of Changes.*

ideology: A body of doctrines and a set of institutions which prescribe a particular way of thinking and living.

immanence: The notion that order inheres in the world and is indwelling rather than independent of the world.

King Wen and King Wu: The founders of the Chou dynasty (ca. 1111 B.C.); father and son, renown for their civil and military virtue.

malleability: Able to be shaped by hammering or pressure.

Mao Tse-tung: (also, "Mao Zedong") Mao was the revolutionary leader who founded Communist China in 1949. His ideology continues to influence China even today. In fact, "Mao fever," the worship of Mao as a divine protector, is popular in large parts of China today.

Mencius: The most celebrated disciple of Confucius who lived about 150 years after the Master's death, and whose philosophy is remembered in one of the classics called after him.

Mo Ti: The founder of the Mohist school who challenged many of the basic beliefs of the Confucians with doctrines such as universal love, obedience to superiors, frugality in ritual practices, compliance with the will of Heaven, and so on.

natural law: The belief that there is a foundation for human laws and morality because they are grounded in some ultimate and unquestionable source of value. The first principles which determine human value are discovered, not invented, and exist as a universal and unchanging standard against which human conduct can be measured.

objectivity: The assumption that there is some reality which is independent of human interpretation.

Plato: A fifth-century B.C. Greek philosopher who in many ways set the agenda for the development of Western civilization. His Theory of Forms—a theory that behind the world of change there is a permanent structure of unchanging principles—has, in various renderings, been a basic assumption in systematic philosophy. The twentieth-century Anglo-American philosopher, A. N. Whitehead, said that all of Western philosophy was simply a series of footnotes to Plato.

Principle of Sufficient Reason: Leibniz's doctrine that nothing happens without a reason which was ultimately posited as a proof for the existence of God beyond this universe.

propriety: A familiar translation for ritual practices *(li)* which inform all aspects of communal living in Chinese society, covering all formal conduct from table manners to social roles and institutions.

ritual: See *propriety*.

sages: Persons like Confucius revered in the Chinese tradition for their uncommon wisdom.

scientific method: The belief that a universal method, modeled on impersonal rational systems such as mathematics and formal logic, can be discovered and applied rigorously to yield new ideas in any field of natural science.

shame: A painful feeling that arises when persons believe that they have let their community down; an important impetus for moral conduct in Chinese society.

Spring and Autumn of Mr. Lu: An encyclopedic compendium of knowledge prepared for the Ch'in court compiled in the third century B.C.

tao: The natural cosmology of classical China is not a single-ordered cosmos that returns the Many to a superordinated and independent One; it is a cosmos in which the Many are constitutive of the ever unique and unbounded *tao*. *Tao* is both "what is" (things and their attributes) and "how things are" (actions and their modalities). *Tao* has as much to do with the subjects of knowing and their quality of understanding, as it does with the object of knowledge.

teleology: The belief that natural phenomena are guided in their development by some preassigned design or purpose—some final cause.

universal: Characteristic of all or the whole; a general term or concept, or the generic nature which the term signifies; a Platonic idea or Aristotelian form.

wok: A Chinese pot used for cooking—usually rounded on the bottom.

Yang Chu: A fourth-century B.C. philosopher who is best and probably incorrectly remembered for the doctrine of nurturing one's own life to the extent that one should not remove a single hair from his thigh even if it were to benefit the entire world.

Yao and Shun: Two legendary rulers remembered as symbols of traditional values.

yin and *yang*: The general and most basic language for articulating correlations among things is metaphorical: in some particular aspect at some specific point in time, one person or thing is "overshadowed" by another; that is, made *yin* to another's *yang*. Literally, *yin* means "shady" and *yang* means "sunny," defining in the most general terms those contrasting and hierarchical relationships which constitute indwelling order and regularity. It is important to recognize the *interdependence* and correlative character of the *yin-yang* kind of polar opposites, and to distinguish this contrastive tension from the dualistic opposition implicit in the vocabulary of the classical Greek world, where one primary member of a set stands *independent* of and is more "real" than the other.

FURTHER READINGS

General

DERK BODDE. *Chinese Thought, Society, and Science.* Honolulu: University of Hawaii Press, 1991.

A. C. GRAHAM. *Disputers of the Tao.* La Salle, Ill.: Open Court, 1989.

DAVID L. HALL and ROGER T. AMES. "Understanding Order: The Chinese Perspective," in Robert Solomon and Kathleen Higgins, eds., *From Africa to Zen: An Invitation to World Philosophy,* 1993.

BENJAMIN I. SCHWARTZ. *The World of Thought in Ancient China.* Cambridge, Mass.: Harvard University Press, 1985.

Confucianism

DAVID L. HALL and ROGER T. AMES. *Thinking Through Confucius.* Albany, N.Y.: State University of New York Press, 1987.

D. C. LAU, trans. *Confucius: The Analects.* Hong Kong: Chinese University Press, 1983.

D. C. LAU, trans. *Mencius.* Hong Kong: Chinese University Press, 1984.

Taoism

ROGER T. AMES. *The Art of Rulership.* Honolulu: University of Hawaii Press, 1983.

CHANG CHUNG-YUAN. *Creativity and Taoism*. New York: Harper & Row, 1963.

A. C. GRAHAM, trans. *Chuang-tzu: The Inner Chapters*. London: George Allen & Unwin, 1981.

Book of Changes (I Ching)

HELLMUT WILHELM. *Heaven, Earth, and Man in the Book of Changes*. Seattle: University of Washington Press, 1977.

RICHARD WILHELM, trans. *The I Ching or Book of Changes*, 3d ed. Translated into English by Cary F. Baynes. Princeton: Princeton University Press, 1967.

Mao Tse-tung

DONALD MUNRO. *The Concept of Man in Contemporary China*. Ann Arbor: University of Michigan Press, 1979.

STUDY QUESTIONS

1. What are some of the differences between the Confucian conception of person and that found in the contemporary Western world?
2. Consider the Taoist notion of "religiousness." What would "religion" mean in this tradition?
3. Explore the passages from Mao Tse-tung for additional ways in which he is a traditional Chinese philosopher.

CHAPTER 3

South Asian Philosophy

STEPHEN H. PHILLIPS

Indian philosophy extends for more than 3,000 years. Two world religions, Hinduism and Buddhism, developed and flourished in India, spawning hundreds of texts. These include philosophic defenses of religious theses and ideas, particularly ideas about experiences termed "enlightenment," "awakening," and "liberation," which are viewed as the supreme good. Thus much in Indian philosophy is religiously, or mystically, inspired. Special experiences brought about by meditation or yogic practice (breath control, etc.) are promoted by certain systematic philosophies—Buddhism, Hinduism, and others. The terms "nirvana" and "yoga" are now familiar to most people.

The religious or mystical philosophies attempt to integrate otherworldliness with a view of this world: what are taken to be special mystic indications are aligned with theories about sense perception, language, and everyday life. But in addition to the religious and mystical apologetics, much of Indian philosophy is secular; logic, philosophy of language, the theory of everyday knowledge, and views about the nature of being (ontology) have become increasingly refined through the centuries. Classical logic known as Nyāya represents a sustained, largely secular tradition. In contrast, Vedānta, the mystical philosophy of the Upanishads, is one of the most important religiously motivated philosophies, rivaled only by Buddhism. From claims about what constitutes the best life to meta-disputes over what constitutes a philosophic claim, Indian philosophy presents enormous intellectual wealth that is only beginning to be appreciated in our modern and global times.

So far we have been speaking of Indian philosophy only in the sense of the classical philosophies, which are expressed in Sanskrit, the intellectual language of the ancient and classical civilizations (ca.

What is Nyaya & Vedanta

1500 B.C.E.–1850). Sanskrit is now a dead language, but modern Indian philosophy continues through other media. The capital of the classical heritage is paying special dividends in contemporary India, where students of philosophy have fused traditional wisdom with new insights from Western philosophy.

With the exception of Aurobindo, the selections below are taken from ancient and classical texts. Aurobindo, a nonacademic mystic out of the traditional mold, combines classical and modern perspectives. Many other modern philosophers, both in and out of academia, carry on the traditions of Vedānta and Nyāya. Of those treated below, Nāgārjuna and Cārvāka currently carry huge influence.

The Buddhist Nāgārjuna launches a professionalism within classical philosophies. Some of his arguments are answered in the selection from the *Nyāya-sūtra*. The first four selections—from the Veda, the Upanishads, the *Bhavagad-Gītā*, and the *Yoga-sūtra*—all help shape classical and modern Vedānta, although the metaphysics of the *Yoga-sūtra* is usually identified as a distinct philosophic school. The Cārvāka selection challenges the religious and mystical conceptions current in classical times.

THE VEDAS

Indo-European tribes migrated into the Indian subcontinent over several centuries—as early as 1500 B.C.E. to approximately 1000 C.E.—and established what has come to be known as the Vedic civilization, named after the Vedas. The Vedas, a collection of sacred poems or hymns, are the oldest documents extant in any Indo-European language. They are composed in an early form of Sanskrit, the intellectual language of the classical Indian civilization that stretches up to modern times.

There is much controversy about the context and the meaning of the various hymns and poems of the Vedas. The prevailing opinion is that the oldest of the four Vedas, the *Ṛg Veda*, is the result of a contest of eloquence. The entries are various in theme: many hymns are devoted to praise of gods of a Vedic pantheon; others recount conquests, teach moral lessons, speculate about nature or creation, or are comical; and a few show a philosophic and questioning turn of mind. But they are all good poetry, with complex rhythms and extensive use of rhetorical devices.

The four poems below are taken from a selection translated by A. A. Macdonell, an eminent Sanskritist and Vedic scholar of the early twentieth century. For the latter three poems, portions of Macdonell's introductions are included. The former, however, is the premier Vedic instance of philosophic questioning, and it is pretty easily followed without introductory contextualization. (Macdonell, in any case, provides none.) The poem contains a story of creation. But notice the skepticism of the last two verses.

The Ṛg Veda

I. HYMN OF CREATION

X, 129.

1. Non-being then existed not nor being:
    There was no air, nor sky that is beyond it.
    What was concealed? Wherein? In whose protection?
    And was there deep unfathomable water?
2. Death then existed not nor life immortal;
    Of neither night nor day was any token.
    By its inherent force the One breathed windless:
    No other thing than that beyond existed.
3. Darkness there was at first by darkness hidden;
    Without distinctive marks, this all was water.
    That which, becoming, by the void was covered,
    That One by force of heat came into being.
4. Desire entered the One in the beginning:
    It was the earliest seed, of thought the product.
    The sages searching in their hearts with wisdom,
    Found out the bond of being in non-being.
5. Their ray extended light across the darkness:
    But was the One above or was it under?
    Creative force was there, and fertile power:
    Below was energy, above was impulse.
6. Who knows for certain? Who shall here declare it?

A. A. Macdonell, ed. and trans. *Hymns from the Ṛg Veda*. London: Oxford University Press, 1911.

Whence was it born, and whence came this creation?
The gods were born after this world's creation:
Then who can know from whence it has arisen?
7. None knoweth whence creation has arisen;
   And whether he has or has not produced it:
   He who surveys it in the highest heaven,
   He only knows, or haply he may know not.

VARUṆA

The greatest of the gods of the *Rigveda*, beside Indra, is Varuṇa,   1
though the number of hymns in which he alone (apart from Mitra) is
addressed is only 12, as compared with the 250 to Indra. His physical
features and activities are mentioned: he has face, eye, arms, hands
and feet; he walks, drives, sits, eats and drinks. His eye, with which he
observes mankind, is the sun. He sits on the strewn grass at the sacrifice. He wears a golden mantle or a shining robe. His car, drawn by
well-yoked steeds, gleams like the sun. Varuṇa sits in his mansion surveying the deeds of men; and the Fathers behold him in the highest
heaven. He has spies who sit around him and observe the two worlds.
By his golden-winged messenger the sun is meant. He is often called
a king, but especially a universal monarch. His sovereignty, his divine
dominion, and his occult power (*māyā*) are specially emphasized.
Varuṇa is characteristically an upholder of physical and moral order,
the great maintainer of the laws of nature. He established heaven and
earth, which he keeps asunder. He caused the sun to shine in heaven,
and made for it a wide path. He placed fire in the waters and Soma on
the rock. The wind that resounds through the air is his breath. By his
ordinance the moon shining brightly moves at night, and the stars disappear by day. He is thus lord of light, both by day and by night.
Varuṇa is also a regulator of the waters: he made the rivers flow; by
his occult power they pour swiftly into the ocean without filling it. He
is, however, more frequently connected with the atmospheric waters:
thus he causes the inverted cask (the cloud) to shed its waters on
heaven, earth and air, and to moisten the ground.

The fixity of his laws, which the gods themselves follow, is fre-   2
quently mentioned. His power is so great that neither the birds as they
fly, nor the rivers as they flow, can reach the limits of his dominion.
His omniscience is typical: he knows the flight of the birds in the sky,

the path of the ships in the ocean, the course of the far-travelling wind; he beholds all the secret things that have been or shall be done, and witnesses men's truth and falsehood; no creature can even wink without his knowledge.

Varuṇa is pre-eminent among the Vedic gods as a moral ruler. His anger is aroused by sin, which he severely punishes. The fetters with which he binds sinners are characteristic of him. But he is merciful to the penitent, releasing them from sin, even that committed by their fathers, and from guilt due to thoughtlessness. Every hymn addressed to Varuṇa contains a prayer for forgiveness of sin. Varuna is on a footing of friendship with his worshipper, who communes with him in his heavenly mansion, and sometimes sees him with his mental eye. The righteous hope to behold in the next world Varuṇa and Yama (the god of Death), the two kings who reign together in bliss. 3

Varuṇa seems originally to have represented the encompassing sky. But this conception has become obscured in the *Rigveda*, because it dates from a pre-Vedic period. It goes back to the Indo-Iranian age at least; for the Ahura Mazda, the "wise spirit" of the *Avesta*, agrees closely with the Asura (divine spirit) Varuṇa in character, though not in name. It may be even older, as *Varuṇa* is perhaps identical with the Greek οὐρανός, "sky." At any rate, the name appears to be derived from the root *vṛ*, to "cover" or "encompass." 4

II. VARUṆA

VII, 88.

1. Present to Varuṇa the gracious giver
   A hymn, Vasiṣṭha, bright and very pleasant,
   That he may bring to us the lofty, holy
   And mighty steed that grants a thousand bounties.
2. Now having come to Varuṇa's full aspect,
   I think his countenance like that of Agni;
   May he, the lord, lead me to see the marvel:
   The light and darkness hidden in the cavern.
3. When Varuṇa and I the boat have mounted
   And have propelled it to the midst of ocean;
   When we shall move across the waters' ridges
   We'll waver in the swing to raise its lustre.
4. Varuṇa has placed Vasiṣṭha in the vessel;
   The sage benignant by his mighty power

His praiser in prosperity has settled,
As long as days endure, as long as mornings.
5. What has become of those our former friendships,
When we two held erstwhile unbroken converse?
O sovereign Varuṇa, thy lofty mansion,
Thy home, I entered, with its thousand portals.
6. Who is, O Varuṇa, thy constant kinsman,
Once dear, though sinful now, he claims thy friendships.
As guilty may we not, O wizard, suffer:
Do thou, O sage, grant shelter to thy praiser.
7. O may we, in these fixed abodes abiding,
Now from the lap of Aditi find favour.
May from his noose king Varuṇa release us.
Ye gods protect us evermore with blessings.

SOMA

As the Soma sacrifice forms the centre of the ritual of the *Rigveda*, this
is one of the most prominent deities, coming next in importance to
Agni, as indicated by the number of hymns (120) addressed to him.
His anthropomorphism is little developed, because the plant and its
juice are constantly present to the mind and the vision of the poet.

Soma has sharp and terrible weapons, which he grasps in his
hand; he wields a bow and a thousand-pointed shaft. He has a celestial car drawn by a team like Vāyu's; he is also said to ride on the
same car as Indra; and he is the best of charioteers. He is associated
as a dual divinity in about half a dozen hymns with Indra, Agni, Pūṣan
and Rudra. He is sometimes attended by the Maruts, Indra's close
allies. He comes to the sacrifice to receive the offerings, and seats
himself on the sacred grass.

The intoxicating Soma juice is often called "mead" *(madhu),* but
more often the "drop" *(indu).* Its colour is brown, ruddy, or more usually tawny. The whole of the ninth book of the *Rigveda* consists of
incantations chanted over the tangible Soma, while its stalks are being
pounded by the pressing stones, and the juice, passing through the
strainer of sheep's wool, flows into wooden vats, in which it is offered
to the gods on the sacred grass. These processes are overlaid with
confused and mystical imagery, endlessly varied. The filtered Soma is
mixed with water as well as milk, by which it is sweetened. Soma's
connexion with the waters is expressed in many ways. He is the drop

that grows in the waters; he is the embryo of the waters or their child; they are his mothers or his sisters; he is lord and king of streams; he produces waters and causes heaven and earth to rain. The sound of the flowing juice is often expressed by verbs meaning to roar, bellow, or even thunder. He is therefore frequently called a bull among the cows (representing the waters). He is, moreover, swift, being often compared with a steed, sometimes with a bird flying to the wood. His yellow colour suggests his brilliance, the physical aspect of Soma on which the poets dwell most frequently. He is then often compared with or associated with the sun.

The exhilarating effect of Soma caused it to be regarded as a drink   4
bestowing immortal life, and to be called the draught of immortality *(amṛta)*. All the gods drink Soma; they drank it to gain immortality; it confers immortality not only on the gods, but on men. It also has healing powers, making the blind to see and the lame to walk. As stimulating the voice, Soma is called "Lord of Speech." He awakens eager thought: he is a generator of hymns, a leader of poets, a seer among priests. His wisdom is hence much dwelt on: he is a wise seer, and knows the races of the gods.

The exhilarating powers of Soma are most emphasized in con-   5
nection with Indra, whom it stimulates for the fight with Vṛtra in innumerable ways. Through this association Indra's warlike exploits come to be attributed to Soma himself: he is a victor unconquered in fight, born for battle; as a warrior he wins all kinds of wealth for his worshippers.

Soma is in several passages said to grow or dwell on the moun-   6
tains, but his true origin and abode are thought to be in heaven. Soma is the child of heaven, is the milk of heaven, and is purified in heaven; he is the lord of heaven; he occupies heaven, and his place is the highest heaven. Thence he was brought to earth: the myth embodying this belief is that of the eagle that brings Soma to Indra.

Being the most important of herbs, Soma is said to have been   7
born as the lord of plants, whose king he is; he is the lord of the wood, and has generated all plants.

In a few of the latest hymns of the *Rigveda* Soma begins to be   8
mystically identified with the moon; in the *Atharvaveda* Soma several times means the moon; and in the *Brāhmaṇas* this identification has already become a commonplace.

The preparation and the offering of Soma (the Avestan *Haoma*)   9
were already an important feature in Indo-Iranian worship. In both the

Rigveda and the *Avesta* it is said that the Soma stalks were pressed, that its juice was yellow, and was mixed with milk; in both Soma grows on the mountains, though its mythical home is in heaven, whence it comes down to earth; in both Soma has become a mighty god and is called a king; in both there are many other identical mythological traits.

It is possible that the belief in an intoxicating divine beverage, the home of which was in heaven, goes back to the Indo-European period; if so, it must have been regarded as a kind of honey-mead (Sanskrit *mádhu*, Greek μέθυ, Anglo-Saxon *medu*).   10

The name of Soma means "pressed juice," being derived from *su* (avestan *hu*), "to press."   11

The following hymn does not touch upon the processes of the production of Soma, but dwells on the inspiring, life-giving, remedial, protective, and beneficial powers of the god.   12

XXX. SOMA

VIII, 48.

1. I have partaken wisely of the sweet food
   That stirs good thoughts, best banisher of trouble,
   The food round which all deities and mortals,
   Calling it honey-mead, collect together.
2. Thou shalt be Aditi when thou hast entered
   Within, appeaser of celestial anger.
   May'st thou, O drop, enjoying Indra's friendship,
   Like willing mare the car, to wealth advance us.
3. We have drunk Soma and become immortal;
   We have attained the light the gods discovered.
   What can hostility now do against us?
   And what, immortal god, the spite of mortals?
4. Be cheering to our heart when drunk, O Indu,
   Kindly, like father to his son, O Soma.
   Like friend for friend, far-famed one, wisely
   Prolong our years that we may live, O Soma.
5. These glorious, freedom-giving drops, when drunk by me,
   Have knit my joints together as do thongs a car.
   May these protect me now from fracturing a limb.
   And may they ever keep me from disease remote.
6. Like fire produced by friction, make me brilliant;
   Do thou illumine us and make us richer;

For then I seem in thy carouse, O Soma,
Enriched. Now enter us for real welfare.
7. Of this thy juice pressed out with mind devoted,
We would partake as of paternal riches.
Prolong the years of life for us, King Soma,
As Sūrya lengthens out the days of spring-time.
8. King Soma, gracious be to us for welfare:
We are thy devotees; of that be mindful.
O Indu, might and anger rise against us:
Hand us not over to our foeman's mercies.
9. Thou, as the guardian of our body, Soma,
Surveying men, in every limb hast settled.
If we perchance infringed, O god, thy statutes,
As our good friend for greater wealth be gracious.
10. I would accompany the friend, the wholesome,
Who, Lord of Bays, imbibed, would never hurt me.
I come to Indra to prolong our life-time,
That we may relish Soma placed within us,
11. Away have fled those ailments and diseases;
The powers of darkness have been all affrighted.
With mighty strength in us has Soma mounted:
We have arrived where men prolong existence.
12. The drop drunk deeply in our hearts, O Fathers,
Us mortals that immortal god has entered.
That Soma we would worship with oblation;
We would be in his mercy and good graces.
13. Uniting with the Fathers thou, O Soma,
Hast over Heaven and Earth thyself extended.
So, Indu, we would serve thee with oblation:
Thus we would be the lords of ample riches.
14. Do ye, protecting gods, speak in our favour,
Let neither sleep nor idle talk subdue us;
May we, for evermore, beloved of Soma,
Endowed with hero sons, address the synod.
15. Thou, Soma, givest strength to us on all sides.
Light-finder, watching men, within us enter.
Do thou, O Indu, with thine aids accordant,
Behind for ever and before protect us.

THE GAMBLER

The following is one of a small group among the secular hymns which
have a didactic character. It is the comment of a gambler, who,

unable to resist the fascination of the dice, deplores the ruin he has brought on himself and his household. The dice consisted of the nuts of a large tree, called *Vibhīdaka*, still used for this purpose in India.

XXXV. THE GAMBLER

X, 34.

1. On high trees born and in a windy region
   The danglers, rolling on the diceboard, cheer me.
   Like Soma draught from Mūjavant's great mountain,
   The rousing nut Vibhīdaka has pleased me.
2. She wrangles not with me nor is she angry:
   To me and comrades she was ever kindly.
   For dice that only luckless throws effected
   I've driven away from home a wife devoted.
3. Her mother hates me, she herself rejects me:
   For one in such distress there is no pity.
   I find a gambling man is no more useful
   Than is an aged horse that's in the market.
4. Others embrace the wife of him whose chattels
   The eager dice have striven hard to capture;
   And father, mother, brothers say about him:
   "We know him not; lead him away a captive."
5. When to myself I think, "I'll not go with them,
   I'll stay behind my friends that go to gamble,"
   And those brown nuts, thrown down, have raised
        their voices,
   I go, like wench, straight to the place of meeting.
6. To the assembly hall the gambler sallies,
   And asking, "Shall I win?" he quakes and trembles.
   And then the dice run counter to his wishes,
   Giving the lucky throw to his opponent.
7. The dice attract the gambler, but deceive and wound,
   Both paining men at play and causing them to pain.
   Like boys they offer first and then take back their gifts:
   With honey sweet to gamblers by their magic charm.
8. Their throng in triple fifties plays untrammelled,
   Like Savitar the god whose laws are constant.
   They yield not to the wrath of even the mighty:
   A king himself on them bestows obeisance.
9. Downward they roll, then swiftly springing upward,
   They overcome the man with hands, though handless.

Cast on the board like magic bits of charcoal,
Though cold themselves, they burn the heart to ashes.
10. Grieved is the gambler's wife by him abandoned,
Grieved, too, his mother as he aimless wanders.
Indebted, fearing, he desiring money
At night approaches other people's houses.
11. It pains the gambler when he sees a woman
Another's wife, and their well-ordered household.
He yokes those brown steeds early in the morning,
And when the fire is low sinks down a beggar.
12. To him who's general of your mighty forces,
As king becomes the chief of your battalions,
I hold my fingers ten extended forward:
"No money I withhold, this truth I tell thee."
13. Play not with dice, but cultivate thy tillage,
Enjoy thy riches, deeming them abundant.
There are thy cows, there is thy wife, O Gambler:
This counsel Savitar the noble gives me.
14. Make friends with us, we pray, to us be gracious;
Do not bewitch us forcibly with magic;
Let now your enmity, your anger slumber:
Let others be in brownies' toils entangled.

THE UPANISHADS

The migrations of Indo-European tribes into India were completed and the development of Vedic culture far advanced centuries before the composition of the oldest of the Upanishads (ca. 700 B.C.E.). These are mystical and speculative texts which have enormous influence on all later Indian religious thought and speculative spiritual philosophy, including Buddhism and Jainism. The Upanishads came to be appended to one or another of the four Vedas, but they give evidence of a break with the earlier literature in the freeing of a philosophic intelligence from myth as well as in the flowering of a mystical sensibility.

The Upanishads are the basis of those classical philosophies known as Vedānta, a term that originally was used as an epithet for the Upanishads themselves. Several distinct and complex world-views claim the Vedānta name: there emerge heated controversies about what the Upanishads say. One central issue is whether the Absolute, Brahman, taught throughout these texts, is to be understood as a creator, God, or as only the impersonal basis of being and self. Some moderns, for example, Aurobindo, continue to develop ideas first articulated in the Upanishads. The following selections are passages that commentators have found especially noteworthy.

The first one is from one of the oldest Upanishads, ca. 800 B.C.E. This passage about spiritual aspiration sets the tone for much Upanishadic teaching. (It is not clear who or what is invoked in this entreaty.)

> From non-being [*asat*] to true being [*sat*] lead me.
> From darkness to light lead me.
> From death to immortality lead me.
>   [*Bṛhadāraṇyaka* 1.3.28]*

The seeking expressed in the early Upanishads centers on *brahman*, considered the secret of both ourselves and the universe. The Upanishadic notion of *brahman* is the precursor of the idea of God in later Hindu theism; the idea of the One that dominates much subsequent Vedantic mysticism—a seeking of a Unity underlying all individual selves and things; and the Emptiness and absolutist notions of much Buddhist thought as well. This is taken from a very old passage:

> An ocean, a single seer without duality becomes he whose world [of vision] is *brahman*. This is his supreme attainment. This is his highest fulfillment. This is his best world. This is his supreme bliss. Other creatures subsist on a fragment of this bliss.
>   [*Bṛhadāraṇyaka* 4.3.32]

This Absolute is considered to have a peculiar logic, or nature, unlike that of everyday, finite, and physical things, as we see in these two passages:

> Not moving the One is swifter than the mind. The gods do not reach That running [always] before. . . . That moves; That moves not. It is far, and It is near. It is within all this; It indeed is outside all this. He who experiences all things in the Self and the Self in all things thereupon does not fear.
>   [*Īśā Upaniṣad* 4–6, *Bṛhadāraṇyaka* 5.1.1]

> *Om.* That is the Full. This is the Full. From the Full, the Full proceeds. Taking away the Full of the Full, it is the Full that remains.
>   [*Bṛhadāraṇyaka* 3.7.3–3.7.23 passim]

---

*Translations by Stephen H. Phillips.

The next passage illustrates doctrines that some have called pantheism, an identification of God and nature. Whether it illustrates pantheism or not, a doctrine of divine immanence is expressed, of divine *indwelling* in all things, and a type of transcendentalist theism: the Inner Controller though indwelling everywhere is thought to be in some sense *other* than the things, and selves, in which it indwells.

Who standing in the earth is other than the earth, whom the earth knows not, whose body the earth is, who within controls the earth, that is this, the Self, the Inner Controller, the Immortal.

Who standing in the waters is other than the waters, whom the waters know not, whose body the waters are, that is this, the Self, the Inner Controller. . . .

Who standing in the wind is other than the wind, whom the wind knows not, whose body the wind is, who within controls the wind, that is this, the Self, the Inner Controller, the Immortal. . . .

Who standing in all beings is other than all beings, whom all beings know not, whose body all beings are, that is this, the Self, the Inner Controller, the Immortal. . . .

Who standing in the eye is other than the eye, whom the eye knows not, whose body the eye is, who within controls the eye, that is this, the Self, the Inner Controller, the Immortal.

Who standing in the ear is other than the ear, whom the ear knows not, whose body the ear is, that is this, the Self, the Inner Controller, the Immortal. . . .

Who standing in the understanding is other than the understanding, whom the understanding knows not, whose body the understanding is, who within controls the understanding, that is this, the Self, the Inner Controller, the Immortal. . . .

Who standing in the seed of generation is other than the seed of generation, whom the seed of generation knows not, whose body the seed of generation is, that is this, the Self, the Inner Controller, the Immortal.

Unseen, the seer, unheard, the hearer, unthought, the thinker, unknown, the knower; there is no other seer than this, no other hearer than this, no other thinker than this, no other knower than this. This is that, the Self, the Inner Controller, the Immortal; valueless is anything other.   [*Chāndogya* 6.11]

Finally two passages about the self. The first, repeatedly quoted through the centuries of commentary and discussion, illustrates a spiritually monist view that has had great prominence in India, a view that finds the self (here *ātman*) as the key to life and reality. The second illustrates mystic doctrines about the small worth of worldly desires and attachments in the light of inevitable death and, to be sure, the possibility of an extraordinary knowledge, or experience, that is thought to carry us beyond the "great fear." Note also an interesting development of Upanishadic theism: the indwelling God is said to have "maddening pleasure" and to be free of it as well.

"Were someone to hack the root of this large tree, my dear son, it would bleed but live; were someone to hack its trunk, it would bleed but live; were someone to hack its tops, it would bleed but live. Pervaded by the living self [*ātman*], it stands continually drinking and exulting. If life were to leave one branch, then that branch would dry up; if a second, then that would dry up; a third, then that would dry up; if the whole, then the whole would dry up. Just in this way indeed, my dear son," he [Śvetaketu's teacher] said, "understand: this endowed most surely with life dies; life does not die. That which is this, this the most subtle, everything here has that as its soul [*ātman*]. That is the reality; that is the self [*ātman*]; you are that, O Śvetaketu."

"Please, sir, instruct me even further."

"All right," he said.   [*Kaṭha*]

[Yama, "Death":] "Whatever desires, (even) the most difficult to win in the world of mortals, have them all at your demand. Beautiful women, chariots, music—none like these may be won by mortal men—be entertained by them, O Naciketas, given by me. Do not inquire into dying."

[Naciketas:] Existing only until tomorrow are such desires of a mortal, and, O Bringer-of-the-end, they wear away the splendor and vigor of every sense and power one has. Even all that is alive is of small worth indeed. Yours alone are the chariots; yours the dancing and the singing. A person is not to be satisfied with wealth. Are we to have wealth once we have seen you? But the boon that I wish to choose is this, answer this question: "Will we continue to exist while you rule?" . . .

[Death:] Having seen in your grasp, O Naciketas, the fulfillment of desire and the foundation of the world and an infinity of power, of will, and the safe shore of fearlessness, and great fame sung far and wide, you wisely let it all go. A person who is wise and steadfast, discerning the God through spiritual discipline and study—the God, the one that is difficult to experience, who has plunged deep into the hidden and is established in the secret place, standing in the cavern, the ancient—such a person leaves joy and sorrow behind. . . .

Subtler than the subtle, grander than the grand, the self is set in the secret heart of the creature. One who is without self-will experiences this (and becomes) free of sorrow, through his clearness and purity towards material things [or, "through the grace of the Creator"*]; one experiences the self's greatness and breadth. Seated he travels far; lying down he goes everywhere. Who other than I is fit to know this God, the one that has both maddening pleasure and freedom from maddening pleasure? The wise person, recognizing the bodiless in bodies, the settled in things unsettled, the great and pervasive self [ātman], does not grieve nor suffer. This the self is not to be won by eloquent instruction, nor by intelligence, nor by much study. Just that person whom this chooses, by such a person is this to be won; to such a person this the self reveals, uncovers its very own form and body.   [Kaṭha]

THE GĪTĀ

Hinduism cannot be counted a single religion, unlike Christianity or Buddhism. At best, it is a family of religious beliefs and practices, connected principally through a social organization in which caste plays an important role. For example, one of the classical philosophic schools defends the authority of the Veda (though with a dubious interpretation) and upholds caste, and for these two reasons has every right to be called a Hindu school of thought. However, the school is atheistic and is antagonistic to the idea that "liberation" or any mystical experience is the supreme good. Theism and a doctrine of a mystical supreme goal for a person, are, on the other hand, central to much ancient, classical, and modern Hindu thought. Six distinct schools, some with many contending branches or subschools, were recognized in classical times as "orthodox," though the Sanskrit word for "orthodox" is used to imply only (1) reverence for the Veda, which was rarely read, and (2) participation in a social organization that included caste identity. There are no truly universal Hindu doctrines. Nevertheless, one

---

* The Sanskrit text is ambiguous between these two meanings. The first reading suggests Buddhist doctrines, while the alternative Hindu theism.

may speak of scriptures and ideas that over the centuries have been more at the center of Hindu culture than others. And to be sure, more than any other, a theistic worldview has dominated Hindu belief and guided religious practices. Of all the many, many scriptures and sacred texts that move, or have moved, the hearts of the devotees of God in India over the centuries, the *Bhagavadgītā* ("Song of God") (ca. 200 B.C.E.) stands out as the most important.

The *Gītā* is a small portion of a long epic poem. The epic's story centers on a conflict over the succession to the throne of a princely state in the ancient civilization that extended along the massive Ganges River, which drains the Himalayas. The warrior Krishna is the ruler of a neighboring state, and throughout most of the long poem is an ordinary person, though an able, just, clever, and politically astute leader. The key event of the entire epic is a battle involving not only cousins fighting cousins along with their local armies but the armies of many other kings and princes, such as Krishna's, all drawn into the terrible conflagration. The political issues are complex, but the one side of the warring family, and not the other, has the just claim. The rightful heir with his four brothers and their allies are on one side; the usurper along with many noble and venerable sages and heroes fight against them. Krishna joins the battle line as the charioteer for Arjuna, the third of the five brothers and a champion archer. The *Gītā* is a dialogue between Krishna and Arjuna occurring just minutes before the battle begins. In it, Krishna ceases to present himself as a mere mortal and able warrior and reveals himself to Arjuna as God incarnate, an *avatāra*, literally a divine "descent" or manifestation. His advice to Arjuna is not just the encouragement of a friend or the wise teachings of a guru; his words are the voice of God speaking to a human being in personal crisis—so the *Gītā* is understood by Hindu theists.

Arjuna's crisis is principally ethical, though he also asks Krishna to remove his ignorance about the nature of things, persons, and God. At the beginning of the dialogue, he insists that it cannot be the morally right thing to do to fight and kill his kinsmen, teachers, friends, and loved ones who face him on the far side of the field of Kurukṣetra.

> "No good do I see in killing my own family in battle. I desire not victory, nor rule, nor pleasures, Krishna; what is power to us, enjoyments, or life, Govinda? Those who make rulership desirable

for us, and enjoyments and pleasures, it is they that are arrayed in battle [against us], abandoning life and wealth. Teachers, fathers, sons, grandfathers, uncles, in-laws—these I do not wish to kill even if it means that I must die, Krishna—not even to rule the three worlds, why then for the earth?"   [*Gītā* 1.31b–35]

Despite the passion and sincerity of moral feeling that Arjuna expresses, Krishna insists that the right thing to do in the circumstances is to fight, to kill the opposing warriors, and to win the battle.

There are many dimensions to Krishna's explanation why fighting is for Arjuna the right course of action; more commentary has been elicited by his response to Arjuna's plea than by any other comparably brief text, except perhaps the Christian Gospels. Krishna explains divine incarnation (that is, the *avatāra* doctrine of rebirth whereby everyone is reborn until she or he reaches "liberation," *mukti*, equated with a mystical experience of God or Brahman); the various paths and practices of yoga (that is, self-discipline, especially meditation: more on yoga with the selection from the *Yoga-sūtra* below); the transcendence of God as well as the unity of the world with God (probably the *Gītā*'s central theological doctrine); *nirvāṇa* (considered identical with the mystical experience of God or Brahman, although *nirvāṇa* is a Buddhist word and Buddhism and Hinduism are competing religions); and finally, evil, the purpose of creation, and the destiny of the individual soul. Some modern scholars see the *Gītā* as a grab-bag of competing philosophic and religious ideas, while many of the classical exegetes are at great pains to show a conceptual unity. But to my mind, given the context in the larger poem, what is most striking and most original in the work is the teaching about action and the spiritual attitude to take in acting. *Karma yoga*, the "yoga of action," is the discipline of acting in a spirit of sacrifice without concern for personal benefit. (The law of *karma* mentioned here is the view that any course of action that one undertakes creates a psychological tendency, or habit, to repeat it. One's free will thus becomes limited by one's own dispositions to action, or habits, dispositions that—according to much ancient Indian thought—continue even into a new birth. The inveterate smoker is drawn to the taste of tobacco at a young age in his or her next incarnation.)

Krishna advises Arjuna about the importance of attitude and regard for the soul over the desires that drive worldly actions. Arjuna asks why Krishna, in the face of what he has just said about the soul and worldly desires, is nevertheless encouraging him to such a violent endeavor. The verses below are part of Krishna's reply.

Krishna explains the cosmic foundations of action, evoking a ritual image of sacrifice to which he gives new meaning. Next, he states his own motive in undertaking actions and in his very assuming of a mortal birth as the divine person and model for those who wish to live in the right way and, indeed, yogically transformed lives. He goes on to talk about human action in general and closes with a refrain recurring throughout the *Gītā*, namely, with injunctions about the practice of *yoga*, that is, spiritual discipline. It is through such discipline in general, whether *karma yoga, jñāna yoga*, or *bhakti yoga*—these are the three paths that Krishna lays out: the yoga of action, the yoga of knowledge and meditation, and the yoga of love and devotion—that one may live a transformed life. Thus one would become in the end, like Krishna, a person aware of one's immortal soul as well as of God, or Brahman, the personal/impersonal Absolute.

The Bhagavad Gītā

Arjuna said:
   3.1   Krishna, if you consider understanding superior to action, why then do you urge me on to an action so terrible?
   3.2   It seems you would confuse my understanding with contradictory words. So tell me definitely that whereby I can attain the supreme good.

Krishna said:
   3.3   There are in this world two fundamental stances declared by me of old, Arjuna: the yoga of knowledge for intellectuals, the yoga of action for yogins.
   3.4   By abstaining from works, a person does not enjoy a mystical actionlessness; nor by renunciation alone is perfection attained.
   3.5   For no one is able to remain even for a moment without acting; everyone willy-nilly is made to do work by the impulsions [*guṇas*, "modes"] of nature.

Bhagavadgita, Chaps. 3–4. Translated by Stephen H. Phillips.

3.6   Self-deluded is he who sits controlling the faculties of action while at the same time thinking about the objects of experience. He is a hypocrite.

3.7   But a person controlling his senses with the mind and commencing a disciplined work [*karma yoga*] with his faculties of action, unattached, that person excels, Arjuna.

3.8   Do controlled work, for action is better than inaction. The very maintenance of your body would not be accomplished without work.

3.9   Without personal attachment undertake action, Arjuna, for just one purpose, for the purpose of sacrifice. From work undertaken for purposes other than sacrifice, this world is bound to the law of *karma*.

3.10   Bringing forth creatures along with sacrifice, the Creator said of old, "With this may you bring forth fruit; let it be your horn-of-plenty [literally, "wish-fulfilling cow"].

3.11   "With this, may you make the gods flourish and may the gods make you flourish. Mutually fostering one another, you will attain the supreme good.

3.12   "For made to flourish by sacrifice, the gods will give you the enjoyments you desire. One who without giving to them enjoys their gifts is nothing but a thief."

3.13   Good people eating the remains from sacrifices are free from sin. But those sinners eat evil who cook for their own sake.

3.14   From food beings come to be; the origin of food is from rain. Rain comes to be from sacrifice. Sacrifice has its origin in works.

3.15   Know works to have their origin in Brahman, and Brahman its foundation in the Immutable. Therefore is the omnipresent Brahman established through all time in sacrifice.

3.16   The wheel is thus set in motion. One who does not follow its rounds, evil in intentions, sensual in delights, he lives in vain, Arjuna.

3.17   But the person delighting only in his higher Self and satisfied living in it—for such a person, thoroughly contented in the Self alone, there is nothing that must be done.

3.18   Nor is there for him any gain in what he has done or has not done. Nor do his interests depend in any way on anyone or anything else.

3.19   Therefore, ever unattached do the work that has to be done. For the person who is unattached in performing action attains the supreme good.

3.20   For by work alone did Janaka and others attain perfection. Considering also the holding together of society, you should be doing works.

3.21   Whatever the superior person does that indeed is what other folk try to do. The standard that he sets is what the world follows.

3.22   For me, there is nothing whatsoever that has to be done, Arjuna, in the three worlds; nor anything unattained that I need to attain. Still I continue in action.

3.23   For if I did not continue ever tirelessly in action, my example people would follow, Arjuna, as they always do.

3.24   Societies would come apart if I were not to do works, and I would be the author of chaos in the world. I would destroy these creatures.

3.25   The unenlightened, who are attached to their actions, proceed in works, Arjuna; so should the enlightened, unattached, to hold together society.

3.26   One should not engender a division in the understanding of ignorant folk who are attached to their works; rather, knowing one should inspire them, performing all actions, himself disciplined.

3.27   Works in every fashion are being done by the impulsions [gunas, "modes"] of nature. The person deluded by egotism thinks, "I am the doer of this work."

3.28   But the one who knows what is real, Arjuna, concerning those impulsions and the different types of action, realizing that the impulsions operate on themselves, he is not attached.

3.29   Deluded by the impulsions of nature, people are attached to its works. One whose knowledge is complete should not disturb the dull-witted whose knowledge is incomplete.

3.30   Concentrating on your higher Self, entrust all your actions to me. Be free of expectation and possessiveness. Fight, with your fever departed.

3.31   People who always follow this teaching of mine, with faith and without griping, they too are freed from [the karmic consequences of] their actions.

3.32   But those who finding fault with this teaching of mine do not follow it, know them as confused by every bit of knowledge, lost and unaware.

3.33   Even a person with knowledge acts in accord with his own nature. Beings follow nature; what would coercing it avail?

3.34   Attraction and repulsion are set in the object of each sense. One should not allow oneself to come under their sway, for they are highwaymen endangering the path.

3.35   Better one's own right way [*dharma*] though flawed than the way of another perfectly followed; death following one's own way is better. The way of another is perilous.

Krishna said:

4.1   This imperishable yoga I proclaimed to Vivasvān [the Sun God]; Vivasvān declared it to Manu [the first human]; Manu told it to Ikṣavāku (a primeval king).

4.2   Thus passed from one to another the royal sages and seers knew it. Then with a long lapse of time, Arjuna, the yoga was lost.

4.3   Today that very yoga, that ancient yoga, is by me explained to you. You are beloved to me, and a friend. So this is indeed the highest secret.

Arjuna said:

4.4   Later is your birth, sir; [much] earlier Vivasvān's. How am I to understand that you declared this yoga in the beginning?

Krishna said:

4.5   Many are my part births; yours also, Arjuna. I know them all; you do not.

4.6   Although I exist as the unborn, the imperishable Self and am the Lord of beings, by resorting to and controlling my own nature I come into phenomenal being through my own magical power of self-delimitation.

4.7   Whenever there is a crisis concerning the right way [*dharma*], Arjuna, and a rising up of evil, then I loose myself forth [taking birth].

4.8   For the protection of good people and for the destruction of evil-doers, for the establishment of the right way, I take birth age after age. . . .

4.14   Actions do not stain me; nor do I have desire for the fruits of works. The person who recognizes me as this way is himself not bound by his works.

4.15   So knowing, ancient seekers of liberation and enlightenment carried out works. Therefore simply do actions as were done of old by them.

4.16   What action is, and what inaction, even seer-sages are confused on this score. To you I will explain that kind of action which when understood you will be free from all ill.

4.17   For action must be understood, and wrong action as well; inaction must be understood—deep, dark, and dense is the nature of action.

4.18   Were one to see inaction in action and action in inaction, that person among mortals would be wise; he would be spiritually disciplined [or, yoked in yoga] in all his works.

4.19   One whose instigations and undertakings are all free from the motive of personal desire, the wise see that person as the truly learned, him whose karma has been burned up in the fire of knowledge.

4.20   Having abandoned attachment to the fruits of works, constantly satisfied, independent, one does nothing whatsoever even while thoroughly engaged in works.

4.21   Transcending hope and expectation, controlled in heart and mind, with all possessiveness renounced, one doing simply physical actions accrues no [karmic] adversity.

4.22   Satisfied with whatever gain comes, passed beyond oppositions and dualities, untouched by jealousy, equal-minded and balanced in the face of success and failure, such a person though he acts is not bound.

4.23   All karmic dispositions dissolve and wash away when a person is free from attachment, liberated, with a mind firmly fixed in knowledge, acting in a spirit of sacrifice.

4.24   Brahman is the giving, Brahman the oblation; by Brahman into the Brahman-fire it is poured. It is just to Brahman where one goes achieving the ecstatic trance of Brahman-action.

4.25   Some yogins practice sacrifice directed to the gods; others offer the sacrifice by the sacrifice into the fire of Brahman.

4.26   Others offer the sense organs of hearing and so on into the fires of control; still others offer the sense objects of sound and so on into the fires of the senses.

4.27   And others all the actions of the sense organs and the actions of the life-breaths as well into the yogic fire of self-control kindled by knowledge.

4.28   Likewise, some perform material sacrifices, some sacrifices of austerity, and some sacrifices of yoga; there are seekers who with strict vows perform sacrifices of both religious study and knowledge.

4.29   Similarly, some offer the incoming breath into the outgoing breath and the outgoing breath into the incoming; these restraining the courses of the breaths are devoted to the practice of breath-control [*prāṇāyāma*].

4.30   Others controlled in diet offer the breaths into the breaths. All these understand sacrifice, and through sacrifice reduce the stains [of karma].

4.31   Those who eat the nectar of immortality left over from a sacrificial action, they go to the eternal Brahman. This world does not belong to one who fails to sacrifice, so how could the next, Arjuna?

4.32   In this way, numerous diverse sacrifices are spread wide in the mouth of Brahman. Know them all as born in action. Thus knowing, you will be liberated and enlightened.

4.33   A sacrifice in knowledge, Arjuna, is superior to a sacrifice with material things. All action in its entirety culminates and is fulfilled in knowledge.

4.34   Come to have this knowledge through submission to those who know, by questioning and service; they, the seers of what is real, will initiate and teach you.

4.35   Knowing that, you will not ever be confused again, Arjuna—that whereby you will see beings without exception in the Self and then in Me.

4.36   Even if of all sinners you are now the very worst evil-doer, once in the boat of knowledge you will safely cross over the crookedness of evil.

4.37   As a fire kindled reduces its fuel to ashes, Arjuna, so the fire of knowledge makes ashes all karma.

4.38   For here in this world there is no purifier the equal of knowledge; a person perfected through yoga practice finds it himself in the Self after a time.

4.39   A person of faith obtains that knowledge, concentrated on it, with senses controlled. Having obtained the knowledge, he at once attains to the supreme peace.

4.40   A person not only not knowing but having no faith, his soul full of doubts, is lost; neither this world nor another, nor happiness, comes to the doubting soul.

4.41   Actions do not bind him who has transcended works through yoga and cut through doubt with knowledge; he is Self-possessed, Arjuna.

4.42   Therefore having cut through the doubt that is born of ignorance and set in the heart, having cut through it with the sword of Self-knowledge, in yoga, Arjuna, take your stand; stand up and fight.

THE YOGA-SŪTRA

"Yoga" is an ambiguous term, used as the name of a classical school as well as the general word for a wide range of meditational, devotional, and ascetic practices of self-discipline (breath control, fasting, etc.). The *Yoga-sūtra*, which defines the Yoga school, is an ancient manual of yogic practices framed within a metaphysics. The philosophy of the *Yoga-sūtra* is distinct from the theism of the *Gītā*, though both texts advocate yogic practices. Also, similar mystic themes are elaborated. But the goal of yoga, self-discipline, is differently conceived: the supreme good according to the *Yoga-sūtra* is an absolute rupture separating the soul or conscious being, *puruṣa*, from nature, *prakṛti*. The *Yoga-sūtra* presents a metaphysical dualism of an infinite plurality of souls, on the one hand, and a single nature, on the other. God, according to this text, is an archetypal liberated yogin, never sullied by contact with the world. This is a notion distinct from that of the *Gītā*, where the Supreme Being is conceived along lines not so different from the theology of Western religions.

Thus in addition to its delineation of yogic practices in the style of a how-to book or meditation manual, the *Yoga-sūtra* attends to questions about reality, especially about the relation of souls to nature. Its theory may be interpreted as a view of the ontological underpinnings of the enlightenment or liberational experience—an explanation of how such an experience is possible.

Though portions of the *Yoga-sūtra* probably date to very early, the final version of the text belongs to the period after the Buddhist Nāgārjuna (see below, the next section) provoked a professional turn in Indian philosophies, with more attention to overall coherence as well as supportive argument.

The Yoga-sūtra

1.1.   Now instruction in yoga.

1.2.   Yoga is cessation of the fluctuations of mind and awareness [*citta*, henceforth rendered as "mind"].

1.3.   Then the seer [the conscious being] rests in his true self.

1.4.   At other times, he identifies with the fluctuations.

Translated by Stephen H. Phillips.

1.5.   The fluctuations are of five types, and are either detrimental or nondetrimental.

1.6.   [The five are:] (a) veridical awareness, (b) its opposite, (c) thought and imagination, (d) sleep, and (e) memory. . . .

1.12.   The cessation of the fluctuations is accomplished through practice and disinterestedness.

1.13.   Practice is effort to hold fast the cessation.

1.14.   Practice is firmly grounded only through proper effort uninterrupted and stretching over a long time.

1.15.   Disinterestedness is the intention to control on the part of someone who has no desire either for worldly or revealed objects. . . .

1.33.   Calming illumination of the mind is furthered through friendship, compassion, happiness, and indifference to objects whether pleasant or painful, virtuous or full of vice.

1.34.   Or, this can be brought about by controlled exhalation and retention of the breath.

1.35.   Or, this [calming illumination] is brought about by particular activity centered on an object arresting mentality.

1.36.   Or, it is brought about by activity that is free from sorrow and luminous.

1.37.   Or, it is achieved when the mind contemplates an object devoid of allure.

1.38.   Another means involves the mind brought to a knowledge of sleep and dreams.

1.39.   Or, from meditation as is appropriate. . . .

2.2.   Yoga is practiced to achieve mystic trance as well as to attenuate the detrimental fluctuations or afflictions [kleśa].

2.3.   The afflictions are spiritual ignorance, egoism, passion, hatred, and attachment to life. . . .

2.11.   These [detrimental] fluctuations are banished through meditation.

2.12.   [Action-inducing] karmic latencies, to be experienced in the current or in future births, are rooted in the afflictions.

2.13.   So long as this root endures its fruit will endure, the [triple] fruit, namely, of birth, life, and apparent enjoyment.

2.14.   These three bring joy or suffering according to the merit or lack thereof [in accumulated karmic latencies].

2.15.   A person of discriminating judgment sees all as suffering because of the pain in continual change, in tortured states of mind, and in subliminal latencies. Suffering is caused by conflicting fluctuations.

2.16.   Future suffering is to be banished.

2.17.   That which is to be banished stands caused by a conjunction of the seer [the conscious being] and that to be seen [nature].

2.18.   What is to be seen [that is, nature] is characterized by the [three qualities or strands] of intelligence, activity, and inertia; it includes the gross elements and the sense organs, and has as its *raison d'être* enjoyments for or liberation of the conscious being. . . .

2.22.   Although destroyed [for the liberated] yogin whose purpose is accomplished, nature is not destroyed for others [who are not liberated], because she is common among them.

2.23.   The conjunction between the power of phenomena and the power of their lord [the conscious being] is caused by a perception of the two's identity.

2.24.   Spiritual ignorance is its reason [that is, the reason the conjunction endures].

2.25.   When spiritual ignorance is no longer, the conjunction is no longer. This is the relinquishment, the "aloneness" [*kaivalya*, "salvation"] of the seer [the conscious being].

2.26.   Unbroken practice of discriminative discernment is the way to that relinquishment.

2.27.   For such a yogin, sevenfold wisdom and insight [*prajñā*] arise as the highest foundation.

2.28.   By practice of the "limbs of yoga," impurity is attenuated. Awareness is illuminated up to discriminative discernment.

2.29.   [Ethical] restraints, constraints, āsanas, breath-control, withdrawal of the senses, [and three stages of meditation, viz.] concentration, "meditation," and mystic trance are the eight "limbs of yoga."

2.30.   Of these, the restraints are non-injury [*ahiṃsā*], truthfulness, refraining from stealing, celibacy, and lack of avarice.

2.31.   These practiced universally irrespective of station and circumstance of time and place constitute the "great vow."

2.32.   The constraints are purity, contentment, asceticism, self-study, and focusing on God [as the archetypal liberated yogin]. . . .

3.1.   Concentration is binding the mind down to a single spot.

3.2.   Of the three [stages of meditation], "meditation" [*dhyāna*] is a single ideational focus.

3.3.   Mystic trance is this carried to the point where there is illumination only of the object as object, empty, as it were, of what it essentially is.

3.4.   The three together are called "conscious power" [samyama].
3.5.   Through its mastery comes the light of wisdom and insight [prajñā]. . . .
3.49.   The yogin whose awareness is restricted to the perception of the difference between [the strand of nature called] intelligence [sattva] and the conscious being achieves lordship over all states of being and omniscience as well.
3.50.   Through disinterest in that achievement arises "aloneness" [kaivalya] in the attenuation of the seeds of defects. . . .
3.55.   When the intelligence [sattva] and the conscious being are equal in purity, "aloneness" ensues. . . .
4.15.   Since with regard to one and the same object, mind [citta] differs [on different occasions of perception], the two [citta and objects] have a distinct mode of being.
4.16.   And to exist a thing does not depend on a single mind or awareness [citta]. When it is not cognized by that mind, what then would it be?
4.17.   Something is known or unknown to a particular mind, depending on the coloring conferred.
4.18.   The fluctuations of mind are always known to their lord [the conscious being], since the conscious being [puruṣa] is unchanging.
4.19.   That [citta] is not self-luminous, because it is something to be perceived.
4.20.   And there is no possibility of cognizing both [objects and subject] at the same time.
4.21.   It would be to assume too much to require one intelligence after another in order that a single mind or awareness be perceived. This would also mean memory's [impossibility because of] confusion.
4.22.   Self-awareness occurs when the mind assumes the form of consciousness which [as the nature of the conscious being] is transcendently unchanging.
4.23.   A mind [citta] that is colored by both the seer and that to be seen is capable of cognizing anything.
4.24.   Although the mind is moved by countless subliminal valences, it works by unifying [diversities] for the sake of the other [the conscious being].
4.25.   For one who sees the distinction [between nature and the conscious being], the projection of sense of self in nature ceases.

4.26.   Then the mind settling into deep discrimination is carried on toward [reflecting] the aloneness [of the conscious being].

4.27.   In the gaps [or weaknesses] of discrimination, other ideational presentations [that is, distractions] may arise by force of [unexhausted] subliminal valences.

4.28.   These are banished like the afflictions, in the ways explained. . . .

4.34.   Aloneness [*kaivalya*, the *summum bonum*] entails the reversal of the course of the strands or qualities of nature, now empty of meaning and value for the conscious being. Or, it may be understood as the power of consciousness returned and established in its own true self.

NĀGĀRJUNA'S "AVERTING THE ARGUMENTS"

The Buddha, who flourished in the sixth century B.C.E., also taught a mystical supreme good, achievable partly through practices similar to some listed in the *Yoga-sūtra* but also by living a life of compassion and balance, the "Middle Way." The Buddha himself did not write anything, but he provoked an immense literature among his followers: records of his sermons, biographies, poetry on events of his life, wisdom literature concerning the Buddhist path to enlightenment and perfection, and speculative philosophy. Early Buddhism develops a great complexity of doctrine, although the Buddha himself is said to have considered philosophic speculation a waste of time. There is a famous parable attributed to him about a person who discovers that his house is on fire. The Buddha asks, Would that person wonder about the nature of fire or rush to put the fire out? The implication is that we need not speculate on questions concerning the path, but instead follow it, to put out the fire of passions—the root of misery—in an experience of mystic bliss, namely nirvana. This experience, in turn, grounds, it is said, a life of compassion, exemplified by the Buddha.

The Buddhist philosopher Nāgārjuna, who lived, approximately, in the second century of the Common Era, tried to restore the anti-intellectual emphasis of the Buddha, that is to say, his emphasis on spiritual practice. Nāgārjuna can also be deemed the Indian Socrates, for he, like the Greek philosopher, brought about an intellectual revolution throughout Indian schools by way of the probing questions he asked. He exposed inadequacies in the views of the various schools, both Buddhist and non-Buddhist philosophies. But Nāgārjuna's identification of paradoxes, contradictions, and impossibilities in the positions of the quarreling schools of Buddhist interpretation was motivated by his sense of enlightenment experience, *nirvāṇa*, as a practical end to which thought and mind have no direct access. The term that he uses for what this experience reveals is "Emptiness" (*śūnyāta*), a term that by its negative character is intended to indicate the inherently experiential character of the supreme good and its transcendence to a discursive and distinction-making mentality.

Yet his soteriological motivation notwithstanding, Nāgārjuna achieves fame as a philosopher simply by the difficulty of the questions he raises. In the text below, Nāgārjuna mounts an onslaught on the notion of a "justifier" or "source of knowledge" that is a prominent feature of the Nyāya philosophy of "realist logic" (see below, the section on Nyāya, where a response to Nāgārjuna's attack is presented). Nāgārjuna identifies the meta-epistemological problem of an infinite regress concerning justification. (If it is my sense experience that justifies my belief that I am now typing on a computer keyboard, what justifies my taking my sense experience to play this role? Any answer would seem to invite a further question, ad infinitum.) In this text, *Vigrahavyāvartinī* ("Averting the Arguments"), the first twenty verses are devoted to the views of his opponents, who counterattack with various questions about Nāgārjuna's view of Emptiness and his anti-intellectual stance. The remaining verses are Nāgārjuna's responses, where some of his original attacks on the opponents' views are presented.

Averting the Arguments

Nāgārjuna

PART I

The Arguments of the Opponents

1. If self-existence (*svabhāva*) does not exist anywhere in any existing thing,

Frederick J. Streng. *Emptiness: A Study in Religious Meaning: A translation of Vigrahavyāvartinī: Averting the Arguments.* New York: Abingdon Press, 1967. Reprinted by permission.

Your statement, [itself] being without self-existence, is not able to discard self-existence.

2. But if that statement has [its own] self-existence, then your initial proposition is refuted;
   There is a [logical] inconsistency in this, and you ought to explain the grounds of the difference [between the principle of validity in your statement and others].

3. Should your opinion be that [your statement] is like "Do not make a sound," this is not possible;
   For in this case by a [present] sound there will be a [future] prevention of that [sound].

4. If [your statement] were that: "This is a denial of a denial," that is not true;
   Thus your thesis, as to a defining mark (*lakṣaṇata*)—not mine—is in error.

5. If you deny existing things while being seen by direct perception,
   Then that direct perception, by which things are seen, also does not exist.

6. By [denying] direct perception inference is denied, as also Scripture and analogy.
   [As well as] the points to be proved by inference and Scripture and those points to be proved by a similar instance (*dṛṣṭānta*).

7. The people who know the modes of the *dharmas* know [there is] a good self-existence of good *dharmas*.
   As to the others, the application is the same.

8. There is a self-existence of liberation in those [*dharmas*] mentioned as liberative modes of *dharmas*.
   Likewise, there is that which is non-liberative, etc.

9. And, if there would be no self-existence of *dharmas*, then that would be "non-self-existence";
   In that case the name (*nāma*) would not exist, for certainly there is nothing without substance [to which it refers].

10. If [one asserts:] That which is self-existent exists, but the self-existence of the *dharmas* does not exist,
    One should give the explanation concerning that of which there is self-existence without *dharmas*.

11. As there must be a denial of something that exists, as [in the statement:] "There is not a pot in the house,"
    That denial of yours which is seen must be a denial of self-existence that exists.

12. Or if that self-existence does not exist, what do you deny by that statement?
    Certainly, the denial of what does not exist is proved without a word!

13. Just as children erroneously apprehend that there is "non-water" in a mirage,
    So you would erroneously apprehend a non-existing thing as deniable.
14. If this is so, then there is the apprehension, "what is apprehended" and the one who apprehends,
    Also the denial, "what is denied" and the one who denies—six all together.
15. However, if the apprehension, "what is apprehended" and the one who apprehends do not exist,
    Then is it not true that denial, "what is denied," and the one who denies do not exist?
16. If denial, "what is denied," and the one who denies do not exist,
    Then all existing things as well as the self-existence of them are proved [since you have eliminated their denial].
17. Because of non-self-existence there is no proof of any grounds [of knowledge]; whence are your grounds?
    There is no proof of a "point" possible for you if it has no grounds.
18. If the proof of your denial of a self-existent thing is not a result of grounds of knowledge,
    Then my affirmation of the existence of a self-existent thing is proved without grounds.
19. Or if you maintain: "The real existence of grounds is such that it is a non-self-existent thing (*asvābhava*)"—this is not justified;
    Because no thing whatever in the world exists lacking its own nature (*niḥsvabhāva*).
20. When it is said: The denial precedes "what is denied," this is not justified.
    [Denial] is not justified either later or simultaneously. Therefore self-existence is real.

PART II

Nāgārjuna's Reply to the Arguments of the Opponents

21. If my thesis does not bear on the totality of causes and conditions, or on them separately,
    Is not emptiness proved because of the fact that there is no self-existence in existing things?
22. The "being dependent nature" of existing things: that is called "emptiness."
    That which has a nature of "being dependent"—of that there is a non-self-existent nature.

23. Just as a magically formed phantom could deny a phantom created by its own magic,
    Just so would be that negation.

24. This statement [regarding emptiness] is not "that which is self-existent"; therefore, there is no refutation of my assertion.
    There is no inconsistency and [thus] the grounds for the difference need not be explained.

25. [Regarding] "Do not make a sound"—this example introduced by you is not pertinent,
    Since there is a negation of sound by sound. That is not like [my denial of self-existence].

26. For, if there is prevention of that which lacks self-existence by that which lacks self-existence,
    Then that which lacks self-existence would cease, and self-existence would be proved.

27. Or, as a phantom could destroy the erroneous apprehension concerning a phantom woman that:
    "There is a woman," just so this is true in our case.

28. Or else the grounds [of proof] are that which is to be proved; certainly sound does not exist as real.
    For we do not speak without accepting, for practical purposes, the work-a-day world.

29. If I would make any proposition whatever, then by that I would have a logical error;
    But I do not make a proposition; therefore I am not in error.

30. If there is something, while being seen by means of the objects of direct perceptions, etc.,
    [It is] affirmed or denied. That [denial] of mine is a non-apprehension of non-things.

31. And if, for you, there is a source [of knowledge] of each and every object of proof,
    Then tell how, in turn, for you there is proof of those sources.

32. If by other sources [of knowledge] there would be the proof of a source—that would be an "infinite regress";
    In that case neither a beginning, middle, nor an end is proved.

33. Or if there is proof of those [objects] without sources, your argument is refuted.
    There is a [logical] inconsistency in this, and you ought to explain the cause of the difference [between the principles of validity in your statement and others].

34. That reconciliation of difficulty is not [realized in the claim:] "Fire illumines itself."
    Certainly it is not like the non-manifest appearance of a pot in the dark.

35. And if, according to your statement, fire illumines its own self,
    Then is this not like a fire which would illumine its own self and something else?
36. If, according to your statement, fire would illumine both its "own self" and an "other self,"
    Then also darkness, like fire, would darken itself and an "other self."
37. Darkness does not exist in the glow of a fire; and where the glow remains in an "other individual self,"
    How could it produce light? Indeed light is the death of darkness.
38. [If you say:] "Fire illumines when it is being produced," this statement is not true;
    For, when being produced, fire certainly does not touch darkness.
39. Now if that glow can destroy the darkness again and again without touching it,
    Then that [glow] which is located here would destroy the darkness in "every corner" of the world.
40. If your sources [of knowledge] are proved by their own strength, then, for you, the sources are proved without respect to "that which is to be proved";
    Then you have a proof of a source, [but] no sources are proved without relation to something else.
41. If, according to you, the sources [of knowledge] are proved without being related to the objects of "that which is to be proved,"
    Then these sources will not prove anything.
42. Or if [you say]: What error is there in thinking, "The relationship of these [sources of knowledge to their objects] is [already] proved"?
    [The answer is:] This would be the proving of what is proved. Indeed "that which is not proved" is not related to something else.
43. Or if the sources [of knowledge] in every case are proved in relation to "what is to be proved,"
    Then "what is to be proved" is proved without relation to the sources.
44. And if "what is to be proved" is proved without relation to the sources [of knowledge],
    What [purpose] is the proof of the sources for you—since that for the purpose of which those [sources] exist is already proved!
45. Or if, for you, the sources [of knowledge] are proved in relation to "what is to be proved,"
    Then, for you, there exists an interchange between the sources and "what is to be proved."
46. Or if, for you, there are the sources [of knowledge] being proved

when there is proof of "what is to be proved," and if "what is to
be proved" exists when
The source is proved, then, for you, the proof of them both
does not exist.
47. If those things which are to be proved are proved by those
sources [of knowledge], and those things which are proved
By "what is to be proved," how will they prove [anything]?
48. And if those sources [of knowledge] are proved by what is to be
proved, and those things which are proved
By the sources, how will they prove [anything]?
49. If a son is produced by a father, and if that [father] is produced by
that very son [when he is born],
Then tell me, in this case, who produces whom?
50. You tell me! Which of the two becomes the father, and which the
son—
Since they both carry characteristics of "father" and "son"? In
that case there is doubt.
51. The proof of the sources [of knowledge] is not [established] by
itself, not by each other, or not by other sources;
It does not exist by that which is to be proved and not from
nothing at all.
52. If those who know the modes of the *dharmas* say that there is
good self-existence of good *dharmas*,
That [self-existence] must be stated in contradistinction to
something else.
53. If a good self-existence were produced in relation to [something
else],
Then that self-existence of the good *dharmas* is an "other
existence." How, then, does [self-existence] exist?
54. Or if there is that self-existence of good *dharmas*, while not being
related to something else,
There would be no state of a spiritual way of life.
55. There would be neither vice nor virtue, and worldly practical
activities would not be possible;
Self-existent things would be eternal because that without a
cause would be eternal.
56. Regarding [your view of] bad, "liberative," and undefined
[*dharmas*], there is an error;
Therefore, all composite products (*saṁskṛta*) exist as non-
composite elements (*asaṁskṛta*).
57. He who would impute a really existing name to a really existing
thing
Could be refuted by you; but we do not assert a name.

58. And that [assertion]: "The name is unreal"—would that relate to a real or a non-real thing?
    If it were a real thing, or if it were a non-real thing—in both cases your entire proposition is refuted.

59. The emptiness of all existing things has been demonstrated previously;
    Therefore, this attack is against that which is not my thesis.

60. Or if [it is said]: "Self-existence exists, but that [self-existence] of *dharmas* does not exist"—
    That is questionable; but that which was said [by me] is not questionable.

61. If the denial concerns something real, then is not emptiness proved?
    Then you would deny the non-self-existence of things.

62. Or if you deny emptiness, and there is no emptiness,
    Then is not your assertion: "The denial concerns something real" refuted?

63. Since anything being denied does not exist, I do not deny anything;
    Therefore, [the statement]: "You deny"—which was made by you—is a false accusation.

64. Regarding what was said concerning what does not exist: "The statement of denial is proved without a word,"
    In that case the statement expresses: "[That object] does not exist"; [the words] do not destroy that [object].

65. Regarding the great censure formerly made by you through the instance of the mirage—
    Now hear the ascertainment whereby that instance is logically possible.

66. If that apprehension [of the mirage] is "something which is self-existent," it would not have originated presupposing [other things];
    But that apprehension which exists presupposing [other things]—is that not emptiness?

67. If that apprehension is "something which is self-existent," with what could the apprehension be negated?
    This understanding [applies] in the remaining [five factors: "what is apprehended," the one who apprehends, the denial, "what is denied," and the one who denies]; therefore that is an invalid censure.

68. By this [argument] the absence of a cause [for denying self-existence] is refuted—on the basis of the similarity [with the foregoing]:

Namely, that which was already said regarding the exclusion of
the instance of the mirage.

69. That which is the cause for the three times is refuted from what is
similar to that [given] before;
Negation of cause for the three times affirms emptiness.

70. All things prevail for him for whom emptiness prevails;
Nothing whatever prevails for him for whom emptiness prevails.

MĀDHAVA'S PHILOSOPHIC COMPENDIUM: CĀRVĀKA

In classical India, not all thinkers took their philosophic orientations
from religious or mystical traditions. The most striking opposition
to religious notions comes from a school known as Cārvāka, also
called Lokāyata, a term meaning "those attached to the ways of the
world." Cārvāka philosophers were materialists; that is, they
believed that physical matter is the only reality. And not only did
they attack the religious positions prominent in their time; the
validity of inference was a favorite target. These materialists maintain that we can know only what we perceive through our senses.
Because they reject inference, they are commonly referred to as
skeptics.

The Cārvākas attack ideas of an immortal soul, rebirth, God, a
mystical enlightenment or liberation, and other such notions by
arguing that inferential reasoning cannot establish anything. That is
to say, by showing that inference is unreliable whatever the topic,
these skeptics strip away all excesses of belief beyond the simple
facts of pleasure and pain and the body. The body exists in an inexplicable material world. Opponents retort that the Cārvāka attack is
self-defeating, for it utilizes the very processes of thinking that it
aims to show invalid. The Cārvāka response is that the burden of
proof is on the other side.

The attack presupposes familiarity with an argument form that
had become standard in philosophical debates in the classical age.
Here is a paradigmatic passage.

0 There is fire on yonder hill. (The conclusion to be proved. How?
Because:)
1 There is smoke rising from it.
2 Wherever there's smoke, there's fire.

3 This smoke-possessing-hill is an example of the "wherever" of the universal proposition (2). (Therefore:)
4 There is fire on yonder hill.

Here fire is an example of a major term as referred to in the text below; smoke is a middle term. The universal proposition (2) expresses an invariable connection.
Most Cārvāka texts have been lost, but references to their arguments occur in many of their opponents' works. The selection that follows is taken from a late (ca. 1500) Sanskrit compendium of philosophic views compiled by a person named Mādhava, who was not himself a Cārvāka. Although this text is late, Cārvāka positions were prominent from very early, as we know from citations and discussions of Cārvāka views in several texts of their opponents.

The Chārvāka System

MĀDHAVA

[We have said in our preliminary invocation "salutation to Śiva, the abode of eternal knowledge, the storehouse of supreme felicity,"] but how can we attribute to the Divine Being the giving of supreme felicity, when such a notion has been utterly abolished by Chārvāka, the crest-gem of the atheistical school, the follower of the doctrine of Bṛhaspati? The efforts of Chārvāka are indeed hard to be eradicated, for the majority of living beings hold by the current refrain— 1

While life is yours, live joyously;
None can escape Death's searching eye:
When once this frame of ours they burn,
How shall it e'er again return?

The mass of men, in accordance with the Śāstras [Sciences] of 2
policy and enjoyment, considering wealth and desire the only ends of man, and denying the existence of any object belonging to a future world, are found to follow only the doctrine of Chārvāka. Hence

E. B. Cowell and A. E. Gough, trans. *The Sarva-Darśana Saṃgraha*. London: Kegan Paul, 1904, pp. 2–11.

another name for that school is Lokāyata,—a name well accordant with the thing signified. [Lokāyata may be etymologically analysed as "prevalent in the world."]

In this school the four elements, earth, etc., are the original prin- 3
ciples; from these alone, when transformed into the body, intelligence is produced, just as the inebriating power is developed from the mixing of certain ingredients; and when these are destroyed, intelligence at once perishes also. . . .

The soul is only the body distinguished by the attribute of intelli- 4
gence, since there is no evidence for any soul distinct from the body, as such cannot be proved, since this school holds that perception is the only source of knowledge and does not allow inference, etc.

The only end of man is enjoyment produced by sensual pleasures. 5
Nor may you say that such cannot be called the end of man as they are always mixed with some kind of pain, because it is our wisdom to enjoy the pure pleasure as far as we can, and to avoid the pain which inevitably accompanies it; just as the man who desires fish takes the fish with their scales and bones, and having taken as many as he wants, desists; or just as the man who desires rice, takes the rice, straw and all, and having taken as much as he wants, desists. It is not therefore for us, through a fear of pain, to reject the pleasure which our nature instinctively recognises as congenial. Men do not refrain from sowing rice, because forsooth there are wild animals to devour it; nor do they refuse to set the cooking-pots on the fire, because forsooth there are beggars to pester us for a share of the contents. If any one were so timid as to forsake a visible pleasure, he would indeed be foolish like a beast, as has been said by the poet—

> The pleasure which arises to men from contact with sensible objects,
> Is to be relinquished as accompanied by pain,—such is the reasoning of
>   fools;
> The berries of paddy, rich with the finest white grains,
> What man, seeking his true interest, would fling away because covered
>   with husk and dust?

If you object that, if there be no such thing as happiness in a 6
future world, then how should men of experienced wisdom engage in the agnihotra and other sacrifices, which can only be performed with great expenditure of money and bodily fatigue, your objection cannot be accepted as any proof to the contrary, since the agnihotra, etc., are

only useful as means of livelihood, for the Veda is tainted by the three
faults of untruth, self-contradiction, and tautology. . . .

> The Agnihotra, the three Vedas, the ascetic's three staves, and smearing
>   oneself with ashes,—
> Bṛihaspati says, these are but means of livelihood for those who have
>   no manliness nor sense.

Hence it follows that there is no other hell than mundane pain   7
produced by purely mundane causes, as thorns, etc.; the only
Supreme is the earthly monarch whose existence is proved by all the
world's eyesight; and the only Liberation is the dissolution of the
body. By holding the doctrine that the soul is identical with the body,
such phrases as "I am thin," "I am black," etc., are at once intelligible,
as the attributes of thinness, etc., and self-consciousness will reside in
the same subject [the body]; like and the use of the phrase "my body"
is metaphorical "the head of Rāhu" [Rāhu being really all head].

All this has been thus summed up—   8

> In this school there are four elements, earth, water, fire, and air;
> And from these four elements alone is intelligence produced,—
> Just like the intoxicating power from kinwa [a grain], etc., mixed
>   together;
> Since in "I am fat," "I am lean," these attributes abide in the same
>   subject,
> And since fatness, etc., reside only in the body, it alone is the soul and
>   no other,
> And such phrases as "my body" are only significant metaphorically.

"Be it so," says the opponent; "your wish would be gained if   9
inference, etc., had no force of proof; but then they have this force;
else, if they had not, then how, on perceiving smoke, should the
thoughts of the intelligent immediately proceed to fire; or why, on
hearing another say, 'There are fruits on the bank of the river,' do
those who desire fruit proceed at once to the shore?"

All this, however, is only the inflation of the world of fancy.   10

Those who maintain the authority of inference accept the *sign* or   11
middle term as the causer of knowledge, which middle term must be
found in the minor and be itself invariably connected with the major.
Now this invariable connection must be a relation destitute of any
condition accepted or disputed; and this connection does not possess
its power of causing inference by virtue of its *existence*, as the eye,

etc., are the cause of perception, but by virtue of its being *known.*
What then is the means of this connection's being known?

We will first show that it is not *perception.* Now perception is   12
held to be of two kinds, external and internal [*i.e.,* as produced by the
external senses, or by the inner sense, mind]. The former is not the
required means; for although it is possible that the actual contact of
the senses and the object will produce the knowledge of the particular object thus brought in contact, yet as there can never be such contact in the case of the past or the future, the universal proposition
which was to embrace the invariable connection of the middle and
major terms in every case becomes impossible to be known. Nor may
you maintain that this knowledge of the universal proposition has the
general class as its object, because if so, there might arise a doubt as
to the existence of the invariable connection in this particular case
[as, for instance, in this particular smoke as implying fire].

Nor is internal perception the means, since you cannot establish   13
that the mind has any power to act independently towards an external
object, since all allow that it is dependent on the external senses, as
has been said by one of the logicians, "The eye, etc., have their
objects as described; but mind externally is dependent on the others."

Nor can *inference* be the means of the knowledge of the univer-   14
sal proposition, since in the case of this inference we should also
require another inference to establish it, and so on, and hence would
arise the fallacy of an *ad infinitum* retrogression.

Again, this same absence of a condition [which must be supplied   15
to restrict a too general middle term], which has been given as the
definition of an invariable connection [*i.e.,* a universal proposition],
can itself never be known; since it is impossible to establish that all
conditions must be objects of perception; and therefore, although the
absence of perceptible things may be itself perceptible, the absence of
non-perceptible things must be itself non-perceptible; and thus, since
we must here too have recourse to inference, etc., we cannot leap
over the obstacle which has already been planted to bar them. Again,
we must accept as the definition of the condition, "it is that which is
reciprocal or equipollent in extension with the major term though not
constantly accompanying the middle." These three distinguishing
clauses, "not constantly accompanying the middle term," "constantly
accompanying the major term," and "being constantly accompanied
by it" [*i.e.,* reciprocal], are needed. . . .

But since the knowledge of the condition must here precede the   16 knowledge of the condition's absence, it is only when there is the knowledge of the condition, that the knowledge of the universality of the proposition is possible, *i.e.*, a knowledge in the form of such a connection between the middle term and major term as is distinguished by the absence of any such condition; and on the other hand, the knowledge of the condition depends upon the knowledge of the invariable connection. Thus we fasten on our opponents as with adamantine glue the thunder-bolt-like fallacy of reasoning in a circle. Hence by the impossibility of knowing the universality of a proposition it becomes impossible to establish inference, etc.

The step which the mind takes from the knowledge of smoke,   17
etc., to the knowledge of fire, etc., can be accounted for by its being based on a former perception or by its being an error; and that in some cases this step is justified by the result, is accidental just like the coincidence of effects observed in the employment of gems, charms, drugs, etc.

From this it follows that fate, etc., do not exist, since these can   18
only be proved by inference. But an opponent will say, if you thus do not allow adṛishṭa, the various phenomena of the world become destitute of any cause. But we cannot accept this objection as valid, since these phenomena can all be produced spontaneously from the inherent nature of things. Thus it has been said—

> The fire is hot, the water cold, refreshing cool the breeze of morn;
> By whom came this variety? from their own nature was it born.

And all this has been also said by Bṛihaspati—   19

> There is no heaven, no final liberation, nor any soul in another world,
> Nor do the actions of the four castes, orders, etc., produce any real
>   effect.
> The Agnihotra, the three Vedas, the ascetic's three staves, and smearing
>   one's self with ashes,
> Were made by Nature as the livelihood of those destitute of knowledge
>   and manliness.
> If a beast slain in the Jyotishṭoma rite will itself go to heaven,
> Why then does not the sacrificer forthwith offer his own father?
> If the Śrāddha produces gratification to beings who are dead,
> Then here, too, in the case of travellers when they start, it is needless to
>   give provisions for the journey.
> If beings in heaven are gratified by our offering the Śrāddha here,
> Then why not give the food down below to those who are standing on
>   the housetop?

While life remains let a man live happily, let him feed on ghee even
    though he runs in debt;
When once the body becomes ashes, how can it ever return again?
If he who departs from the body goes to another world,
How is it that he comes not back again, restless for love of his kindred?
Hence it is only as a means of livelihood that Brahmans have
    established here
All these ceremonies for the dead,—there is no other fruit anywhere.
The three authors of the Vedas were buffoons, knaves, and demons.
All the well-known formulæ of the pandits, jarpharī, turpharī, etc.
And all the obscene rites for the queen commanded in the Aśwamedha,
These were invented by buffoons, and so all the various kinds of
    presents to the priests, [or "and all the various other things to be
    handled in the rites,"]
While the eating of flesh was similarly commanded by night-prowling
    demons.

Hence in kindness to the mass of living beings must we fly for   20
refuge to the doctrine of Chārvāka. Such is the pleasant consummation.

THE NYĀYA-SŪTRA

Three realist schools opposed the dialectic of Nāgārjuna and the
materialist skepticism of Cārvāka as well: Nyāya, which is usually
translated, "logic"; Vaiśeṣika, "atomism"; and Mīmāṃsā, "exegesis"
(viz. concerning the Vedic revelation). But it is in the *Nyāya-sūtra*
(ca. 200 C.E.), the root text of the logic school, and commentaries
thereon, that the most sustained response is to be found. Logicians
are also concerned with what we know and not just with how we
know it, and their positions come to be increasingly in line with the
atomist ontology. The atomists recognize atomic material substances but also irreducible composites and wholes. The logicians
argue—again, principally against Buddhists—that some wholes are
not to be reduced to their parts, that a clay pot, for example, is more
than the collection of atoms of which it is composed. The first love
of the logicians remains, however, the number and nature of "justi-
fiers" or "sources of knowledge" (*pramāṇa*), and they organize their
ontological reflection around their reflection on these. What there is
(the concern of ontology) is to be analyzed on the basis of how we
know it (the concern of epistemology). The *Nyāya-sūtra* recognizes
four separate sources of knowledge: perception, inference, analogical acquisition of vocabulary, and reliable testimony.

In the selection below from the *Nyāya-sūtra* and the commentary or Bhāṣya by Vātsyāyana (ca. 450), we have a response to Nāgārjuna's skepticism. Nāgārjuna has attacked the logicians' epistemology in several ways, and their realism about the external world as well (see above, "Averting the Arguments"). I repeat, the logicians take the sources of knowledge to be the means whereby we know what there is, and these show, they claim, the real existence of the objects of the everyday world, pots, cloth, human beings, and so on. In the passage below, the Buddhist position that world appearances are to be compared to dream objects is refuted. To explain illusions, a distinction between an experience's phenomenological object ("the object imputed") and the actual object in the world is maintained. On this basis and causal suppositions, illusions can be explained. Thus the possibility of illusion is no reason to throw out the Nyāya's theory of sources of knowledge.

Nyāya-sūtra

COMMENTARY BY VĀTSYĀYANA

Sutra 30: (The opponent's thesis "all is non-existent" is illogical), because (it can be justified by admitting) neither the presence nor the absence of independent *pramāṇa* [justifier, source of knowledge] establishing it. [iv. 2.30]

Bhāṣya: If it be so (*i.e.,* if it be accepted that a *pramāṇa* [source of   1 knowledge] rightly indicates the essential nature of an object), the thesis that all is non-existent cannot be justified. Why? Because (it can be justified by admitting) neither the presence nor the absence of an independent *pramāṇa* [source of knowledge] establishing it. If there be an independent *pramāṇa* establishing the thesis "all is non-existent," the very thesis "all is non-existent" would be contradicted, for the opponent would have to admit the reality of that *pramāṇa* [source of knowledge] at least. If, on the other hand, there be no independent *pramāṇa* [source of knowledge], how would the thesis "all is non-exis-

Mrinalkanti Gangopadhyaya, trans. *Nyāya-sūtra.* Calcutta: India Studies, 1982, pp. 360–367.

tent" be established at all? If, however, you admit that the thesis) is   2
established without the help of any independent *pramāṇa* [source of
knowledge], how is it that the thesis "all is existent" is not established
(in the same way)?

> *Sūtra 31:* (Objection) The notion of *pramāṇa* [source of knowledge]
> and *prameya* [object of knowledge] (is wrong), just like the false
> awareness of an object in the state of dream. [iv. 2.31]

> *Sūtra 32:* (Objection) Or, (the notion of *pramāṇa* [source of knowl-
> edge] and *prameya* [object of knowledge] is wrong), just like the
> false perceptions of (the non-existent as "existent") due to "magi-
> cian's trickery" of "castles in the sky" and of water in a mirage [iv.
> 2.32]

Bhāṣya: (Objection) Just as, in the state of dream, there is no   3
object really; yet one wrongly perceives them, so also there is really
nothing called *pramāṇa* [source of knowledge] or *prameya* [object of
knowledge], yet one has wrong notions about them.

> *Sūtra 33:* (Answer) (The thesis of the opponent) is not established (by
> the said instances), because there is no proper ground for it. [iv.
> 2.33]

Bhāṣya: (Answer) There is no ground to establish the thesis that   4
the notion of *pramāṇa* [source of knowledge] and *prameya* [object of
knowledge] is similar to wrong awareness of an object in the state of
dream, and not to the (right) cognition of an object in the waking state
and hence, due to the lack of a proper ground, the thesis is not established. There is also no ground to establish that in the state of dream
absolute non-entities only are apprehended.

> *Sūtra 35:* False cognition can be removed by right knowledge, just
> like the removal of the false awareness of an object in a dream when
> one is awakened from sleep. [iv. 2.35]

Bhāṣya: An ascertainment of the form "this is a man" in respect of   5
a post is false cognition, (for) it is the knowledge of "that" (= man) in
what is "not-that" (= post). An ascertainment of the form "this is a
post" in respect of a post is right knowledge. And right knowledge
only removes false cognition but does not (negate the reality of) the
objects known, such as posts or human beings in general; just as, the
awareness produced in the waking state negates only the false awareness of an object in a dream, but not (the reality of) the things dreamt
of, that is, objects in general. Similarly, the cognitions produced in the

cases of a magician's trickery, castles in the sky and a mirage are only ascertainments of "that" in what is "not-that" (*i.e.,* are only false perceptions). In these cases also false cognition only is removed, in the same manner as indicated above, by right knowledge, but (the reality of) the object (of false cognition) is not negated.

Moreover, the false cognitions in the cases of a magician's trick- 6 ery and the like are due to specific causes. The person who has got the means (for effecting a trickery) takes up an object similar to the particular object he intends to show (artfully to the spectator) and leads others into false perceptions; this is what is known as trickery. When, in the sky, the cloud etc. assume the form similar to a castle, one has the (false) cognition of a castle (in the sky) from a distance. Otherwise (*i.e.* when the cloud etc. do not assume the form of a castle) there is no such cognition. When the rays of the sun intermingled with the heat radiating from the surface of the earth begin to flicker, one has (from a distance) the (false) perception of water (in them), for one perceives in them characteristics similar (to those of water). Otherwise (*i.e.* if the similarity of water in the rays of the sun is not perceived), as in the case of one who is nearer, there is no such cognition. A false cognition is produced in respect of a particular person at a particular place at a particular moment, (and not in respect of every person, everywhere and always). Hence it cannot be produced without a specific cause. . . .

> *Sūtra 37:* There is difference between the "actual object" and the "object imputed" (upon the real one); hence, the dual character of false cognition is justified. [iv. 2.37]

Bhāṣya: (In the illusory perception of a post as a human being), the 7 actual object is represented by a post and the object imputed upon by a human being. Both the actual object and the object imputed upon exist really and there is difference between the two; and that is why there may arise a false cognition characterising a post as a human being, when one apprehends the similarity between the two. Similar is the case with the illusory perceptions of a banner as a row of cranes and of a (similarly shaped) lump of earth as a pigeon. But then, all the illusory cognitions do not converge upon the same object, because there is regularity as regards the perception of similarity. (That is, one takes a post for a human being, but not for a row of crane or a pigeon, because one perceives in a post the similar characteristics of a human being only—and not of a row of crane or a pigeon). One who thinks that all objects are without any essential nature of their own and are absolute non-entities only would be led to the absurdity of a convergence (of all illusory cognitions) upon the same object.

(Even) when the objects of knowledge like "smell" etc. are cognised as "smell" etc., the cognitions are considered to be false (by the opponent). But in such cases no (distinction between) an "actual object" and an "object imputed upon" can be made and there is moreover no apprehension of similarity (between the two). As such, they all become nothing but valid cognitions. Therefore, it is illogical to claim that the notions of *pramāṇa* [source of knowledge] and *prameya* [object of knowledge] are false.

8

THE WORKS OF SRI AUROBINDO

Philosophers known as Vedāntins base their speculations on the teachings of the Upanishads. Understood in a broad fashion, Vedānta stretches beyond the classical age—where there flourish several distinct Vedānta schools—to the modern period. Some may be called "folk Vedāntins," such as Swami Vivekananda (1863–1902) and Sri Aurobindo (1872–1950), who have no strict allegiance to a school of classical philosophy but draw on the Upanishads and works influenced by Vedāntic conceptions. Aurobindo affirms an allegiance to the Upanishads, but he is also commonly regarded as the most original Indian metaphysician of modern times.

Aurobindo was born August 15, 1872, in Calcutta, the third son of an "England-returned" physician. A confirmed anglophile, Aurobindo's father sent his sons to an English-medium convent school in Darjeeling and then to England. After several years in Manchester, Aurobindo entered St. Paul's School in London and later won a scholarship to King's College, Cambridge University. At Cambridge, he excelled in classics, winning college prizes for Greek and Latin verse.

Aurobindo returned to India in 1893 and was employed by the maharaja of Baroda. Studious and reclusive, he read widely during his thirteen years in Baroda's civil service and college. Through translations he had already studied some of the traditional Hindu scriptures, in particular the Upanishads. Aurobindo reports that though he was an agnostic when he returned from England, his

Upanishadic reading led him to embrace the idea of Brahman, the Absolute, World Ground, or God. He also came to accept the traditional belief that meditation and other practices of self-discipline could bring about "union" (*yoga*, in a later, theistic sense of the word) of the individual consciousness with the Divine.

Around the turn of the century—a time when the idea of a perpetual British Empire was taken for granted by most of the Indian intelligentsia—Aurobindo became a passionate spokesman for India's independence. Beginning in 1902 he helped form a revolutionary organization in Bengal, and in 1906 he quit his job in Baroda to become principal of the newly founded Bengal National College in Calcutta. At the same time he became the editor and chief writer of *Bande Mataram,* a "seditious" newspaper in English that had great influence on the development of Indian nationalism. Toward the end of 1907 a secret society led by Aurobindo's younger brother began a campaign of terrorism. A botched attempt to murder an unpopular British judge led to the arrest of many conspirators, including Aurobindo. After a sensational year-long trial—during which Aurobindo remained in prison, often in solitary confinement—he was acquitted on grounds of insufficient evidence. In prison Aurobindo was absorbed in yogic practices and upon his release he declared that he saw the Divine "as all beings and all that is." Ten months later, learning that the British again planned to arrest him, he left Calcutta and took refuge in the nearby French enclave of Chandernagore. From there he went secretly to Pondicherry, another French settlement south of Madras.

Originally intending to stay in Pondicherry for only a short period, Aurobindo remained there the rest of his life. In 1914, he began publishing a monthly "review of pure philosophy." During the next six years, most of his major works were published serially, although he revised his philosophic *chef d'oeuvre* twenty years later and wrote an epic poem throughout the remainder of his life. The poem, *Savitri,* is one of the longest in English, but was unfinished when Aurobindo died, in 1950.

The selection below is the first chapter of Aurobindo's long (more than 1,000 pages) philosophic masterpiece, *The Life Divine.* Though not developed in the passage, Aurobindo presents a theory integrating a view of biological evolution with a metaphysics centered on God or Brahman and an ethics of yogic practice. This is perhaps the most striking feature of his thought.

The Human Aspiration

Sri Aurobindo

*She follows to the goal of those that are passing on beyond,
she is the first in the eternal succession of the dawns that are
coming,—Usha widens bringing out that which lives, awakening someone who was dead. . . . What is her scope when
she harmonises with the dawns that shone out before and
those that now must shine? She desires the ancient mornings
and fulfils their light; projecting forwards her illumination she
enters into communion with the rest that are to come.*

KUTSA ANGIRASA—*Rig Veda*

*Threefold are those supreme births of this divine force that is
in the world, they are true, they are desirable; he moves there
wide-overt within the Infinite and shines pure, luminous and
fulfilling. . . . That which is immortal in mortals and possessed
of the truth, is a god and established inwardly as an energy
working out in our divine powers. . . . Become high-uplifted,
O Strength, pierce all veils, manifest in us the things of the
Godhead.*

VAMADEVA—*Rig Veda*

The earliest preoccupation of man in his awakened thoughts and, as it   1
seems, his inevitable and ultimate preoccupation,—for it survives the
longest periods of scepticism and returns after every banishment,—is
also the highest which his thought can envisage. It manifests itself in
the divination of Godhead, the impulse towards perfection, the search
after pure Truth and unmixed Bliss, the sense of a secret immortality.
The ancient dawns of human knowledge have left us their witness to
this constant aspiration; today we see a humanity satiated but not satisfied by victorious analysis of the externalities of Nature preparing to
return to its primeval longings. The earliest formula of Wisdom
promises to be its last,—God, Light, Freedom, Immortality.

Sri Aurobindo (Ghose). *The Life Divine.* Sri Aurobindo Birth Centenary Library, vol.
18. Pondicherry: Sri Aurobindo Ashram Trust, 1973.

These persistent ideals of the race are at once the contradiction of   2
its normal experience and the affirmation of higher and deeper experiences which are abnormal to humanity and only to be attained, in
their organised entirety, by a revolutionary individual effort or an evolutionary general progression. To know, possess and be the divine
being in an animal and egoistic consciousness, to convert our twilit or
obscure physical mentality into the plenary supramental illumination,
to build peace and a self-existent bliss where there is only a stress of
transitory satisfaction besieged by physical pain and emotional suffering, to establish an infinite freedom in a world which presents itself as
a group of mechanical necessities, to discover and realise the immortal life in a body subjected to death and constant mutation,—this is
offered to us as the manifestation of God in Matter and the goal of
Nature in her terrestrial evolution. To the ordinary material intellect
which takes its present organisation of consciousness for the limit of
its possibilities, the direct contradiction of the unrealised ideals with
the realised fact is a final argument against their validity. But if we
take a more deliberate view of the world's workings, that direct opposition appears rather as part of Nature's profoundest method and the
seal of her completest sanction.

For all problems of existence are essentially problems of harmo-   3
ny. They arise from the perception of an unsolved discord and the
instinct of an undiscovered agreement or unity. To rest content with
an unsolved discord is possible for the practical and more animal part
of man, but impossible for his fully awakened mind, and usually even
his practical parts only escape from the general necessity either by
shutting out the problem or by accepting a rough, utilitarian and unil-
lumined compromise. For essentially, all Nature seeks a harmony, life
and matter in their own sphere as much as mind in the arrangement
of its perceptions. The greater the apparent disorder of the materials
offered or the apparent disparateness, even to irreconcilable opposition, of the elements that have to be utilised, the stronger is the spur,
and it drives towards a more subtle and puissant order than can normally be the result of a less difficult endeavour. The accordance of
active Life with a material of form in which the condition of activity
itself seems to be inertia, is one problem of opposites that Nature has
solved and seeks always to solve better with greater complexities; for
its perfect solution would be the material immortality of a fully organised mind-supporting animal body. The accordance of conscious
mind and conscious will with a form and a life in themselves not

overtly self-conscious and capable at best of a mechanical or sub-conscious will is another problem of opposites in which she has produced astonishing results and aims always at higher marvels; for there her ultimate miracle would be an animal consciousness no longer seeking but possessed of Truth and Light, with the practical omnipotence which would result from the possession of a direct and perfected knowledge. Not only, then, is the upward impulse of man towards the accordance of yet higher opposites rational in itself, but it is the only logical completion of a rule and an effort that seem to be a fundamental method of Nature and the very sense of her universal strivings.

We speak of the evolution of Life in Matter, the evolution of Mind   4 in Matter; but evolution is a word which merely states the phenomenon without explaining it. For there seems to be no reason why Life should evolve out of material elements or Mind out of living form, unless we accept the Vedantic solution that Life is already involved in Matter and Mind in Life because in essence Matter is a form of veiled Life, Life a form of veiled Consciousness. And then there seems to be little objection to a farther step in the series and the admission that mental consciousness may itself be only a form and a veil of higher states which are beyond Mind. In that case, the unconquerable impulse of man towards God, Light, Bliss, Freedom, Immortality presents itself in its right place in the chain as simply the imperative impulse by which Nature is seeking to evolve beyond Mind, and appears to be as natural, true and just as the impulse towards Life which she has planted in certain forms of Matter or the impulse towards Mind which she has planted in certain forms of Life. As there, so here, the impulse exists more or less obscurely in her different vessels with an ever-ascending series in the power of its will-to-be; as there, so here, it is gradually evolving and bound fully to evolve the necessary organs and faculties. As the impulse towards Mind ranges from the more sensitive reactions of Life in the metal and the plant up to its full organisation in man, so in man himself there is the same ascending series, the preparation, if nothing more, of a higher and divine life. The animal is a living laboratory in which Nature has, it is said, worked out man. Man himself may well be a thinking and living laboratory in whom and with whose conscious co-operation she wills to work out the superman, the god. Or shall we not say, rather, to manifest God? For if evolution is the progressive manifestation by Nature of that which slept or worked in her, involved, it is also the overt realisation of that which she secretly is. We cannot, then, bid her pause at a given stage of her evolution, nor have we the right to condemn with the religionist as perverse and presumptuous or with the rationalist as a disease or hallucination any intention she may evince or effort she may make to go beyond. If it be true that Spirit is involved in Matter and apparent Nature is secret God, then the manifestation of the divine in himself and the realisation of God within and without are the highest and most legitimate aim possible to man upon earth.

Thus the eternal paradox and eternal truth of a divine life in an 5 animal body, an immortal aspiration or reality inhabiting a mortal tenement, a single and universal consciousness representing itself in limited minds and divided egos, a transcendent, indefinable, timeless and spaceless Being who alone renders time and space and cosmos possible, and in all these the higher truth realisable by the lower term, justify themselves to the deliberate reason as well as to the persistent instinct or intuition of mankind. Attempts are sometimes made to have done finally with questionings which have so often been declared insoluble by logical thought and to persuade men to limit their mental activities to the practical and immediate problems of their material existence in the universe; but such evasions are never permanent in their effect. Mankind returns from them with a more vehement impulse of inquiry or a more violent hunger for an immediate solution. By that hunger mysticism profits and new religions arise to replace the old that have been destroyed or stripped of significance by a scepticism which itself could not satisfy because, although its business was inquiry, it was unwilling sufficiently to inquire. The attempt to deny or stifle a truth because it is yet obscure in its outward workings and too often represented by obscurantist superstition or a crude faith, is itself a kind of obscurantism. The will to escape from a cosmic necessity because it is arduous, difficult to justify by immediate tangible results, slow in regulating its operations, must turn out eventually to have been no acceptance of the truth of Nature, but a revolt against the secret, mightier will of the great Mother. It is better and more rational to accept what she will not allow us as a race to reject and lift it from the sphere of blind instinct, obscure intuition and random aspiration into the light of reason and an instructed and consciously self-guiding will. And if there is any higher light of illumined intuition or self-revealing truth which is now in man either obstructed and inoperative or works with intermittent glancings as if from behind a veil or with occasional displays as of the northern lights in our material skies, then there also we need not fear to aspire. For it is likely that such is the next higher state of consciousness of which Mind is only a form and veil, and through the splendours of that light may lie the path of our progressive self-enlargement into whatever highest state is humanity's ultimate resting-place.

SANSKRIT PRONUNCIATION

All consonants are voiced. Sibilants with diacritics sound like English "sh"; for example, "Śvetaketu" is pronounced *shvaytukaytoo*. Unmarked "a" sounds like English "u" in "but"; long "a" (*ā*) like "a" in "father"; Sanskrit "i," both long and short, like English "ee"; "u" like "oo" in "moon"; "e" like "ay" in "may"; "ai" like "i" in "mine"; and "au" like "ow" in "cow." Other letters are roughly equivalent to the transliterated counterparts as they sound in English.

GLOSSARY

Proper Names

Buddhism: A world religion founded by Siddhārtha Gautama (the Buddha, or the "Awakened One") who taught that a supreme felicity and end to suffering occur in a special experience termed *nirvāṇa*, and who laid out a way or ways to attain it.

Cārvāka: A materialist and skeptical school also known as Lokāyata, "those who follow the way of the world."

Jainism: An ancient Indian religion founded by Mahāvīra, ca. 500 B.C.E., who like the Buddha taught a philosophy of a "supreme personal good." In later periods, Jaina philosophers addressed a broad range of issues.

Nyāya: "Logic"; a school of realism and common sense prominent throughout the classical period, from the *Nyāya-sūtra* (ca. 200), developing out of canons of debate and informal logic.

Upanishads: "Secret doctrines"; various prose and verse texts (appended to the Vedas) with mystic themes centered on an understanding of the self and its relation to the Absolute or God, called Brahman; the primary sources for classical Vedānta philosophy.

Vedānta: Originally an epithet for the Upanishads; in the classical period, any of several schools defending Upanishadic views.

Vedas: "Revealed Knowledge"; the oldest texts composed in Sanskrit (possibly as early as 1500 B.C.E.) comprised principally of hymns to various Indo-European gods, in particular: Aditi (the infinite Mother), Agni (Fire), Indra (the chief of the gods), the Maruts (wind gods), Mitra (the Friend), Soma (the god of the immortal and mystical nectar, *soma*), Varuṇa (Lord of the righteous), Vāyu (Air), and Yama (Death).

Yoga: A classical philosophy of a "supreme personal good," proposing various exercises of "self-discipline" (i.e., *yoga*) as the means thereto.

Terms

ātman: Self or soul; the Upanishadic term for an individual's true or most basic consciousness.

avatāra: An incarnation of God; e.g., Krishna.

brahman: Brahman *(brahma)* the Absolute; the key concept of the Upanishads and all Vedānta philosophy.

buddha: The awakened; an epithet of Siddhārtha Gautama, the founder of Buddhism, after his enlightenment.

dharma: Duty; right (religious) practice; quality or state of awareness (in Buddhism).

karma: "Action"; psychological dispositions to act in a certain manner accrued through previous actions; habit.

karma yoga: The yoga of action and sacrifice.

mukti: Liberation, enlightenment.

nirvāṇa: Extinction (of suffering); enlightenment.

pramāṇa: Justifier; source of knowledge; means to veridical awareness; according to Nyāya, there are four *pramāṇa*, veridical perception, cogent inference, analogical vocabulary acquisition, and authoritative testimony.

prameya: Object of veridical cognition; the knowable.

śūnyatā: "Emptiness," the Vibrant Void; the reality that *nirvāṇa* experience is said to reveal.

sūtra: Literally "thread"; a philosophic aphorism.

yoga: Self-discipline.

FURTHER READINGS

Veda

Louis Renou. *Religions of Ancient India.* New York: Schocken, 1968.

118   *Stephen H. Phillips*

Upanishads

ROBERT E. HUME. *The Thirteen Principal Upanishads,* 2d ed. London: Oxford
University Press, 1971.

Bhagavad Gītā

BARBARA STOLLER MILLER, trans. *The Bhagavad-Gita,* New York: Bantam, 1986.

Yoga-sūtra

GEORG FEUERSTEIN. *The Encyclopedic Dictionary of Yoga.* New York: Paragon
House, 1990.

Nāgārjuna

CHRISTIAN LINDTNER. *Nagarjuniana.* Delhi: Motilal Banarsidass, 1986.

Cārvāka

DEBIPRASAD CHATTOPADHYAYA. *Cārvāka/Lokāyata.* New Delhi: Indian
Council of Philosophical Research, 1990.

Nyāya-sūtra

KARL H. POTTER. *Encyclopedia of Indian Philosophies,* vol. 2: *Nyāya-Vaiśeṣika.*
Princeton: Princeton University Press, 1977.

Aurobindo

STEPHEN H. PHILLIPS. *Aurobindo's Philosophy of Brahman.* Leiden: Brill, 1986.

STUDY QUESTIONS

1. Reconstruct the exchange between Nyāya and Nāgārjuna
regarding whether the Buddhist thesis "All is nonexistent" is
contradicted by the act of philosophic debate and assertion. In
particular, try to identify Nāgārjuna's anticipation of the *Nyāya-
sūtra* argument.

2. Discuss the concept of Brahman (alternatively, of the self)—or family of concepts of Brahman—found in the Upanishads and the *Gītā*. How do the teachings differ among themselves on this topic, as well as from what the *Yoga-sūtra* says about a "conscious being"?

3. What is the Cārvāka view of the self? How does Cārvāka regard the religious teaching of an after-death destiny for the self or soul? What objections are laid at the feet of those who would use perception, inference, et cetera, to prove the reality of a self or soul transcending death and the body?

4. Aurobindo believes that natural oppositions between sentience and insentient matter, life and inanimate matter, human imperfection and "aspiration"—other "contradictions" as well—are indications of inevitable future development or even "evolution" of consciousness. What is his reasoning, and what are its strongest and weakest points?

5. *Ṛg Veda* 10.129, "Hymn of Creation," presents a way (or ways) that things might have arisen. Just what view is presented? And how should we understand the skepticism expressed in the last verse?

CHAPTER 4

Arabic Philosophy

ERIC L. ORMSBY

The writing of philosophical works in classical Arabic, for millennia the language of unlettered nomadic tribes in the Arabian Peninsula, came about gradually as a result of the translation, from Greek via Syriac (a Christian dialect of Aramaic) into Arabic, of key works on medicine, logic, and philosophy by ancient thinkers. The very process of translation, begun in the eighth century and given patronage and support by certain Abbasid caliphs, compelled Arabic speakers to forge a new vocabulary suitable for abstract expression. The rise and spread of a number of indigenous disciplines, particularly grammar, jurisprudence, and dialectical theology, strengthened and enriched early attempts at philosophical thinking in Arabic. Disputation and controversies between Muslims and Jews, or Muslims and Christians, hastened the development of more sophisticated and precise terminology and modes of argument. The year 622, the date of the prophet Mohammed's "flight," or *hijrah*, to Medinah from Mecca together with his most trusted followers, marks the official, historical beginning of Islam; but by this date, Christians and Jews had long been versed in the techniques and strategies of debate and polemic. Muslims as representatives of a younger faith had to acquire, and often to invent, these intellectual tools in Arabic, the language of conquest.

Muslims were not the only users of Arabic. As the language grew in refinement and subtlety, it became the preferred means of expression for ever more groups—not merely for various ethnic groups (Turks, Persians, Berbers, and others) but also for members of different religions (Jews, Christians, and Zoroastrians).

Thus, the following extracts contain a passage by the tenth-century Christian Aristotelian Yaḥyā ibn ʿAdī as well as excerpts from the *Guide of the Perplexed* of the twelfth-century Jewish philosopher Maimonides, both of whom wrote major works in Arabic.

120

The fact that within a relatively short time classical Arabic became the common language of philosophical discourse from Spain in the west to India and beyond in the east bears witness both to the immensely rich capacity of Arabic for word building and nuanced distinction as well as to the growing importance of philosophy itself within the medieval Islamic world. Though the philosophers themselves usually earned their livings by other professions, most often medicine and astronomy, philosophy exerted a strong and decisive influence on other disciplines. For example, Aristotelian logic, especially the syllogistic method introduced and espoused by the philosophers, eventually became, despite protracted opposition, pervasive and indispensable not only to philosophy but to Islamic theology as well.

The extracts which follow from seven important philosophers writing in Arabic have been selected to illustrate both the richness and the diversity of the Arabic philosophical tradition.

ABŪ YŪSUF YA'QŪB IBN ISHĀQ AL-KINDĪ

Al-Kindī (ca. 800–866) was born in Kufa, one of the early cantonment cities of southern Iraq, and enjoyed official, caliphal support for much of his career. He is said to have written some 242 works, of which only 40 survive today. Al-Kindī wrote not only on philosophy but also on such diverse subjects as mathematics, medicine, meteorology, glass making, jewelry, astronomy, and music. Apparently allied with the powerful and influential theological movement of the Muʿtazilites, who emphasized the efficacy of human reason, al-Kindī fell into disfavor at around the same time as this sect fell from grace at the caliphal court.

On God

AL-KINDĪ

In things evident to the senses—may God make hidden things evident   1
to you!—a supremely clear indication exists of the governance of a

M. Abū Ridā, ed. *Rasāʾil al-Kindī al-falsafīyah*, vol. 1. Cairo, 1950, pp. 214–215. Translated by Eric L. Ormsby.

prime mover (and by this I mean, a mover for everything that is moved, an agent for every agent, and an originator for everything that is originated, a first to every first and a cause for every other cause) for anyone whose senses are instruments leading to the illumination of his reason and whose quest it is to discover the truth. . . . That which he possesses which attests to the truth . . . is the intellect. Whoever is like this has the veils of dark ignorance torn away from his eyes, his soul is cured from the turbid waterholes of vanity and disdains the debility of recourse to pride. [His soul] is averse to the entry of gloomy doubts, and emerges from reliance on which is not clear and feels shame for craving to acquire what does not exist and to relinquish what does exist. . . .

Be like this, therefore—may God be your help!—O you praise-   2
worthy form and precious substance! Let God become manifest to you—glorious is His praise!—since He is the true ipseity which admits no nonbeing and is not not forever. His being has not ceased and will not cease forever. He is the living, the one who is utterly indivisible. He is the first cause which has no other cause, the agent who has no other agent, the perfect who has no perfector, who confers is-ness to all out of is-not-ness, who produces certain things for other things as causes and effects, (as has already been made plain in our writings on First Philosophy . . .).

Indeed, in the very order of this world and in its arrangement, in   3
the action of one part of it upon another, in the obedience of one part to another and in the subordination of one part to another, in the perfection of its form in the optimal manner for the generation of each existent and for the corruption of every corruptible thing, the enduring of all that endures, and the transience of all that passes away—in all these, there is a mighty sign of the most consummate order. But all order is accompanied by one who creates order, and this is the most sagacious wisdom. But wisdom presupposes a wise [agent], for these things, in their entirety, are interconnected.

ABŪ BAKR MUḤAMMAD IBN ZAKARĪYĀ AL-RĀZĪ

Al-Rāzī (865–ca. 925), or Rhazes, as he was known to the Latin Scholastics, was born in Rayy, near present-day Tehran, and achieved fame as a physician. Indeed, his books on medicine have long eclipsed his distinction as a philosopher. Al-Rāzī's philosophical thought is distinctive, controversial, and original. An avowed Platonist and deeply influenced by late Greek neo-Platonic writings, al-Rāzī held the view that reason, and not revelation, should be human beings' chief instrument for ascertaining truth. Al-Rāzī's love of reason led him to criticize revealed religions, including Islam, for their "evil codes and laws." Al-Rāzī's philosophical works survive in fragmentary form, often embedded in the texts of his opponents.

On Reason

AL-RĀZĪ

I say that the Creator—His name be exalted!—gave us reason and favored us with it solely in order that we be granted, and attain by means of it, benefits in both this world and the next to the furthest extent of that, the bestowal and attainment of which lies in our essential natures. [Reason] is the most magnificent of God's favors to us, and it is the most useful and advantageous of objects for us. Through reason we gain precedence over speechless beasts so that we may own them, manage them, subdue them, and dispose of them in ways which redound both to our benefit and to theirs. Through reason we grasp all that which exalts us and which enhances and sweetens our lives. Through reason we obtain what we desire and intend. Through reason we apprehend the craft of ships and their practical application so that we arrive by their means at whatever the sea divides and interposes between ourselves and it. Through reason we partake of medicine wherein lie many advantages for our bodies, as well as all the other disciplines by which benefit accrues to us. By means of reason we grasp hidden, distant things which are concealed and veiled from us. By reason we know the form of the earth and the heavenly sphere, the magnitude of the sun and the moon and the other stars, as well as their distances and motions. By reason we arrive at knowledge of the

1

Paul Kraus, ed. *Rasā'il falsafīyah/Opera Philosophica.* Cairo, 1939, pp. 17–18. Translated by Eric L. Ormsby.

Creator—He is mighty and glorious!—who is the loftiest object of our contemplation and the most beneficial object of our striving.

In sum, reason is something without which our state would be the state of beasts, of unreasoning infants, and of the insane. Reason is something by which we form a mental image of our intellectual activities before they are manifest to the senses, for we see them as though we had already perceived them sensorially. Then, we make our perceptible actions like the mental representation of them so that there becomes manifest a congruence to what we are imagining and fancying of them. This being reason's extent and place, its significance and loftiness, it is right and just that we not lower it from its high rank nor abase it from its eminence and that we not make it the object of judgment when it is itself the judge, nor rein it in when it is what holds the reins; nor that we make it subordinate when it is itself that to which subordination is due. On the contrary, we refer matters to reason and by means of reason, we give utterance to them, and we rely on reason in addressing them.

2

ABŪ NAṢR AL-FĀRĀBĪ

Perhaps the greatest philosopher in the Islamic tradition, al-Fārābī (ca. 870–950) was of Turkish origin and spent most of his career in Baghdad, where he learned philosophy under Christian teachers. Though he is most famous for his works of political philosophy, and especially the *Opinions of the Inhabitants of the Virtuous City,* a strongly Platonic work, it was as a commentator and logician that al-Fārābī had the greatest impact. His presentation of Aristotelian logic in Arabic was of major significance for later thinkers.

On Hierarchies of Existence

AL-FĀRĀBĪ

The substance of the First is a substance from which every existent emanates, however it may be, whether perfect or deficient. But the

1

Richard Walzer, trans. and ed. *Al-Fārābī on the Perfect State.* Oxford: Oxford University Press, 1985, pp. 95–96. Reprinted by permission of the publisher.

substance of the First is also such that all the existents, when they emanate from it, are arranged in an order of rank, and that every existent gets its allotted share and rank of existence from it. It starts with the most perfect existent and is followed by something a little less perfect than it. Afterward it is followed successively by more and more deficient existents until the final stage of being is reached beyond which no existence whatsoever is possible. . . . Inasmuch as the substance of the First is a substance from which all the existents emanate, . . . it is generous, and its generosity is in its substance; and inasmuch as all the existents receive their order of rank from it, . . . the First is just.

On Aristotle's De Interpretatione

AL-FĀRĀBĪ

The learned Abū Naṣr Muḥammed ibn Muḥammed al-Fārābī—may   1
he find favour with God!—continues:
    [First Section]   2
    One of the first things anyone taking up logic must know is that   3
there are sense-objects or, more generally, entities outside the soul; furthermore thoughts, pictures, and representations within the soul; and [finally] speech and script. We must know how they relate to one another; for the logician considered thought as relating to both sides, namely, to the entities outside the soul and to speech. He also studies speech by itself, but always in terms of its relation to thought.
    Aristotle begins by explaining the relation of speech to thought   4
and that of script to speech.

> [16^{a}1–4] First we must settle what is a noun and a verb; after that we
> must settle what is an affirmation, a negation, a statement, and a sen
> tence. We say that what comes out in the voice signifies traces in the
> soul, and what is written signifies what comes out in the voice.

By *what comes out in the voice,* Aristotle means speech. He points   5
out that speech *signifies* thoughts *in the soul.* When reading this, you

F. W. Zimmerman, trans. *Al-Fārābī's Commentary and Short Treatise on Aristotle's De Interpretatione.* London: Oxford University Press, 1981, pp. 10–12. Reprinted by permission of the publisher.

should add to it as follows: *what comes out in the voice,* i.e. speech, *signifies* in the first place thoughts *in the soul,* where "in the first place" means "without anything in between." In other words, speech signifies thoughts in the soul, without anything in between.

He says *traces in the soul* rather than "thoughts" because he 6
means to cover all that arises in the soul after the sense-objects have withdrawn from the senses. For among the things that arise in the soul there are, apart from thoughts, also images of sense-objects according to the sensation one has had of them, like the sense-image of Zayd, and other things, like the goat-stag and similar things, which the soul invents by combining images. Aristotle wants to cover all these, so he calls them *traces in the soul.*

In saying, *what is written signifies what comes out in the voice,* he 7
refers to script. Again you should add to it and read: . . . *signifies* in the first place *what comes out in the voice.* Further, you should add as your own contribution that what comes out in the voice signifies in the second place the sense-objects which the thoughts are thoughts of, which means that the thoughts are in between; and that what is written signifies in the second place the traces in the soul.

The *traces in the soul* are likenesses of the referents which exist 8
outside the soul. The commentators claim that the thoughts in the soul signify the entities outside the soul. They say that the entities outside the soul are signified without signifying and that the script signifies without being signified, while speech and thought are each both signifying and signified. Aristotle does not here go into the relation of thought to the entities outside the soul. But it is clear that the thoughts, which are said by the commentators to signify, do not signify sense-objects in the same way as speech signifies thought. If they can be said to signify at all, they merely convey the sense-object's essence or some other aspect that can be conveyed. Expressions, on the other hand, signify by virtue of being common signs. When someone hears them, the thing of which the expression in question has been made a sign actually comes to his mind. This is all there is to their signification. They are similar to other signs man creates to remind him of what he needs to remember. To say that expressions signify means no more than this. Similarly with script: this is all there is to its signification of speech. But the way thoughts convey entities outside the soul is not signification in this sense, and it should not be put on a par with the way expressions signify referents.

In this passage, Aristotle wants to inform us of the way speech sig-   9
nifies thoughts in the soul, namely, that it is similar to the way script
signifies speech.

[16ª5–6] And just as writing is not the same for all, so too what   10
comes out in the voice is not the same for them.

Aristotle wants to explain how it is with speech: that its signification is   11
based on convention. Script, where this is more evident than in
speech, resembles speech in matters of signification. And just as
scripts are not the same for all communities, their scripts being, in
fact, different, so too the expressions signifying thoughts are not the
same with all communities, their languages differing just like their
scripts. If man had been given his expressions by nature they would
be the same for all communities, just as the thoughts expressed by different languages are the same with all communities, and just as the
sense-objects which these thoughts are thoughts of are also common
to all communities.

Everything that can be put in words can be put in writing as well.   12
And just as script signifies speech by convention, speech signifies the
thoughts in the soul by convention and legislation. I say "by legislation" because communities have their expressions prescribed for
them. That is to say, communities introduce expressions in a legislative manner, just as they introduce legislation on actions and other
things. Those who impose expressions are also lawgivers. And just as
laws of conduct may be agreed upon by a group of representatives of
the total population of a nation or a city, or else may be given them by
one or several leaders imposing the laws on them, so too with language and script. The relation of the thoughts within the soul to the
entities outside the soul is based on nature. By contrast, the relation of
thought to speech, i.e. the relation of being signified by speech, is
based on sheer legislation.

YAḤYĀ IBN ʿADĪ

A pupil of al-Fārābī, Yaḥyā ibn ʿAdī (d. 972) was a Christian
Monophysite theologian and an Aristotelian philosopher. He spent
most of his career in Baghdad. His writings on Islamic ethics have
been especially influential.

On Cultivation of Character

YAḤYĀ IBN ʿADĪ

Know that man among all other animals is endowed with thought and   1
judgment, and of all things, he always loves what is most excellent, of
degrees, the noblest and of possessions, the most precious, as long as
he does not swerve from judgment in his choice, and passion does not
conquer him in the pursuit of his aims.

The most appropriate object a man may choose for himself, when   2
he does not fall below attainment of his utmost nor remain satisfied
with falling short of his end, is his own completion and perfection. It
is inherent to man's completion and perfection that he be pleased
with the noble traits and merits of good character and that he keep
aloof from ignoble traits and repugnant qualities in his character, and
that he take in all his circumstances the directives of virtues and avoid
in all his actions the pathways of vice.

This being so, it is incumbent upon man to take as his goal the   3
acquisition of every trait safe from defect and to direct his zeal
towards obtaining every noble tendency that is devoid of flaw, and to
give his effort to avoidance of every vicious reprehensible quality and
to make every exertion to discard every base, blameworthy characteristic, so that he may attain perfection by means of cultivating his character and may attire himself in the garments of goodness . . . and vie
by truth with those who are powerful and proud, and cling to the
highest steps of vigilance and nobility.

Character is a state of the soul by which man performs his acts with-   4
out either forethought or choice. Character may be innate and instinctive in some people while in others it may not occur except through
training and effort. So, for example, generosity may exist in many people without training and effort, and bravery, equanimity, continence,
justice and their like, among praiseworthy traits, may also occur.
Among people are many in whom that exists, and so among them are
those, too, who come to it by training; among them are those who
remain entrenched in habits of virtue, and those who live a life based
on ethical precepts.

Yahyā ibn ʿAdī. *Tahdhīb al-akhlāq.* In Muhammed Kurd ʿAlī, *Rasāʾil al-bulaghāʾ*. (Cairo, 1954, pp. 483–485, 512). Translated by Eric L. Ormsby.

Reprehensible traits exist in many people; for example, stinginess, 5 cowardice, injustice and evil-doing. These habits are predominant in most people and are their usual, ingrained pattern of behavior. There are few people free from distasteful traits and free from all defects, but they contend with one another in [doing bad]. So, too, with laudable qualities of character: people may differ and contend with each other for superiority, but those who by their natures are good are very few, while the odious are numerous. As for those who by their natures are vicious, these are the majority of people since evil prevails over the nature of most people. This is because when man acts unconstrainedly from his inborn nature, he uses neither thought nor discernment, neither shame nor prudence, and the characteristics of the beasts dominate him. This is because man is distinguished from beasts solely by thought and discernment; whenever he does not employ these, he partakes with beasts of their habits. . . .

It remains for us now to mention the attributes of the perfect man 6 which comprise the good qualities of character, as well as the way by which he arrives at perfection. Hence we say: The perfect man is he whom virtue has not abandoned and whom vice has not disfigured. A man rarely reaches this extreme but whenever man does reach this limit, he is more comparable to the angels than to men. For man is imprinted with varieties of defect; all sorts of evil overwhelm him in accord with his inmost nature; rarely does he ever purify himself from all of these or is his soul free from every defect and deficiency. . . .

Nevertheless, perfection, although precious and difficult to par- 7 take of, is possible. It is the ultimate toward which man strives and a final end which has a limit. Whenever human resolve is sincere and man gives his striving its due, he is worthy to reach to his final end, . . . and to arrive at his desire.

ABŪ ᶜALĪ IBN SĪNĀ

Ibn Sīnā (980–1037) (Avicenna to the Latin West) was one of the greatest and most influential of Islamic philosophers. He was born in northwest Iran and achieved lasting fame as a physician; his Arabic work on medicine entitled *al-Qānūn* was for centuries a fundamental text consulted in both East and West. He wrote some 276 works, many of which are lost today, in Arabic and Persian. His great summa of philosophy, entitled *al-Shifā*, "The Healing," is a systematic compendium of philosophical knowledge.

Autobiography

IBN SĪNĀ

My father was a man of Balkh; he moved from there to Bukhārā in the   1
days of Amīr Nūḥ ibn Manṣūr, during whose reign he worked in the
administration, being entrusted with the governing of a village in one
of the royal estates of Bukhārā. . . . Near it is a village called Afshanah,
where my father married my mother and where he took up residence
and lived. . . . A teacher of the Qur'ān and a teacher of literature were
provided for me, and when I reached the age of ten I had finished the
Qur'ān and many works of literature, so that people were greatly
amazed at me. . . .

At that time Abū ʿAbd Allāh al-Nātilī, who claimed to know phi-   2
losophy, arrived in Bukhārā; so my father had him stay in our home
and he devoted himself to educating me. Before his arrival I had
devoted myself to jurisprudence. . . . I was a skillful questioner, having become acquainted with the methods of prosecution and the procedures of rebuttal. . . . Then I began to read the *Isagoge* under
al-Nātilī, and when he mentioned to me the definition of genus, as
being that which is predicated of a number of things of different
species in answer to the question "What is it?," I evoked his admiration by verifying this definition in a manner unlike any he had heard
of. He was extremely amazed at me; whatever problem he posed I
conceptualized better than he, so he advised my father against my
taking up any occupation other than learning. . . .

Thus I mastered the logical, natural, and mathematical sciences,   3
and I had now reached the science of metaphysics. I read the
Metaphysics [of Aristotle], but I could not comprehend its contents,
and its author's object remained obscure to me, even when I had gone
back and read it forty times and had got to the point where I had
memorized it. . . . One day in the afternoon when I was at the book-

William E. Gohlman, trans. and ed. *The Life of Ibn Sīnā*. Albany, N.Y.: State University of New York Press, 1974, pp. 17–19, 21–23, 31–35. Reprinted by permission of the publisher.

sellers' quarter a salesman approached with a book in his hand which he was calling out for sale. He offered it to me, but I refused it with disgust, believing that there was no merit in this science. But he said to me, "Buy it, because its owner needs the money and so it is cheap. I will sell it to you for three *dirhams.*" So I bought it and, lo and behold, it was Abu Nasr al-Fārābī's book on the objects of the *Metaphysics.* I returned home and was quick to read it, and in no time the objects of that book became clear to me because I had got to the point of having memorized it by heart. I rejoiced at this and the next day gave much in alms to the poor in gratitude to God, who is exalted.

The Soul Does Not Die with the Death of the Body; It Is Incorruptible

IBN SĪNĀ

We say that the soul does not die with the death of the body and is 1
absolutely incorruptible. As for the former proposition, this is because everything which is corrupted with the corruption of something else is in some way attached to it. And anything which in some way is attached to something else is either coexistent with it or posterior to it in existence or prior to it, this priority being essential and not temporal. If, then, the soul is so attached to the body that it is coexistent with it, and this is not accidental but pertains to its essence, then they are essentially interdependent. Then neither the soul nor the body would be a substance; but in fact they are substances. And if this is an accidental and not an essential attachment, then, with the corruption of the one term only the accidental relationship of the other term will be annulled, but its being will not be corrupted with its corruption. If the soul is so attached to the body that it is posterior to it in existence, then, in that case, the body will be the cause of the soul's existence. Now the causes are four; so either the body is the efficient cause of the soul and gives it existence, or it is its receptive and material

Fazlur Rahman, trans. and ed. *Avicenna's Psychology.* London: Oxford University Press, 1952, pp. 58–59, 62–63. Reprinted by permission of the publisher.

cause—maybe by way of composition as the elements are for the body or by way of simplicity as bronze is for the statue—or the body is the soul's formal or final cause. But the body cannot be the soul's efficient cause, for body, as such, does not act; it acts only through its faculties. If it were to act through its essence, not through its faculties, every body would act in the same way. Again, the bodily faculties are all of them either accidents or material form, and it is impossible that either accidents or forms subsisting in matter should produce the being of a self-subsisting entity independent of matter or that of an absolute substance. Nor is it possible that the body should be the receptive and material cause of the soul, for we have clearly shown and proved that the soul is in no way imprinted in the body. The body, then, is not "informed" with the form of the soul, either by way of simplicity or composition so that certain parts of the body are composed and mixed together in a certain way and then the soul is imprinted in them. It is also impossible that the body should be the formal or the final cause of the soul, for the reverse is the more plausible case.

Thus the attachment of the soul to the body is not the attachment 2 of an effect to a necessary cause. The truth is that the body and the temperament are an accidental cause for the soul, for when the matter of a body suitable to become the instrument of the soul and its proper subject comes into existence, the separate causes bring into being the individual soul, and that is how the soul originates from them. . . .

So if the soul is absolutely simple and is not divisible into matter 3 and form, it will not admit of corruption. But if it is composite, let us leave the composite and consider only the substance which is its matter. We say: either that matter will continue to be divisible and so the same analysis will go on being applied to it and we shall then have a regress *ad infinitum,* which is absurd; or this substance and base will never cease to exist. But if so, then our present discourse is devoted to this factor which is the base and origin (i.e. the substance) and not to the composite thing which is composed of this factor and some other. So it is clear that everything which is simple and not composite, or which is the origin and base (i.e. the substance) of the composite thing, cannot in itself possess both the actuality of persistence and the potentiality of corruption. If it has the potentiality of corruption, it cannot possibly have the actuality of persistence, and if it has the actuality of persistence and existence, it cannot have the potentiality of corruption. Obviously, then, the substance of the soul does not have the potentiality of corruption. Of those things which come to be and are corrupted, the corruptible is only the concrete composite. The potentiality of corruption and of persistence at the same time does not belong to something which gives unity to the composite, but to the matter which potentially admits of both contraries. So the corruptible composite as such possesses neither the potentiality of persistence nor that of corruption, let alone both. As to the matter itself, it either has persistence not due to any potentiality, which gives it the capacity for persistence—as some people think—or it has persistence through a potentiality which gives it persistence, but does not have the potentiality of corruption; this latter being something which it acquires. The potentiality of corruption of simple entities which subsist in matter is due to matter and is not in their own substance. The argument which proves that everything which comes to exist passes away on account of the finitude of the potentialities of persistence and corruption is relevant only to those things whose being is composed of matter and form. Matter has the potentiality that this form may persist in it, and at the same time the potentiality that this form may cease to exist in it. It is then obvious that the soul is absolutely incorruptible. This is the point which we wanted to make, and this is what we wanted to prove.

MAIMONIDES

The great codifier of Jewish law and a renowned physician, Maimonides (1135–1204) wrote his philosophical works in Judeo-Arabic, Arabic written in Hebrew letters. His masterpiece is *The Guide of the Perplexed,* which Maimonides wrote while living in Egypt whence he had moved from Muslim Spain.

The Guide of the Perplexed

MAIMONIDES

Often it occurs to the imagination of the multitude that there are more   1
evils in the world than there are good things. As a consequence, this

Maimonides. *The Guide of the Perplexed.* Translated by Shlomo Pines. Chicago: University of Chicago Press, 1969, pp. 441–445, 471–472. Reprinted by permission of the publisher.

thought is contained in many sermons and poems of all of the religious communities, which say that it is surprising if good exists in the temporal, whereas the evils of the temporal are numerous and constant. This error is not found only among the multitude, but also among those who deem that they know something.

Rāzī has written a famous book, which he has entitled "Divine   2
Things." He filled it with the enormity of his ravings and his ignorant notions. Among them there is a notion that he has thought up, namely, that there is more evil than good in what exists; if you compare man's well-being and his pleasures in the time span of his well-being with the pains, the heavy sufferings, the infirmities, the paralytic afflictions, the wretchedness, the sorrows, and the calamities that befall him, you find that his existence—he means the existence of man—is a punishment and a great evil inflicted upon him. He began to establish this opinion by inductively examining these misfortunes, so as to oppose all that is thought by the adherents of the truth regarding the beneficence and manifest munificence of the deity and regarding His being, may he be exalted, the absolute good and regarding all that proceeds from Him being indubitably an absolute good. The reason for this whole mistake lies in the fact that this ignoramus and those like him among the multitude consider that which exists only with reference to a human individual. Every ignoramus imagines that all that exists exists with a view to his individual sake; it is as if there were nothing that exists except him. And if something happens to him that is contrary to what he wishes, he makes the trenchant judgment that all that exists is an evil. However, if man considered and represented to himself that which exists and knew the smallness of his part in it, the truth would become clear and manifest to him. For this extensive raving entertained by men with regard to the multitude of evils in the world is not said by them to hold good with regard to the angels or with regard to the spheres and the stars or with regard to the elements and the minerals and the plants composed of them or with regard the various species of animals, but their whole thought only goes out to some individuals belonging to the human species. If someone has eaten bad food and consequently was stricken with leprosy, they are astonished how this great ill has befallen him and how this great evil exists. They are also astonished when one who frequently copulates is stricken blind, and they think it a marvelous thing the calamity of blindness that has befallen such a man and other such calamities.

Now the true way of considering this is that all the existent indi-   3 viduals of the human species and, all the more, those of the other species of the animals are things of no value at all in comparison with the whole that exists and endures. It has made this clear, saying: *Man is like unto vanity, and so on. Man, that is worm; and the son of man, that is a maggot. How much less in them that dwell in houses of clay, and so on. Behold, the nations are as a drop of a bucket, and so on.* There are also all the other passages figuring in the texts of the books of the prophets concerning this sublime and grave subject, which is most useful in giving man knowledge of his true value, so that he should not make the mistake of thinking that what exists is in existence only for the sake of him as an individual. According to us, on the other hand, what exists is in existence because of the will of its Creator; and among the things that are in existence, the species of man is the least in comparison to the superior existents—I refer to the spheres and the stars. As far as comparison with the angels is concerned, there is in true reality no relation between man and them. Man is merely the most noble among the things that are subject to generation, namely, in this our nether world; I mean to say that he is the noblest thing that is composed of the elements. Withal his existence is for him a great good and a benefit on the part of God because of the properties with which He has singled him out and perfected him. The greater part of the evils that befall its individuals are due to the latter, I mean the deficient individuals of the human species. It is because of our own deficiencies that we lament and we call for aid. We suffer because of evils that we have produced ourselves of our free will; but we attribute them to God, may He be exalted above this; just as He explains in His book, saying: *Is corruption His? No; his children's is the blemish, and so on. Solomon* too has explained this. saying: *The foolishness of man perverteth his way; and his heart fretteth against the Lord.* The explanation of this lies in the fact that all the evils that befall man fall under one of three species.

The first species of evil is that which befalls man because of the nature of coming-to-be and passing-away, I mean to say because of his being endowed with matter. Because of this, infirmities and paralytic afflictions befall some individuals either in consequence of their original natural disposition, or they supervene because of changes occurring in the elements, such as corruption of the air or a fire from heaven and a landslide. We have already explained that divine wisdom has made it obligatory that there should be no coming-to-be except through passing-away. Were it not for the passing-away of individuals, the coming-to-be relating to the species would not continue. Thus that pure beneficence, that munificence, that activity causing good to overflow, are made clear. He who wishes to be endowed with flesh and bones and at the same time not be subject to impressions and not to be attained by any of the concomitants of matter merely wishes, without being aware of it, to combine two contraries, namely to be subject to impressions and not to be subject to them. . . . Galen has put it well in the third of the books of "Utilities," saying: Do not set your mind on the vain thought that it is possible that out of menstrual blood and sperm there should be generated a living being that does not die, is not subject to pain, is in perpetual motion, or is as brilliant as the sun. This dictum of Galen draws attention to one particular case falling under a general proposition. That proposition is as follows: Everything that is capable of being generated from any matter whatever, is generated in the most perfect way in which it is possible to be generated out of that specific matter; the deficiency attaining the individuals of the species corresponds to the deficiency of the particular matter of the individual. Now the ultimate term and the most perfect thing that may be generated out of blood and sperm is the human species with its well-known nature consisting in man's being a living, rational, and mortal being. Thus this species of evils must necessarily exist. Withal you will find that the evils of this kind that befall men are very few and occur only seldom. For you will find cities, existing for thousands of years, that have never been flooded or burned. Also thousands of people are born in perfect health whereas the birth of an infirm human being is an anomaly, or at least—if someone objects to the word anomaly and does not use it—such an individual is very rare; for they do not form a hundredth or even a thousandth part of those born in good health.

The evils of the second kind are those that men inflict upon one 5 another, such as tyrannical domination of some of them over others. These evils are more numerous than those belonging to the first kind, and the reasons for that are numerous and well known. The evils in question also come from us. . . .

The evils of the third kind are those that are inflicted upon any 6 individual among us by his own action; this is what happens in the majority of cases, and these evils are much more numerous than those of the second kind. All men lament over evils of this kind; and it is only seldom that you find one who is not guilty of having brought them upon himself. He who is reached by them deserves truly to be blamed.

As for my own belief with regard to this fundamental principle, I mean divine providence, it is as I shall set forth to you. In this belief that I shall set forth, I am not relying upon the conclusion to which demonstration has led me, but upon what has clearly appeared as the intention of the book of God and of the books of our prophets. This opinion, which I believe, is less disgraceful than the preceding opinions and nearer than they to intellectual reasoning. For I for one believe that in this lowly world—I mean that which is beneath the sphere of the moon—divine providence watches only over the individuals belonging to the human species and that in this species alone all the circumstances of the individuals and the good and evil that befall them are consequent upon the deserts, just as it says: *For all His ways are judgment.* But regarding all the other animals and, all the more, the plants and other things, my opinion is that of Aristotle. For I do not by any means believe that this particular leaf has fallen because of a providence watching over it; nor that this spider has devoured this fly because God has now decreed and willed something concerning individuals; nor that the spittle spat by Zayd has moved till it came down in one particular place upon a gnat and killed it by divine decree and judgment; nor that when this fish snatched this worm from the face of the water, this happened in virtue of a divine volition concerning individuals. For all this is in my opinion due to pure chance, just as Aristotle holds. According to me, as I consider the matter, divine providence is consequent upon the divine overflow; and the species with which this intellectual overflow is united, so that it became endowed with intellect and so that everything that is disclosed to a being endowed with intellect was disclosed to it, is the one accompanied by divine providence, which appraises all its actions from the point of view of reward and punishment. If, as he states, the foundering of a ship and the drowning of those who were in it and the falling-down of a roof upon those who were in the house, are due to pure chance, the fact that the people in the ship went on board and that the people in the house were sitting in it is, according to our opinion, not due to chance, but to divine will in accordance with the deserts of those people as determined by His judgments, the rule of which cannot be attained by our intellects.

7

138 *Eric Ormsby*

ABŪ AL-WALĪD IBN RUSHD

Ibn Rushd (1126–1198), or Averroës as he was known in the West, was the last great representative in the *falsafah* tradition. A native of Cordoba in Muslim Spain, Ibn Rushd came from a long and distinguished tradition of judges and imams. A universal man, Ibn Rushd was equally learned in Islamic law, medicine, astronomy, and philosophy. The extracts which follow are from his great rebuttal of the mystic Abū Ḥamid al-Ghazālī (d. 1111), who had attacked a number of premises of the philosophers as being incompatible with Islamic revelation.

On Creation

IBN RUSHD

Most people who accept a temporal creation of the world believe   1 time to have been created with it. Therefore his [i.e., al-Ghazālī's] assertion that the duration of His inactivity was either limited or unlimited is untrue. For what has no beginning does not finish or end. And the opponent does not admit that the inactivity has any duration at all. What one has to ask them about the consequence of their theory is: Is it possible, when the creation of time is admitted, that the term of its beginning may lie beyond the real time in which we live? If they answer that it is not possible, they posit a limited extension beyond which the Creator cannot pass, and this is, in their view, shocking and absurd. If, however, they concede that its possible beginning may lie beyond the moment of its created term, it may further be asked if there may not lie another beyond the second. If they answer in the affirmative—and they cannot do otherwise—it will be said: Then we shall have here a possible creation of an infinite number of durations, and you will be forced to admit—according to your argument about the spherical revolutions—that their termination is a

Averroes' Tahāfut al-tahāfut (The Incoherence of the Incoherence), vol. 1. Translated by Simon van den Bergh. London: Luzac, 1969, pp. 17–18, 57, 111–112. Reprinted by permission of the publisher.

condition for the real age which exists since them. If you say what is infinite does not finish, the arguments you use about the spherical revolutions against your opponents your opponents will use against you on the subject of the possibility of created durations. If it is objected that the difference between those two cases is that these infinite possibilities belong to extensions which do not become actual, whereas the spherical revolutions do become actual, the answer is that the possibilities of things belong to their necessary accidents and that it does not make any difference, according to the philosophers, if they precede these things or are simultaneous with them, for of necessity they are the dispositions of things. If, then, it is impossible that before the existence of the present spherical revolution there should have been infinite spherical revolutions, the existence of infinite possible revolutions is equally impossible. If one wants to avoid these consequences, one can say that the age of the world is a definite quantity and cannot be longer or shorter than it is, in conformity with the philosophical doctrine about the size of the world. Therefore, these arguments are not stringent, and the safest way for him who accepts the temporal creation of the world is to regard time as of a definite extension and not to admit a possibility which precedes the possible; and to regard also the spatial extension of the world as infinite. Only, spatial extension forms a simultaneous whole; not so time. . . .

I say:

2

3

The man who assumes that before the existence of the world there was one unique, never-ceasing possibility must concede that the world is eternal. The man who affirms, like Ghazali in his answer, that before the world there was an infinite number of possibilities of worlds, has certainly to admit that before this world there was another world and before this second world a third, and so on *ad infinitum,* as is the case with human beings, and especially when it is assumed that the perishing of the earlier is the necessary condition for the existence of the later. For instance, if God had the power to create another world before this, and before this second world yet another, the series must continue infinitely, or else we should arrive at a world before which no other world could have been created (however, the theologians do not affirm this nor use it as a proof for the temporal production of the world). Although the assumption that before this world there might be an infinite number of others does not seem an impossible one, it appears after closer examination to be absurd, for it would follow from it that the universe had the nature of an individual person in this transitory world, so that its procession from the First Principle would be like the procession of the individual person from Him—that is to say, through an eternal moving body and an eternal motion. But then this world would be part of another world, like the transient beings in this world, and then necessarily either we end finally in a world individually eternal or we have an infinite series. And if we have to bring this series to a standstill, it is more appropriate to arrest it at this world, by regarding it as eternally unique. . . .

The true theory of the ancient philosophers is that there are principles   4
which are the celestial bodies, and that the principles of the celestial bodies, which are immaterial existents, are the movers of those celestial bodies, and that the celestial bodies move towards them in obedience to them and out of love for them, to comply with their order to move and to understand them, and that they are only created with a view to movement. For when it was found that the principles which move the celestial bodies are immaterial and incorporeal, there was no way left to them in which they might move the bodies other than by ordering them to move. And from this the philosophers concluded that the celestial bodies are rational animals, conscious of themselves and of their principles, which move them by command. And since it was established—in the *De Anima*—that there is no difference between knowledge and the object of knowledge, except for the latter's being in matter, of necessity the substance of immaterial beings—if there are such—had to be knowledge or intellect or whatever you wish to call it. And the philosophers knew that these principles must be immaterial, because they confer on the celestial bodies everlasting movement in which there is no fatigue or weariness, and that anything which bestows such an everlasting movement must be immaterial, and cannot be a material power. And indeed the celestial body acquires its permanence only through these immaterial principles. And the philosophers understood that the existence of these immaterial principles must be connected with a first principle amongst them; if not, there could be no order in the world. You can find these theories in the books of the philosophers and, if you want to make sure of the truth in these matters, you will have to consult them. It also becomes clear from the fact that all the spheres have the daily circular movement, although besides this movement they have, as the philosophers had ascertained, their own special movements, that He

who commands this movement must be the First Principle, i.e. God, and that He commands the other principles to order the other movements to the other spheres. Through this heaven and earth are ruled as a state is ruled by the commands of the supreme monarch, which, however, are transmitted to all classes of the population by the men he has appointed for this purpose in the different affairs of the state. As it says in the Koran: "And He inspired every Heaven with its bidding." This heavenly injunction and this obedience are the prototypes of the injunction and obedience imposed on man because he is a rational animal. What Avicenna says of the derivation of these principles from each other is a theory not known amongst the ancients, who merely state that these principles hold certain positions in relation to the First Principle, and that their existence is only made real through this relation to the First Principle. As is said in the Koran: "There is none amongst us but has his appointed place." It is the connexion which exists between them which brings it about that some are the effect of others and that they all depend on the First Principle. By "agent" and "object," "creator" and "creature," in so far as it concerns this existence nothing more can be understood than just this idea of connexion. But what we said of this connexion of every existent with the One is something different from what is meant by "agent" and "object," "maker" and "product" in this sublunary world. If you imagine a ruler who has many men under his command who again have others under their command, and if you imagine that those commanded receive their existence only through receiving this command and through their obedience to this command, and those who are under those commanded can only exist through those commanded, of necessity the first ruler will be the one who bestows on all existents the characteristic through which they become existent, and that which exists through its being commanded will only exist because of the first ruler. And the philosophers understood that this is what is meant by the divine laws when they speak of creation, of calling into existence out of nothing, and of command. This is the best way to teach people to understand the philosophical doctrine without the ignominy attaching to it, which seems to attach when you listen to the analysis Ghazali gives of it here. The philosophers assert that all this is proved in their books, and the man who, having fulfilled the conditions they impose, is able to study their works will find the truth of what they say—or perhaps its opposite—and will not understand Aristotle's theory or Plato's in any other sense than that here indicated. And their philosophy is the highest point human intelligence can reach. It may be that, when a man discovers these explanations of philosophical theory, he will find that they happen not only to be true but to be generally acknowledged, and teachings that are generally acceptable are pleasing and delightful to all.

PRONUNCIATION GUIDE

A Semitic language related to Hebrew, Aramaic, and Ethiopic, classical Arabic contains a number of consonants whose sounds do not exist in English. These sounds are represented by special accents when Arabic is transliterated from the Arabic alphabet into English letters. For example, six emphatic sounds are indicated by a dot beneath the letter, e.g., ḥ, a sharp "h" marked by a slight hissing sound, as when you blow on your glasses to clean them; or ṣ, ḍ, ṭ, and ẓ, like English s, d, t, and z, except "palatized," i.e., pronounced with the tongue flattened against the roof of the mouth. The apostrophe represents the "glottal stop," perceptible between the words in "ticket taker," while the raised ᶜ stands for the Arabic letter ᶜ*ayin*, pronounced by a contraction of the throat.

Unlike English, Arabic is a quantitative language: Arabic vowels are either long or short, and a long vowel takes twice as long to pronounce as a short vowel. Long vowels are represented by the macron in transliteration: Abū, Kindī, Qur'ān. Short vowels are unmarked.

GLOSSARY

Abbasid Caliphate: The Arab dynasty, centered in Baghdad, which lasted from 750 to 1258 and comprised Islam's "Golden Age."

concomitants: Accompanying states or qualities of things, e.g., heat is a concomitant of fire.

De Anima: "On the Soul," a work by Aristotle which was translated early into Arabic and was highly influential.

dirham: A coin, usually silver, which was widespread in Islamic lands; the word comes from Greek *drachma*.

falsafah: The Arabic word for "philosophy" taken from Greek *philosophia*. The *"falsafah* tradition" denotes those philosophers from al-Kindī to

Ibn Rushd whose inspiration came from Ancient Greek thinkers, such as Plato and Aristotle.

hijrah: The Arabic word for the "emigration" of the prophet Mohammed and his companions from Mecca to Medina in 622, the official beginning of Islam itself.

imām: A prayer leader and, by extension, a spiritual leader of the Muslim community; the term is fraught with religious and historical significance.

ipseity: A technical term from Latin *ipse*, "itself" or "himself," used by Scholastic philosophers to denote essential, individual identity.

Isagoge: A Greek work whose title means "Introduction," written by the third-century philosopher Porphyry as a guide to Aristotle's logic.

Koran: See Qur'an.

Monophysite: The Eastern Christian theological sect, considered heretical in the West, which taught that Christ possessed only a single divine and perfect nature, and no human nature.

Muʿtazilites: A varied group of Muslim theologians, active from the eighth to the seventeenth centuries, who stressed God's oneness and justice as well as the primacy of human reason.

neo-Platonists: Those later Greek philosophers, such as Plotinus, Proclus, and their followers, who elaborated the thought of Plato in new and influential ways.

"overflow" (divine): The notion, essentially neo-Platonic, that all things emanate, or flow, from the divine in a descending hierarchy of being down to our sublunary world.

Qur'an: The sacred scripture of Islam revealed to the prophet Mohammed by the angel Jibrīl (Gabriel).

regress ad infinitum: A fallacious form of argumentation from one cause backward to another, and so on, to no final cause or conclusion.

Scholastics: Those medieval European theologians and philosophers, such as Abelard and Thomas Aquinas, who wrote in Latin and dominated Western thought from the ninth to the sixteenth centuries.

sublunary world: This lowest world, our transient world "beneath the moon."

summa: A comprehensive summation of a philosophical or theological system, such as the *Summa theologica* of Thomas Aquinas.

syllogistic: The method of reasoning invented by Aristotle which depends upon the syllogism, an argument consisting of three propositions linked in such a way that if the first two are posited, the third necessarily follows as true.

Zayd: A common name in Arabic for a man, used as an example in grammatical and philosophical texts.

Zoroastrian: A member of the dualistic world religion founded in Persia by the priest and prophet Zoroaster in the sixth century B.C.E.

FURTHER READINGS

GUSTAVE E. VON GRUNEBAUM. *Medieval Islam.* Chicago: University of Chicago Press, 1966. Provides a detailed cultural history.
ALBERT HOURANI. *A History of the Arab Peoples.* Cambridge, Mass.: Harvard University Press, 1991. The most thorough and readable recent book on Islamic history, culture, and thought.
BERNARD LEWIS. *The Arabs in History,* rev. ed. New York: Harper, 1966. An excellent brief history.
ROY MOTTAHEDEH. *The Mantle of the Prophet: Religion and Politics in Iran.* New York: Simon & Schuster, 1985. A good inside account written like a novel but based on careful scholarship.
ERIC ORMSBY. "Arabic Philosophy," in Robert C. Solomon and Kathleen M. Higgins, eds., *From Africa to Zen: An Invitation to World Philosophy.* Lanham, Md.: Rowman & Littlefield, 1993. A brief history of Arabic philosophy.
FAZLUR RAHMAN. *Islam,* 2d ed. Chicago: University of Chicago Press, 1979. The best account of Islamic religion from a Muslim viewpoint.

STUDY QUESTIONS

1. Why was formal, Aristotelian logic both attractive and controversial in the Islamic tradition? What factors led to the assimilation of this logic within Arabic philosophy?
2. Why was philosophy so often connected with both medicine and astronomy in the Islamic tradition?
3. Why was it necessary to formulate proofs for God's existence if the Qur'ān had already revealed this? Was rational proof superfluous?

CHAPTER 5

Persian Philosophy

JANET McCRACKEN AND
HOMAYOON SEPASI-TEHRANI

Persia is known today, as it was in ancient times, as Iran. Although its borders have been redefined many times over its long history, Iran is nonetheless one of the oldest identifiable cultures in the world. The original Iranians were Indo-European tribespeople that moved in Neolithic times from western Europe onto the Iranian plateau. The first Iranian nation, the Medians, was established in the second millennium B.C.E.

From that time until the seventh century A.D.—over 2,500 years—the Persians were one of the major powers in the world, with wide and long-lasting influence upon other cultures. The first Persian Empire, the Achaemenid empire, ruled Assyria and Babylonia and was the major opponent of the Greeks. The Persian Parthians were the rivals of the Roman Empire. And the second Persian Empire, the Sassanid empire, was the rival of Byzantium. Until the Arab conquest of Iran and the conversion of Iranians to Islam, the Persian religion, Zoroastrianism, was the main rival—and an important theological influence—on Christianity and Judaism.

Because of this long tradition of political and religious power, and the resulting development of the arts and sciences, Persia retained an influential position in the world even after the Arab conquest. Persian soil fertilized and nurtured both of the major factions within Islam (Shi'ism and Sufism, which differed from Sunni Islam, the major branch of Islam elsewhere in the Middle East) and prominent Islamic theology, as well as widely influential alternatives to Islam, Christianity, and Judaism (particularly Manichaeism and Mazdakism, as well as Zoroastrianism, which remained popular until the ninth century and still has followers today).

Medieval Persian poetry has been widely recognized as an artistic triumph, and it influenced both the romantic poets and the

European philosophers of the nineteenth century. Many poets used their art as vehicles for philosophical, religious, and political commentary, particularly the Sufi sects.

Because of their achievements throughout the Middle Ages, Persians established a great Renaissance power in their Safavid dynasty, which made Shi'ism the state religion of Iran. Over the 200 years of Safavid rule, Persia gained a worldwide reputation as a cultural and political hub. However, Persia's later Qajar dynasty, like so much of the world in the nineteenth century, played a weaker role in world politics than had its predecessors. Persia was no longer admired for its cultural affluence, but was coveted by both Britain and czarist Russia because of its strategic geographical position. With the discovery of oil and the establishment of the Anglo-Persian Oil Company in 1908, Iran became politically and economically dependent on the world powers.

In 1921, Reza Khan took Iran by *coup d'état.* In his new Pahlavi dynasty the shah of Iran pursued a policy of "modernization," which in its essence was only Westernization—whirlwind industrialization and enforced separation of church and state. Mounting opposition to these policies, which were pressed further by the shah's son under alliance with the United States, culminated in the Iranian revolution of 1979. After the defeat of the shah, the various revolutionary groups were gathered under the umbrella of the Islamic Republic, originally led by the Ayatollah Khomeini, an outspoken Shi'ite leader. Despite some successes for the Islamic Republic (still in power today), dissent in Iran is still widespread and without legal recourse.

In this chapter, we have collected some basic readings in several of the major movements in Persian thought, described above. Included are selections on Zoroastrianism, Manichaeism, Mazdakism, early Shi'ism, Sufism, and modern Shi'ite theology. We have included some introductory passages of our own to help readers fit the selections together and focus on the major philosophical themes in Persian thought.

PRE-ISLAMIC PERSIAN THOUGHT

Zoroastrianism

The religion of the ancient Persians, which was widely practiced in Iran from the sixth century B.C.E. until the seventh century C.E., was called Zoroastrianism, after its founding prophet, Zarathustra. The readings below give a general picture of this fascinating and influential religion, and highlight some interesting details of its liturgy and practice.

In the first selection, Mary Boyce, a prominent scholar in the field of Persian studies, introduces us to the political and social background within which Zoroastrianism first appeared, the significance of the prophet, and the pantheon of divinities in which Zoroastrians believe.

Zoroastrians

Zoroastrianism is the oldest of the revealed world-religions, and it has probably had more influence on mankind, directly and indirectly, than any other single faith. In its own right it was the state religion of three great Iranian empires, which flourished almost continually from the sixth century B.C. to the seventh century A.C., and dominated much of the Near and Middle East. Iran's power and wealth lent it immense prestige, and some of its leading doctrines were adopted by Judaism, Christianity and Islam, as well as by a host of Gnostic faiths, while in the East it had some influence on the development of northern Buddhism. Today external forces have reduced the Zoroastrians themselves to tiny scattered minorities, living mostly in Iran and India; but beliefs first taught by their prophet are still subscribed to by other peoples throughout the world.   1

Zoroastrianism was already old when it first enters recorded history; and it has its roots in a very distant past. Indeed, so tenacious are the Iranians of tradition that there are elements in living Zoroastrianism which go back, it seems, to Indo-European times. These elements, blended with later revealed doctrines, make it a richly complex faith, knowledge of which increases understanding of man's spiritual progress over millennia. It is also a noble one, with some unique and remarkable doctrines, which has been able to give its adherents purposeful and satisfying lives, awaking in them deep devotion. It is thus   2

Mary Boyce. *Zoroastrians: Their Religious Beliefs and Practices.* London: Routledge & Kegan Paul, 1979, pp. 1–3.

fully deserving of study for its own sake, as well as for its place in man's religious history.

Zoroastrianism has been so named in the West because its 3 prophet, Zarathushtra, was known to the ancient Greeks as Zoroaster. He was an Iranian, and lived in what for his people were prehistoric times. It is impossible, therefore, to establish fixed dates for his life; but there is evidence to suggest that he flourished when the Stone Age was giving way for the Iranians to the Bronze Age, possibly, that is, between about 1700 and 1500 B.C. . . .

Eventually—it is thought early in the third millennium—the proto- 4 Indo-Iranians drifted apart, to become identifiable by speech as two distinct peoples, the Indians and Iranians. They were still pastoralists; and they had contact, presumably through trade, with the settled peoples to the south of them. From Mesopotamia they learnt the use first of wooden carts pulled by oxen, and then of the war-chariot. To draw these chariots they lassoed and tamed the wild horses of the steppes; and at about the same time bronze came into use. The mountains flanking the Inner Asian steppes—notably the Altai—contained rich deposits of copper and tin; and so the steppe-dwellers were able to equip themselves formidably as fighting-men.

The Gathas

The Gathas (the oldest section of the Zoroastrian scripture, the *Avesta*) appear to be Zarathustra's own words, and they give us our primary clue as to the religious beliefs of the prophet himself. Like any prophet, Zarathustra is believed to have received direct revelation from his God, called Ahura Mazda. Zarathustra's claim to direct divine authority was a fortunate defense for his religious teachings, which were in radical disagreement with those of his contemporaries. Zarathustra proclaimed a monotheistic religion amidst a thriving polytheism.

The ancient Indo-Iranians who lived in Iran before Zarathustra's time worshiped two types of deity, "devas" and "ahuras." Zarathustra denounced the worship of the devas, and venerated only one of the ahuras, "Ahura Mazda," or "wise Lord." After fleeing his homeland and years of wandering, he took refuge under the patronage of a king Vishtaspa, in northeastern Iran. He sings, "To what land to turn; aye, whither turning shall I go?"

The Gathas

Sometimes the warrior's booty consisted of herds of cattle, carried off   1
by force; and the fame of a great champion had to be paid for with the
blood of the slain, and the sufferings of the weak and unprotected. It
was during this turbulent and restless age, it seems, when might ruled
rather than law, that Zoroaster lived, and sought a revelation of the
purpose of man's troubled days on earth.

Zoroaster himself was a priest; and to understand the nature of his   2
revelation it is necessary to learn what one can of the old religion
which nurtured him. Fortunately much can be discovered through a
comparison of the most ancient elements in the Zoroastrian scriptures
and cult with the oldest religious works of India (notably the Rigveda)
and the Brahmanic rituals. The Zoroastrian scriptures are known collectively as the "Avesta" (a title which probably means something like
"Authoritative Utterance"); and the language in which they are composed is called simply "Avestan," since it is known only from this
source. . . .

According to Zoroastrian tradition, he spent years in a wandering   3
quest for truth; and his hymns suggest that he must then have witnessed acts of violence, with war-bands, worshippers of the Daevas,
descending on peaceful communities to pillage, slaughter and carry
off cattle. Conscious himself of being powerless physically, he
became filled with a deep longing for justice, for the moral law of the
Ahuras to be established for strong and weak alike, so that order and
tranquillity could prevail, and all be able to pursue the good life in
peace. . . .

It is said that Zoroaster, being at a gathering met to celebrate a   4
spring festival, went at dawn to a river to fetch water for the haoma-
ceremony [a pre-Zoroastrian ritual in which an intoxicating drink,
haoma, was used]. He waded in to draw it from midstream; and when
he returned to the bank—himself in a state of ritual purity, emerging
from the pure element, water, in the freshness of a spring dawn—he
had a vision. He saw on the bank a shining Being, who revealed himself as Vohu Manah "Good Purpose"; and this Being led Zoroaster
into the presence of Ahura Mazda and five other radiant figures,

Mary Boyce. *Zoroastrians: Their Religious Beliefs and Practices.* London: Routledge &
Kegan Paul, 1979, p. 19.

before whom "he did not see his own shadow upon the earth, owing to their great light." And it was then, from this great heptad, that he received his revelation.

The Zoroastrian Pantheon

Existence was revealed to Zarathustra to be a pantheon of interdependent entities, each with a distinct character and a distinct role to play in the drama of history. Ahura Mazda, the Lord, created everything by thought and ex nihilo ("from nothing") in seven steps or stages. He created through his Spenta Mainyush (the "Holy" or "Beneficent" Spirit). The first step is the creation of six other, lower divinities, the Amesha Spentas. They become Ahura Mazda's helpers in the creation of the natural world. The Amesha Spentas are persons, both one with Ahura Mazda and distinguishable from Him, but they are also lesser gods in their own right. Each one represents one of the good characteristics of the all-good Ahura Mazda, and personifies one of his attributes. The process of creation culminates, at the seventh step, in the creation of material things. Each Amesha Spenta is associated with an aspect of the material world.

The most important of the Amesha Spentas, as we have seen, is Vohu Manah ("Good Mind" or "Purpose"). Through Vohu Manah each individual (apparently even Ahura Mazda himself) instantiates the good or right. This "Righteousness" (or "Truth") which is associated with the element fire is the Amesha Spenta named Asha Vahista. Allegiance to Asha distinguishes the devoted worshipper of Mazda from the adherents of other immoral religions. Fire was an especially important element in the Zoroastrian worldview; consequently, outsiders sometimes mistakenly referred to Zoroastrians as "fire worshippers."

In the following passages, William Malandra translates and interprets two of the most familiar stories from the *Avesta*. Together, they outline some basic Zoroastrian tenets. In the first passage, thought to be Zarathustra's first revelation, we learn the fundamental moral insight of Zoroastrianism: humanity's stewardship of the herds and fields. In the second passage, the Zoroastrian doctrine of the origin and nature of evil is given in the story of the Twins. Zoroastrianism is monotheistic: that is, it espouses the existence of only one God, the creator of everything. The moral doctrine of Zoroastrianism, however, is dualist: Zoroastrians believe that nature is fundamentally *both* good and evil.

The Cow's Lament

Probably the best known and in many ways the most interesting of the   1
Gāthās is the so-called "Cow's Lament" (Yasna 29). In the form of dramatic dialogue it expresses the suffering of the Cow at the hands of the
forces of the Lie. She cries out to Ahura Mazdā and the other Ahuras
(i.e., the Amesha Spentas) for an explanation of her wretched condition. In particular, she despairs over her abandonment, her lack of an
adequate herdsman for her protection. After some discussion born of
indecision, since the Ahuras seem unable to find her a proper protector, Zarathushtra is recognized as the only one fit for the job. . . .

Until recent years there has been general agreement that, along   2
broad lines, the "Lament of the Soul of the Cow" is an allegorical por-
trayal of the conflict of two ways of life and religion in eastern Iran,
and of Zarathushtra's struggle to establish his religious way of life.
Zarathushtra, the Soul of the Cow, and the Ahuras represent a peace-
loving, sedentary form of agriculture in which animal husbandry
played an important role. Pitted against them are the wild, lawless
nomads and persistent followers of the old ways, all worshippers of
the Daēwas. On this level, the conflict is one that recurs at different
historical moments throughout Iranian history. The conflict is essentially sociological. On another level, the conflict is seen as not so
much sociological as religious, and specifically ritualistic. That is, the
daēwas who have chosen Falsehood perform violent, orgiastic, and
bloody sacrifices, whereas Zarathushtra and the followers of Truth
respect the Cow, treating her in a ritually proper manner. . . .

To sum up, then, one may say that the "Cow's Lament" is based   3
on an ancient mythic theme of the Cow's suffering at the hands of
raiders. Zarathushtra has reworked the myth to reflect his perception of
the world, a world where the peace-loving followers of Ahura Mazdā
are pitted against foes who practice cattle raiding. Although the conclusion can be drawn from other Gāthic contexts that the daēwas
required ritual treatment of the Cow, abhorrent to Zarathushtra, this
element is not apparent in the "Lament." Further, one must entertain
the possibility that for Zarathushtra the theme of the "Cow's Lament"
was to be understood on a spiritual as well as this more mundane

William W. Malandra, trans. and ed. *An Introduction to Ancient Iranian Religion.*
Minneapolis: University of Minnesota Press, 1983, pp. 35–40.

level. Here the myth has become an allegory for the vicissitudes suffered by the righteous man's soul in its quest for the "good vision."

YASNA 29

1. The Soul of the Cow lamented to you: For whom have you determined me? Who fashioned me? Wrath and Violence, Harm, Daring, and Brutality (each) have bound me! I have no other pastor than you—so appear to me with good husbandry!
2. Then the Fashioner of the Cow asked Asha (Truth): Hast thou a *ratu* for the Cow such that you are able to give him, together with a herdsman, zeal for fostering the Cow? Whom do you want as a lord for her, who, hostile toward Liars, may repel Wrath? . . .
5. Thus we both are calling out to the Lord with outstretched hands, my (soul) and the Soul of the pregnant Cow, in order that we may address (?) Mazdā with questions. (For, as matters now stand,) there is no possibility of) continuing life for the righteously living husbandman (residing) among Liars. . . .
8. Here I have found this one who alone listens to our commandments, Zarathushtra the Spitamid. He wants, O Mazdā, to recite hymns of praise for us and Asha, if I should bestow on him sweetness of speech.
9. The Soul of the Cow lamented: Must I suffer a powerless caretaker—the speech of a man without strength—whom I wish to be a powerful ruler? When ever shall he come to exist who can give him a helping hand?

The Two Spirits

The stanzas in Yasna 30, together with 45.2, allude to the encounter between the two Spirits, the primordial Twins. The mythology of the Twins . . . extends back into proto-Indo-European religion and is to be found in other variants elsewhere in Iranian myth. . . . With Zarathushtra the myth has undergone a reinterpretation, which accords well with his general propensity to rework inherited ideas in order to express his own vision of the dualistic cosmological and ethical situation facing mankind. . . .

Whereas one tends to regard all events, whether mythological or 2 not, as taking place in a nonrecurring historical order, archaic man understood mythical events, which took place in mythological time, as being everpresent. To say that the two primordial Spirits chose good and evil "in the beginning" implies that they do so in the present as well. This is not to imply that archaic man had no real notion of past, present, and future: rather, it is a recognition of his awareness of an atemporal dimension that cuts across historical time. In reading the text, therefore, one must understand that the myth of the two Spirits is also a present reality. Furthermore, it is present reality in the sense that the two Spirits now contend with each other not only on an individual level but also in the cosmos. Bearing in mind that Zarathushtra uses abstractions (for example, "Good Mind" or "Devotion") to refer to states of mind as well as to divine entities, one comprehends that for him the macrocosmic struggle is simultaneously occurring in the human microcosm. Each one of us recapitulates the cosmic drama, and, as in the case of the two Spirits, man holds the keys to his own destiny in his free exercise of choice between good and evil, between Truth and the Lie.

YASNA 30.3–6

3. Now, these are the two original Spirits who, as Twins, have been perceived (by me?) through a vision. In both thought and speech, (and) in deed, these two are what is good and evil. Between these two, the pious, not the impious, will choose rightly.
4. Furthermore, the two Spirits confronted each other; in the beginning (each) create(d) for himself life and nonlife, so that (?) in the end there will be the worst existence for the Drugwants, but the best Mind for the Righteous.
5. Of these two Spirits, the deceitful (drugwant) chose the worst course of action, (while) the most beneficent Spirit who is clothed in the hardest stones (chose) Truth, (as) also (do) those who believingly propitiate Ahura Mazdā.
6. Between these two (Spirits) the daēwas did not choose rightly at all since, while they were taking council among themselves, delusion came upon them, so that they chose the worst Mind. Then, all together, they ran to Wrath with which they infect the life of man.

YASNA 45.2

2. Now I shall proclaim the original two Spirits of existence. About the two, the very beneficent would have spoken thus to the evil one: Neither our minds nor (our) pronouncements nor (our) intellects nor yet (our) choices nor (our) words nor yet (our) deeds, nor (our) visions (daēnā), nor (our) souls (urwan) are in agreement.

Manichaeism

Manichaeism was a descendent of Zoroastrianism, although considered heretical by orthodox Zoroastrians. This doctrine, preached by Mani (b. 216 C.E.), the founder of Manichaeism, held that two primordial principles, one of Darkness and one of Light, battled for control of the world. Manichaeans aimed to ally themselves with the principle of Light, and thereby to attain redemption.

The Fihrist of Al-Nadim

Thus saith Muḥammad ibn Isḥāq [al-*Nadīm*]: Mānī appeared during 1 the second year of the reign of *Callus* the Roman. . . .

Mānī asserted that he was the paraclete about whom Jesus, for 2 whom may there be peace, preached. Mānī derived his doctrine from the Magians and Christians. In a similar way, the script with which he wrote books about religious subjects was derived from Syriac and Persian.

Mānī said, "The origin of the world was [composed of] two ele- 3 ments, one of which was light and the other darkness. Each of them was separated from the other. Light is the great [element] and the first, but not in quantity. It is the deity the King of the Gardens of Light. It has five worlds: forbearance, knowledge, intelligence, the unperceivable, and discernment. It has also five other spiritual qualities, which are love, faith, fidelity, benevolence, and wisdom."

He [Mānī] stated, "Together with his attributes he [Light] is eter- 4

Bayard Dodge, trans. and ed. *The Fihrist of al-Nadim: A Tenth-Century Survey of Muslim Culture.* New York: Columbia University Press, 1970, nal. With him are two externals, one of which is the sky (atmosphere) and the other the earth." Mānī also said, "The worlds of the sky are five: forbearance, knowledge, intelligence, the unperceivable, and discernment. The worlds of the earth are the ether (zephyr), wind, light, water, and fire. The other existence, which is Darkness, has five worlds: clouds, flame, pestilential wind, poison, and obscurity."

Mānī said, "The light shining existence was contiguous with the dark existence, with no barrier between them. The Light contacted the Darkness on its surface." 5

Mānī said, "From this land of Darkness there was Satan (al-Shayṭān), who is not eternal in his own person, but the elements of his ingredients are eternal. These elements of his ingredients became compounded and brought Satan into existence. After this Satan, who is called the Ancient Devil, had been formed from the Darkness and had swallowed, gulped down, and corrupted, passing from right to left and descending below, while all the time corrupting and slaying anyone who opposed him, he coveted the upper regions, seeing the flashings of the Light and contesting them. Then beholding them raised on high, he trembled and they intermingled with him, coming into contact with his ingredients. Thus as he coveted the upper regions, the Light World discerned Satan's state of mind and what he desired of slaving and corruption." 6

He [Mānī] said, "Then it [the Light World] informed the King of the Gardens of Light about him and plotted for his subjection." He said, "These warriors of his were able to defeat him [and generated the Primal Man]." 7

He said, "The Primal Man clad himself with five principles, which are the five deities: the ether (zephyr), wind, light, water, and fire. He took them as armament. 8

"Thereupon the Ancient Devil repaired to his five principles, which are the smoke, flame, obscurity, pestilential wind, and clouds, arming himself with them and making them a protection for him. Upon his coming into contact with the Primal Man, they joined in battle for a long time. The Ancient Devil mastered Primal Man and took a swallow from his light, which he surrounded with his principles and ingredients." 9

Mānī said, "When the Ancient Devil was entangled with Primal Man in battle, the five ingredients of Light were mixed with the five ingredients of Darkness. 10

". . . What there was in them of purity, beauty, cleanliness, and 11 usefulness, was from the light. What there was in them of filth, grime, grossness, and harshness was from the darkness."

Mānī said, "The King of the World of Light commanded one of his   12
angels to create this world and to build it from those mixed particles, so as to rescue the particles of Light from those of Darkness."

Mānī said, "This conflagration will last for a period of one thou-   13
sand, four hundred and sixty-eight years." He said, "If this state of affairs comes to an end and the bold chieftainess, the Spirit of Darkness, sees the rescue of the Light and the exaltation of the angels while the warriors and guards [of Darkness] are surrendering, and if she sees the battle and the warriors about her accusing her, she will retreat to a tomb prepared for her and this tomb will be blocked with a rock the size of the world, which will barricade her in it [the tomb], so that the Light will be set free from anxiety due to the Darkness and its injury."

HOW A MAN MUST ENTER INTO THE CULT

He [Mānī] said, "He who would enter the cult must examine his soul.   14
If he finds that he can subdue lust and covetousness, refrain from eating meats, drinking wine, as well as from marriage, and if he can also avoid [causing] injury to water, fire, trees, and living things, then let him enter the cult. But if he is unable to do all of these things, he shall not enter the cult. If, however, he loves the cult, but is unable to subdue lust and craving, let him seize upon guarding the cult and the Elect, that there may be an offsetting of his unworthy actions, and times in which he devotes himself to work and righteousness, nighttime prayer, intercession, and pious humility (supplication)."

THE SACRED LAW WHICH MĀNĪ BROUGHT AND THE ORDINANCES WHICH HE ORDAINED

Mānī prescribed ten ordinances for the Hearers, which he followed   15
up with three seals and a fast of seven days without fail during every month. The ordinances represent faith in the four great beings: God, His Light, His Power, and His Wisdom. God, may His name be magnified, is the King of the Gardens of Light. His Light is the sun and the

moon, His Power the five angels: ether (zephyr), wind, light, water, and fire. His Wisdom is the holy religion with its five significations: teachers, the sons of forbearance; deacons, the sons of knowledge; priests, the sons of intelligence; the Elect, the sons of the unperceivable, and the Hearers, the sons of discernment.

THE TEN ORDINANCES

Renouncing the worship of idols; renouncing the telling of lies; renouncing avarice; renouncing killing; renouncing adultery; renouncing: stealing; the teaching of defects; magic; the upholding of two opinions, which is about the faith; neglect and lassitude in action.   16

Mazdakism

Around the turn of the fifth and sixth centuries, Persia witnessed the emergence, consolidation, and brutal persecution of a revolutionary, protocommunist doctrine—Mazdakism. Named after its chief advocate, Mazdak Bamdadan, Mazdakism is a gnostic doctrine based, like Manichaeism and some versions of later Zoroastrianism, on the dualism of Light and Darkness. Mazdakism, however, recognizes three fundamental substances.

Mazdakism is consistently more materialist than the Persian religions that preceded it. According to Mazdakite doctrine, in the beginning of time, there were three substances: water, earth, and fire. Out of their mingling, two "Cosmic Managers" emerged, one of good and one of evil. Without denying the existence of spiritual qualities, Mazdakites claimed that the origin of all things was material, or physical. The three physical substances, earth, water, and fire, rather than One Immaterial God, are the fountain from which good and evil spring.

The Light, or good, principle of Mazdakism is wise and endowed with consciousness. The Dark, or evil, principle is blind, ignorant, and lacking in volition. Thus, through rationality, it is hoped we will be able to be good and overcome evil.

Goodness, in Mazdakism, was a matter of distributive justice. Mazdakite doctrine stipulated that the resources provided by the earth were intended for people to use collectively. Human needs, the Mazdakites claimed, could and should be met in a cooperative manner, without resorting to violence, competition, or domination of any one over any other. Evil disrupted this proper process by instigating in people a blind, irrational passion to own property and an equally blind sexual desire such that men would be enticed by the prospect of dominating their mates. Thus, 1,200 years before the German philosopher Karl Marx offered a similar argument, the Mazdakites pinpointed the ownership of private property as the "origin of evil."

Mazdakites also believed in the possibility of becoming perfect. The "perfect man," able independently to know and to instantiate the good, is exempt from participation in the religious rituals. Such a person, of course, will no longer be subject to any authority other than his own knowledge of the good. This anti-authoritarianism added to the earthly materialism of their cosmology to mark Mazdakism as politically radical, and Mazdakites were considered heretics by the Zoroastrian orthodoxy of Persia in the Second Empire.

POST-ISLAMIC PERSIAN THOUGHT

Early Islam

The prophet of Islam, Mohammed, received his first revelations from Allah in the year 610 C.E., in Mecca, Arabia. These revelations continued throughout his life. The texts were copied down according to Mohammed's order and comprise the Muslim scripture, the Qur'an.

Mohammed's revelations conferred upon him the mission of unifying the disparate Arab families into a nation by redirecting their familial loyalties toward the one proper object of faith, Allah. Among other things, this was achieved through a redefinition of the concept of justice in terms of personal responsibility. The unification of the Arabs, however, was considered to be but the first step in the mission of spreading to everyone the One True Faith. Despite its clear designation of the Arabs as a "chosen" people, Islam is also for the ears of Christians and Jews. The Qur'an is the "final" comment from the Judeo-Christian God.

The original Muslims, with the prophet as their guide, were assured that their actions were just, that their policies were rational, and that they knew God's law. When in 632 the prophet died, however, leaving no heir and no instructions for how to choose his successor, religious schisms arose and centered on questions of justice, truth, and the will of Allah. The resulting Islamic sects distinguished themselves by their different interpretations—and different theories of what counted as proper interpretation—of the Qur'an.

The Shi'ites

In modern times, Iran has been associated most closely with Shi'ite Islam. Shi'ism became the state religion in Persia in the sixteenth century, and today's Islamic Republic of Iran is also a Shi'ite nation.

Among Shi'ites, the Qur'an is understood to be only the written articulation of a divine message. It is said to contain not just expression and meaning but also multiple levels of meaning. The apparent, or literal, meaning is called "exoteric." But there is also a hidden, secret meaning in scripture, called "esoteric." This esoteric meaning is thought by Shi'ites to be veiled from those uninitiated in the Qur'anic mysteries and cannot be understood through the "usual" human faculties of reason.

The Shi'ites consider the prophet's role in revelation to have been unique and inimicable by ordinary human beings. Mohammed, they believe, united the exoteric with the esoteric meaning of scripture, and he was the last person able to do so. Only the members of a new "cycle of sainthood," called the "imams," have been able to render the esoteric meaning of scripture intelligible to us, through their proper interpretation of it. The Shi'ites trace the lineage of the imams through Mohammed's daughter, Fatemah, and recognized the authority of Ali, her husband and the first imam, to be the ruler of Islam after Mohammed's death.

There are sectarian disputes even within Shi'ism. The sects can be categorized according to the number of imams in which each believes, as Twelvers, Seveners, Fivers, and Fourers. The most important distinction is that between Twelver and Sevener Shi'ites.

The Seveners believed that the esoteric meaning of the Qur'an is much more important than the exoteric meaning. Seveners believe that Allah's creation is mediated by a series of Intellects, the first of which was the archetype of Adam. According to the Seveners, the world, and us in it, is evolving through seven intermediate intellects toward a restoration of its original, unfallen state in which we will have immediate knowledge of God. Until that time, so the Seveners claim, the imams must mediate between us and God.

The Twelvers gave equal weight to the exoteric and the esoteric meanings of scripture. They believe that the imams are distinguished not just by their lineage and their closeness to God but also by their absolute infallibility as interpreters of God's will. Therefore, rather than being just spiritual leaders and teachers, as they are in Sevener Shi'ism, the imams in Twelver Shi'ism are also absolute legislators of the Islamic community. Their infallibility qualifies them for both spiritual and political leadership.

Belief in the Mahdi, the hidden Twelfth Imam, is particularly characteristic of Twelver Shi'ism. Mahdi, the last descendent of Mohammed through Fatemah and the only child of the Eleventh Imam, is believed by Twelvers to be the Messiah. Mahdi, they believe, is awaiting resurrection, at which time there will be a final judgment by God, a restoration of justice and peace, and a definitive revelation to us of God's will.

The state religion of Iran, in the sixteenth century as today, is Twelver Shi'ism. Seveners, however, are also closely associated with Iran. Nasir-i Khusraw, a selection of whose poetry, called "divan," follows, was a Sevener. His work is still widely respected and celebrated among Iranian Shi'ites.

The first selection, from the poem "Speech," is a moral instruction on the path through the Seven Intellects to perfection. It describes the relationship between the exoteric word—by which Khusraw means everything in creation which is visible and obvious—to the esoteric word, which is a silent and imperceivable truth. (In one line, Khusraw uses "Logos," a word borrowed from ancient Greek philosophy, to describe it.)

The second selection, from the poem "Free Will and Determination," explains how it is possible for human beings to be free and responsible for their actions even though God creates and determines everything.

Persian poetry, you will notice, is neither delicate nor pussyfooting. It is passionate, romantic, and stirring, as well as exceptionally playful and clever. We will look at more Persian poetry below; Nasir-i Khusraw is an early master.

Speech

NASIR-I KHUSRAW

My son this corpse of yours, this prison
will never be lovely even draped in silk brocades;
embellish your soul with the jewel of Speech
for the soul is ugly even in silk brocades.
Can you not see God's chains on your ankles   5
(only awakened souls can see them)?
Be a man in your chains and cinch your belt
nor dream your cell the realm of Darius:
those who act in moderation find
kingdoms wider far than his.   10
Patience! no one finds heart's desire
but a man of patience;
and for sexual lust open the Quran
to the story of Adam and Eve. . . .

The world's a cunning devil whom the wise   15
have never cultivated for companionship;
if you've an ounce of sense don't swagger
in its sulphurous wake like a drunken clot.
The world's a bottomless mudchoked well—
don't lose your purified soul in its cloudy depths   20
(your soul purified by Speech—as the wise
through Logos have flown from well's-bottom to the stars).
Take pride in speech as the Prophet (who willed
not even a camel to his heirs) treasured his eloquence; . . .

Tell me for the Prophet's sake! who told Him   25
to entrust the hermeneutic to the wise, words to the rabble?
The diver surfaces with a handful of slime
perhaps because he sees in you an enemy . . .
look for the pith of Revelation, don't follow the herd
content with husks like asses with their braying. . . .   30

A day comes in which is no shelter nor refuge
from the arbitration of a just and equitable Judge;

Nasir-i Khusraw. *Forty Poems from the Divan.* Translated and with notes by Peter Lamborn Wilson and Gholam Reza Aavani. Tehran: Imperial Iranian Academy of Philosophy, 1955.

at that hour all shall be paid for their deeds
both the just and the unjust receive justice;
on that day of tumult in that turbulent crowd   35
before the martyrs of God I shall take refuge with
                    The Daughter of Muhammad
              so that God the Almighty may decide
                          between me
                          and the enemies   40
                      of the household
                      of the Prophet.

Free Will and Determination

NASIR-I KHUSRAW

The wiseman treads midway
between Fate and Freewill
the path of the learned threads between hope and fear.
Seek you the Straight Way likewise
for either extreme leads to pain and suffering.   5
Straight indeed is that Way in religion
approved by Intellect, the gift of God to Man.
Justice is the cornerstone of the Cosmos
—and consider!—by what faculty is justice
distinguished from tyranny except by Reason?   10
If man follows the tracks of Reason
it would not be wrong to expect to see
pearls spring up in his footprints from the soil.
Reason—Wisdom—only for this
and its radiant dignity does the Lord   15
of the Universe applaud and deign to address
his creature Man. Wisdom is the prop
for every weakness, relief from every sorrow
comfort in every fear, balm for each ill
noble companion, bulwark in the way of the world   20
and in religion a trusty guide, a stout staff.

Nasir-i Khusraw. *Forty Poems from the Divan.* Translated and with notes by Peter Lamborn Wilson and Gholam Reza Aavani. Tehran: Imperial Iranian Academy of Philosophy, 1955.

Even if the whole Universe were free
it would be in bondage—but the wiseman
even in chains would be at liberty.
The Sage! Study him well with an awakened eye   25
and see by contrast with what black plague
this ignorant world is afflicted.
This one tells you "All actions are performed
by God—the servant's duty is silence
submission and contentment." That one replies   30
"All good is from God, all evil, O World
your work alone." But both parties
Agree on one thing at least, that a Great Day
is coming, a day of reward and punishment.
But if the work is not mine, how   35
shall I be rewarded? Look: Illogic!!!
Where's the justice in chastising the innocent?
You may see it but I am nonplussed. No,
this arbitrator of *your* judgement day
is the Drunkard of Sodom, not the Wise Being   40
who has built the vault of Heaven.
True wisdom would never lead us astray
in such error—then follow Wisdom's manifest Way.

Sufism

Muslim mystics, many of whom had moral objections to the Islamic rulership, eventually distinguished themselves as a group, called the Sufis, because of the coarse woolen (or *suf*) garments that some wore, reminiscent of the Christian monks' hair shirts.

Sufism's emphasis is essentially moral and practical. Sufism is a "way of being" whose theological doctrines were for some Sufis best put in terms of Shi'ism and for others, Sunnism. Sufism is diverse, fickle in its theological alliances, and intimate and interpersonal in its method of its teaching. Nonetheless, we can say that Sufism is more influential in Iran than in the other nations of the Middle East. Here, we will excerpt some readings in some of the theologies allied with Sufism, as well as some of its poetic literature. The Sufis' esoteric version of Islam followed the Shi'ite epistemology in their belief that the Qur'anic text contained exoteric and esoteric levels of meaning. To unlock the mysteries of the Qur'an, however, Sufis considered it essential that one rely upon the grace of God. According to Sufis, God and He alone is real. Everything else is an illusion, a veil that obscures the divine meaning hidden behind created things. Only through *qalb* ("heart") can a person become capable of finding this hidden meaning, which is God. To succeed in finding God, it is essential that one perfect one's spirit, which is to cleanse one's heart.

Most Sufis believe that spiritual perfection is achieved in stages. The stage of *shari'a*—ordinary obedience to the Islamic law—is a prelude to the higher stage of mystical experience. In the second stage of *tariqqa*, ("the path"), the Sufi lives in poverty, renouncing the world and its physical attractions; the individual suppresses his or her desire and, ultimately, will, in anticipation of achieving union with the One. The third stage is that of *ma'rifa* ("gnosis"), in which it becomes possible for the Sufi, having rid him or herself of will or ego, to attain isolated moments of "unity with the One." These are supreme moments of *hal* ("ecstasy"). The last stage is *fana* ("vanishing"). In the last stage of unity with the One, it becomes possible to know the full, hidden truth. This truth is so beautiful that the Sufi loses all desire to be a self, or ego, distinguishable from the One.

Abu ibn-Mansur, known as al-Hallaj, is said to have uttered his famous cry, "Ana al haq!" ("I am God!") in the final stage of mystic experience. He was put to death as a heretic for this in 922. The Sufis, however, regard the remark as extremely pious. The Sufi poet Rumi interprets al-Hallaj in one of his *Discourses:*

> Take the famous utterance, "I am God." Some men reckon it as a great pretension; but "I am God" is in fact a great humility. The man who says, "I am the servant of God" asserts that two exist, one himself and the other God. But he who says "I am God" has naughted himself and cast himself to the winds. He says, "I am God": that is, "I am not, He is all, nothing has existence but God, I am pure non-entity, I am nothing." In this the humility is greater.*

Suhrawardi and Illuminationism

The idea of communion with God in the state of ecstasy later became the basis of the Illuminationist, or *Ishraqi*, school of Persian philosophy, founded by the Sufi Sheikh al-Suhrawardi. He was also executed for heresy in approximately 1191. Hence, Suhrawardi is

---

*Jalaluddin Rumi. *Discourses of Rumi.* Translated by A. J. Arberry. New York: Samuel Weiser, 1972, p. 55.

more often called "al-Maghtul," ("the Assassinated"). Suhrawardi expounded a metaphysics based in a mystic epistemology.

Suhrawardi and his followers claimed that Light was the foundation of all existence. Knowledge of the truth, therefore, was achieved through an intuition of Light, or an "illumination." He called the mystic stages a "trip to the East," where the sun rises, whose final destination, however, was beyond the world of material things. The "Occident" from which one embarks upon the mystic journey is the world of matter, darkness, and illusion. The "Orient" proper is beyond the material world. It is the realm of light and the home of the Archangels.

For Suhrawardi, the essence of any particular thing, its definitive characteristic, is just a higher, or more "luminous," level of its existence, and there are degrees of existence which differ according to their illumination. God is the highest essence of all, and pure Light. For Suhrawardi, then, the term "reflection" is an important one. It has the dual meaning of "mirroring" and "thinking."

An introduction to his compelling mixture of philosophical argument and mystic revelation is given in the following excerpts from two of his treatises. In both, he describes conversations that took place during visions.

The Sound of Gabriel's Wing

YAHYA SUHRAWARDI

In the name of God, the Compassionate, the Merciful. . . . 1

Ten old men of beautiful countenance [were] seated on a bench. 2
I was so amazed by their magnificence and splendour and so staggered by the sight of their throne, their beauty, their white hair, their garments and trappings that I could not speak. . . .

"Naïve child," [one] said, "the sun is always in its sphere. Yet, if 3
a blind man cannot feel or perceive the sun's attitude, his lack of sensation does not mean that the sun does not exist or that it is standing

Yahya Suhrawardi. *The Mystical and Visionary Treatises of Shihabuddin Yahya Suhrawardi.* Translated by W. M. Thackston, Jr. London: Octagon Press, 1982, pp. 27–32.

still in its place. If the blind man's handicap is removed, he has no right to chide the sun for not existing in the world prior to that or for not shining on him before, because it was always constant in its motion. The change will have been his, not the sun's. Likewise, we have always been on this bench: the fact that you did not see us does not mean that we were not here, nor does it mean that we have changed or moved. The change has been in you."

(11) "Do you worship God?" I asked.   4

"No," he said, "our total absorption in the act of witnessing   5
existence leaves us no leisure for worship. If we were to worship, it would not be by the tongue but by a limb that knows no movement. . . .

"God has several Great Words. They are luminous from the   6
Splendour of his August Face, and some are higher than others. The first light is the Highest Word, than which there is none greater. Its relation in light and brilliance to the other words is like the relation of the sun to the stars. This is what the Prophet meant when he said, 'Even if the face of the Sun were uncovered, it would fall short of [the brilliance of] God.' From the rays of this word another word [comes to be], and so on until the perfect number is reached. These words are the Incoherents.

(15) "The last of these words is Gabriel, and the spirits of human   7
beings are from this last word, as the Prophet said in a long narrative on human nature, 'God sends an angel who blows the spirit into it.' In the Divine Word it is said:

> It is he who hath made everything which he hath created exceeding good; and first created man of clay and afterwards made his posterity of an extract of despicable water; and then formed him into proper shape, and breathed of his spirit into him. (Koran, 32:7–9)

(18) "Tell me of Gabriel's wing," I said.   8
"Gabriel has two wings," he replied. "The right wing is pure light,   9
the totality of which is an abstraction of the relation between his being and God. The left wing has traces of darkness, like the dark spots on the surface of the moon that resemble peacock's feet. That is a sign that his being has one side toward not-being. If you look at the relation of his being to God's being, it has the attribute of His being. When you look at the realization of his essence it is the realization of non-existence and a concomitant to possible existence. These two intrinsic meanings stand on the level of two wings: the relation to God

on the right and the mental positing of the realization in the soul on the left ."

A Tale of Occidental Exile

YAHYA SUHRAWARDI

"We saw the hoopoe enter through the small window and bring us greetings on a moonlit night. In his beak was a letter sent from 'the right side of the valley in the blessed field, from the tree." . . .

I rejoiced at what he said. Then he said to me, "Know that this is Mount Sinai. Above this is Mount Sinin, where my father, your grandfather, dwells. I stand in relation to him as you stand in relation to me. We have other ancestors until the line reaches the king who is the great progenitor without father or grandfather. We are all his servants. We take our light from him and are modelled on him. His is the greatest splendour, his the highest glory and the most forceful light. He is above above, the light of light, above light ever and eternally. It is he who is manifested to everything, and 'everything perishes except his face.' ". . .

May God save us from the captivity of nature and the bonds of matter. Say, "Praise be unto God! he will show you his signs, and ye shall know them; and thy Lord is not regardless of that which ye do." And say, "God be praised!" But the greater part of them do not understand. And prayers upon His prophet and his family all.

Sufi Poetry

As may already be apparent, the notion of love is central to Sufism generally. Love of God is an effort on the part of the lover to join with that which creates him or her as a lover; to join with the beautiful, the beloved. Love joins the Sufi to the wisdom which is God. The overflow of God's love into His creation is a devolution, a "sending away." God's love is like a beautiful woman who inspires

Yahya Suhrawardi. *The Mystical and Visionary Treatises of Shihabuddin Yahya Suhrawardi.* Translated by W. M. Thackston, Jr. London: Octagon Press, 1982, pp. 102–108.

a lover only to spurn him, or a mother who gives birth to a son only to send him on his own way.

The indirect medium of poetry rather than direct philosophical prose was often the forum for the Sufi message. Its effect is like the indirect vision of a face in a mirror as opposed to a direct glance at it.

Certain metaphors have been so often repeated in Sufi poetry that their interpretation is unequivocal. Allah is universally represented as the Beloved, the beautiful. The Beloved's beauty, and the lover's nearness to her, are most often represented in visual terms. Beauty is described as Light, and the knowledge acquired by the lover's closeness to her as vision. God and the human heart are figured as mirrors of each other. Drunkenness is the most common image used for the ecstasy of the Sufi in the last stage of mystical union.

Sufi poetry also makes allusions of political import, often including biographical notes on particular Sufi masters who bettered their political leaders by exemplifying the teachings of the esoteric level of scripture.

Here are a few Sufi poems by some great Persian masters of the late Middle Ages. The best known in the West of the Sufi masters is Jalaluddin Rumi, whose interpretation of Hallaj appears above.

Divan a Shamsi-Tabriz

JALALUDDIN RUMI

XXXI.

What is to be done, O Moslems? for I do not recognise myself.
I am neither Christian, nor Jew, nor Gabr, nor Moslem.
I am not of the East, nor of the West, nor of the land, nor of the
      sea;
I am not of Nature's mint, nor of the circling heavens.   5
I am not of earth, nor of water, nor of air, nor of fire;
I am not of the empyrean, nor of the dust, nor of existence, nor of
      entity.

Jalaluddin Rumi. *Divan a Shamsi-Tabriz.* Translated by R. Nicholson. Lahore: Islamic Book Services, 1989.

I am not of India, nor of China, nor of Bulgaria, nor of Saqsīn;
I am not of the kingdom of Irāqain, nor of the country of   10
    Khorāsān.
I am not of this world, nor of the next, nor of Paradise, nor of
    Hell;
I am not of Adam, nor of Eve, nor of Eden and Rizwān.
My place is the Placeless, my trace is the Traceless;   15
'Tis neither body nor soul, for I belong to the soul of the
    Beloved.

I have put duality away, I have seen that the two worlds are
    one;
One I seek, One I know, One I see, One I call.   20
He is the first, He is the last, He is the outward, He is the inward;
I know none other except "Yā Hū" and "Yā man Hū."
I am intoxicated with Love's cup, the two worlds have passed
    out of my ken;
I have no business save carouse and revelry.   25
If once in my life I spent a moment without thee,
From that time and from that hour I repent of my life.
If once in this world I win a moment with thee,
I will trample on both worlds, I will dance in triumph for ever.
O Shamsi Tabrīz, I am so drunken in this world,   30
That except of drunkenness and revelry I have no tale to tell.

The Dullard Sage

'ATTAR

    when the sun
        reached noon
            I disappeared.
I have no news
       of my coming   5
          or passing away—
       In the candle flame
of his face

Peter Lamborn Wilson and Nasrollah Pourjavady, trans. and eds. *The Drunken Universe: An Anthology of Persian Sufi Poetry.* Grand Rapids: Phanes Press, 1987. Reprinted with the permission of the publisher.

I have forgotten
    all the answers.   10
In the way of love
    there must be knowledge
      and ignorance

so I have become
both a dullard   15
    and a sage;

one must be
an eye and yet
    not see

so I am blind   20
and yet I still
    perceive . . .

'Attār
    watched his heart
      transcend both worlds   25
and under its shadow
    now is gone mad
      with love.

Lover's Craft

Forughi

Again and again I polished my eye—now look:
it's become such a mirror that with a single glance
I can make you fall in love with yourself. Now look,
look deep into this glass and be aware
of other worlds.   5
        Now like a drunken reveler
pass by the monastery and the mosque:
you will be worshiped as the niche for prayer
by Muslim and Christian alike. . . .

In Love's atelier my craftsmanship   10

Peter Lamborn Wilson and Nasrollah Pourjavady, trans. and eds. *The Drunken Universe: An Anthology of Persian Sufi Poetry*. Grand Rapids: Phanes Press, 1987. Reprinted with the permission of the publisher.

reaches an unearthly beauty when
I contemplate your face.
                    The whole world knows
I am a reprobate in love—but God forbid
I ruin your reputation as well, my love.   15

The Drunken Universe

SAVAJI

In Preeternity
        already the reflection
                of your ruby wine
                        colored
                                the cup   5
already poor lovers
        fell into raging
                thirst—
Lip of the cup
        crystaled with sugar   10
                from your garnet lips,
the hidden secret
        of the jug
                poured out
                        into Everybody's   15
                                mouth—

The Tale of the Uniquely Beautiful
Mirror Maker

HASHEMI

There was an idol once (by which we mean
To say, a youth whose beauty could inspire

Peter Lamborn Wilson and Nasrollah Pourjavady, trans. and eds. *The Drunken Universe: An Anthology of Persian Sufi Poetry.* Grand Rapids: Phanes Press, 1987. Reprinted with the permission of the publisher.

Idolatrous praise) who lived in Syria
And earned his keep by making mirrors in
The city of Aleppo. Sweet were his lips.   5
His mouth a rosebud, cheeks as fresh as rain
Upon the desert, and his face was called
The Mecca of true lovers. Like the vault of heaven
His eyebrows curved, or like two crescent moons.
The sun in shame before his loveliness   10
Drew close upon its face a veil of cloud
And at his kiss the Fount of Life might flow
From sterile rock. No one can tell, no pen
Of poet celebrate such perfect grace.

Now no one in Aleppo loved this youth   15
As much as he himself; so fond was he
Of his own beauty that he wished no bliss
But to admire himself unceasingly
As with a hundred eyes. So, to that end,
He set out to construct a palace which   20
Would be unique as he who planned to live
In it. All arts, of mason, architect
And carpenter, he orchestrated in
His work; but last and most important he
Himself set out with all his skill to make   25
The interior of his castle one vast hall
Of mirrors: . . .

The bright house was complete but empty still
Till he, the mirror maker, entered in
To view it—and himself. Ah, then the veil,   30
The curtain of sweet unity was torn
From the face of eternity. Ah, then
The companionship of the mirror-hearted ones
Began. His face, reflected in each glass
Found its own reflection in the next   35
And next and next. Then, and only then
Were his exquisite down, his beauty spot
At last revealed in all their purity
And grace. At last the beauty that he owned
Was finally unfolded to his sight   40
In every sweet detail . . . in ecstasy.
O Hāshemi! This place of vision, like the sky,
Is nothing but the reflection in one place
Of one supreme and perfect Beauty. We

Are like mirrors of this mirror house 45
Gazing from Above as from Below
Like the eye grown simple. So be cut
Off from yourself, that the sun of His grace might shine
According to the polish of your soul.
For nothing but the One is to be seen 50
Reflecting to infinity in all
This carnival of mirrors, where the form
Of every glance is but the shadow of
That Form Divine, and all the world is but
The double of His Essence, Space, and Time 55
The Book wherein He writes His magic signs.
    And if our mirror has gone dark
    Our treacherous eyes grown dim with cloud
    It is our faults that veil the spark
    Of His perfection. Cry aloud 60
        O Hāshemi
        Then woe is me!

The Mathnawi

JALALUDDIN RUMI

PREFACE

In the Name of God the Compassionate, the Merciful.

This is the Book of the *Mathnawí,* which is the roots of the roots of the 1
roots of the (Mohammedan) Religion in respect of (its) unveiling the
mysteries of attainment (to the Truth) and of certainty; and which is
the greatest science of God and the clearest (religious) way of God
and the most manifest evidence of God.

    The likeness of the light thereof is *as a niche in which is a candle* 2
shining with a radiance brighter than the dawn. It is the heart's
Paradise, having fountains and boughs, one of them a fountain called
Salsabíl amongst the travellers on this Path; and in the view of the pos-

Jalaluddin Rumi. *The Mathnawi.* Translated by Reynold Nicholson. Lahore: Islamic Book Service, 1989.

sessors of (mystical) stations and (Divine) graces; it (the *Mathnawí*) is *best as a station and most excellent as a (spiritual) resting-place.* Therein the righteous eat and drink, and thereby the (spiritually) free are gladdened and rejoiced.

PROEM

In the Name of God the Merciful, the Compassionate.

Listen to the reed how it tells a tale, complaining of separations—
Saying, "Ever since I was parted from the reed-bed, my lament
    hath caused man and woman to moan.
I want a bosom torn by severance, that I may unfold (to such a
    one) the pain of love-desire.   5
Every one who is left far from his source wishes back the time
    when he was united with it. . . .

My secret is not far from my plaint, but ear and eye lack the light
    (whereby it should be apprehended).
Body is not veiled from soul, nor soul from body, yet none is   10
    permitted to see the soul.
This noise of the reed is fire, it is not wind: whoso hath not this
    fire, may he be naught!
'Tis the fire of Love that is in the reed, 'tis the fervor of Love that
    is in the wine.   15
The reed is the comrade of every one who has been parted from a
    friend: its strains pierced our hearts.
Who ever saw a poison and antidote like the reed? Who ever saw
    a sympathiser and a longing lover like the reed? . . .

Hail, O Love that bringest us good gain—thou that art the   20
    physician of all our ills,
The remedy of our pride and vainglory, our Plato and our Galen!
Through Love the earthly body soared to the skies: the mountain
    began to dance and became nimble.
Love inspired Mount Sinai, O lover, (so that) Sinai (was made)   25
    drunken *and Moses fell in a swoon.*
Were I joined to the lip of one in accord with me, I too, like the
    reed, would tell all that may be told;
(But) whoever is parted from one who speaks his language
    becomes dumb, though he have a hundred songs.   30

When the rose is gone and the garden faded, thou wilt hear no
    more the nightingale's story.
The Beloved is all and the lover (but) a veil; the Beloved is
    living and the lover a dead thing.
When Love hath no care for him, he is left as a bird without   35
    wings. Alas for him then!

BOOK II, THE UNITIVE STATE

The miracles of Ibráhím son of Adham—may God sanctify his holy spirit!—on the sea-shore.

Thus, it is related of Ibráhím son of Adham that after a journey
    he sat down (to rest) by the edge of the sea.
(Whilst) he was stitching his Ṣúfí mantle, an Amír, walking on
    the shore, suddenly came to that spot.
That Amír had been one of the Shaykh's servants; he recognized   5
    the Shaykh and at once bowed low.
He was astounded at the Shaykh and at his dervish garb—(for)
    his nature and outward guise had become transformed—
(Marvelling) that he gave up such a grand kingdom, and chose
    that very pettifogging (spiritual) poverty;   10
(And why) he lets the sovereignty of the Seven Climes be lost (by
    him), and plies the needle on his dervish-cloak, like a beggar.
The Shaykh became aware of his thought: a Shaykh is as the lion,
    and (people's) hearts are his jungle.
He is entering, like hope and fear, into (their) hearts: not hid   15
    from him are the secrets of the world.
Keep watch over your hearts, O fruitless ones, in the presence
    of the majesty of the men of heart (saints).
Before the men of body (worldlings), respect is (shown)
    outwardly, for God is veiling the occult from them.   20
Before the men of heart (saints), respect is (shown) inwardly,
    because their hearts have insight into the secret thoughts.

The School of Esphahan and Mulla Sadra

The important school of Esphahan concentrated on Shi'ite theology.
It produced one of the most important philosophers of later Islam,
Sadra al-Din Mohammad Shirazi, known as Mulla Sadra (ca.

1571–1641). Like Suhrawardi before him (an explicit influence on Sadra) Sadra integrated the "Western" categories and discursive technique with Islamic mysticism. He remains one of the central figures in Persian and Shi'ite theology.

Sadra shares concerns about "substance" and "knowledge" with Western philosophers of the same period, but his solutions to these problems are thoroughly Islamic and heavily influenced by Sufi mysticism. Because he integrates such a wide range of philosophical traditions into his own work, Sadra's writing is famously complex and intricate. Consequently, we have excerpted only a very small part of only one of his works and break the text often to explicate and comment upon it.

Sadra's longest and best-known work is known as the *Afsar*, or "Journeys." The following excerpts are from a shorter and more accessible work on some of the same subjects covered in the *Afsar*. It is called *The Wisdom of the Throne*. The throne referred to in the title is the seat of God. By titling the work this way, Sadra marks it as written from the point of view of the mystic in transcendent union with God. He thereby makes in a literary way one point he argues in the work, namely, that transcendent knowledge of God is indeed possible. Sadra's philosophy, then, is an investigation and demonstration of what Being and Knowledge must be like if the union of knower and known is to be possible.

The Wisdom of the Throne

MULLA SADRA

CONCLUDING TESTAMENT

Know that to attain the true inner divine knowledge one must follow   1
a *proof* or "unveiling" by immediate vision, just as He—May He be exalted!—said: *Say: "Bring your proof, if you are among those who speak truthfully!"* and He—May He be exalted!—said: *Whoever calls upon another god together with God has no proof for that.* This *proof* is a Light that God casts on the Heart of the man of true faith, a Light

The Wisdom of the Throne. Translated and edited by James Winston Morris. Princeton: Princeton University Press, 1981.

that illuminates his inner vision so that he "sees things as they really are," as it was stated in the prayer of the Prophet—May God's blessings and peace be with him!—for himself and the elect among his community and his close disciples: "O my God, cause us to see things as they really are!"

Know, too, that those questions concerning which the commonality of the philosophers have disagreed with the prophets—May God bless them!—are not matters that can easily be grasped and attained; nor can they be acquired by rejecting our rational, logical intellects, with their (intrinsic) measures and their contemplative activities of learning and investigating. If this were so, then there would never have been any disagreement (with the prophets) concerning these questions on the part of those intelligent men who were busy all their lives using the tool of thought and reflection to acquire a (true) conception of things; those (philosophers) would never have fallen into error in these questions and there would have been no need for the sending of the prophets (if these metaphysical realities were so easy to grasp). So it should be known that these questions can only be comprehended by taking over Lights from the Lamp-niche of Prophecy, and by earnestly seeking Them. For these are the Secrets which are the true inner meaning of Discipleship and Sainthood.

By "taking over the lights from the lamp-niche of prophecy," Sadra means to follow somewhat the Illuminationists in his theory of knowledge. Knowledge of God is an illumination of the knower by Him; the prophet Mohammed was illumined most purely and directly of human beings; by correctly interpreting scripture we are, in a sense, illumined by God through the prophet.

FIRST PLACE OF ILLUMINATION, CONCERNING KNOWLEDGE OF GOD, OF HIS ATTRIBUTES, HIS NAMES, AND HIS SIGNS

§1. Principle (deriving from) the divine Presence, concerning the divisions of Being and the establishment of the Primary Being

That which exists is either the Reality of Being or something else. By the Reality of Being we mean That which is not mixed with anything but Being, whether a generality or a particularity, a limit or a bound, a quiddity [a thing's essential quality], an imperfection, or a privation—and this is what is called the "Necessary Being." Therefore we say that if the Reality of Being did not exist, then nothing at all would exist. But the consequence (of this conditional statement) is self-evidently false; therefore its premise is likewise (false).

The "first place" of illumination is the knowledge that God's existence is "necessary," in other words, that for God not to exist is impossible. God is the origin and the very content of all things. God's existence, unlike the existence of created things, is pure and unmixed. This is what Sadra means by saying that He exists before any "qiddity, imperfection, or privation." Created things are limited, divided into kinds and individuals. God is completely unlimited, and therefore He is of no kind, has no essence, and not a token of a kind, either. But all kinds of things, and all individuals, nonetheless find their origin in God.

As for showing the necessity (of the actual existence) of this   4
Primary Being, this is because everything other than this Reality of Being is either a specific quiddity or a particular being, mixed with privation and imperfection. . . .

So privation (or "nonbeing") does not enter into the existence and   5
actual occurrence of a thing, although it may enter into its definition and its concept. For to affirm any concept of something and to predicate it of that thing—whether (the concept be) a quiddity or some other attribute, and whether it be affirmed or denied of something—always presupposes the being of that thing. Our discussion always comes back to Being: either there is an infinite regression (of predications and subjects) or one arrives in the end at an Absolute Being, unmixed with anything else.

Thus it has become evident that the Source of existence of every-   6
thing that exists is this Pure Reality of Being, unmixed with anything other than Being. This Reality is not restricted by any definition, limitation, imperfection, contingent potentiality, or quiddity; nor is It mixed with any generality, whether of genus, species, or differentia, nor with any accident, whether specific or general. For Being is prior to all these descriptions that apply to quiddities, and That which has no quiddity other than Being is not bound by any generality or specificity. It has no specific difference and no particularity apart from Its own Essence (or Self); It has no form, nor has It any agent or end. On the contrary, It is Its own Form, and That which gives form to every thing, because It is the completion of the essence of every thing. And It is the completion of every thing because Its Essence is actualized in every respect.

No one can describe Him or reveal Him but He Himself, and   7
there is no demonstration of Him but His own Essence (or Self).
Therefore He gave witness through His Self to Himself and to the
Unicity of His Self when He said: *God gives witness that there is no
god but He.* For His Unity is not the particular unity that is found in an
individual of a (particular) nature; nor is It the generic or specific unity
that is found in any general notion or any quiddity. Neither is It the
conjunctive unity that is found when a number of things become
assembled or unified into a single thing; nor is It the unity of contigu-
ity found in quantities and measurable things. Nor, as you will learn,
is It any of the other relative unities, such as unity by resemblance,
homogeneity, analogy, correspondence, reduplication—although
(certain) philosophers have allowed that—congruence, or any of the
other kinds of unity that are not the True Unity. No, His Unity is other
(than these relative ones), unknowable in Its innermost core, like His
Essence—May He be exalted!—except that His Unity is the Source of
all (these other) unities, just as His being is the Source of all (particular) beings. Hence *He has no second.*

Sadra argues that knowledge must necessarily be a transcendent unification of the knower with the known. All knowledge,
then, is like sensation, like seeing, hearing, etc. In sensation, light
or sound (the sensed object) is sensed "through itself"; the knower knows a sound by "having" or "being with" the sound in hearing. Similarly, argues Sadra, when we know something (and since
all things are part of God, the object of knowledge is always, in
a sense, God), our knowledge is the very joining of our soul with
God.

§10. Principle (deriving from) the divine Throne (concerning the unity of knower and known)

Everything that is intelligible in its being is also actively intelligizing.   8
Indeed, every form in perception—whether it be intelligible or sensible—is unified in its being with that which perceives it.

The proof of this, emanating from God's Presence, is that every   9
form in perception—even if it is sensible, for example—has some sort
of separation from matter, so that its being in itself and its being
sensible are really only one thing and do not differ at all. Thus one
cannot suppose that the specific form might have a mode of being
with respect to which it would not be sensible, because its very being

is a being *in sensation*—quite different from the being of the heavens or earth or anything else which is in external (material being). For the being of those (material) things is not in sensation, and they are grasped by sense or by the intellect only in an accidental manner and in consequence of a form in sensation corresponding to them. . . .

No, the essence of the form existing in sensation is sensible by its   10
very essence. Therefore its very being is sensible by essence—whether or not there exists in the world a sensing substance which is separate from it. Indeed, even if we completely ignored everything else (but this form in sensation) or supposed that there did not exist in the world any separate sensing substance—even in that condition and under that supposition this form would still be sensible in essence. For its essence is sensible for itself, so that its essence in itself is at once the thing sensed, that which senses, and that which is sensed. This is because one of the terms of the relation (between that which senses and that which is sensed), insofar as it is part of the relation, cannot be separated from its partner in their being, at any of the levels of (intensity of) that being. And the same rule holds for the status of the form in imagination or intellection with respect to its being identical with that which imagines or intelligizes.

The soul's unification with the "Productive (or Active) Intellect" is   11
nothing but its becoming in its essence an intellect actually productive of forms. For the Intellect cannot be many in number (like corporeal things). Rather, it has another, comprehensive Unity that is not like that numerical unity which applies generally to the particular individuals of a species. The Productive Intellect, at the same time as It produces (or "brings into actuality") these souls which are connected with bodies, is also an End of perfection, ordering them, and an intellective Form for them, encompassing them all. And these souls are like delicate and subtle threads radiating from It to the bodies, and then returning to It when the souls become perfected and immaterial (or "transcendent").

But the (complete) verification of these topics would require a   12
detailed discussion that cannot be contained in this treatise.

The second part of the treatise is called the "Return," signifying its subject matter as the effect and nature of the knowledge of God upon the life of the knower. Since the knower is made a better person by his or her union with God, we may understand the second part of the treatise as a sort of moral theory.

SECOND PLACE OF ILLUMINATION, CONCERNING KNOWLEDGE OF THE RETURN

§2. Principle (concerning the levels of the soul)

The human soul has many levels and stations, from the beginning of   13
its generation to the end of its goal; and it has certain essential states
and modes of being. At first, in its state of connection (with the body)
it is a corporeal substance. Then it gradually becomes more and more
intensified and develops through the different stages of its natural constitution until it subsists by itself and moves from this world to the
other world, and so *returns to its Lord.*

Thus the soul is originated in a corporeal (state), but endures in a   14
spiritual (state). The first thing to be generated in its state (of connection with the body) is a corporeal power; next is a natural form; then
the sensible soul with its levels; then the cogitative and recollective;
and then the rational soul. Next, after the practical intellect, it
acquires the theoretical intellect according to its various degrees, from
the rank of the intellect in potency to that of the intellect in actuality
and the Active Intellect—which is the same as that "Spirit" of the
divine Command which is ascribed to God in His saying: *Say: "The
Spirit is from my Lord's Command!"* This last degree occurs only in a
very small number of individuals of the human species. Moreover,
(merely human) effort and labor do not suffice to acquire it, since a
certain divine attraction is also necessary for its attainment, as it is
mentioned in the Prophetic tradition: "A single attraction from God
outbalances all the efforts of men and jinn."

Rhazes' Platonism

Thus far, we have stressed the philosophies we consider particularly "Iranian" in their character, those which strive for truth along a
path very different from that traveled by Western philosophers. Yet
we have also stated that Persia is characterized by a cosmopoli-
tanism and synchretism of different themes from Western and
Eastern cultures, and that this is part of what gives Persian culture
its special flavor. In closing, then, we thought it would be nice to
look at a philosopher who gives a distinct Persian spin on themes
with which you may be familiar from classes in Western philosophy. In the following passage, Rhazes, an eighth-century Persian

Platonist, gives his own interpretation of Socrates' notion of "the examined life." Like many of the Persian thinkers we have seen so far, Rhazes stresses how the practical, physical concerns of the ordinary person play into the life of the mind: by doing so, he fleshes out the bare bones of the traditional, Western interpretations of Socrates' notion.

After all the Islamic Aristotelianism above, it may also be refreshing to read one example of an Islamic use of Platonic philosophy. Like Plato's dialogues themselves, Rhazes leads the reader back to him or herself and reminds us that knowledge and justice are the concern and the obligation of the philosopher, whatever his or her nationality or culture.

On the Philosophic Life

RHAZES

Certain men there be, speculative and discriminating and of undoubted attainments, who have therefore criticised and found fault with us, asserting that we have swerved away from the Philosophic Life and in particular that of our leader Socrates. For of him it is recorded that he frequented not the company of kings, and treated them with scant respect if ever they sought his; that he ate no tasty food, wore no fine raiment, raised no edifice, acquired not wealth, begat no issue; that he consumed no meat, drank no wine, and attended no amusements, but contented himself with eating herbs, wrapping himself in threadbare garments, and sheltering in a barrel in the waste. It is further reported that he practised dissimulation neither before the common people nor in the presence of authority, but confronted all with the truth as he conceived it, and that in the frankest and bluntest language.   1

We on the other hand are, they say, the opposite of all that. . . .   2

Now we are by no means at variance with the more laudable part   3
of Socrates' life, even though we ourselves fall far short of him in that respect and readily confess our failure perfectly to practise the just life, to suppress passion, and to be in love with and eager for knowledge. Where we differ from Socrates is not regarding the quality but rather the quantity of that life.

A. J. Arberry, trans. *The Asiatic Review*; 45(163), (July 1949): 703ff.

It is obvious that the reckless indulgence of the passions is not the 4
better and nobler way: this we have clearly stated in our book *On
Spiritual Physick*. True virtue consists in taking of every need so much
as is indispensable, or so much as will not involve pain exceeding the
pleasure thereby obtained.

Since this has now all been sufficiently dealt with, let us proceed 5
to discourse upon the Philosophic Life, for the benefit of the true
lovers of knowledge.

The supreme end for which we were created and towards which 6
we have been led is not the gratification of physical pleasures but the
acquisition of knowledge and the practice of justice: these two occu-
pations are our sole deliverance out of the present world into the
world wherein is neither death nor pain.

Nature and passion prompt us to prefer present pleasure, but rea- 7
son frequently urges us to eschew present pleasures for the sake of
other objects which it prefers.

Our Ruler, for Whose reward we hope (while fearing His punish- 8
ment), is watching over us with compassion, and does not desire that
we should suffer pain. It is hateful to Him that we should be unjust
and ignorant: He loves us to have knowledge and to be just. This
same Ruler will punish those of us who inflict pain, and those who
deserve to be pained, each according to his deserts. . . .

This being so, it likewise necessarily follows that we ought not to 9
seek any pleasure, the attainment of which would inevitably involve
us in the commission of an act barring our deliverance into the World
of Spirit, or that would oblige us in this present world to suffer pain
exceeding both quantitively and qualitively the pleasure we have chosen. All other pleasures are of course free for us to take, except that
the philosopher may sometimes eschew many of these lawful pleasures in order thus to train and habituate his soul, so that it may be
easier and simpler for him so to do when the occasion requires.

Accordingly it is incumbent upon us not to cause pain to any sen- 10
tient being whatsoever except it deserve so to be pained, or in order
that we may thereby avert from it a yet severer pain.

This generalisation likewise comprehends a wide range of detail, 11
and embraces every manner of wrongful act, alike the pleasure kings
take hunting animals and the excessive labour men impose on their
domestic beasts. All this ought to be done in moderation and according to a certain code and method, a just and reasonable manner
which must not be exceeded or transgressed. . . .

It is not right to exterminate and destroy domestic and herbivo- 12 rous animals; on the contrary, domestic animals are to be handled gently as we have described, and taken as little as possible for food, neither should they be bred in such quantities as to necessitate excessive slaughtering, but rather in moderation and as need arises. If it were not for the fact that there is no hope for a soul to escape save from the human body, the judgment of reason would not have permitted their slaughter at all.

Since the arbitrament of both reason and justice is against a man   13
inflicting hurt upon another, it follows from this that he may not hurt himself either.

People are by no means alike in this respect, and in fact there is a   14
very great difference between them. . . .

It is therefore not possible for all men to be charged with an equal   15
burden, but this must differ according to their different circumstances.

There is however a certain limit which cannot be transgressed. All   16
men must refrain from such pleasures as may not be gratified without perpetrating some injustice or committing murder—in short, all such acts as may anger God and are condemned by reason and justice. Short of this, all things are lawful to be enjoyed. This then is the upper limit, that is to say in regard to the luxury that may be properly indulged.

Noble spirits, though they may be associated with bodies used to   17
luxurious food, have ever brought their bodies down gradually to accept the lower limit. But to surpass the lower limit is to quit philosophy and to fall into those Indian and Manichean and monkish and ascetic practices which we have mentioned; it is to abandon the just life, and to anger God Himself, by paining the spirit to no purpose. Such conduct truly merits expulsion from the name of philosophy. This is of course equally true when the upper limit is transgressed. And we ask God, the Giver of reason and Deliverer from grief and sorrow, to assist, direct and aid us to that life which is higher and more pleasing unto Him.

PRONUNCIATION GUIDE

Key: r = trilled r; kh = soft ch (sounded in the back of the throat); q = glottal gh; ' = glottal stop
Note: in Farsi (the Persian language), all R's are trilled (i.e., rolled on the tongue, not growled in the back of the throat); all H's appearing

by themselves (i.e., not as "SH" or "CH" or "KH" or "OH") are pronounced.

Achaemenid: Aw-khem-en-id
'Attar: 'At-tawr
Divan: Dee-vawn
Esphahan: Es-fa-hawn
Fihrist al-Nadim: Fee-hreest al-Na-deem
Forughi: Foh-hroo-qi
Hashemi: Haw-shem-ee
Imam: Ee-mawm
Ishraqi: Eesh-raw-qee
Khan: Khawn
Khomeini: Khoh-may-nee
Mahdi: Mah-dee
Mani: Ma-nee
Manichaeism: Maw-nee-khee-ism
Mathnawi: Math-naw-vee
Mazdak: Maz-dak
Mulla: Mul-law
Nasir-i Khusraw: Na-seer-ee Khus-raw
Pahlavi: Pa-hla-vee
Qajar: Qa-jawr
Qalb: Qalb
Rhazes: R-haw-zeez
Rumi (Jalaluddin): Roo-mee (Jal-al-ood-deen)
Sadra: Sa-draw
Savaji: Sa-vaw-jee
Sufi: Soo-fee
Suhrawardi (Yahya): Soo-hra-vawr-dee (Ya-h-ya)
Zarathustra: Zar-a-thoo-shtraw

GLOSSARY

Achaemenid empire: The first Persian Empire, begins sixth century B.C.E.
Ahura Mazda (later, Ormazd): The god of the ancient Persian religion, Zoroastrianism.
Asha: Divinity in the Zoroastrian pantheon, represented by fire, and translated as "truth" or "right."
Avesta (Zend Avesta): The scripture of the ancient Persian religion, Zoroastrianism.
divan: A type of Persian poetry; a particular meter.

Esphahan: Iranian city and cultural center during the Safavid and Qajar dynasties.

imams: The descendents of 'Ali, Mohammed's son-in-law, believed by Shi'ite Muslims to have been the successors to the prophet.

haoma: Intoxicating beverage used in ancient religious rituals in Persia.

Ishraqi: "Illuminationist" philosophers of the late Middle Ages, following Suhrawardi.

Khomeini: Shi'ite leader who took control of Iran after the 1979 revolution.

Mahdi: The hidden Twelfth Imam, whom Twelver Shi'ites believe to be the messiah.

Manichaeism: An ancient religion (second century) which believed in a fundamental spiritual duality between good and evil, understood as "light and dark," and "spirit and body."

Mazdakism: An ancient religion (fifth century) which believed in the abolition of private property.

Medians: The first Persian peoples in the Iranian plateau, second millennium B.C.E.

Pahlavi dynasty: Twentieth-century Persian dynasty, prior to the 1979 revolution (the government of the shahs of Iran).

Qajar dynasty: Weak Persian dynasty of the nineteenth century.

qalb ("Heart"): The source of the path to divine knowledge, according to the Sufis, Islamic mystics.

Safavid dynasty: Powerful Persian dynasty (sixteenth to eighteenth century) which made Shi'ism the state religion of Iran

Sassanids: The second Persian Empire, begins second century B.C.E.

Shi'ism: The sect of Islam which followed Mohammed's son-in-law, 'Ali, calling him the first imam, and claiming a special status for the imams in interpreting scripture.

Sufism: Islamic mysticism.

Sunnism: The major branch of Islam, practiced in most Arab nations; Sunnis followed an elected successor to Mohammed after the prophet's death.

Vohu Manah: Divinity in the Zoroastrian pantheon; represented by the cow and translated as "Good Purpose."

Zarathustra (Zarathushtra): Prophet of the ancient Persian religion, Zoroastrianism.

Zoroastrianism: The ancient religion of Persia.

FURTHER READINGS

A. J. ARBERRY. *Classical Persian Literature*. London: Allen & Unwin, 1962.

———. *Tales from the Masnavi*. London: Allen & Unwin, 1962.

MARY BOYCE. *Zoroastrians: Their Beliefs and Practices*. London: Routledge & Kegan Paul, 1979.

WILLIAM W. MALANDRA. *An Introduction to Ancient Iranian Religion.* Minneapolis: University of Minnesota Press, 1983.

R. C. ZAEHNER. *Concise Encyclopedia of Living Faiths.* Boston: Beacon Press, 1962.

STUDY QUESTIONS

1. What are some of the similarities and differences between Zarathustra and his teachings and those of the religion in which you were raised? What can your reflections tell us about the historical influences of Zoroastrianism upon other religions? Be sure to take into consideration the characters of Zarathustra and of the different gods in the Zoroastrian pantheon.

2. Manichaeism, and many later Persian religions which felt its influence, makes an association between Light and moral Goodness and, similarly, between Darkness and Evil. These associations are extremely common ones, right down to our own day. Why, in your opinion? Use some examples from Manichaeism, and from our own culture, in your response. Do you think we ought to abandon this association? Why or why not?

3. Sectarian disputes within Islam tend to revolve around the question of authority in interpreting scriptures. In "Speech," Nasir-i Khusraw asks: "Why told [the Prophet] to entrust the hermeneutic to the wise, words to the rabble?" What is his answer to this question, and how does it mark him as a "Sevener" Shi'ite? What is *your* answer? Does everyone have equal access to God's will through scripture, or is it a mystery that some people are better able to interpret than others?

4. Using passages from the readings on Sufism and Illuminationism, discuss the relationship between knowledge and love in these thinkers. Is love, for them, a practical activity or a paralyzing passion? Draw out the consequences of your answer for an understanding of knowledge. What do you think is the relation between knowledge and love, after reading them?

5. Sadra believes that mystical revelation is consistent with demonstrative reasoning. Give an example from *The Wisdom of the Throne* that exemplifies this belief. Does he convince you? Is revelation "just another way" to God, no better or worse than a proof of God's existence, or are the two inconsistent with each other? Why, in either case?

CHAPTER 6

American Indian
Philosophy

J. BAIRD CALLICOTT AND
THOMAS W. OVERHOLT

The Americas may have been inhabited by 100 million people some 500 years ago when they were "discovered" by Columbus—a population equal to or greater than that of contemporaneous Europe. Some 350 years ago, the first English colony was established on the east coast of North America in what had become a "desolate and howling" wilderness. Contact was disastrous for American Indian peoples. Their numbers plummeted, not because of warfare with the better-armed European intruders, though that took its toll, but mainly because of Old World diseases, against which the Indians had evolved no immunities.

After half a millennium, we are just now beginning to realize that before 1492 the Western Hemisphere was not a wilderness. It was richly peopled. For at least 10,000 years, the original Americans had evolved culturally (as well as biologically) in complete isolation from the peoples of Europe, Asia, and Africa. And like people everywhere, American Indians developed rich cognitive, as well as material, cultures. What did American Indians think about their world and how they, as human beings, fit into it? Isolated as they were for so long, American Indian thought must have been really different from the familiar European and Asian legacy of ideas.

Traditional American Indian peoples spoke hundreds of mutually unintelligible languages and lived in diverse material and cognitive cultures adapted to ecosystems that ran the gamut from hot southern deserts to wet northern tundra. However varied, American Indian thought centered, generally speaking, on nature. The following three sets of selections from the rich vein of indigenous

American natural philosophy offer temporal as well as g variety. The two Ojibwa (Oh-JIB-wuh) stories hark back immemorial and provide a window into one of the oldest ᵢ   ᵤₒₛₜ venerable forms of human thinking still alive on planet Earth. And they represent the traditional woodland worldview of the upper Great Lakes. The excerpts from the autobiographical narratives of two famous Sioux or, more properly, Lakota (La-KOH-tah) holy men represent the philosophy of the Plains Indians of the American heartland after they acquired the horse, a European import, and established a way of life centered on buffalo hunting. The piece by Oxford-educated Kiowa (KAI-oh-wuh) Indian N. Scott Momaday, winner of the Pulitzer Prize for fiction in 1969, expresses the environmental philosophy of a contemporary Native American who is deeply imbued with the experience of his ancestors.

189-155

THE OJIBWA BIOTIC COMMUNITY

Among the woodland Indians, stories had a dual function: to amuse and to educate. In the absence of formal schooling, folktales were the principal vehicle for instructing the young and reminding the old of the group's worldview. Hence they are a gold mine of tribal attitudes and values.

These two stories are about opposite sides of the same coin of mutual obligation: the obligations that people have to animals, in the first story, specifically to the beaver; and the reciprocal obligations that animals, in the second story, specifically the moose, have to people. Dozens of other stories in the Ojibwa narrative cycle provide variations on this basic theme of mutual obligation and respect between people and nature. The characters differ and the plot varies, but the overall message remains constant.

The first of these stories is based upon a premise that seems very strange indeed to modern Western sensibilities—a human woman marries a beaver man. But in tribal societies, clans (or extended families) are distinguished from one another through totem representation. Entertaining the notion of interspecies marriages would doubtless seem less weird to people who think of themselves in terms of totem identities—the bear people, the snake people, the crane people, etc.

Intermarriage facilitates the exchange of goods and services between clans which, in the absence of a market, proceeds by gift giving. The odd-couple marriage in the first of these stories thus establishes an alliance that has economic implications between the people and these important rodents. Gifts are exchanged which are mutually beneficial.

The woman who married a beaver acts as a kind of emissary from her in-laws to the Indians. In this story the main message she brings back to her people is that the beavers demand respect. Otherwise they will not allow themselves to be taken home, skinned, and eaten. Yes, allow themselves! The Indians believed that game animals gave themselves up voluntarily to human hunters. But why would they do that? As the story suggests, in order to obtain products that can be gotten only from human beings—tobacco, clothing, and other things that people grow or make. But how could they possibly enjoy the use of such goods if they were dead? As the story explains, the slain beavers come back to life. So everyone is better off. The people get meat and fur, the reincarnated beavers get human stuff.

A couple of details in "The Woman Who Married a Beaver" may need explaining. When the story begins the young woman is on her quest for an empowering vision. That is why she has "blackened" her face, presumably with charcoal. Later in the story, when she is discovered by a man, down in the beaver lodge, he thinks she may be a "manitou" (MAN-ih-too)—an Ojibwa word meaning, roughly, a nature spirit.

"A Moose and His Offspring" suggests what might befall a game animal that does not respect and submit to human hunters who keep their end of the human-animal pact. The first part of the story informs the audience that the young moose is a typical adolescent—headstrong and reckless. He has perfect contempt for human beings and infinite confidence in his own prowess. But he is defeated by circumstance. In late winter a crust forms on deep snow. The sharp hooves of moose and deer plunge through and the animals' movement is hampered, but men on snowshoes and their dogs can run unencumbered on the hardened surface.

Notice that when his pursuer catches him, the young moose is not killed. Instead he is beaten and his nose is cut off to punish his insolence. The other members of his family, on the other hand, voluntarily and gladly subject themselves to slaughter. They come back to life, of course. A little later, they are invited to the hunters' lodge to eat and smoke and collect their gifts, which are all lovingly detailed in the story. Needless to say, the foolhardy young moose gets none of these.

"Bird-hawks and swans" refers to the spirit power that the human hunters use to make them speedy, in the tangible form of the feathers or skins of these swift creatures. When the pipe suddenly comes in to the moose lodge, as if on its own, that indicates that the hunters are properly inviting the moose over for dinner, so to speak. When all the moose, except for the antihero of our story, take it and smoke, that indicates that they have accepted the invitation. Drumming is a further sign of the manitou power that the hunters use to woo their prey. The extraordinarily strange fact that the hunter's entrails were exposed to the family of moose may mean that he is signaling his hunger and thus the dire necessity of his act.

There is a remarkable similarity to contemporary ecology in the way that the traditional Ojibwa represent nature and the human place in the natural order of things. Ecology pictures the living world as a "biotic community" in which plants and animals perform various vital roles in the "economy of nature." The Ojibwa also represent the natural world as a vast multispecies society in which human beings are, in the words of ecology's great philosopher, Aldo Leopold (1887–1948), "plain members and citizens." For the Ojibwa and other traditional woodland Indians, membership in the natural community implied an environmental ethic. The animals and plants upon which they depended for survival ought to be treated with respect, used with restraint, and compensated in order to maintain a balance of trade. According to Leopold, ecology's portrait of nature and the human-nature relationship implies a similar "respect for fellow members and . . . for the community as such," if we are to maintain the balance of nature. Of course, there are important dissimilarities between the traditional woodland Indian environmental ethic and the contemporary Leopold "land ethic." The community concept is expressed mythically by traditional woodland Indians, not scientifically. And Leopold did not think that animals could return human respect and assume reciprocal obligations. But the similarities appear to be greater than the differences.

The Woman Who Married a Beaver

Once on a time a certain young woman went into a long fast, black-   1
ening (her face). Far off somewhere she wandered about. In course of
time she beheld a man that was standing, (and) by him was she
addressed, saying: "Will you not come along with me to where I
live?"

Whereupon she went along with him who was in the form of a   2
human being. And when they got to where he dwelt, very pretty was
the home of the man; every kind of thing he had in clothing and food.
Very well provided for was the man. And this she was told: "Will you
not become my wife? In this place will we spend our life," she was
told.

And the woman said: "Perhaps sad might be my father and my   3
mother."

"They will not be sad," she was told.   4

Thereupon, in truth, she freely consented to marry him, whereat   5
the woman lost the memory of her parents. Very beautiful was the
clothing given her by him to whom she was married. It was where
there was a certain lake that they passed their life. A long while did
she have the man for her husband. When they beheld their (first)
young, four was the number of them. Never of anything was the
woman in want. Of every kind of fish that was, did the man kill;
besides, some small animal-kind he slew; of great abundance was
their food. Outside of where they dwelt (was) also some fire-wood.
And the woman herself was continually at work making flag-reed
mats and bags; in very neat order was it inside of where they dwelt.
Sometimes by a human being were they visited; but only roundabout
out of doors would the man pass, not within would the man come.
Now, the woman knew that she had married a beaver.

From time to time with the person, that had come to where they   6
were, would the children go back home; frequently, too, would the
man return home with the person. And back home would they always
return again. All sorts of things would they fetch,—kettles and bowls,
knives, tobacco, and all the things that are used when a beaver is

Thomas W. Overholt and J. Baird Callicott. *Clothed in Fur and Other Tales: An Introduction to an Ojibwa World View.* Washington: University Press of America, 1982, pp. 74–75, 81–84.

eaten; such was what they brought. Continually were they adding to their great wealth. Very numerous were the young they had; and as often as the spring came round, then was when off went their brood two by two, one male and one female. And this they said to them: "Somewhere do you go and put up a shelter. Do you rear a numerous offspring, to the end that greater may be the number of beavers." Save only the smaller of their young would they watch over for still another year; not till the following spring would their young go away.

Now and then by a person were they visited; then they would go 7 to where the person lived, whereupon the people would then slay the beavers, yet they really did not kill them; but back home would they come again. Now, the woman never went to where the people lived; she was forbidden by her husband. That was the time when very numerous were the beavers, and the beavers were very fond of the people; in the same way as people are when visiting one another, so were (the beavers) in their mental attitude toward the people. Even though they were slain by (the people), yet they really were not dead. They were very fond of the tobacco that was given them by the people; at times they were also given clothing by the people.

And when they were growing old, the woman was addressed by 8 her husband saying: "Well, it is now time, therefore, for you to go back home. I too am going away to some other land. But do you remain here in my house. Eventually, as time goes on, there will arrive some people, (and) you should speak to them."

And the woman all the while continued at her work, making 9 twine. In very beautiful order was her home. Now, once sure enough, (she saw) a man arriving there; on top of the beaver dwelling the man sat down. Thereupon he heard the sound of some creature sawing in the beaver lodge beneath, the sound of some one pounding. When the woman picked up a piece of wood, she made a tapping-noise, so that her presence might be found out by the man. And he that was seated out on top learned that some creature was down inside of the beaver-lodge. And so up he spoke, saying: "Who (are) you?"

"(It is) I," came the voice of the woman speaking. "Come, do you 10 force an opening into this beaver-dwelling! I wish to get out," was the sound of her voice as she spoke.

Now, the man was afraid of her. "It might be a manitou," he 11 thought. Then plainly he heard the sound of her voice saying to him: "Long ago was I taken by the beavers. I too was once a human being. Please do break into this beaver-dwelling!"

Thereupon truly then did he break into that beaver-wigwam. And   12
when he was making the hole into it, "Be careful lest you hit me!"
(she said). And when he was breaking an opening, in the man reached
his hand; whereupon he found by the feel of her that she was a
human being; all over did he try feeling her,—on her head; and her
ears, having on numerous ear-rings, he felt. And when he had forced
a wide opening, out came the woman; very white was her head. And
beautiful was the whole mystic cloth that she had for a skirt; worked
all over with beads was her cloak; and her moccasins too were very
pretty; and her ear-rings she also had on; she was very handsomely
arrayed.

Thereupon she plainly told the story of what had happened to her   13
while she lived with the beavers. She never ate a beaver. A long while
afterwards lived the woman. There still lived after her one of her
younger sisters; it was she who used to take care of her. And she was
wont to say: "Never speak you ill of a beaver! Should you speak ill of
(a beaver), you will not (be able to) kill one."

Therefore such was what the people always did; they never spoke   14
ill of the beavers, especially when they intended hunting them. Such
was what the people truly know. If any one regards a beaver with too
much contempt, speaking ill of it, one simply (will) not (be able to) kill
it. Just the same as the feelings of one who is disliked, so is the feeling
of the beaver. And he who never speaks ill of a beaver is very much
loved by it; in the same way as people often love one another, so is
one held in the mind of the beaver; particularly lucky then is one at
killing beavers.

A Moose and His Offspring

The Moose was about to go into camp for the winter, and also his   1
wife. Two (in number) were their children, and there was a youth
among them; therefore they were in fear. On very long journeys frequently went the youth, whereupon continually was the old man trying to dissuade him (not to go so far). "Upon your trail might come
the people." But (the youth) paid no heed. Once (he saw) the tracks of
another Moose; he knew it was a cow. Accordingly he followed after
her, whereat, on seeing her, he took her to wife. During this time that

he had her for wife, by another Moose were they visited; and by her, as by the other, was he desired for a husband; to be sure, he married her. Therefore two were the wives he had.

In truth, very frequently did they fight. And once he went away, to his father he went. After he was come, he spoke to his father, saying: "Verily, my father, two (are) the women I have." He was addressed by him saying: "My son, do not bring it about that there be two women for you to have. Perhaps they might do harm to each other." 2

"Ay," he said to his father. And then on the morrow he went back home; in a while he arrived at where they dwelt. Whereupon, sure enough, (he found) that one of his wives had been killed. 3

And once there arrived two other Moose. Presently they spoke to him, saying: "Why did you have two wives? You should not have done so." 4

Thereupon he became exceedingly ill, hardly was he able to go back to his father. In time he arrived within (the wigwam), whereupon then he began to undergo treatment from his father. "Such was the reason why I tried to dissuade you from your purpose. Because of this disobedience you became sick. Therefore now you should remain quietly by." 5

By this time the winter was halfway gone. In certain places roundabout where they lived wandered the calves. When it snowed, (then) sang the young Moose. Truly happy they were when it snowed:— 6

"May more snow fall, may some more snow fall!
May more snow fall, may some more snow fall!
May more snow fall, may some more snow fall!
May more snow fall, may some more snow fall!"

Thus sang the young Moose. They were heard by their mother, by whom they were then addressed: "Do not sing such a song, lest perhaps you be laid low with a club on the hardened crust, if much snow falls." 7

Thereupon they ceased. 8

And in course of time to very much better health was the youth restored. Therefore then he started off, trying to see how he could travel; and very comfortably did he walk along. And once he saw where the cloud had cast a shadow; in truth, he believed that he could outstrip it. Accordingly, when he ran it a race, a very great distance behind he left it. Truly pleased was he to have outrun the cloud. 9

Then on his homeward way he went. When he entered into where they lived, he spoke to his father, saying: "My father, of a truth, you deceived me when you said that speedy is a human being. On this day now past I raced with the cloud, far behind I outran it. Not so swift as that would a human being be." Thereupon he was addressed by his father saying: "My dear son, of a truth, you are greatly to be pitied for regarding with contempt a human being. Of the nature of a manitou is a human being. To-day you shall learn, if very far you intend to go, how it is that a human being is of the nature of a mani-tou. He makes use of bird-hawks and swans, and on that account speedy is a human being."

It was then growing dark when (the youth) departed, for away   10
went the Moose. And once, while travelling along, he saw the tracks of some one; it seemed as if some one had been dragging two poles, such was the mark of some one's trail. "It must be a human being that has made the trail," he thought. Then he followed in the path behind him. Of a truth, he made great fun (of the human being), he held him in contempt because of the tracks he made. "It is impossible for him ever to overtake any one, too ungainly are his tracks." And then back home he went; when he arrived, a heap of fun he made of his father: "My father, now perhaps"—while at the same time he was laughing at his father—"upon the tracks of a person did I come. No doubt, you must have been beside yourself, my father, when you said that a human being was speedy. When I was on his trail, two poles was he dragging behind. Verily, never anything could that good-for-nothing human being overtake." Thereupon then again he was addressed by his father saying: "In a little while we shall be visited by a human being."

It was now growing dark. And suddenly in came a pipe. First to   11
the girl's mouth came the stem, whereupon then the girl smoked; next to the old woman, and she also smoked; next to the boy, likewise to the old man, who smoked; then next to the youth. The moment that the stem was entering into his mouth, he dealt it a hard blow. Thereupon then he said: "Never can I be slain by a human being." Thereupon then he was addressed by his father saying: "Oh, my dear son! therefore now have you played the mischief with yourself."

And then in a while they lay down to sleep. After they had lain   12
down to sleep, they heard the sound of a kettle-drum beating; and it was on their account that it was beating; they were being overcome with manitou power. The old man then rose from his bed. "It is in the

morning that we shall be sought for. My dear son, come, harken to what I tell you! Don't think of trying to flee away, for I am really telling you the truth in what I am saying to you. Of bird-hawks and swans (the people) make use, such are the things the people use."

Early in the morning, while it was yet dark, there came a sudden crunching of the crust of the snow. Not even did he see any one. Very close he heard the sound of some one. "Halloo!" exclaimed the other. It so happened that the dogs were scattered about everywhere barking. The calves rose to their feet; they saw some one walking hitherward. Not at all did they fail to make out every part of him, and exposed to view were his entrails. (They saw) him point the gun at them, whereupon they were then shot at. Now, there were two human beings. When they all had been shot at, then in that place were they all killed. Then for tracks did the man seek. In truth, one (he found) trailing off the other way. Before (following it up), he turned about, he went to where his father was. "Therefore you had better look after the dressing of these moose." Then away he started, following after the lone moose. On his way went the man, keeping over on the trail of the moose. Now, two (in number) were his dogs, and so upon them he depended. Now, with an easy gait at first did the moose move along; and later, while on his way he went traveling, (he) suddenly (heard the dogs) as they came barking. And then with great speed went the moose. And as he was on the point of slowing up, already again was he being overtaken. In lively manner was he barked at, whereupon truly as fast as he could go he went. For a little while he got out of sound (of the dogs' barking). Now, by this time he was very much out of wind, but yet of a truth he tried running. It was impossible for him to outstrip the dogs, for by this time he was very much out of strength. And by and by, "$Kan'kan$, $kan'kan$, $kan'kan$!" he heard. Then it was that he became mindful of what he had been told by his father, who had tried in vain to dissuade him from going. Thereupon truly he tried with all his might to go, but he was not at all able to outrun the dogs. At the same time he cried as he went walking along. And once, when unable to go, he saw back on his trail a human being walking hitherward, he came saying: "Well, Moose, does it seem that you have walked far enough?"

"Not at all have I yet walked enough."

Then at yonder place (the man) leaned his gun; an axe he drew (from his belt), a stick he cut. After cutting the stick, he came over to where (the Moose) was; a hard blow on the back was dealt the

13

14

15

Moose. He was addressed by (the man) saying: "Go on! not yet have you walked enough."

Poor fellow! In spite of his efforts, he tried to go, but he was not   16
even able to take a step.

Next (the man) drew a knife from his scabbard. Then he went up   17
to (the Moose); taking him by the nose, he cut it off. After hanging the
nose to his belt, he turned the head (of the Moose) about, and said to
him: "Yonder is where you shall be eaten by your fellow-dogs."
Forthwith then away went the man.

Accordingly then, in truth, he was much disturbed in mind, fear-   18
ing lest he might bleed to death. Then he became mindful of what
in vain he had been told by his father; and of his mother he also
thought.

And now, after those were disposed of that had been killed at   19
yonder place, then back again to life they came. Forthwith they fixed
up the place where they lived. It was now growing dark. And after a
while there came some one to invite them, whereupon all that were
there were asked to come. They departed on their way to where the
people dwelt. After they had gone inside, then they smoked. They also
were fed, and they were given raiment. Truly happy were they. The
old woman was given ear-rings and leggings. And all the various
things that people have they were given. And the boy was given a
cedar-bark pouch to keep powder in. Ever so pleased was the boy
after putting over his shoulder the powder-pouch.

And in a while back home they went; after they were come at   20
home, gone was their youth. In a while it began to grow dark, but they
would not go to sleep. And by and by in the night the old woman
heard the sound of somebody out of doors coming softly up (and)
stopping by the door. "That may be my dear son," she thought. "Some
evil fate, perhaps, may have befallen my dear son." Rising to her feet,
she then went outside.

Poor thing! there he was with his hand over his nose.   21

"Ah, me! my dear son, what has been done to you?"   22

"Nothing (is left of) my nose."   23

When the old woman saw him, very bitterly she wept. After she   24
had finished weeping, she took up some earth that was very black;
when she rubbed (it over) his nose, then back as it used to look
became his nose. When within entered the old woman, she spoke to
her son, saying: "Come inside!" Of a truth, the man accordingly
entered.

Then spoke the old woman, saying: "Verily, with m
casin will I strike at a human being if he purposes to shoc.

Thereupon spoke the old man, saying: "Hush! speak not thus oɪ
the people, for they are truly endowed with manitou power."

THE LAKOTA'S RELATIVES

155-207

The traditional Lakota lived in open country. There is the sky, the earth, and, on the horizon, the four quarters—north, south, east, and west. Mirroring the expansive landscape of the Great Plains, the Lakota philosophy of nature was simple and beautiful. The sky above is like a father; the earth beneath is like a mother. And therefore all living things—the plants and trees, the animals and the birds—are like relatives to one another. Each of the cardinal directions is a "power" that has characteristics peculiar to itself. There is an obvious environmental ethic in this representation of nature. One lives with one's relatives in a community of love and generosity as well as mutual respect and obligation.

Black Elk Speaks is the story of one of the world's foremost religious geniuses related by a masterly writer of English prose. The synergy of this collaboration resulted in a book that ranks among the great classics of American literature. *Lame Deer: Seeker of Visions* belongs to the same literary genre, but it is set in the mid-twentieth century. *Lame Deer* helps to deepen our understanding of the Lakota worldview against the background of modern Western civilization.

Like the Ojibwa worldview, the Lakota exhibits some remarkable similarities to certain morally relevant aspects of our current understanding of the natural environment. A fundamental implication of Darwin's evolutionary epic is that we human beings are in fact literally kin to all other living things. They are our cousins in geological measures of time and relationship. And according to Leopold, once again, "This new knowledge should have given us a sense of kinship with fellow-creatures; a wish to live and let live." Black Elk (1863–1950) and Lame Deer (1903–1984) both wax eloquently on the Indian symbol of the circle. Contemporary ecology confirms Black Elk's claim that "the Power of the World always works in circles." We are now aware of the great natural cycles of water, carbon, oxygen, and so on. And some contemporary environmental philosophers argue that in order to live in harmony with nature we must realign our own, presently linear, human economy with the cyclical patterns of nature's economy and recycle our raw materials. Lame Deer even expresses an insight at the leading edge of contemporary theoretical ecology. The various natural circles that he mentions are hierarchically embedded within one another; they are "circles within circles." That is, the larger cycles of nature (such as global climate change, from cooler to warmer and back again) turn over more slowly and act as constants for the smaller ones (such as the annual revolution of the seasons).

Wasichu is a Lakota term for persons of European extraction, but does not refer to color. It literally means "countless many" and thus laconically comments on the overpopulation which led to the European colonization of North America. A *Yuwipi* man is a certain type of Lakota medicine man. The Lakota term *Wakan Tanka* may be translated "Great Spirit." While the Lakota recognize six major powers or spirits, both Black Elk and Lame Deer affirm that these are all parts or aspects of the one Great Spirit. In technical theological terms, the Lakota worldview is pantheistic.

Black Elk Speaks

JOHN G. NEIHARDT

My friend, I am going to tell you the story of my life, as you wish; and if it were only the story of my life I think I would not tell it; for what is one man that he should make much of his winters, even when they bend him like a heavy snow? So many other men have lived and shall live that story, to be grass upon the hills.   1

It is the story of all life that is holy and is good to tell, and of us two-leggeds sharing in it with the four-leggeds and the wings of the air and all green things; for these are children of one mother and their father is one Spirit. . . .   2

So I know that it is a good thing I am going to do; and because no good thing can be done by any man alone, I will first make an offer-   3 ing and send a voice to the Spirit of the World, that it may help me to be true. See, I fill this sacred pipe with the bark of the red willow; but before we smoke it, you must see how it is made and what it means. These four ribbons hanging here on the stem are the four quarters of the universe. The black one is for the west where the thunder beings live to send us rain; the white one for the north, whence comes the great white cleansing wind; the red one for the east, whence springs the light and where the morning star lives to give men wisdom; the yellow for the south, whence come the summer and the power to grow.

But these four spirits are only one Spirit after all, and this eagle   4 feather here is for that One, which is like a father, and also it is for the thoughts of men that should rise high as eagles do. Is not the sky a father and the earth a mother, and are not all living things with feet or wings or roots their children? And this hide upon the mouthpiece here, which should be bison hide, is for the earth, from whence we came and at whose breast we suck as babies all our lives, along with all the animals and birds and trees and grasses. And because it means all this, and more than any man can understand, the pipe is holy. . . .

Now I light the pipe, and after I have offered it to the powers that   5 are one Power, and sent forth a voice to them, we shall smoke together. Offering the mouthpiece first of all to the One above—so—I send a voice:

Hey hey! hey hey! hey hey! hey hey!   6

Grandfather, Great Spirit, you have been always, and before you   7 no one has been. There is no other one to pray to but you. You yourself, everything that you see, everything has been made by you. The star nations all over the universe you have finished. The four quarters of the earth you have finished. The day, and in that day, everything you have finished. Grandfather, Great Spirit, lean close to the earth that you may hear the voice I send. You towards where the sun goes down, behold me; Thunder Beings, behold me! You where the White Giant lives in power, behold me! You where the sun shines continually, whence come the day-break star and the day, behold me! You where the summer lives, behold me! You in the depths of the heavens, an eagle of power, behold! And you, Mother Earth, the only Mother, you who have shown mercy to your children!

Hear me, four quarters of the world—a relative I am! Give me the   8 strength to walk the soft earth, a relative to all that is! Give me the eyes to see and the strength to understand, that I may be like you. With your power only can I face the winds.

Great Spirit, Great Spirit, my Grandfather, all over the earth the   9
faces of living things are all alike. With tenderness have these come up out of the ground. Look upon these faces of children without number and with children in their arms, that they may face the winds and walk the good road to the day of quiet.

This is my prayer; hear me! The voice I have sent is weak, yet   10
with earnestness I have sent it. Hear me!

It is finished. Hetchetu aloh!   11

Now, my friend, let us smoke together so that there may be only   12
good between us. . . .

A long time ago my father told me what his father told him, that   13
there was once a Lakota holy man, called Drinks Water, who dreamed what was to be; and this was long before the coming of the Wasichus. He dreamed that the four-leggeds were going back into the earth and that a strange race had woven a spider's web all around the Lakotas. And he said: "When this happens, you shall live in square gray houses, in a barren land, and beside those square gray houses you shall starve." They say he went back to Mother Earth soon after he saw this vision, and it was sorrow that killed him. You can look about you now and see that he meant these dirt-roofed houses we are living in, and that all the rest was true. Sometimes dreams are wiser than waking. . . .

After the heyoka ceremony, I came to live here where I am now   14
between Wounded Knee Creek and Grass Creek. Others came too, and we made these little gray houses of logs that you see, and they are square. It is a bad way to live, for there can be no power in a square.

You have noticed that everything an Indian does is in a circle, and   15
that is because the Power of the World always works in circles, and everything tries to be round. In the old days when we were a strong and happy people, all our power came to us from the sacred hoop of the nation, and so long as the hoop was unbroken, the people flourished. The flowering tree was the living center of the hoop, and the circle of the four quarters nourished it. The east gave peace and light, the south gave warmth, the west gave rain, and the north with its cold and mighty wind gave strength and endurance. This knowledge came to us from the outer world with our religion. Everything the Power of the World does is done in a circle. The sky is round, and I have heard that the earth is round like a ball, and so are all the stars. The wind, in

its greatest power, whirls. Birds make their nests in circles, for theirs is the same religion as ours. The sun comes forth and goes down again in a circle. The moon does the same, and both are round. Even the seasons form a great circle in their changing, and always come back again to where they were. The life of a man is a circle from childhood to childhood, and so it is in everything where power moves. Our tepees were round like the nests of birds, and these were always set in a circle, the nation's hoop, a nest of many nests, where the Great Spirit meant for us to hatch our children.

But the Wasichus have put us in these square boxes. Our power is gone and we are dying, for the power is not in us any more. You can look at our boys and see how it is with us. When we were living by the power of the circle in the way we should, boys were men at twelve or thirteen years of age. But now it takes them very much longer to mature. . . . 16

You want to know why we always go from left to right like that. I can tell you something of the reason, but not all. Think of this: Is not the south the source of life, and does not the flowering stick truly come from there? And does not man advance from there toward the setting sun of his life? Then does he not approach the colder north where the white hairs are? And does he not then arrive, if he lives, at the source of light and understanding, which is the east? Then does he not return to where he began, to his second childhood, there to give back his life to all life, and his flesh to the earth whence it came? The more you think about this, the more meaning you will see in it. 17

Lame Deer: Seeker of Visions

BY JOHN (FIRE) LAME DEER AND RICHARD ERDOES

What do you see here, my friend? Just an ordinary old cooking pot, black with soot and full of dents. 1

It is standing on the fire on top of that old wood stove, and the water bubbles and moves the lid as the white steam rises to the ceil- 2

John (Fire) Lame Deer and Richard Erdoes. *Lame Deer: Seeker of Visions.* New York: Pocket Books, 1976, pp. 96–97, 100–101, 145–146, 153.

ing. Inside the pot is boiling water, chunks of meat with bone and fat, plenty of potatoes.

It doesn't seem to have a message, that old pot, and I guess you   3
don't give it a thought. Except the soup smells good and reminds you that you are hungry. Maybe you are worried that this is dog stew. Well, don't worry. It's just beef—no fat puppy for a special ceremony. It's just an ordinary, everyday meal.

But I'm an Indian. I think about ordinary, common things like this   4
pot. The bubbling water comes from the rain cloud. It represents the sky. The fire comes from the sun which warms us all—men, animals, trees. The meat stands for the four-legged creatures, our animal brothers, who gave of themselves so that we should live. The steam is living breath. It was water; now it goes up to the sky, becomes a cloud again. These things are sacred. Looking at that pot full of good soup, I am thinking how, in this simple manner, Wakan Tanka takes care of me. We Sioux spend a lot of time thinking about everyday things, which in our mind are mixed up with the spiritual. We see in the world around us many symbols that teach us the meaning of life. We have a saying that the white man sees so little, he must see with only one eye. We see a lot that you no longer notice. You could notice if you wanted to, but you are usually too busy. We Indians live in a world of symbols and images where the spiritual and the commonplace are one. To you symbols are just words, spoken or written in a book. To us they are part of nature, part of ourselves—the earth, the sun, the wind and the rain, stones, trees, animals, even little insects like ants and grasshoppers. We try to understand them not with the head but with the heart, and we need no more than a hint to give us the meaning. . . .

You know, it always makes me laugh when I hear young white   5
kids speak of some people as "squares" or "straights"—old people, hardened in their ways, in their minds, in their hearts. They don't even have to be old. You can be an "old square" at eighteen. Anyway, calling these people "squares"—an Indian could have thought it up. To our way of thinking the Indians' symbol is the circle, the hoop. Nature wants things to be round. The bodies of human beings and animals have no corners. With us the circle stands for the togetherness of people who sit with one another around the campfire, relatives and friends united in peace while the pipe passes from hand to hand. The camp in which every tipi had its place was also a ring. The tipi was a

ring in which people sat in a circle and all the families in the village were in turn circles within a larger circle, part of the larger hoop which was the seven campfires of the Sioux, representing one nation. The nation was only a part of the universe, in itself circular and made of the earth, which is round, of the sun, which is round, of the stars, which are round. The moon, the horizon, the rainbow—circles within circles within circles, with no beginning and no end.

To us this is beautiful and fitting, symbol and reality at the same time, expressing the harmony of life and nature. Our circle is timeless, flowing; it is new life emerging from death—life winning out over death. 6

The white man's symbol is the square. Square is his house, his office buildings with walls that separate people from one another. Square is the door which keeps strangers out, the dollar bill, the jail. Square are the white man's gadgets—boxes, boxes, boxes and more boxes—TV sets, radios, washing machines, computers, cars. These all have corners and sharp edges—points in time, white man's time, with appointments, time clocks and rush hours—that's what the corners mean to me. You become a prisoner inside all these boxes. 7

More and more young white people want to stop being "straight" and "square" and try to become round, join our circle. That is good. . . . 8

Every day in my life I see symbols in the shape of certain roots or branches. I read messages in the stones. I pay special attention to them, because I am a Yuwipi man and that is my work. But I am not the only one. Many Indians do this. 9

Inyan—the rocks—are holy. Every man needs a stone to help him. There are two kinds of pebbles that make good medicine. One is white like ice. The other is like ordinary stone, but it makes you pick it up and recognize it by its special shape. You ask stones for aid to find things which are lost or missing. Stones can give warning of an enemy, of approaching misfortune. The winds are symbolized by a raven and a small black stone the size of an egg. . . . 10

Nothing is so small and unimportant but it has a spirit given to it by Wakan Tanka. Tunkan is what you might call a stone god, but he is also part of the Great Spirit. The gods are separate beings, but they are all united in Wakan Tanka. It is hard to understand—something like the Holy Trinity. You can't explain it except by going back to the "circles within circles" idea, the spirit splitting itself up into stones, trees, tiny insects even, making them all *wakan* by his ever-presence. And in 11 turn all these myriad of things which make up the universe flowing back to their source, united in the one Grandfather Spirit. . . .

The more I think about it, the more I believe that the only real medicine man is the *wićaśa wakan*—the holy man. Such a one can cure, prophesy, talk to the herbs, command the stones, conduct the sun dance or even change the weather, but all this is of no great importance to him. These are merely stages he has passed through. The *wićaśa wakan* has gone beyond all this. He has the *wakanya wowanyanke*—the great vision. 12

The *wićaśa wakan* wants to be by himself. He wants to be away from the crowd, from everyday matters. He likes to meditate, leaning against a tree or rock, feeling the earth move beneath him, feeling the weight of that big flaming sky upon him. That way he can figure things out. Closing his eyes, he sees many things clearly. What you see with your eyes shut is what counts. 13

The *wićaśa wakan* loves the silence, wrapping it around himself like a blanket—a loud silence with a voice like thunder which tells him of many things. Such a man likes to be in a place where there is no sound but the humming of insects. He sits facing the west, asking for help. He talks to the plants and they answer him. He listens to the voices of the *wama kaśkan*—all those who move upon the earth, the animals. He is as one with them. From all living beings something flows into him all the time, and something flows from him. I don't know where or what, but it's there. I know. . . . 14

In order to be a medicine man one should find the visions there, in nature. To the west a man has the power from the buffalo. From the north he gets the power from the thunder-beings. From the east his strength comes from the spirit horse and the elk. From the south he has the ghost power. From above, from the sky, he will receive the wisdom of the great eagle. From beneath, from the earth, he will receive the mother's food. This is the way to become a *wićaśa wakan*, to learn the secret language, to speak about sacred things, to work with the stones and herbs, to use the pipe. 15

Much power comes from the animals, and most medicine men have their special animal which they saw in their first vision. One never kills or harms this animal. Medicine men can be buffalo, eagle, elk or bear dreamers. Of all the four-legged and winged creatures a medicine man could receive a vision from, the bear is foremost. The bear is the wisest of animals as far as medicines are concerned. If a 16

man dreams of this animal he could become a great heale
is the only animal that one can see in a dream acting like
man, giving herbs to people. It digs up certain healing roots with its
claws. Often it will show a man in a vision which medicines to use.

207-217

FROM AN INDIAN LAND AESTHETIC TO A LAND ETHIC

N. Scott Momaday takes us back in imagination to a time shortly
after the arrival of the ancestors of American Indians in the Western
Hemisphere across the Bering land bridge from northwest Asia.
That first, original human discovery of America coincided with the
extinction of many large native American animals—the mammoth,
the mastodon, the camel, and the long-horned bison that figures in
Momaday's opening sketch, among others. No one knows for sure
what role the immigrant Siberian big game hunters played in this
episode of mass extinction. Momaday suggests that it may have
been significant. If so, an ancient American environmental crisis
could have precipitated an eventual American Indian environmental ethic.

How so? Momaday argues that if the ancient Siberian immi-
grants did not have a moral relationship with their new landscape,
they could certainly perceive its beauty. After they had hunted out
the big game (if indeed they did), that aesthetic perception of nature
evolved into an ethical and religious conception. Such a view was
adaptive. It helped keep the eventual American Indian peoples from
overexploiting their natural resources as their ancestors may have
done. He also argues that the eventual American Indian aesthetic-
moral-religious relationship with nature grows out of the investment of many generations in a particular landscape. Momaday's
word for this relationship is "appropriate," which as an adjective
means "right" or "correct," but as a verb means "to take possession." The appropriation of a natural environment implies appropriate behavior in respect to it, he suggests, a lesson that contemporary Euro-American culture is only now just beginning to learn.
Perhaps traditional American Indian environmental philosophy
may help teach it to us.

A First American Views His Land

N. Scott Momaday

First Man
behold:
the earth
glitters
with leaves;
the sky
glistens
with rain.
Pollen
is borne
on winds
that low
and lean
upon
mountains.
Cedars
blacken
the slopes—
and pines.

One hundred centuries ago. There is a wide, irregular landscape in   1
what is now northern New Mexico. The sun is a dull white disk, low
in the south; it is a perfect mystery, a deity whose coming and going
are inexorable. The gray sky is curdled, and it bears very close upon
the earth. A cold wind runs along the ground, dips and spins, flaking
drift from a pond in the bottom of a ravine. Beyond the wind the
silence is acute. A man crouches in the ravine, in the darkness there,
scarcely visible. He moves not a muscle; only the wind lifts a lock of
his hair and lays it back along his neck. He wears skins and carries a
spear. These things in particular mark his human intelligence and distinguish him as the lord of the universe. And for him the universe is
especially *this* landscape; for him the landscape is an element like the
air. The vast, virgin wilderness is by and large his whole context. For
him there is no possibility of existence elsewhere.

N. Scott Momaday. "A First American Views His Land." *National Geographic*, July
1976.

Directly there is a blowing, a rumble of breath deeper than the   2
wind, above him, where some of the hard clay of the bank is broken
off and the clouds roll down into the water. At the same time there
appears on the skyline the massive head of a long-horned bison, then
the hump, then the whole beast, huge and black on the sky, standing
to a height of seven feet at the hump, with horns that extend six feet
across the shaggy crown. For a moment it is poised there; then it lum-
bers obliquely down the bank to the pond. Still the man does not
move, though the beast is now only a few steps upwind. There is no
sign of what is about to happen; the beast meanders; the man is frozen
in repose.

Then the scene explodes. In one and the same instant the man   3
springs to his feet and bolts forward, his arm cocked and the spear
held high, and the huge animal lunges in panic, bellowing, its whole
weight thrown violently into the bank, its hooves churning and chipping earth into the air, its eyes gone wide and wild and white. There
is a moment in which its awful, frenzied motion is wasted, and it is
mired and helpless in its fear, and the man hurls the spear with his
whole strength, and the point is driven into the deep, vital flesh, and
the bison in its agony staggers and crashes down and dies.

This ancient drama of the hunt is enacted again and again in the   4
landscape. The man is preeminently a predator, the most dangerous of
all. He hunts in order to survive; his very existence is simply, square-
ly established upon that basis. But he hunts also because he can,
because he has the means; he has the ultimate weapon of his age, and
his prey is plentiful. His relationship to the land has not yet become a
moral equation.

But in time he will come to understand that there is an intimate,   5
vital link between the earth and himself, a link that implies an intricate
network of rights and responsibilities. In some unimagined future he
will understand that he has the ability to devastate and perhaps
destroy his environment. That moment will be one of extreme crisis in
his evolution.

The weapon is deadly and efficient. The hunter has taken great   6
care in its manufacture, especially in the shaping of the flint point,
which is an extraordinary thing. A larger flake has been removed from
each face, a groove that extends from the base nearly to the tip.
Several hundred pounds of pressure, expertly applied, were required
to make these grooves. The hunter then is an artisan, and he must
know how to use rudimentary tools. His skill, manifest in the manu-

facture of this artifact, is unsurpassed for its time and purpose. By means of this weapon is the Paleo-Indian hunter eminently able to exploit his environment.

Thousands of years later, about the time that Columbus begins his 7 first voyage to the New World, another man, in the region of the Great Lakes, stands in the forest shade on the edge of a sunlit brake. In a while a deer enters into the pool of light. Silently the man fits an arrow to a bow, draws aim, and shoots. The arrow zips across the distance and strikes home. The deer leaps and falls dead.

But this latter-day man, unlike his ancient predecessor, is only 8 incidentally a hunter; he is also a fisherman, a husbandman, even a physician. He fells trees and builds canoes; he grows corn, squash, and beans, and he gathers fruits and nuts; he uses hundreds of species of wild plants for food, medicine, teas, and dyes. Instead of one animal, or two or three, he hunts many, none to extinction as the Paleo-Indian may have done. He has fitted himself far more precisely into the patterns of the wilderness than did his ancient predecessor. He lives on the land; he takes his living from it; but he does not destroy it. This distinction supports the fundamental ethic that we call conservation today. In principle, if not yet in name, this man is a conservationist.

These two hunting sketches are far less important in themselves 9 than is that long distance between them, that whole possibility within the dimension of time. I believe that in that interim there grew up in the mind of man an idea of the land as sacred.

At dawn
eagles
lie and
hover
above
the plain
where light
gathers
in pools.
Grasses
shimmer
and shine.
Shadows
withdraw
and lie
away
like smoke.

"The earth is our mother. The sky is our father." This concept of   10
nature, which is at the center of the Native American world view, is
familiar to us all. But it may well be that we do not understand entirely what that concept is in its ethical and philosophical implications.

I tell my students that the American Indian has a unique invest-   11
ment in the American landscape. It is an investment that represents
perhaps thirty thousand years of habitation. That tenure has to be
worth something in itself—a great deal, in fact. The Indian has been
here a long time; he is at home here. That simple and obvious truth is
one of the most important realities of the Indian world, and it is integral in the Indian mind and spirit.

How does such a concept evolve? Where does it begin? Perhaps   12
it begins with the recognition of beauty, the realization that the physical world *is* beautiful. We don't know much about the ancient
hunter's sensibilities. It isn't likely that he had leisure in his life for the
elaboration of an aesthetic ideal. And yet the weapon he made was
beautiful as well as functional. It has been suggested that much of the
minute chipping along the edges of his weapon served no purpose but
that of aesthetic satisfaction.

A good deal more is known concerning that man of the central   13
forests. He made beautiful boxes and dishes out of elm and birch bark,
for example. His canoes were marvelous, delicate works of art. And
this aesthetic perception was a principle of the whole Indian world of
his time, as indeed it is of our time. The contemporary Native
American is a man whose strong aesthetic perceptions are clearly evident in his arts and crafts, in his religious ceremonies, and in the stories and songs of his rich oral tradition. This, in view of the pressures
that have been brought to bear upon the Indian world and the drastic
changes that have been effected in its landscape, is a blessing and an
irony.

Consider for example the Navajos of the Four Corners area. In   14
recent years an extensive coal-mining operation has mutilated some of
their most sacred land. A large power plant in that same region spews
a contamination into the sky that is visible for many miles. And yet, as
much as any people of whom I have heard, the Navajos perceive and
celebrate the beauty of the physical world.

There is a Navajo ceremonial song that celebrates the sounds that   15
are made in the natural world, the particular voices that beautify the
earth:

Voice above,

Voice of thunder,
Speak from the
dark of clouds;
Voice below,
Grasshopper voice,
Speak from the
green of plants;
So may the earth
be beautiful.

There is in the motion and meaning of this song a comprehension   16
of the world that is peculiarly native. I believe, that is integral in the
Native American mentality. Consider: The singer stands at the center
of the natural world, at the source of its sound, of its motion, of its
life. Nothing of that world is inaccessible to him or lost upon him. His
song is filled with reverence, with wonder and delight, and with confidence as well. He knows something about himself and about the
things around him—and he knows that he knows. I am interested in
what he sees and hears; I am interested in the range and force of his
perception. Our immediate impression may be that his perception is
narrow and deep—vertical. After all, "voice above . . . voice below,"
he sings. But is it vertical only? At each level of his expression there is
an extension of his awareness across the whole landscape. The voice
above is the voice of thunder, and thunder rolls. Moreover, it issues
from the impalpable dark clouds and runs upon their horizontal
range. It is a sound that integrates the whole of the atmosphere. And
even so, the voice below, that of the grasshopper, issues from the
broad plain and multiplicity of plants. And of course the singer is
mindful of much more than thunder and insects; we are given in his
song the wide angle of his vision and his hearing—and we are given
the testimony of his dignity, his trust, and his deep belief.

This comprehension of the earth and air is surely a matter of   17
morality, for it brings into account not only man's instinctive reaction
to his environment but the full realization of his humanity as well, the
achievement of his intellectual and spiritual development as an individual and as a race.

In my own experience I have seen numerous examples of this   18
regard for nature. My grandfather Mammedaty was a farmer in his
mature years; his grandfather was a buffalo hunter. It was not easy for
Mammedaty to be a farmer; he was a Kiowa, and the Kiowas never
had an agrarian tradition. Yet he had to make his living, and the old,

beloved life of roaming the plains and hunting the buffalo was gone forever. Even so, as much as any man before him, he fitted his mind and will and spirit to the land; there was nothing else. He could not have conceived of living apart from the land.

In *The Way to Rainy Mountain* I set down a small narrative that   19
belongs in the oral tradition of my family. It indicates something essential about the Native American attitude toward the land:

"East of my grandmother's house, south of the pecan grove, there   20
is buried a woman in a beautiful dress. Mammedaty used to know where she is buried, but now no one knows. If you stand on the front porch of the house and look eastward towards Carnegie, you know that the woman is buried somewhere within the range of your vision. But her grave is unmarked. She was buried in a cabinet, and she wore a beautiful dress. How beautiful it was! It was one of those fine buckskin dresses, and it was decorated with elk's teeth and beadwork. That dress is still there, under the ground."

It seems to me that this statement is primarily a declaration of love   21
for the land, in which the several elements—the woman, the dress, and this plain—are at last become one reality, one expression of the beautiful in nature. Moreover, it seems to me a peculiarly Native American expression in this sense: that the concentration of things that are explicitly remembered—the general landscape, the simple, almost abstract nature of the burial, above all the beautiful dress, which is wholly singular in kind (as well as in its function within the narrative)—is especially Indian in character. The things that are *not* explicitly remembered—the woman's name, the exact location of her grave—are the things that matter least in the special view of the story-teller. What matters here is the translation of the woman into the landscape, a translation particularly signified by means of the beautiful and distinctive dress, an *Indian* dress.

When I was a boy, I lived for several years at Jemez Pueblo, New   22
Mexico. The Pueblo Indians are perhaps more obviously invested in the land than are other people. Their whole life is predicated upon a thorough perception of the physical world and its myriad aspects. When I first went there to live, the cacique, or chief, of the Pueblos was a venerable old man with long, gray hair and bright, deep-set eyes. He was entirely dignified and imposing—and rather formidable in the eyes of a boy. He excited my imagination a good deal. I was told that this old man kept the calendar of the tribe, that each morning he stood on a certain spot of ground near the center of the town

and watched to see where the sun appeared on the skyline. By means of this solar calendar did he know and announce to his people when it was time to plant, to harvest, to perform this or that ceremony. This image of him in my mind's eye—the old man gazing each morning after the ranging sun—came to represent for me the epitome of that real harmony between man and the land that signifies the Indian world.

One day when I was riding my horse along the Jemez River, I   23
looked up to see a long caravan of wagons and people on horseback and on foot. Men, women, and children were crossing the river ahead of me, moving out to the west, where most of the cultivated fields were, the farmland of the town. It was a wonderful sight to see, this long procession, and I was immediately deeply curious. I wanted to investigate, but it was not in me to do so at once, for that racial reserve, that sense of propriety that is deep-seated in Native American culture, stayed me, held me up. Then I saw someone coming toward me on horseback, galloping. It was a friend of mine, a boy of my own age. "Come on," he said. "Come with us." "Where are you going?" I asked casually. But he would not tell me. He simply laughed and urged me to come along, and of course I was very glad to do so. It was a bright spring morning, and I had a good horse under me, and the prospect of adventure was delicious. We moved far out across the eroded plain to the farthest fields at the foot of a great red mesa, and there we planted two large fields of corn. And afterward, on the edge of the fields, we sat on blankets and ate a feast in the shade of a cottonwood grove. Later I learned it was the cacique's fields we planted. And this is an ancient tradition at Jemez. The people of the town plant and tend and harvest the cacique's fields, and in the winter the hunters give to him a portion of the meat that they bring home from the mountains. It is as if the cacique is himself the translation of man, every man, into the landscape.

I have not forgotten that day, nor shall I forget it. I remember the   24
warm earth of the fields, the smooth texture of seeds in my hands, and the brown water moving slowly and irresistibly among the rows. Above all I remember the spirit in which the procession was made, the work was done, and the feasting was enjoyed. It was a spirit of communion, of the life of each man in relation to the life of the planet and of the infinite distance and silence in which it moves. We made, in concert, an appropriate expression of that spirit.

One afternoon an old Kiowa woman talked to me, telling me of   25 the place in Oklahoma in which she had lived for a hundred years. It was the place in which my grandparents, too, lived; and it is the place where I was born. And she told me of a time even further back, when the Kiowas came down from the north and centered their culture in the red earth of the southern plains. She told wonderful stories, and as I listened, I began to feel more and more sure that her voice proceeded from the land itself. I asked her many things concerning the Kiowas, for I wanted to understand all that I could of my heritage. I told the old woman that I had come there to learn from her and from people like her, those in whom the old ways were preserved. And she said simply: "It is good that you have come here." I believe that her word "good" meant many things; for one thing it meant *right,* or *appropriate.* And indeed it was appropriate that she should speak of the land. She was eminently qualified to do so. She had a great reverence for the land, and an ancient perception of it, a perception that is acquired only in the course of many generations.

It is this notion of the appropriate, along with that of the beautiful, 26 that forms the Native American perspective on the land. In a sense these considerations are indivisible; Native American oral tradition is rich with songs and tales that celebrate natural beauty, the beauty of the natural world. What is more appropriate to our world than that which is beautiful?

> At noon
> turtles
> enter
> slowly
> into
> the warm
> dark loam.
> Bees hold
> the swarm.
> Meadows
> recede
> through planes
> of heat
> and pure
> distance.

Very old in the Native American world view is the conviction that 27 the earth is vital, that there is a spiritual dimension to it, a dimension in which man rightly exists. It follows logically that there are ethical imperatives in this matter. I think: Inasmuch as I am in the land, it is appropriate that I should affirm myself in the spirit of the land. I shall celebrate my life in the world and the world in my life. In the natural order man invests himself in the landscape and at the same time incorporates the landscape into his own most fundamental experience. This trust is sacred.

The process of investment and appropriation is, I believe, preeminently a function of the imagination. It is accomplished by means of an act of the imagination that is especially ethical in kind. We are what we imagine ourselves to be. The Native American is someone who thinks of himself, imagines himself in a particular way. By virtue of his experience his idea of himself comprehends his relationship to the land.   28

And the quality of this imagining is determined as well by racial and cultural experience. The Native American's attitudes toward this landscape have been formulated over a long period of time, a span that reaches back to the end of the Ice Age. The land, *this* land, is secure in his racial memory.   29

In our society as a whole we conceive of the land in terms of ownership and use. It is a lifeless medium of exchange; it has for most of us, I suspect, no more spirituality than has an automobile, say, or a refrigerator. And our laws confirm us in this view, for we can buy and sell the land, we can exclude each other from it, and in the context of ownership we can use it as we will. Ownership implies use, and use implies consumption.   30

But this way of thinking of the land is alien to the Indian. His cultural intelligence is opposed to these concepts; indeed, for him they are all but inconceivable quantities. This fundamental distinction is easier to understand with respect to ownership than to use, perhaps. For obviously the Indian does use, and has always used, the land and the available resources in it. The point is that *use* does not indicate in any real way his idea of the land. "Use" is neither his word nor his idea. As an Indian I think: "You say that I *use* the land, and I reply, yes, it is true; but it is not the first truth. The first truth is that I *love* the land; I see that it is beautiful; I delight in it; I am alive in it."   31

In the long course of his journey from Asia and in the realization of himself in the New World, the Indian has assumed a deep ethical regard for the earth and sky, a reverence for the natural world that is antipodal to that strange tenet of modern civilization that seemingly   32 has it that man must destroy his environment. It is this ancient ethic of the Native American that must shape our efforts to preserve the earth and the life upon and within it.

> At dusk
> the gray
> foxes
> stiffen
> in cold;
> blackbirds
> are fixed
> in white
> branches.
> Rivers
> follow
> the moon,
> the long
> white track
> of the
> full moon.

GLOSSARY

cacique: A Pueblo Indian chief.

ecology: A subdiscipline of biology devoted to the study of relationships between organisms and their environments.

environmental ethic: Moral attitudes and values toward the natural environment.

inyan: Lakota word meaning "stones" or "rocks."

Leopold land ethic: The environmental ethic sketched by Aldo Leopold in *A Sand County Almanac.*

manitou: Ojibwa word meaning (roughly) "spirit."

totem: The animal that a clan or tribe identifies with.

Wakan Tanka: Lakota word usually translated as "Great Spirit;" *wakan* = holy, sacred; *tanka* = big, great.

wama kaskan: Lakota word meaning "moving beings," i.e., animals.

wicasa wakan: Lakota word meaning "holy man" or "shaman."

worldview: A group of people's shared conceptual framework and conscious beliefs that give order and structure to common human experience.

Yuwipi man: A Lakota medicine man or shaman who conducts the *Yuwipi* ceremony.

FURTHER READINGS

JOSEPH E. BROWN. *The Sacred Pipe: Black Elk's Account of the Seven Rights of the Oglala Sioux.* Norman: University of Oklahoma Press, 1953.

A. IRVING HALLOWELL. *Culture and Experience.* Philadelphia: University of Pennsylvania Press, 1955.

DONALD E. HUGHES. *American Indian Ecology.* El Paso: Texas Western Press, 1983.

CALVIN MARTIN. *Keepers of the Game: Indian-Animal Relationships and the Fur Trade.* Berkeley: University of California Press, 1978.

JOHN G. NEIHARDT. *When the Tree Flowered: An Authentic Tale of the Old Sioux World.* New York: Macmillan, 1951.

CHRISTOPHER VECSEY AND ROBERT W. VENABLES, eds. *American Indian Environments: Ecological Issues in Native American History.* Syracuse: Syracuse University Press, 1980.

STUDY QUESTIONS

1. If American Indians really had an environmental ethic and respected other forms of life, how could they have hunted and killed animals for food?
2. What are the similarities and what are the differences between the modern scientific and the Ojibwa or Lakota portraits of nature?
3. How is a Lakota "holy man" similar to and different from a holy man in other religious traditions, such as Christianity, Buddhism, or Hinduism?
4. Can the environmental attitudes and values of traditional American Indians be useful to us today as we confront the environmental crisis?

CHAPTER 7

Latin American Philosophy

JORGE VALADEZ

Since the cultures of Latin America are the union of Spanish and indigenous cultures, it is not possible to understand the Latin American *Lebenswelt* (life world) without taking indigenous pre-Columbian cultural perspectives into account. Some of the contemporary cultures of Latin America have internalized certain views of these indigenous cultures, such as their views on death. As Nobel Prize recipient Octavio Paz explains in one of the following excerpts, we can discern certain pre-Columbian views of death in the attitudes of contemporary Mexicans. Also, some of these indigenous cultures developed intellectual traditions in which different views of truth and the nature of the universe were proposed and debated. In one of the following excerpts, ethnophilosopher Miguel León-Portilla argues that in the Aztec culture the *tlamatinime* (Aztec wise men) developed epistemological doctrines according to which truth was attainable not through reason but through the process of artistic inspiration and expression.

Modern philosophy in Latin America has been affected to a far greater degree by sociopolitical and cultural factors than philosophy in Europe and the United States. The legacy of European colonialism and, at a later time, U.S. imperialism, affected Latin American thought and culture in indelible ways. During the colonial period scholasticism, a philosophical and theological tradition based on the works of Aristotle and his commentators, was the dominant philosophical perspective in most of Latin America. To some extent, scholasticism was used as an elaborate philosophical justification for the Christian ideology that was imposed by the Spanish on the people of Latin America.

After the countries of Latin America attained their independence, positivism emerged as the most influential philosophical movement. The great advances in the natural sciences that occurred in the middle of the nineteenth century inspired the development of positivism, which is based on the scientific observation of physical phenomena and the application of reason in resolving social and political problems. Positivists believed that social and political interactions were governed by universal scientific laws of human behavior, and that by discovering these laws it would be possible to create a utopian society in which the problems facing society would be resolved. Positivism seemed an attractive alternative to Latin American intellectuals because it provided a way to raise the socially and politically underdeveloped countries of Latin America to a new level of social and scientific enlightenment.

However, although positivism was adopted as the official government policy in several countries in Latin America, it failed to live up to expectations. Positivism, as it was interpreted and applied in Latin America, was essentially an elitist philosophy that placed great emphasis on political order and on governance by the members of the privileged classes. It was sometimes used, as in the regime of Mexican dictator Porfirio Diaz, as the official state philosophy and as a rationale for the political status quo. Positivism, like scholasticism before it, was a philosophical perspective that had been imported from Europe and that failed to meet the social, intellectual, and political needs of Latin America.

The initial stage in the liberation and self-affirmation of Latin American philosophers was the critique and rejection of positivism, which occurred in the early 1900s. Philosophers like Alejandro Korn of Argentina and José Vasconcelos of Mexico criticized the excessive scientific rationalism of positivism and articulated new directions in Latin American thought. In the latter half of the twentieth century Latin American philosophers expressed their philosophical autonomy by addressing problems and questions of particular concern to Latin Americans. The selections that follow are from this period onward, since it is at this point that Latin American philosophers started to address philosophical questions from a uniquely Latin American standpoint. One of these questions concerned the character of Latin American philosophical identity: Was there, and could there be, such a thing as a Latin American philosophy? Some philosophers answered in the negative and argued that philosophy is by its very nature universal and transcultural. Others, like

Leopoldo Zea, argued that since philosophy is an activity grounded in concrete cultural and historical contexts, one could correctly characterize as Latin American any philosophy arising from the particular existential circumstances facing Latin Americans. In one of the selections that follow, Peruvian author Augusto Salazar Bondy addresses and expands on this issue, which has been of major concern to Latin American philosophers.

The effort to clarify the relation between philosophical reflection and the Latin American cultural experience was one of the factors that led to an examination of the intellectual, economic, and political dependency status that Latin America has had *vis-à-vis* Europe and the United States. An increased awareness of the historical exploitation of Latin America by the industrial powers of the North gave rise in the 1960s and 1970s to two similar intellectual traditions: the theology of liberation and the philosophy of liberation. These doctrines sought to articulate, respectively, theological and philosophical positions from the perspective of the poor and oppressed people of Latin America. Of these two intellectual movements, the theology of liberation has had the most impact in Latin America and the most influence on a worldwide scale. The philosophy of liberation and the theology of liberation are perhaps the most prominent examples of the attempt by Latin American thinkers to break away from European and North American theoretical influences and see the world from the perspective of the marginalized people of Latin America. In the final excerpt in this chapter, Gustavo Gutierrez, one of the seminal figures in the theology of liberation, outlines some of the central themes of this perspective.

Even though feminist thought has not played a prominent role in the philosophical perspectives of Latin America, in recent years there has been an increased interest in women's issues. The seventeenth-century Mexican nun Sor Juana Inez de la Cruz is historically the most important precursor of Latin American feminist thought. She was perhaps the first Latin American intellectual who was concerned with the issue of the domination of women. Since 1981 women throughout Latin America have met every two years at the Encuentro Feminista Latinoamericano y del Caribe (Feminist Encounter of Latin America and the Caribbean) to address issues of importance to women. Works such as Isabel Larguia's *Towards a Scientific Conception of the Emancipation of Women*, which appeared in 1983, attempt to develop comprehensive feminist philosophical perspectives. One of the most distinctive feminist views developing in Latin America seeks the equality of women in the public sphere while maintaining their connection with their families and communities. Perhaps this movement is an expression of the efforts of Latin American women to integrate the feminist search for equality with their own culturally specific standpoint, which values greatly the role of the family and the community in an individual's life.

INTEGRATING LIFE AND DEATH

Nobel laureate Octavio Paz is the quintessential Latin American *pensador* (thinker). For over forty years Paz has been a prolific poet, essayist, philosopher, and social critic. He has also been passionately involved with Mexico's political life and has even served as his country's ambassador to India. A man of strong humanist convictions, he resigned his post as ambassador to protest the massacre of hundreds of unarmed dissident students by Mexican troops shortly before the 1968 Olympics. He has been harshly critical of Marxism and leftist politics in Latin America and, unlike other prominent Latin American intellectuals, has defended democracy and free enterprise. However, Paz is far from being a conservative ideologue; he believes that the demise of communism as a viable ideology has made the role of intellectuals as social critics all the more important.

In the early phase of his development as a writer Paz was greatly influenced by surrealism. In later years he has explored the possibility of grounding meaning, in the face of existential solitude, on artistic creativity and eroticism. Among the most important of his thirty books are the following: *The Labyrinth of Solitude, Sunstone, Alternating Current, Conjunctions and Disjunctions, The Collected Poems of Octavio Paz, 1957–87,* and *Sor Juana: Or, The Traps of Faith.* In the selection that follows, taken from *The Labyrinth of Solitude,* Paz discusses how the Mexican thinks about, and deals with, death. Paz makes interesting connections between pre-Columbian perceptions of death and those of the contemporary Mexican. He also compares the European's tendency to avoid confronting the reality of death with the Mexican's embracing of it, particularly during the national observance of la Dia de los Muertos ("Day of the Dead"), when one's dead relatives and friends are remembered and death is taunted and celebrated.

The Labyrinth of Solitude

OCTAVIO PAZ

The opposition between life and death was not so absolute to the   1
ancient Mexicans as it is to us. Life extended into death, and vice versa. Death was not the natural end of life but one phase of an infinite cycle. Life, death and resurrection were stages of a cosmic process which repeated itself continuously. Life had no higher function than to flow into death, its opposite and complement; and death, in turn, was not an end in itself: man fed the insatiable hunger of life with his death. Sacrifices had a double purpose: on the one hand man participated in the creative process, at the same time paying back to the gods the debt contracted by his species; on the other hand he nourished cosmic life and also social life, which was nurtured by the former.

Perhaps the most characteristic aspect of this conception is the   2
impersonal nature of the sacrifice. Since their lives did not belong to them, their deaths lacked any personal meaning. The dead—including warriors killed in battle and women dying in childbirth, companions of Huitzilopochtli the sun god—disappeared at the end of a certain period, to return to the undifferentiated country of the shadows, to be melted into the air, the earth, the fire, the animating substance of the universe. Our indigenous ancestors did not believe that their deaths belonged to them, just as they never thought that their lives were really theirs in the Christian sense. Everything was examined to determine, from birth, the life and death of each man: his social class, the year, the place, the day, the hour. The Aztec was as little responsible for his actions as for his death.

Space and time were bound together and formed an inseparable   3
whole. There was a particular "time" for each place, each of the car-

Octavio Paz. *The Labyrinth of Solitude.* Translated by Lysander Kempt, Yara Milos, and Rachel Phillips Belash. New York: Grove Press, 1985. Reprinted with the permission of the publisher.

dinal points and the center in which they were immobilized. And this complex of space-time possessed its own virtues and powers, which profoundly influenced and determined human life. To be born on a certain day was to pertain to a place, a time, a color and a destiny. All was traced out in advance. Where we dissociate space and time, mere stage sets for the actions of our lives, there were as many "space-times" for the Aztecs as there were combinations in the priestly calendar, each one endowed with a particular qualitative significance, superior to human will.

Religion and destiny ruled their lives, as morality and freedom   4
rule ours. We live under the sign of liberty, and everything—even Greek fatality and the grace of the theologians—is election and struggle, but for the Aztecs the problem reduced itself to investigating the never-clear will of the gods. Only the gods were free, and only they had the power to choose—and therefore, in a profound sense, to sin. The Aztec religion is full of great sinful gods—Quetzalcóatl is the major example—who grow weak and abandon their believers, in the same way that Christians sometimes deny God. The conquest of Mexico would be inexplicable without the treachery of the gods, who denied their own people.

The advent of Catholicism radically modified this situation.   5
Sacrifice and the idea of salvation, formerly collective, became personal. Freedom was humanized, embodied in man. To the ancient Aztecs the essential thing was to assure the continuity of creation; sacrifice did not bring about salvation in another world, but cosmic health; the universe, and not the individual, was given life by the blood and death of human beings. For Christians it is the individual who counts. The world—history, society—is condemned beforehand. The death of Christ saved each man in particular. Each one of us is Man, and represents the hopes and possibilities of the species. Redemption is a personal task.

Both attitudes, opposed as they may seem, have a common note: 6
life, collective or individual, looks forward to a death that in its way is a new life. Life only justifies and transcends itself when it is realized in death, and death is also a transcendence, in that it is a new life. To Christians death is a transition, a somersault between two lives, the temporal and the otherworldly; to the Aztecs it was the profoundest way of participating in the continuous regeneration of the creative forces, which were always in danger of being extinguished if they were not provided with blood, the sacred food. In both systems life

and death lack autonomy, are the two sides of a single reality. They are references to the invisible realities.

Modern death does not have any significance that transcends it or that refers to other values. It is rarely anything more than the inevitable conclusion of a natural process. In a world of facts, death is merely one more fact. But since it is such a disagreeable fact, contrary to all our concepts and to the very meaning of our lives, the philosophy of progress ("Progress toward what, and from what?" Scheler asked) pretends to make it disappear, like a magician palming a coin. Everything in the modern world functions as if death did not exist. Nobody takes it into account, it is suppressed everywhere: in political pronouncements, commercial advertising, public morality and popular customs; in the promise of cut-rate health and happiness offered to all of us by hospitals, drugstores and playing fields. But death enters into everything we undertake, and it is no longer a transition but a great gaping mouth that nothing can satisfy. The century of health, hygiene and contraceptives, miracle drugs and synthetic foods, is also the century of the concentration camp and the police state, Hiroshima and the murder story. Nobody thinks about death, about his own death, as Rilke asked us to do, because nobody lives a personal life. Collective slaughter is the fruit of a collectivized way of life.

7

Death also lacks meaning for the modern Mexican. It is no longer a transition, an access to another life more alive than our own. But although we do not view death as a transcendence, we have not eliminated it from our daily lives. The word death is not pronounced in New York, in Paris, in London, because it burns the lips. The Mexican, in contrast, is familiar with death, jokes about it, caresses it, sleeps with it, celebrates it; it is one of his favorite toys and his most steadfast love. True, there is perhaps as much fear in his attitude as in that of others, but at least death is not hidden away: he looks at it face to face, with impatience, disdain or irony. "If they are going to kill me tomorrow, let them kill me right away."

8

The Mexican's indifference toward death is fostered by his indifference toward life. He views not only death but also life as nontranscendent. Our songs, proverbs, fiestas and popular beliefs show very clearly that the reason death cannot frighten us is that "life has cured us of fear." It is natural, even desirable, to die, and the sooner the better. We kill because life—our own or another's—is of no value. Life and death are inseparable, and when the former lacks meaning, the latter becomes equally meaningless. Mexican death is the mirror of

9

Mexican life. And the Mexican shuts himself away and ignores both of them.

Our contempt for death is not at odds with the cult we have made 10
of it. Death is present in our fiestas, our games, our loves and our thoughts. To die and to kill are ideas that rarely leave us. We are seduced by death. The fascination it exerts over us is the result, perhaps, of our hermit-like solitude and of the fury with which we break out of it. The pressure of our vitality, which can only express itself in forms that betray it, explains the deadly nature, aggressive or suicidal, of our explosions. When we explode we touch against the highest point of that tension, we graze the very zenith of life. And there, at the height of our frenzy, suddenly we feel dizzy: it is then that death attracts us.

Another factor is that death revenges us against life, strips it of all 11
its vanities and pretensions and converts it into what it really is: a few neat bones and a dreadful grimace. In a closed world where everything is death, only death has value. But our affirmation is negative. Sugar-candy skulls, and tissue-paper skulls and skeletons strung with fireworks . . . our popular images always poke fun at life, affirming the nothingness and insignificance of human existence. We decorate our houses with death's heads, we eat bread in the shape of bones on the Day of the Dead, we love the songs and stories in which death laughs and cracks jokes, but all this boastful familiarity does not rid us of the question we all ask: What is death? We have not thought up a new answer. And each time we ask, we shrug our shoulders: Why should I care about death if I have never cared about life?

AN ARTISTIC VISION OF METAPHYSICAL TRUTH

In order to obtain an inclusive understanding of the philosophical perspectives of Latin American cultures, it is important to take into account the thought of the pre-Columbian people who lived in the areas now known as Latin America. The pre-Columbian native cultures, which had been isolated from the Old World for many millennia, developed elaborate and intriguing cosmologies and philosophical perspectives. In discussions of the philosophical perspectives of the ancient cultures of Latin America, the name of Miguel León-Portilla invariably arises. He is particularly well known for his meticulous studies of the narratives provided by native Nahuatl

(Aztec) elders shortly after the arrival of the Spanish in the New World. León-Portilla has written extensively on the philosophical views of the ancient Nahuatl thinkers. His most important publications include *Aztec Thought and Culture, The Broken Spears, Pre-Columbian Literatures of Mexico,* and *Native Mesoamerican Spirituality.* Among other theses, he maintains that there is sufficient evidence to conclude that Aztec culture had developed its own philosophical traditions. According to León-Portilla, Aztec wise men called *tlamatinime* proposed and debated in centers of higher learning various doctrines concerning the nature of ultimate reality and our capacity to know it.

In the selection that follows, which is taken from his classic text, *Aztec Thought and Culture,* León-Portilla discusses how the *tlamatinime* developed doctrines that were alternatives to the militaristic-theological perspective (which included human sacrifice) that was dominant in Aztec culture. According to the cosmology of the Aztecs, human sacrifice was necessary in order to maintain the cosmic order. But some of the Aztec wise men developed doctrines which cast doubt on the need to preserve the existence of the universe through human sacrifice, and proposed glimpsing at divine wisdom through artistic inspiration.

Aztec Thought and Culture

MIGUEL LEÓN-PORTILLA

Aztec religion, on the mystico-militaristic level, sought to preserve the life of the Sun, threatened by a fifth and final cataclysm, through ceremonial warfare and human sacrifice. The supreme ideal of the Aztec warriors was to fulfill their mission as the chosen people of Tonatiuh, the Sun, who needed the precious liquid if he were to continue to shine over *Cemanáhuac,* the world. At the same time, however, many of the wise men, living in the shadow of the great symbol of Nahuatl wisdom, Quetzalcóatl, attempted to discover the meaning of life on   1

Miguel León-Portilla. *Aztec Thought and Culture.* Translated by Jack Emory Davis. Norman: University of Oklahoma Press, 1963. Reprinted with the permission of the publisher.

an intellectual plane. These almost diametrically opposed attitudes toward life and the universe existed side by side—a situation similar to that of Nazi Germany in our time, where a mystico-militaristic world view and a genuinely humanistic philosophy and literature coexisted. Indeed, such a mixture of humanism and barbarism seems to be an inherent quality of the so-called rational animal.

In the face of this duality of attitudes, it is necessary to isolate that   2
fundamental element which colored and gave direction to Nahuatl thought.

The *tlamatinime*'s point of departure was the ephemeral and frag-   3
ile quality of all that exists. "Although it be jade, it is broken; although it be gold, it is crushed; although it be quetzal plumes, it is torn asunder." Obviously, "this is not the place where things are made; here nothing grows green," and "we only dream, all is like a dream."

Convinced of the evanescence of earthly life, the Nahuatl wise   4
men posed two questions, one of a practical nature, the other more speculative: "On earth, is the striving for anything really worth while?"; "Do we perhaps speak any truth here?" Since truth is that which gives support or foundation to all things, the second question led to two even more urgent problems: "What is it perchance that stands?" "Are men really true?" In other words, do things and men have a real truth or foundation, or are they merely dreamlike, as are those things which come into one's semiconscious mind at the moment of awakening?

The problems were formulated cosmologically in the language of   5
the ancient myths, and they were given impetus by the need of finding an answer before the imminent end of the Fifth Sun. For man, here on earth without "a well-formed face and heart," the question of his own truth is the most pressing, since this reality embraces his origin, his personality, and his final destiny.

Lengthy and profound were the meditations of the Nahuatl wise   6
men. Instead of creating numerous hypotheses, they first asked themselves—in spite of their religious beliefs—whether it were at all possible "to speak the truth on earth." Giving their thought a metaphysical turn, they concluded that if everything on earth is temporary and dreamlike, then "it is not here where truth is to be found." Truth must be sought "farther on," "beyond the visible and tangible," "in that place that lies beyond us, in the region of the dead and of the gods."

But how to find this road to the beyond, to reach "that which is   7
true"? The religious approach, through sacrifice and offerings, was

rejected by some because the Giver of Life seemed to them to be always inexorable and inscrutable. Nor could the problem be solved satisfactorily by the attempt of human reason to reach the essence of things. For if everything on earth "changes, perishes, and is like a dream," the Nahuas' ultimate question—"How many say that the truth is or is not here?"—must remain unanswerable.

Thus the *tlamatinime* crossed the borders of doubt. Some of them, despairing of ever finding an answer, formulated a Nahuatl version of Epicureanism—to live pleasurably this short while on earth. 8

In opposition to this attitude of intellectual despair, there finally appeared a philosophical answer to the question of metaphysical knowledge. The answer came through intuition; there is only one way by which we may babble the "truth" occasionally, and that is through poetic inspiration—"flower and song." By means of metaphors conceived within the very depths of one's being or perhaps emanating from the "interior of heaven," one may attain certain glimpses of the truth. 9

"Flower and song," then, could reveal the universe to man and allow him to explain it in poetry. There was first the supreme metaphor of Ometéotl, God of Duality, the self-created, the generating-conceiving cosmic principle, Lord of the Close Vicinity, invisible as the night and the wind—origin, foundation, and goal of all things and of man. 10

Many aspects had Ometéotl: "mother and father of the gods"; "in his circle of turquoise, in the waters colored as the bluebird; it is he who dwells in the clouds, on earth and in the realm of the dead, the Lord of fire and of the year"; "in whose hands rests Anáhuac." He is the mirror of night and day, able both to conceal and to illuminate; he gives all things their truth and then makes them vanish "into the region of oblivion." He is "the inventor of man, the one who drops him into the maternal womb; he holds men and the world in the palm of his hand and, rocking them to and fro, amuses himself and laughs." This then is Ometéotl, the metaphysical configuration of God, seen through "flower and song." 11

The wise men then conceived a theory about man himself; he is "face and heart." Concerning man's free will, his destiny, and his moral goodness, the sages felt that his supreme ideal should be the development of "a wise countenance and a heart firm as a rock." Man, in reality a beggar, needed a light, a truth. These he could find, perhaps, through the symbols of and along the path of "flower and song." 12

Oh stealer of songs, my heart!
Where will you find them?
You are needy and poor,
but grasp firmly the black and red ink [wisdom],
And perhaps you will no longer be a beggar.
[*MSS Cantares Mexicanos,* fol. 68,r.]

In order to escape this poverty, this lack of metaphysical knowl- 13
edge, the Nahuatl sages meditated. Their final answer was that
"flower and song" placed God in man's heart, making it true and
causing it to create what today we call art. So, for instance, in the
description of the painter, the artist appears as a man with God in his
heart, a man in possession of the truth and of the very roots of his
being. Having a deified heart, he converses with it so that he can
"give a divine quality to things"; he creates art:

The good painter is wise;
God is in his heart.
He puts divinity into things;
he converses with his own heart.
He paints the colors of all the flowers
as if he were a Toltec.
[*Códice Matritense de la Real
Academia,* VIII, fol. 117,v.]

The painter, the singer, the sculptor, the poet, and all those wor- 14
thy of the title Toltec, artist, were "deified hearts," visionaries who,
having truth themselves, were empowered to create divine things.
Such men, having realized the supreme Nahuatl ideal, were called
upon to fill high posts, such as that of director of the *Calmécac,* the
greatest centers of learning.

Memorizing the divine hymns, contemplating the heavens and 15
"the orderly motions of the stars," admiring painting and sculpture,
the students of the *Calmécac* were taught to awaken in their hearts a
thirst for the light and the creative power of Ometéotl. They began to
see the world and man actively through "flower and song." They
became aware that only this "calms and delights men."

Opening his own window to the universe, a youthful student 16
described the essence of his being as a spring from which inspiration
flowed:

Who am I?
As a bird I fly about,
I sing of flowers;

I compose songs,
butterflies of song.
Let them burst forth from my soul!
Let my heart be delighted with them!
[*MSS Cantares Mexicanos,*
fol. 11,v.]

17

By allowing the "butterflies of song" to be born in himself, the Nahuatl wise man began to express "that which is true on earth." And the painter, "the artist of the black and the red"; the sculptor, carver of the signs that measured time and of the images of gods and myths; all of the philosophers, musicians, architects, and astronomers sought the same thing—their own truth and that of the universe.

18

Nahuatl philosophic thought thus revolved about an aesthetic conception of the universe and life, for art "made things divine," and only the divine was true. To know the truth was to understand the hidden meanings of things through "flower and song," a power emanating from the deified heart.

LATIN AMERICAN PHILOSOPHICAL IDENTITY

One of Bondy's principal philosophical concerns was articulating the nature of Latin American philosophy. The issue of whether there is, and whether there can be, a Latin American philosophy has concerned philosophers in Latin America for the past fifty years. This issue raises inquiries concerning the nature of philosophical thought, the character of Latin American culture, and the nature of the relation between the two. Bondy believes that philosophical reflection should have both a theoretical and an anthropological component; that is, it should be concerned with conceptual issues and with the particular sociopolitical and historical contexts in which it occurs. Like many other Latin American intellectuals, Bondy believes that to understand Latin American culture one must take into account the relations of economic, political, and cultural dependence that Latin America has had on Europe and the United States. As Bondy maintains in the following excerpt, taken from *The Meaning and Problem of Hispanic American Thought*, this dependency status has affected in significant ways the manner in which philosophy has developed in Latin America.

At different phases in his intellectual development Bondy, who was born and educated in Peru, was influenced by phenomenology,

Marxism, and analytic philosophy. His conception of philosophy as a broad discipline that incorporates a variety of approaches and interdisciplinary insights exemplifies the view of other Latin American philosophers who reject the notion of philosophy as a narrowly delimited intellectual enterprise. Among his major works we find *Irrealidad e idealidad, Breve antologia filosofica, Existe una filosofia de nuestra America?*, and *Sentido y problema del pensamiento filosofico hispanoamericano.* In the following essay philosophical and sociopolitical insights converge to provide some insights into the question of Latin American philosophical identity.

The Meaning and Problem of Hispanic American Thought

AUGUSTO SALAZAR BONDY

Following the direction of current Hispanic American thought, let us inquire about the quality and scope of the intellectual products of the philosophizing of four-hundred-years of evolution. . . . Our balance cannot fail to be negative, as has been that of practically all historians and interpreters of ideas in Hispanic America. In fact, it is impossible to extract clearly from this process an articulation of ideas, a well-structured dialectic of reflections and expositions, and of concepts and solutions nurtured by its historical and cultural circumstance. On the contrary, what we find in all our countries is a succession of imported doctrines, a procession of systems which follows European, or, in general, foreign unrest. It is almost a succession of intellectual fashions without roots in our spiritual life and, for this very reason, lacking the virtue of fertility. Just as scholastic colonial thought . . . was imposed by the interests of the mother country, so also the systems that replaced it responded to an historical logic that was foreign to the conscience of our peoples. For this reason these systems were abandoned as quickly and easily as they were embraced, having been chosen by the upper class and the intellectual sectors of Hispanic

1

Augusto Salazar Bondy. *The Meaning and Problem of Hispanic American Thought.* Translated by John P. Angelli. Lawrence, Kan.: Center of Latin American Studies at the University of Kansas, 1969. Reprinted with the permission of the publisher.

Americans according to their immediate preferences and momentary affinities. To review the process of Hispanic American philosophy is to relate the passing of Western philosophy *through* our countries, or to narrate European philosophy *in* Hispanic America. It is not to tell the history of a natural philosophy *of* Hispanic America. In our historical process there are Cartesians, Krausists, Spencerians, Bergsonians and other European *"isms."* But this is all; there are no creative figures to found and nurture their own peculiar tradition, nor native philosophic *"isms."* We search for the original contributions of our countries in answer to the Western challenge—or to that of other cultures—and we do not find them. At least we find nothing substantial, worthy of a positive historical appraisal. No one, I believe, can give testimony to its existence if he is moderately strict in his judgment.

The characteristics which, according to this balance, stand out in boldest relief in Hispanic American thought are the following: 2

1. *Imitative sense of thought.* Thinking is done according to theoretical molds already shaped in the pattern of Western thought—mainly European—imported in the form of currents, schools and systems totally defined in their content and orientation. To philosophize is to adopt a pre-existent foreign *"ism,"* to incorporate into one's thought theses adopted during the process of reading, and to repeat more or less faithfully the works of the most resounding figures of the period. 3

2. *Universal receptivity.* An indiscriminate disposition to accept all manner of theoretical product coming from the most diverse schools and national traditions, with extremely varied styles and spiritual purposes. This, of course, always provided that they will have obtained a certain reputation, a perceptible ascendancy in some important country of Europe. This receptivity, which betrays a lack of substance in ideas and convictions, has often been taken for an Hispanic American virtue. 4

3. *Absence of a characteristic, definitive tendency,* and of an ideological, conceptual proclivity capable of founding a tradition of thought, of sketching a profile in an intellectual manner. Notice the "empiricist" seal that Britannic thought has, perceptible even in the work of its speculative idealists. There is no solid basis upon which to define a similar style in Hispanic American philosophy. At times one speaks of a practical inclination in the Hispanic American, at others, of a speculative vein. Apart from the fact that these two traits are contradictory, their manifestations—weak and confusing—have disap- 5

peared rapidly and almost completely each time that contrary influences have prevailed. The only alternative is to count as a distinctive
character precisely the absence of definition and the nebulous state of
conceptions, which is merely to confirm the thesis.

4. *Correlative absence of original contributions,* capable of being   6
incorporated into the tradition of world thought. There is no philosophic system of Hispanic American roots, or doctrine with meaning
in the entirety of universal thought. Neither are there polemic reactions to the affirmations of our thinkers, nor sequels and doctrinary
effects of them in other philosophies. All of this is an additional proof
of the inexistence of our own ideas and theses. The most relevant
philosophical figures of Hispanic America have been commentators
or professors, but, no matter how fruitful their action in this field may
have been for the educational process of our countries, it has not had
an effect beyond our own cultural circle.

5. *Existence of a strong sense of intellectual frustration* among   7
cultivators of philosophy. It is symptomatic that, throughout the history of our culture, its most lucid interpreters have planted time and
again the question of the existence of their own philosophic thought.
Responding to it, as we said, almost unanimously with a complete
negation, they have formulated projects for the future construction of
such thought. Significantly, this unrest and reflection are not found, or
are rarely found, among those nations that have made fundamental
contributions to the development of philosophy. They are, so to speak,
well installed in the territory of philosophic theory and move within it
as in their own dominion. Hispanic Americans, on the other hand,
have always, in this regard, felt themselves to be in alien territory, as
one who makes furtive and clandestine incursions, for they have had
a vivid consciousness of their lack of speculative originality.

6. *There has existed permanently in Hispanic America a great*   8
distance between those who practice philosophy and the whole of the
community. There is no way to consider our philosophies as national
thought, with a differential seal, as one speaks of a German, French,
English, or Greek philosophy. It is also impossible for the community
to recognize itself in these philosophies, precisely because we are
dealing with transplanted thought, the spiritual products of other men
and other cultures, which a refined minority makes an effort to understand and to share. We do not deny that there is a universal factor in
philosophy, nor do we think that philosophy has to be popular.
However, when an elaborate intellectual creation is genuine, it

reflects the conscience of a community finding in it profound resonance especially through its ethical and political derivations.

7. *The same scheme of historic development and the same constellation of traits—although negative—are suitable to the activity unfolded during more than four centuries by the men dedicated to philosophy in a plurality of countries,* often far removed physically and socially from each other as is the case of Hispanic America. Not only does it permit a general judgment of Hispanic American thought—without ignoring the existence of special cases and regional variants resulting from divergent influences within the common framework—it also demonstrates that in order to comprehend the thought of our countries it is necessary to define the basic cultural-historical reality that links them beneath their nearly always artificial confrontations and political separations. 9

In his *Lectures on the History of Philosophy,* Hegel wrote: "Philosophy is the philosophy of its time, a link in the great chain of universal evolution, from whence it derives that it can only satisfy peculiar interests of its time." In another place, confronted with the existence of systems that pretend to reproduce doctrines of the past, that is, to make a kind of transfer from one mode of thinking to another, he formulated this bitter disqualification: "These attempts are simple translations, not original creations; and the spirit only finds satisfaction in the knowledge of its own and genuine originality." With this the great master of the history of philosophy underscored a very important fact in the dominion of thought. To wit, philosophy as such expresses the life of the community, but it can fail in this function, and, instead of manifesting its uniqueness, it can detract from it or conceal it. Accordingly, an unauthentic philosophy, or a mystified thought may develop. 10

To what extent a philosophy can be unauthentic will be made clear in an attempt to specify the purpose and meaning of philosophic thought. As we understand it, a philosophy is many things, but among them it cannot fail to be the manifestation of the rational conscience of a community. It is the conception that expresses the mode in which the community reacts before the whole of reality and the course of existence, and its peculiar manner of illuminating and interpreting the being in which it finds itself installed. Because it comprises the whole of reality, it deals with that which is essential to man, with his vital commitment. In this respect it differs from science 11 which does not commit the whole man. On the other hand, to the extent that philosophy is a rational conscience, an attempt to make the world and life intelligible, it is not confused with religious faith, which operates through feeling and suggestion. Thus, philosophy deals with the total truth of a rationally clarified existence, that appeals to the totality of the personal human being and its full lucidity. The latter are the two means of referring to that which is most unique in each man. . . .

Where is the cause, the determining complex of this condition of   12
Hispanic America as an entity and also of each of its constituent nations? If we are aware that this condition is not peculiar to Hispanic American countries, but is largely similar to that of other communities and regional groups of nations, belonging to what today is called the Third World, then it is clear that, to explain it, we must utilize the concept of underdevelopment, with the correlative concept of domination. In fact, underdeveloped countries present an aggregate of basically negative characteristics which, one way or the other, are related to dependent bonds with other centers of economic and political power. These centers of power—which direct the activities of the dependent countries according to their own interests—are situated in the developed nations, in the mother countries or in great industrial powers. And these negative characteristics correspond to factors which easily explain the phenomena of a culture like that of Hispanic America. It was not by accident that our countries were first subject to Spanish power and that they evolved from this situation as Spanish political colonies to that of factories and supply centers or markets of the British Empire, subject to their economic control. The United States inherited this empire, with a closer and more effective network of power. As dependents of Spain, England, or the United States, we have been and continue to be underdeveloped—if I may use the expression—*under* these powers, and, consequently, countries with a *culture of domination*. . . .

Our thought is defective and unauthentic owing to our society   13
and our culture. Must it necessarily remain so? Is there no alternative to this prospect? That is to say, is there no way of giving it originality and authenticity? Indeed there is, because man, in certain circumstances rises above his present condition, and transcends in reality toward new forms of life, toward unheard-of manifestations. These will endure or will bear fruit to the degree that the initiated movement

can expand and provoke a general dialectic and totalization of development. In the socio-political field this is what constitutes revolutions. This means that that part of man which rises above his circumstances can not do so fruitfully and in a lasting manner unless the movement is capable of articulating itself with the rest of reality and provoking in it an overall change. If this is valid for society and culture in general, it is also true of philosophy, for the latter, being the focus of man's total awareness, could, better than other spiritual creations, be that part of humanity that rises above itself, and overcomes the negativity of the present as it moves toward new and superior forms of reality. But, to achieve this, it must possess certain valences capable of turning theory into live reality. It must operate in such a way that, through an effective and prudent utilization of historical resources, it will produce the most fruitful dialectical reactions in the proper areas of social life. Hegel said that the owl of Minerva took flight at dusk, thus giving philosophy the character of a theory that elucidates the meaning of facts already accomplished. It is not always so. Contrary to what Hegel thought, we feel that philosophy can be, and on more than one historic occasion has had to be, the messenger of the dawn, the beginning of historic change through a radical awareness of existence projected toward the future.

Philosophy in Hispanic America has a possibility of being authentic in the midst of the unauthenticity that surrounds and consumes it, and to convert itself into the lucid awareness of this condition and into the thought capable of unleashing the process to overcome it. It must be a meditation *about* our anthropological status and *from* our own negative status, with a view to its cancellation. Consequently, Hispanic American philosophy has before it—as a possibility of its own recuperation—a destructive task that, in the long run, will be destructive to its current form. It must be an awareness that cancels prejudice, myths, idols; an awareness that will awaken us to our subjection as peoples and our depression as men. In consequence, it must be an awareness that liberates us from the obstacles that impede our anthropological expansion, which is also the anthropological expansion of the world. It must be, in addition, a critical and analytical awareness of the potentialities and demands of our affirmation as humanity. All of which requires a thought that from the beginning will cast aside every deceptive illusion and, delving into the historical substance of our community, will search for the qualities and values that could express it positively. These qualities and values must be precisely those capable of finding resonance in the entirety of Hispanic America, and, along with other convergent forces, unleashing a progressive movement that will eliminate underdevelopment and domination.

THROUGH THE EYES OF THE OPPRESSED

The theology of liberation has been one of the most influential movements in Latin America in the last quarter century. Its pioneering figure, Gustavo Gutierrez, articulated not only a new way of doing theology but also a novel way of thinking about Christian spirituality. According to the theology of liberation, to accept and to know God is to do justice through solidarity with the poor and marginalized. Gutierrez maintains that the real measure of one's faith in the teachings of Christ is determined by one's commitment to alleviating the plight of the poor and the oppressed members of society. A deep concern for the poor and disfranchised, which Christ himself exemplified in his own life, is at the core of living a Christian life. As Gutierrez has repeatedly pointed out, this theological perspective was not developed in an academic, intellectual setting; rather, it evolved out of the struggles of the poor of Latin America to attain justice.

Gustavo Gutierrez, who was born and raised in Peru, received a traditional theological education in Europe. After completing his formal education, he returned to minister in the working-class neighborhood of Rímac in Lima, Peru. His pioneering efforts in developing the theology of liberation have had a significant impact on the poor Christian communities of Latin America and on the hierarchy of the Catholic church. The influence of the theologians of liberation can be discerned in the documents written by the Latin American bishops in their conference held in Puebla, Mexico, in 1979. The bishops recognized the importance of having a "preferential option for the poor." In recent years, theology of liberation movements have also emerged in Africa and Asia.

Gutierrez's works include *The Theology of Liberation, The Power of the Poor in History,* and *El Dios de la Vida.* In the following selection, Gutierrez articulates some central ideas underlying the perspective of the theology of liberation.

The Power of the Poor in History
GUSTAVO GUTIERREZ

CONFRONTING THE REAL SITUATION OF LATIN AMERICA

The self-awareness of the Christian community is conditioned histori-   1
cally by the world of which it is a part, and by its way of viewing this
world.

Moving Out of the Ghetto

We need not begin from scratch to work up our own private vision of   2
reality. In the case of Latin America, which is what concerns us here,
we must rather become really involved in the way that the people of
Latin America see themselves and their course in history. Thus we
must start by opening our ears and listening to them—which presupposes that we are willing to move out of our own narrow world.

From the past right up to today, the Christian community in Latin   3
America has lived largely in its own ghetto world. Born at a time
when the Catholic Church was leading a Counter-Reformation movement, the Latin American church has always been marked by an attitude of defense. This defensive posture has led it to engage in silent
retreat on numerous occasions, to act as a quiet refuge for all those
who felt fearful and in need of protection as they tried to follow God's
lead. This posture was reinforced by the occasional attacks from liberal and anticlerical factions during the period that followed political
independence in the last century. It was further reinforced by the
harsh criticism of more recent social movements, which have sought
to introduce radical social change and which have regarded the
church as an obstacle to such change.

All this led the church to solidify its ties with established authori-   4
ty, thus enjoying the latter's support and forming a common front
against their presumed enemies. It also led it to create and maintain
costly educational institutions, social services, and charitable works
that were practically duplicates of those in the world around it. It was

Gustavo Gutierrez. *The Power of the Poor in History.* Translated by Robert R. Barr.
Maryknoll, N.Y.: Orbis Books, 1983. Reprinted with the permission of the publisher.

a futile, perhaps last-ditch effort to prolong an outdated brand of Christianity in a society that no longer evinced religious oneness and that had clearly and openly entered a period of ideological pluralism. The church thus became an easy and compliant prey for those who used it to protect their own selfish interests and the established order, in the name of the "Christian West."

Probing the Real Causes

Moving out of the ghetto is one aspect of a broader attitude: opening   5
up to the world. It involves sharing, in a more positive and unreserved way, the vision that Latin Americans have of their situation. It also involves contributing in an effective way to the elaboration and development of this vision, and committing ourselves wholeheartedly to the activities it entails.

Recent years have been critical ones in this respect. We have   6
come out of a long period when ignorance about the real Latin American situation prevailed, and we have also left behind the brief period when false optimism was promoted by vested interests. We are abandoning the sketchy and hazy views of the past for an overall, integrated understanding of our real situation.

The true face of Latin America is emerging in all its naked ugli-   7
ness. It is not simply or primarily a question of low educational standards, a limited economy, an unsatisfactory legal system, or inadequate legal institutions. What we are faced with is a situation that takes no account of the dignity of human beings, or their most elemental needs, that does not provide for their biological survival, or their basic right to be free and autonomous. Poverty, injustice, alienation, and the exploitation of human beings by other human beings combine to form a situation that the Medellin conference did not hesitate to condemn as "institutionalized violence."

This phrase might well seem strange in a pronouncement by the   8
hierarchy. But it should be emphasized that it is not something thrown in as an aside, for the whole Medellin document on peace is focused on this concept. It is a commonplace for all experts on Latin America, and a reality that is known and experienced daily by most of those who live in Latin America. It is only within this real context that one can honestly raise the complex question of the moral rightness or wrongness of putting down violence. No double standard will do. We cannot say that violence is all right when the oppressor uses it to

maintain or preserve "order," but wrong when the oppressed use it to overthrow this same "order."

The most important change in our understanding of the Latin   9
American situation, however, has to do with its deeper, underlying causes. These are now seen in the context of a broader historical process. It is becoming ever more clear that underdevelopment, in a total sense, is primarily due to economic, political, and cultural dependence on power centers that lie outside Latin America. The functioning of the capitalist economy leads simultaneously to the creation of greater wealth for the few and greater poverty for the many. Acting in complicity with these outside power centers, the oligarchies of each nation in Latin America operate through various mechanisms to maintain their dominion over the internal affairs of their own countries.

This new awareness of the Latin American situation shines   10
through various documents in varying degrees of clarity. It finds authoritative and clear-cut expression in the Medellin document on peace, which forthrightly speaks of "internal colonialism" and "external neocolonialism." In Latin America these are the ultimate causes of the violence that is committed against the most basic human rights.

Our new vision, attentive to structural factors, will help Christians   11
to avoid the fallacy of proposing a personal change detached from concrete conditions, as a necessary prerequisite to any social transformation. If any of us remain wedded to this fallacy, in the name of some hazy humanism or disembodied spiritualism, we shall only prove to be accomplices in the continuing postponement of the radical changes that are necessary. Such changes call for simultaneous work on both persons and structures, for they condition each other mutually.

Involvement in the Liberation Process

When we characterize the Latin American situation as one of depen-   12
dence and unfair domination, we are naturally led to talk about liberation, and to participate in the process that will lead to it. We are in fact dealing with a term that expresses the new stance adopted by Latin Americans, a stance that is gradually taking concrete shape in official documents. It is recapitulated forcefully in the Medellin conference and in the Thirty-Sixth Episcopal Assembly of Peru. Expressions such as "development" and "integration," with their

attendant retinue of international alliances, agencies, and experts, are relegated to the shadows; for they involve a different vision of the Latin American situation.

But to stress the need for liberation presupposes far more than simply differences in our analyses of the situation. At a deeper level, it means that we see the ongoing development of humanity in a particular perspective, and in terms of a specific philosophy and theology of history. It means that we see it as a process of human emancipation, aiming toward a society where men and women are truly free from servitude, and where they are the active shapers of their own destiny. Such a process does not lead us simply to a radical transformation of structures—to a revolution. It goes much further, implying the perduring creation of a wholly new way for men and women to be human. 13

There is an urgent need for Christians to involve themselves in the work of liberating this oppressed continent, by establishing real solidarity with the oppressed persons who are the chief victims. The first step is for the church as a whole to break its many ties with the present order, ties that it has maintained overtly or covertly, wittingly or unwittingly, up to now. This will not be an easy task, for it will mean abandoning outworn traditions, suspicions, viewpoints, advantages, and privileges, as well as the forces of inertia. It will also mean accepting the fact that the future cast of the church will be radically different from the one we know today. It will mean incurring the wrath of the groups in power—with all the risks that entails. Above all, it will mean believing in the revolutionary and liberating power of the gospel—believing in the Lord—and authentic faith, a faith that goes beyond the mere recitation and acceptance of codified truths. This will not be easy. We know it, of course, and we have said it countless times. But perhaps we have not been sufficiently aware of the fears and vacillations of the vast majority of the Christian community in Latin America. Perhaps we have not realized how much they bore ironic witness to this truth. 14

One manifestation of our break with injustice and exploitation, which the present economic and social structures foist upon the vast majority of our people under the guise of law, should come from the bishops. They must turn to the oppressed, declaring their solidarity with them and their desire to join with them in their struggle. This is what they must do instead of what they have done in the past, when they turned to those in power and called for necessary reforms while implying that their own position need not be affected by such change. 15

*PRONUNCIATION GUIDE**

The vowels in Mesoamerican words are pronounced as follows:

a is pronounced "ah," as in b*a*rk

e is pronounced "eh," as in b*e*t

i is pronounced "ee," as in p*ee*k

o is pronounced "oh," as in t*o*ld

u is pronounced "oo," as in b*oo*r. When it comes before a vowel, however, it is pronounced as an English *w*

The consonants are pronounced as in modern Spanish, with the exception of *ll* and *x*.

ll is pronounced as a prolonged English *l*

x is pronounced "sh" (Oaxaca, however, is pronounced *wah hah kah*)

c is pronounced as English *k* except when it comes before *e* or *i;* in that case it is pronounced as the English *s*

hu is pronounced as the *w* in *w*ent

qu is pronounced as *k* in English when it comes before *e* or *i*

tl is pronounced as a unit as in met*tl*e

GLOSSARY

calmecac: Aztec center of higher learning where the moral codes, history, and arts of Aztec culture were taught. In these institutions Aztec wise men proposed and debated questions concerning the ultimate meaning of human existence.

cemanahuac: Aztec word referring to the world.

comunidades de base: Grass-roots communities of poor people in Latin America that serve as organizing centers for addressing social, economic, and political issues faced by the poor.

Dia de los Muertos: Day of the Dead celebrations that occur in many parts of Latin America at the end of October and beginning of

*This guide to pronunciation is based on the guide given in *The Flayed God: The Mesoamerican Mythological Tradition*, San Francisco: Harper, 1992, p. xv.

November. In these celebrations the dead are propitiated, remembered, and honored so that they will intercede on behalf of the living with God, Christ, the Virgin Mary, and other supernatural beings.

Huitzilopochtli: The sun and war god of the Aztecs.

Medellin conference: A conference that took place in Medellin, Colombia, in 1968 in which the bishops of Latin America drafted a document that expressed their "preferential option for the poor." This document signaled the willingness of the Catholic Church to stand in solidarity with the poor and oppressed in Latin America.

Nahuas: The people of the Valley of Mexico that spoke the Nahuatl language.

Nahuatl: The language spoken by the people of the Valley of Mexico before the arrival of the Spaniards.

Ometeotl: The god of the Aztecs with a dual male-female identity who is the creator and sustainer of the universe.

philosophy of liberation: A school of philosophical thought in Latin America that sees philosophy as an interdisciplinary enterprise that is an instrument of social change and that conceptualizes the world from the perspective of the marginalized and oppressed.

positivism: A philosophical perspective that predominated in Latin America in the nineteenth century. This perspective, which was based on the work of Auguste Comte and his followers, saw reason and the scientific method as the basis for developing social policies that would lead to universal human progress.

Quetzalcóatl: The man-god of the Aztecs who created the people who live in the present era under the Fifth Sun. He is often depicted as a feathered serpent.

theology of liberation: A theological perspective that understands Christian faith and the Gospel message in terms of a commitment to alleviate the suffering of the poor and oppressed in society.

tlamatinime: Aztec wise men who studied and interpreted Aztec legends and who proposed and debated theories about the possibility of obtaining knowledge of the ultimate nature of reality.

FURTHER READINGS

Luis Aquilar, ed. *Marxism in Latin America*, rev. ed. Philadelphia: Temple University Press, 1978.

Marcelo Dascal. *Cultural Relativism and Philosophy: North and Latin American Perspectives*. New York: E. J. Brill, 1991.

Enrique Dussel. *Philosophy of Liberation*. Translated by A. Martinez and M. Morkovsky. New York: Orbis Books, 1985.

JORGE J. E. GRACIA. *Latin American Philosophy in the Twentieth Century.* Buffalo: Prometheus Books, 1986.

GUSTAVO GUTIERREZ. *A Theology of Liberation.* Translated by Sister Caridad Inda and John Eagleson. Maryknoll, N.Y.: Orbis Books, 1983.

JOSE INGENIEROS. *Obras Completas,* 3d ed. Buenos Aires: L. J. Rosso, 1917.

MIGUEL JORRIN and JOHN D. MARTZ. *Latin-American Political Thought and Ideology.* Chapel Hill: University of North Carolina Press, 1970.

ALEJANDRO KORN. *Obras.* Buenos Aires: Universidad de la Plata, 1938.

ISABEL LARGUIA and JOHN DUMOULIN. *Hacia una Concepcion Cientifica de la Emancipacion de la Mujer.* Habana: Editorial de Ciencias Sociales, 1983.

LEÓN-PORTILLA. *Aztec Thought and Culture.* Norman: University of Oklahoma Press, 1963.

JOSE CARLOS MARIATEGUI. *Siete Ensayos de Interpretacion de la Realidad Peruana: Escritos de Mundial y Amauta.* Lima: Ediciones Amauta, 1928.

OCTAVIO PAZ. *The Labyrinth of Solitude.* Translated by Lysander Kemp, Yara Milos, and Rachel Phillips Belash. New York: Grove Press, 1985.

FRANCISCO ROMERO. *Theory of Man.* Berkeley: University of California Press, 1964.

AUGUSTO SALAZAR BONDY. *Existe una filosofia de nuestra America?* Mexico: Siglo XX, 1968.

JOSÉ VASCONCELOS. *Obras Completas,* vol. 4: *Todologia.* Mexico: Libreros Mexicanos Unidos, 1961.

LEOPOLDO ZEA. *The Latin American Mind.* Translated by J. H. Abbot and L. Dunham. Norman: University of Oklahoma, 1963.

STUDY QUESTIONS

1. Does the identification of a philosophy that is uniquely Latin American undermine the claim that philosophy involves the search for answers to questions that are universal and transcultural? Do Latin American philosophers limit themselves as philosophers by trying to articulate a philosophy that is uniquely Latin American? Why have Latin American philosophers been so concerned with the issue of Latin American philosophical identity?

2. In what ways does Gustavo Gutierrez provide a different understanding of the nature of Christian faith? Do Christians in the United States have a tendency to separate their faith from their political orientations? Does the fact that Gutierrez is a Catholic priest mean that his perspective is not authentically Latin American?

3. Do you agree with Paz that people in the United States and in western Europe avoid confronting the reality of death? If Paz is correct, what does this say about North American and western European cultures? Is it important for the members of a culture to come to terms with death? Why or why not?

4. Is it possible to understand the nature of reality through artistic creation and inspiration instead of rational thought? Why or why not? Do you think that the Western tradition has placed excessive emphasis on rationality as a means of understanding the world? If so, how has this emphasis affected other aspects of our culture?

CHAPTER 8

African Philosophy

JACQUELINE TRIMIER

It is a peculiar sensation, this double-consciousness, this sense of always looking at one's self through the eyes of others, of measuring one's soul by the tape of a world that looks on in amused contempt and pity. One ever feels his twoness—an American, a Negro; two souls, two thoughts, two unreconciled strivings; two warring ideals in one dark body, whose dogged strength alone keeps it from being torn asunder.

W. E. B. DU BOIS, *The Souls of Black Folk*

Du Bois laments a situation faced by *all* people of African descent. Wrenched from Africa and deposited as human cargo throughout the world by the slave trade, Africans confronted a hostile, white Western culture that ridiculed their indigenous cultures. However, the Africans remaining on their continent have had to reconcile on their own soil the immense tensions of their "peculiar sensation" of "twoness." Colonialism slammed together the two different African and Western heritages, a trauma resonating even in today's post-colonial Africa. Primarily an economic system, the colonial powers stole Africa's natural resources and raw materials to manufacture products for Western markets. To justify colonialism, eighteenth- and nineteenth-century European missionaries, anthropologists, ethnologists, and sociologists created a dualistic, racist mythology which contrasted a superior "whiteness" with an inferior "blackness." Whiteness signified humanity, modernity, civilization, rationality, Christianity, and scientism; blackness symbolized barbarism, traditionalism, savagery, primitiveness, irrationality, mysticism, and paganism. With this racist ideology, colonialism brutally and systematically attempted to erase the indigenous African cultures by imposing European political, economic, cultural, and social institutions throughout Africa and making Europe the yardstick against which non-Europe must measure itself. Moreover, this acculturation alienated Africans from their precolonial way of life and deeply implanted a psychological inferiority complex which made them ashamed of their blackness.

Squashed for centuries by the foot of oppression, Africans began to rise up and clamor for independence from colonialism. This feverish nationalistic spirit, reaching its zenith in the 1960s, had three distinct but connected elements. *Political nationalism* demanded the right to establish independent nations from colonial territories. This political agenda often celebrated the precolonial African past unsullied by colonialism. Therefore, political nationalism has mostly mirrored, if not intertwined with, *cultural nationalism.* Cultural and political nationalism formed the theoretical and methodological background of African intellectual activity. An *intellectual nationalism* emphasized that precolonial Africa should be the subject matter of African scholarship and motivated Africans to produce and control knowledge about Africa, activities historically manipulated by the West.

This tripartite history of "twoness" especially frames most postcolonial African philosophy. The African philosopher is unsure how to negotiate between the two African and Western cultures which colonialism savagely thrust together. The postcolonial African philosopher confronts certain deconstructive and reconstructive challenges in his or her situation of twoness.* The deconstructive challenge tries to understand the malignant Eurocentrism inherited from colonialism that infects contemporary Africa. Complementing this challenge, the reconstructive challenge critically revitalizes the modern reality of Africa's broken historical and cultural heritage.

For the last thirty years, African philosophers' major concerns, reflected in numerous publications, have been these: What is and is not African philosophy? Is it different from Western philosophy? What does philosophizing as an African and as a Black person really mean? Contemporary African philosophers have struggled to answer these questions in four main ways: ethnophilosophy, professional philosophy, philosophic sagacity, and national-ideological philosophy.

---

*Tsenay Serequeberhan, ed. *African Philosophy: The Essential Readings.* New York: Paragon House, 1991.

Ethnophilosophy, combining philosophy and ethnology, includes the works of Placide Tempels, Léopold Sédar Senghor, John Mbiti, and Alexis Kagamé. Ethnophilosophy embodies two primary aims: to describe ethnological concepts like time, ethics, personhood, and cosmology in the religion, mythology, and folklore of traditional African culture and to use these descriptions to prove that a unique and authentic African philosophy exists that is distinctly different from Western philosophy. Thus, ethnophilosophy directly links cul-- ture and philosophy: an authentic (that is, a traditional and precolonial) African culture creates an authentic African philosophy. Three characteristics differentiate ethnophilosophy from Western philosophy. While Western philosophy has individuals called "philosophers," African philosophy has a group, folk, or collective philosophy shared by all members in a culture. Unlike Western philosophy which emphasizes reason, logic, analysis, and system, ethnophilosophy is emotive, intuitive, mystical, and spiritual. Finally, authentic African philosophy is carried through the generations by the oral tradition, while Western philosophy has a written corpus of literature.

Professional philosophy ferociously challenges ethnophilosophy's uncritical acceptance of an authentic, traditional, precolonial Black African culture and philosophy. Professional philosophers like Kwasi Wiredu, Peter Bodunrin, Henry Odera Oruka, and Paulin Hountondji assert that the ideology of "authenticity" is simply an extension of the colonial mythology of blackness versus whiteness and that there is a difference between Philosophy (academic and second-order thought) and philosophy (cultural worldviews, first-order thought, or folk philosophy).

According to professional philosophers, an "authentic" African philosophy based on an "authentic" African culture is an extension of the colonial myth. To construct a mythical racial nature, colonialism needed to categorize *authentic* African cultures as monolithic, incapable of developing, and frozen in the past. Consequently, colonialist ideology exalts the idea of a folk philosophy—*first-order* thought or a body of unreflected and uncritiqued ideas commonly underlying a culture's values, beliefs, and institutions. Being university-trained academics in the Western philosophical tradition, they often make a distinction between Philosophy and philosophy. As defined by academia, Philosophy rationally, systematically, and rigorously analyzes commonly held cultural ideas and raises them to *second-order* thought. Describing African philosophy as first-order thought, or philosophy in a debased sense, implies that Africans are not capable of genuine philosophy. Moreover, real (academic) philosophy is not oral but written, as it is in the West. Finally, philosophy, a universal and culturally neutral discipline, should not be limited to discussing "authentic, precolonial Africa," but should be free to address problems in contemporary Africa and in other cultures.

Being preoccupied with ethnophilosophy, many professional philosophers often talk more about philosophy instead of actually doing it. However, some professional philosophers travel far beyond the ethnophilosophical debate and use Western philosophy to elucidate the African situation. This trend has been particularly fruitful in hermeneutics (the theory and methodology of interpretation), reflected in the works of Theophilus Okere, Okonda Okolo, Jeki Kinyongo, and P. I. Laleye.

The third trend of *philosophic sagacity* mediates a middle position between the squabbling of ethnophilosophers and professional philosophers. Some professional philosophers, while rejecting ethnographic and colonialist mythologies, still believe traditional, precolonial African culture is philosophically relevant and interesting to African philosophical discourse. Moreover, they strive to show that there are individuals in traditional cultures who are capable of second-order analysis and reflection. Henry Odera Oruka and J. O. Sopido, philosophic sagacity's primary exponents, focus on the sages or wise men in traditional African cultures who critically and systematically analyze unreflected cultural worldviews. Through a dialogue with such sages, the trained philosopher can uncover a second-order philosophy within traditional culture.

National-ideological philosophy expresses the political, economic, cultural, and social aspirations of the African liberation struggle. Kwame Nkrumah, Amilcar Cabral, Aimé Césaire, Frantz Fanon, Julius Nyerere, and Léopold Sédar Senghor—the most notable theorists—had often appropriated revolutionary Western theories to overthrow colonialism and establish autonomous African political, economic, and social structures. Three connecting themes dominate national-ideological literature: Marxist socialism, nationalism, and pan-Africanism. Basic Marxist socialist doctrine asserts that capitalism divides society into two antagonistic classes: the proletariat (the exploited workers) and the bourgeoisie (the exploiting owners of production). Colonialism extends this fundamental oppressive relationship on an international scale in which the colonized proletariat works to produce goods for the material benefit and consumption of the bourgeois colonial power. Thus, African socialists maintain that the only way Africa can reach full independence from colonial dominance is by overthrowing capitalism in a revolutionary struggle and adopting a socialist society without class exploitation. Nationalism represents the wish to dismantle colonial political administrations and build sovereign African nations. Colonialism, pan-Africanists believe, exploits the entire African continent. Therefore, all Africans should band together in solidarity to fight colonialism.

For years, African philosophers have been trying to decide which of the four approaches should become the foundation of postcolonial African philosophy. The readings in this chapter represent each of the four positions in the works of Placide Tempels and Léopold Sédar Senghor (ethnophilosophy), Paulin Hountondji and Theophilus Okere (professional philosophy), Henry Odera Oruka and J. O. Sopido (philosophic sagacity), and Kwame Nkrumah and Frantz Fanon (national-ideological philosophy).

ETHNOPHILOSOPHY

Ironically, the African philosophy debate springs from a book that was not written by either an African or a philosopher. "Ethnophilosophy" was a label originally given to *Bantu Philosophy*, written by the Belgian missionary Father Placide Franz Tempels who worked in the Congo from 1933 to 1962. As a missionary, Tempels' main concern was to understand Bantu culture so he could better "civilize" them with Christianity. Tempels believed he had uncovered a Bantu philosophy with five main points (Mudimbe, 1988, pp. 138–139). First, the Bantu have an organized belief system constituting a legitimate philosophy. Second, Bantu philosophy's primary metaphysical category is force, reflecting a dynamic and vitalist conception of the universe. Third, being is force—vital forces order all beings in the universe into a strict cosmological hierarchy of mineral, vegetable, animal, human, ancestral, and divine. Fourth, only Westerners—not the Bantu themselves—have the necessary philosophical knowledge to properly understand Bantu philosophy. Finally, Bantu philosophy, a "primitive philosophy," characterizes the nature of philosophy in all non-Western societies. In the following reading Tempels explains the Bantu notion of being as force.

Bantu Philosophy

Placide Tempels

Christian thought in the West, having adopted the terminology of Greek philosophy and perhaps under its influence, has defined this reality [metaphysics] common to all beings, or, as one should perhaps say, being as such; "the reality that is," "anything that exists," "what is." Its metaphysics has most generally been based upon a fundamentally *static* conception of being.   1

Herein is to be seen the fundamental difference between Western thought and that of the Bantu and other primitive people. (I compare only systems which have inspired widespread "civilizations.")   2

We can conceive the transcendental notion of "being" by separating it from its attribute, "Force," but the Bantu cannot. "Force" in his thought is a necessary element in "being," and the concept "force" is inseparable from the definition of "being." There is no idea among Bantu of "being" divorced from the idea of "force." Without the element "force," "being" cannot be conceived.   3

We hold a *static* conception of "being," they a *dynamic*.   4

What has been said above should be accepted as the basis of Bantu ontology [the branch of philosophy dealing with the nature of being]: in particular, *the concept "force" is bound to the concept "being" even in the most abstract thinking upon the notion of being.*   5

At least it must be said that the Bantu have a double concept concerning being, a concept which can be expressed: "being is that which has force."   6

But I think we go further. Our statement of Bantu philosophy should press as closely as possible its distinctive characteristics. It   7

Placide Tempels. *Bantu Philosophy*. Paris: Présence Africaine, 1959.

seems to me that we shall not attain this precision by formulating the notion of being *in Bantu thought: "being* is that which *possesses* force."

I believe that we should most faithfully render the Bantu thought in European language by saying that Bantu speak, act, live as if, for them, beings were forces. Force is not for them an adventitious, accidental reality. Force is even more than a necessary attribute of beings: *Force is the nature of being, force is being, being is force.* 8

When we think in terms of the concept "being," they use the concept "force." Where we see concrete beings, they see concrete forces. When we say that "beings" are differentiated by their essence or nature, Bantu say that "forces" differ in their essence or nature. They hold that there is the divine force, celestial or terrestrial forces, human forces, animal forces, vegetable and even material or mineral forces. . . . 9

In contradistinction to our definition of being as "that which is," or *"the thing insofar as it is,"* the Bantu definition reads, *"that which is force,"* or *"the thing insofar as it is force,"* or *"an existent force."* We must insist once again that "force" is not for Bantu a necessary, irreducible attribute of being: no, the notion of "force" takes for them the place of the notion "being" in our philosophy. Just as we have, so they have a transcendental, elemental, simple concept: with them "force," with us "being." 10

It is because all being is force and exists only in that it is force, that the category "force" includes of necessity all "beings": God, men living and departed, animals, plants, minerals. . . . 11

It would be a misuse of words to call the Bantu "dynamists" or "energists," as if the universe were animated by some universal force, a sort of unique magical power encompassing all existence, as certain authors seem to believe. . . . Such is a European presentation of a primitive philosophy that is but imperfectly understood. The Bantu make a clear distinction and understand an essential difference between different beings, that is to say, different forces. Among the different kinds of forces they have come to recognize, just as we do, unity, individuality but individuality clearly understood as meaning individuality of forces. 12

Few people have caused such intense controversy in contemporary African intellectual discourse as the Senegalese theorist Léopold Sédar Senghor (b. 1906). Besides being president of the West African country of Senegal from 1961 to 1980, Senghor developed in the 1930s the philosophical, political, cultural, and literary theory called *negritude* (a term coined by the Martinique writer Aimé Césaire). Although Senghor has defined negritude in many often contradictory ways, he has consistently emphasized one element which has provoked the most heated debates within African scholarship: negritude is a metaphysics of a Black identity, an African personality, and a Black soul. Senghor believed that a racial essence created an "authentic, traditional, and pre-colonial, black African culture" shared by all Black people throughout the diaspora. Race as biology, therefore, determined one's essential cultural, political, and social being. The following reading explains these controversial views. Throughout the essay, Senghor manipulates the subject/object distinction pervasive in Western philosophy—objectivity (the material, physical, concrete world apprehended by the senses) is separate from and superior to subjectivity (the unconscious, inner, and psychological world of feeling and emotion). Senghor inverts this duality and privileges subjectivity as essentially Black and African, embodied in his famous assertion that analysis, system, and logic belong to the "white race," whereas, emotion, intuition, sensuality, and spirituality belong to the "black race."

On Negrohood

LÉOPOLD SÉDAR SENGHOR

The African negro . . . reacts more faithfully to stimulation by the   1
object: he espouses its rhythm. This carnal sense of *rhythm*, that of
movement, form and color, is one of his specific characteristics. For
rhythm is the very essence of energy. It is rhythm which is at the bottom of imitation, which plays such a prominent role in the "generative" or "creative" activities of man: in memory, language and art.

　　Let us pause for a moment to illustrate this proposition about the   2
rhythm of a movement in music and dance. When I see a team in
action, at a soccer game for example, I take part in the game with my

Léopold Sédar Senghor. "On Negrohood: Psychology of the African Negro." *Diogenes*
32 (1962): 1–15.

entire body. When I listen to a jazz tune or an African negro song, I have to make every effort not to break into song or dance, for I am now a "civilized" person. George Hardy wrote that the most civilized negro, even in a dinner jacket, always stirred at the sound of a tom-tom. He was quite right. The reason for all this is that team play reproduces the gestures natural to man, and that African negro music and dance (which are one, like music and dance in general) reproduce the movements of the human body, which are in turn attuned to the movements of the brain and of the world: to heart-beat, respiration, the rhythms of marching and making love, ebb and flow, the succession of days and seasons, and in general, all the rhythms of the universe. . . .

Let no one decry this as eroticism. *Sensuality* would be the more 3 accurate term. But *spirituality* would be better still; for the spirituality of the negro is rooted in sensuality: in his physiology. . . .

In dark Africa, people always dance because they feel, and they 4 always dance someone or something. Now to dance is to discover and to *re-create,* to identify oneself with the forces of life, to lead a fuller life, and in short, to *be.* It is, at any rate, the highest form of knowledge. . . . *The reason of classical Europe is analytic through utilization, the reason of the African negro, intuitive through participation.*

PROFESSIONAL PHILOSOPHY

Paulin Hountondji is a professor of philosophy at the National University of Benin, Cotonou. Hountondji's strident articles critiquing ethnophilosophy have presented the African philosophy debate to an international audience, and some of these articles have been collected into *African Philosophy: Myth and Reality.* Hountondji asserts that African philosophy does indeed exist, but it is both a myth *and* a reality. It is a myth because the common definition of African philosophy uses the colonial mythology of African culture as collective and unanimous (everyone agrees with everyone else). Therefore a philosophy based on this myth can only be a myth as well. Yet, African philosophy is also a reality because a body of literature written by Africans on philosophical issues exists and is continually developing.

African Philosophy: Myth and Reality

PAULIN J. HOUNTONDJI

THE POPULAR CONCEPT OF AFRICAN PHILOSOPHY

Without being motivated quite so restrictively as the church   1
ethnophilosophers, these authors [Senghor and his disciples] were
nonetheless intent on locating, beneath the various manifestations of
African civilization, beneath the flood of history which has swept this
civilization along willy-nilly, a solid bedrock which might provide a
foundation of certitudes: in other words, a system of beliefs. In this
quest, we find the same preoccupation as in the negritude movement—a passionate search for the identity that was denied by the colonizer—but now there is the underlying idea that one of the elements
of the cultural identity is precisely "philosophy," the idea that every
culture rests on a specific, permanent, metaphysical substratum.

Let us now ask the crucial question: is this the usual meaning of   2
the word "philosophy"? Is it the way it is understood, for instance, in
the phrases "European philosophy," "nineteenth-century philosophy,"
etc.? Clearly not. It seems as though the word automatically changes
its meaning as soon as it ceases to be applied to Europe or to America
and is applied to Africa. This is a well-known phenomenon. As our
Kenyan colleague Henry Odera humorously remarks:

> What may be a superstition is paraded as "African religion," and the
> white world is expected to endorse that it is indeed a religion but an
> African religion. What in all cases is a mythology is paraded as
> "African philosophy," and again the white culture is expected to
> endorse that it is indeed a philosophy but an African philosophy.
> What is in all cases a dictatorship is paraded as "African democra-
> cy," and the white culture is again expected to endorse that it is so.
> And what is clearly a dedevelopment or pseudo-development is
> described as "development," and again the white world is expected
> to endorse that it is development—but of course "African develop-
> ment." ["Mythologies as African Philosophy"]

Words do indeed change their meanings miraculously as soon as   3
they pass from the Western to the African context, and not only in the

Paulin J. Hountondji. *African Philosophy: Myth and Reality.* Translated by Henri Evans, with Jonathan Rée. London: Hutchinson University Library for Africa, 1983.

vocabulary of European or American writers but also, through faithful imitation, in that of Africans themselves. That is what happens to the word "philosophy": applied to Africa, it is supposed to designate no longer the specific discipline it evokes in its Western context but merely a collective world-view, an implicit, spontaneous, perhaps even unconscious system of beliefs to which all Africans are supposed to adhere. This is a vulgar usage of the word, justified presumably by the supposed vulgarity of the geographical context to which it is applied.

Behind this usage, then, there is a myth at work, the myth of prim-   4
itive unanimity, with its suggestion that in "primitive" societies—that is to say, non-Western societies—everybody always agrees with everybody else. It follows that in such societies there can never be individual beliefs or philosophies but only collective systems of belief. The word "philosophy" is then used to designate each belief-system of this kind, and it is tacitly agreed among well-bred people that in this context it could not mean anything else.

One can easily detect in this one of the founding acts of the "sci-   5
ence" (or rather the pseudo-science) called ethnology, namely, the generally tacit thesis that non-Western societies are absolutely specific, the silent postulate of a difference in *nature* (and not merely in the *evolutionary stage* attained, with regard to particular types of achievement), of a difference in *quality* (not merely in quantity or *scale*) between so-called "primitive" societies and developed ones. Cultural anthropology (another name for ethnology) owes its supposed autonomy (notably in relation to sociology) to this arbitrary division of the human community into two types of societies which are taken, arbitrarily and without proof, to be fundamentally different.

But let us return to the myth of unanimity. It would seem at first   6
sight that this theoretical consensus postulated by ethnophilosophy among all members of each "primitive" community should produce a parallel consensus, at the level of results if not of methods, among all ethnophilosophers studying the same community. But, curiously enough, instead of an ideal consensus, a fine unanimity of all those "primitive philosophers," ethnophilosophical literature offers us a rich harvest of not only diverse but also sometimes frankly contradictory works.

But I can see the objection being raised that such differences are nor-   7
mal [as those between ethnophilosophers such as Tempels and Alexis

Kagamé], that the diversity of works is a source of wealth and not of weakness, that the internal contradictions of ethnophilosophy can be found in any science worthy of the name—physics, chemistry, mathematics, linguistics, psychoanalysis, sociology, etc.—that they are a sign of vitality, not inconsistency, a condition of progress rather than an obstacle in the path of discovery. It may be added that, as in all sciences, a reality may exist without being immediately understood, and that consequently it is not surprising if an implicit system of thought can be reconstructed only as a result of long, collective and contradictory research.

The only thing this objection overlooks is the "slight difference"   8 between the sciences cited and ethnophilosophy that they do not postulate anything remotely comparable with the supposed unanimity of a human community; that in these sciences, moreover, a contradiction is never stagnant but always progressive, never final or absolute but indicative of an *error,* of the *falsity* of a hypothesis or thesis, which is bound to emerge from a rational investigation of the object itself, whereas a contradiction between two ethnophilosophical theses is necessarily circular, since it can never be resolved by experimentation or any other method of verification. The point is that an ethnophilosophical contradiction is necessarily *antinomal* in the Kantian sense [i.e., the idea can be both affirmed and denied]; thesis and antithesis are equally demonstrable—in other words, equally gratuitous. In such a case contradiction does not generate synthesis but simply demonstrates the need to re-examine the very foundations of the discipline and to provide a critique of ethnophilosophical reason and perhaps ethnological reason too.

Ethnophilosophy can now be seen in its true light. Because it has   9 to account for an imaginary unanimity, to interpret a text which nowhere exists and has to be constantly reinvented, it is a science without an object, a "crazed language" accountable to nothing, a discourse that has no referent, so that its falsity can never be demonstrated. Tempels can then maintain that for the Bantu being is power, and Kagamé can beg to differ: we have no means of settling the quarrel. It is clear, therefore, that the "Bantu philosophy" of the one is not the philosophy of the Bantu but that of Tempels, that the "Bantu-Rwandais philosophy" of the other is not that of the Rwandais but that of Kagamé. Both of them simply make use of African traditions and oral literature and project on to them their own philosophical beliefs, hoping to enhance their credibility thereby.

That is how the functioning of this thesis of collective African phi- 10
losophy works: it is a smokescreen behind which each author is able
to manipulate his own philosophical views. It has nothing beyond this
ideological function: it is an indeterminate discourse with no object.

TOWARDS A NEW CONCEPT OF AFRICAN PHILOSOPHY

If we now return to our question, namely, whether philosophy resides 11
in the world-view described or in the description itself, we can now
assert that if it resides in either, it must be the second, the description
of that vision, even if this is, in fact, a self-deluding invention that
hides behind its own products. African philosophy does exist therefore, but in a new sense, as a literature produced by Africans and
dealing with philosophical problems.

A contradiction? Oh no! Some may be surprised that, having 12
patiently dismantled the ethnophilosophical machine, we should now
be trying to restore it. They have simply failed to understand that we
are merely recognizing the existence of that literature as *philosophical
literature,* whatever may be its *value* and *credibility*. What we are
acknowledging is what it *is*, not what it *says*. Having laid bare the
mythological assumptions on which it is founded (these having suppressed all question of its status), we can now pay greater attention to
the fact of its existence as a determinate form of philosophical literature which, however mystified and mystifying it may be (mystifying
became mystified), nevertheless belongs to the history of African literature in general.

Let us be accurate: the issue here is only *African* ethnophilosophy. 13
A work like *Bantu Philosophy* does not belong to African philosophy,
since its author is not African; but Kagamé's work is an integral part of
African philosophical literature. In other words, speaking of African
philosophy in a new sense, we must draw a line, within ethnophilosophical literature in general, between African and non-African writers, not because one category is better than the other, or because both
might not, in the last analysis, say the same thing, but because, the
subject being *African* philosophy, we cannot exclude a geographical
variable, taken here as empirical, contingent, extrinsic to the content
or significance of the discourse and as quite apart from any questions
of *theoretical connections*. Thus Tempels' work, although it deals with
an African subject and has played a decisive role in the development

of African ethnophilosophy, belongs to *European* scientific literature, in the same way as anthropology in general, although it deals with non-Western societies, is an embodiment of Western science, no more and no less.

A happy consequence of this demarcation is that it emphasizes   14 certain subtle nuances and occasional serious divergences which might otherwise have passed unnoticed and which differentiate African authors whom we initially grouped together as ethnophilosophers. It is thus possible to see the immense distance which separates, for instance, Bahoken's *Clairières métaphysiques africaines,* justifiably assessed as a perfect example of ideological twaddle designed by an apparently nationalistic African to flatter the exotic tastes of the Western public, from Kwame Nkrumah's *Consciencism,* written chiefly for the African public and aimed at making it aware of its new cultural identity, even though Nkrumah's book, unfortunately, partakes of the ethnological conception that there can be such a thing as a collective philosophy.

Another even more important consequence is that this African   15 philosophical literature can now be seen to include philosophical works of those African authors who do not believe in the myth of a collective philosophy or who reject it explicitly. . . .

But more than that: African philosophical literature includes   16 works which make no attempt whatever to broach the problem of "African philosophy," either to assert or to deny its existence. In fact, we must extend the concept to include all the research into Western philosophy carried out by Africans. This broadening of the horizon implies no contradiction: just as the writings of Western anthropologists on African societies belong to Western scientific literature, so the philosophical writings of Africans on the history of Western thought are an integral part of African philosophical literature. So, obviously, African philosophical works concerning problems that are not specially related to the African experience should also be included.

The essential point here is that we have produced a radically new def-   17 inition of African philosophy, the criterion now being the geographical origin of the authors rather than an alleged specificity of content. The effect of this is to broaden the narrow horizon which has hitherto been imposed on African philosophy and to treat it, as now conceived, as a methodical inquiry with the same universal aims as those of any other philosophy in the world. In short, it destroys the dominant mythological conception of Africanness and restores the simple,

being

obvious truth that Africa is above all a continent and the concept of Africa an empirical, geographical concept and not a metaphysical one. The purpose of this "demythologizing" of the idea of Africa and African philosophy is simply to free our faculty for theorizing from all the intellectual impediments and prejudices which have so far prevented it from getting off the ground.

The Nigerian philosopher Theophilus Okere was one of the first African philosophers to investigate the relevance of hermeneutical theory and method for developing African philosophy. Ethnophilosophy's main fault, Okere insists, lies in its failure to see that the philosophy is primarily hermeneutical—that is, it grows out of and depends on a cultural-historical background. Thus, by understanding the hermeneutical relationship between culture and philosophy, African philosophers can begin to lay a proper and nonethnophilosophical foundation for contemporary African philosophy. The following reading explores the German philosopher Hans-Georg Gadamer's concepts of "prejudice" and the "hermeneutical circle." Human understanding and interpretation is, by nature, informed by our prejudices—our presuppositions and prejudgments—that are themselves created from our particular historical and cultural background. The past always shapes the present and future; understanding and interpretation can only evolve against a past or a tradition even when it attempts to leave that past behind. Thus, human beings are locked in a circular play among the past, present, and future in which there is no absolute culturally or historically neutral knowledge.

The Role of Prejudice and the Hermeneutical Circle

THEOPHILUS OKERE

Hans-Georg Gadamer, in his two major works on hermeneutics— 1
Wahrheit und Methode, Grundzuge einer philosophischen Hermeneutik ["Truth and Method Characteristics of a Philosophical

Theophilus Okere. *African Philosophy: A Historico-Hermeneutical Investigation of the Conditions of Its Possibility.* Lanham, Md.: University Press of America, 1983.

Hermeneutic"], and *Kleine Schriften I, Philosophie, Hermeneutik* *["Short Writings I, Philosophy Hermeneutic"]*—has developed and explicated the insights reached by Heidegger. What the latter cryptically calls the *vor-Struktur of Verstehen* ["Pre-structure of Understanding"], Gadamer names by the prosaic expression Prejudice. His studies of . . . Prejudices contain the kernel of the thesis we have been trying to establish. Gadamer does not hide the fact that . . . Prejudices are in disrepute in present usage. But this is a historical accident due, in fact, to the prejudices of the Enlightenment which tended to understand *Praejudicium (Vorurteil, préjugé,* prejudgment*)* merely negatively.

The Enlightenment understood it as its mission to accomplish the   2 liberation of human thought from superstition and prejudice in order to effect the triumph of Logos over Mythos. The antithesis Logos/Mythos was taken over but conversely evaluated by the Romantics in the programme of the cult of the noble savage and the quest of original innocence. Such an antithesis is artificial. "As a matter of fact," says Gadamer,

> the presupposition of the secret darkness in which lies the mythical collective consciousness existing before all thought, is just as dogmatically abstract as that of a perfect state of a finished Enlightenment or that of absolute knowledge. The primeval wisdom is only the antipodes of the "primeval stupidity." All mythical consciousness is always already knowledge and by the very fact that it knows of divine powers it already exceeds the mere trembling before the power . . . but also goes beyond a collective life, spell-bound in a magical ritual. [H. G. Gadamer, *Wahrheit und Methode*, p. 258]

Just like the Romantics, the historical school took over the   3 schemata of the Enlightenment. But to realise the finitude of human knowledge and existence is to realise that it is always bounded and limited and that the idea of absolute knowledge is impossible to historical humanity.

Therefore there can be no question of getting rid of all prejudices.   4 Taken etymologically, *praejudicium* is not necessarily negative. It simply means those predispositions and anticipations which precede the actual and definitive judgment. There are legitimate prejudices. The fact that authority is substituted for one's judgment makes authority a source of prejudices. But if this authority is based on knowledge, as it should be, the resulting prejudice need not be negatively disqualified as a source of error. It is indeed a source of truth. The authority of persons is finally based on their judgment to ours. Authority has thus more to do with knowledge than with obedience. It is based on a presumption of intelligence and is legitimised in the person. Tradition is only a form of authority. No amount of emancipation can free one from one's culture and heritage.

Tradition, Authority, Prejudice, all three terms are ambiguous and one can view them negatively as a source of error or positively as the necessary accompaniment of all human knowledge and experience. Tradition, authority and prejudice are just other words for pre-experience and pre-knowledge which become indeed the conditions of all our future experiences and knowledge. They underline the essential historicity of man, the fact that he is born into and limited within a culture from which limits he can soar, though always in a limited way.

Thus there can be no experience, no knowledge, no interpretation, no philosophy without presuppositions *(voraussetzungslos).* This is what Heidegger meant by the term *vor-Struktur.* These presuppositions work at the three levels of . . . tradition, *Weltanschauung* [worldview] and language. In other words, our respective cultures provide the mines from where we have all our presuppositions. Contradicting the epistemological tradition since Aristotle, Gadamer affirms that it is not so much our judgment as our prejudgment (prejudices) which make up our Being.

The vain quest of historians who pursue the goal of history without presuppositions only in fact hides the dogged obstinacy of the presuppositions which remain undiscovered but continue to influence and determine the historian.

With the gift of illustration by simple but perceptive examples so characteristic of his work, Gadamer proves how laden with presuppositions are those who cry out loudest against presuppositions: "We know this phenomenon sufficiently from the way historians work. They claim to be critical, that is, to examine sources and witnesses on a historical question with the superior justice of a judge, in order to get behind the matter. But does not the silent effectivity of guiding presuppositions not always already underlie such pretended criticism? At the end of all criticism of sources and witnesses, there always exists a final criterion of credibility, which depends on nothing else than on what one regards as possible and is prepared to believe. . . . Yes, indeed, there is more to say at the end. Just as real life so also does history speak to us only if and when it speaks into our prior judgments about things, men and times. All understanding of the meaningful presupposed that we bring along a complex of such prejudgments.

5

6

7

8

Heidegger has designated this fact as the hermeneutical circle. We understand only what we already know; we get out of a thing only what we read into it."

If interpretation means grasping something explicitly and themat-   9 ically, i.e. in its *als-Struktur* (as-structure) [the structure of something which has already been made explicit through interpretation], the fact is that it is the hallmark of human finitude, that one cannot grasp everything thematically and simultaneously. While some things are grasped and made manifest others remain in the background in order even to make the grasping and manifestation possible. Without this background nothing would show in the foreground. Without the framework there would be no apparition. Without the prejudgment there would be not judgment. Gadamer puts it thus:

> "In truth, it lies in the historicity of our existence that prejudgments in the literal sense of the word make up the prior orientedness of all our capacity to experience. They are the prejudices (biases) of our openness to the world which are precisely the conditions for the fact that we experience something, for the fact that what we experience says something to us. . . . We are . . . prepossessed by something and precisely thanks to this prepossession we are open-minded for something new, something other, something true. It is as Plato explained it with the lovely comparison between bodily good and spiritual nourishment: while the one can be rejected, for instance at the behest of the doctor, the other is already irrevocably assimilated."

It is thus clear that the concept of prejudice is at the very heart of the hermeneutical problem, bound up, as it is, with the hermeneutical circle. Without its negative overtone, prejudice is another word for all the background—historical, linguistic, cultural, etc. from which no philosophical speculation, be it ever so rarified, can be free, because in it and by it, it is, moves and has its being.

The *vor-Struktur,* the pre-structure of understanding . . . together   10 with the *als-Struktur* (as-structure) of interpretation represents the so-called hermeneutical circle. "All interpretation that is meant to accompany understanding must have understood the object before hand" [Heidegger, *Being and Time,* p. 152].

But this circle is not a vicious circle which is unavoidable and   11 merely to be tolerated. It is of the essence of understanding itself and the aim should not be to get out of it but to enter into it properly. This circle is not an orbit in which any type of knowledge at all moves but it is the expression of the existential *vor-Struktur*—prestructure of

Dasein [the human being's ontological essence] himself. It is no vicious circle. Its positive nature can only then become fruitful if and when interpretation "grasps that its first, its continuous and its last task remains not to allow *Vorhabe, Vorsicht and Vorgriff* [prior acquisition, prior view, and preconception: the three elements of the *vor-Struktur*] to be prejudged by lucky ideas due to chance or by popular conception but rather the assuring of the scientific theme through the working out of this *vor-Struktur* from the object itself" [Heidegger, *Being and Time*, p. 153]. The circle of understanding belongs to the structure of meaning itself, a phenomenon that is rooted in the existential constitution of *Dasein*, the interpreting understanding.

PHILOSOPHIC SAGACITY

Henry Odera Oruka is a professor of philosophy at the University of Nairobi, Kenya, and his main contribution to African philosophy is his formulation of the concept of philosophic sagacity. In the reading below Oruka criticizes professional philosophy's belief that philosophical sagacity is no different from ethnophilosophy by showing the difference between philosophical sagacity (second-order thought) and culture philosophy (first-order thought).

Sagacity in African Philosophy

HENRY ODERA ORUKA

THE FOUR TRENDS

Recently I characterized four trends in current African philosophy: [1] ethnophilosophy, philosophic sagacity, nationalist-ideological philosophy, and professional philosophy. These four trends appear to characterize the crossroads of philosophy in modern Africa. There are some who feel that no approach except that of ethnophilosophy represents the right path. This claim is already well refuted by the literature ema-

Henry Odera Oruka. "Sagacity in African Philosophy." *International Philosophical Quarterly* 23(4) (1983): 383–393.

nating from professional philosophy. Yet, the latter also has an arrogant claim of its own. The claim is not representative of all those who subscribe to this school. It is the claim that authentic African philosophy can and must only be a scientific (i.e., systematic) and/or written philosophy. It thus rules out philosophic sagacity as part of African philosophy, since this trend is largely unwritten and apparently "pre-scientific." Within our ranks the position of Prof. P. Bodrunin and that of Prof. P. Hountondji are representative of this claim. . . .

Philosophic sagacity . . . is still widely unknown as a proper 2 aspect of philosophy in Africa. Nevertheless, it is the only trend that it seems to me can give an all-acceptable decisive blow to the position of ethnophilosophy. None of the other two trends can objectively decisively play this role. And the reason is because they (i.e., professional philosophy and nationalist-ideological philosophy) are generally suspected of smuggling Western techniques into African philosophy. Those who make this charge can hardly be convinced, say, that professional philosophy in Africa is a refutation of the presuppositions of ethnophilosophy. They would maintain that it is a fallacy to use professional philosophy (in their view a "foreign philosophy") to reject ethnophilosophy.

It should be noted that ethnophilosophy implies that traditional 3 Africa is free from (1) philosophic, rational discourse and (2) personalized philosophical activity. Philosophy here is treated as a general communal activity in which ready-made beliefs and emotions rather than reflection decide the outcome. Philosophic sagacity stands to prove the contrary. It shows that the problem in traditional Africa is not lack of logic, reason, or scientific curiosity, since we can find many sages there with a system of thought employing a rigorous use of these mental gifts. It shows that communal consensus, a fact typical of most traditional societies, should not be seen as a hindrance for individual critical reflection. Just as religion and all kinds of dogmatic fanaticism did not kill philosophy in the West, traditional African folk wisdoms and taboos left some room for real philosophic thought. . . .

PHILOSOPHIC SAGACITY AND CULTURE PHILOSOPHY

Let me make a distinction between "philosophic sagacity" on the one 4 hand and "culture philosophy" (a philosophy of culture) on the other. Philosophic sagacity is a reflection of a person who is (1) a sage and

(2) a thinker. As a sage the person is versed in the wisdoms and traditions of his people, and very often he is recognized by the people
themselves as having this gift. In certain cases, however, he may not
be so recognized. Being a sage, however, does not necessarily make
one a philosopher. Some of the sages are simply moralists and the disciplined die-hard faithfuls to a tradition. Others are merely historians
and good interpreters of the history and customs of their people. In
short, they are *wise* within the conventional and historical confines of
their culture. But they may not be wise (rational) in understanding or
solving the inconsistencies of their culture nor coping with the foreign
innovations that encroach on it. In other words, they are the spokesmen of their people, but they speak what after all is known to almost
every average person within the culture.

Some sages go beyond mere sagacity and attain a philosophic   5
capacity. As sages they are versed in the beliefs and wisdoms of their
people. But as thinkers, they are rationally critical and they opt for or
recommend only those aspects of the beliefs and wisdoms which satisfy their rational scrutiny. In this respect they are potentially or con-
temporarily in clash with the die-hard adherents of the prevailing
common beliefs. Such sages are also capable of conceiving and rationally recommending ideas offering alternatives to the commonly
accepted opinions and practices. They transcend the communal wisdom. They are lucky if the people recognize this special gift in them.
Then they are treated with special respect and their suggestions
peacefully and positively reform the people. Should the people fail to
recognize their gift, then their safety in the community would demand
that they remain silent and keep mum. Socrates is a good example of
the unrecognized sage who failed to keep silence. And so he came to
the expected logically predictable fate.

So much for philosophic sagacity. Now, something about culture   6
philosophy. Every culture has ideas and beliefs which underlie and
justify it. Let us for the sake of simplicity refer to these as the *mythos*
of a culture. To be really conversant with a culture one must be familiar with its *mythos*. The *mythos* forms a system which in a broad and
loose sense can be referred to as the people's philosophy. Its contents
make up the "philosophy" as underlying the culture in question and
acting as its immediate and ultimate justification. Sages and every reasonable man in society are supposed to be conversant with the philosophy of their culture, i.e. with its *mythos*. To distinguish such
mythos from philosophy proper, let us refer to it as "a culture philoso-

phy." To have expertise in a culture philosophy is often the mark of the sages of the culture in question. However, in a free or well-informed society every reasonable person is conversant with the prevailing culture philosophy.

Beliefs or truth-claims with a culture philosophy are generally treated as "absolutes." Anything outside or contradictory to the culture is treated with indifference and even hostility. Those sages or persons who are experts in the culture defend this philosophy and the structure of their society with the zeal of fanatical ideologists defending their political line.   7

Philosophic sagacity, however, is often a product and a reflective reevaluation of the culture philosophy. The few sages who possess the philosophic inclination make a critical assessment of their culture and its underlying beliefs. Using the power of *reason* rather than the celebrated beliefs of the communal consensus and explanation, the sage philosopher produces a system within a system, and order within an order.   8

The first order is that of the culture philosophy. It is absolute in its ideas and truth-claims and has an ideological war with anything to the contrary. Ordinary sages (the nonphilosophic sages) are specialists in explaining and maintaining this order. They may even distinguish themselves in various aspects of the system. Some may be poets, herbalists, medicine men, musicians, fortune tellers, etc., etc. The common thing they have is that their explanations or thought do not go beyond the premises and conclusions given by the prevailing culture.   9

In contrast, the second order is that of philosophic sagacity. It is a critical reflection on the first order. In many other cases it is a critical rebellion against the first order conformity and anachronism. While the first order glorifies the communal conformity, philosophic sagacity is skeptical of communal consensus, and it employs reason to assess it. While the first order is purely absolutist and ideological, the second order is generally open-minded and rationalistic. Its truths are given as tentative and ratio-cinative, not as God-sent messages.   10

APPENDIX: AN EXAMPLE OF "AFRICAN SAGACITY"

Theme: God
by Paul Mbuya K'akoko

1. The Luos had no Religion *(Dini)* in the European sense before the whites came to Kenya.
2. In the European sense religion is an organized group way of worship.
3. The Luos did not organize worship. But the Luos knew of and worshipped God. They did so individually and in various ways. They generally did so by turning their faces towards the Sun or Moon. The Sun was the symbol (Fire) of God.
4. I believe God is one, both for the Whites and Blacks.
5. I also believe no one is capable of knowing really what God is. Those who claim to do so are wrong.
6. The Existence of God is necessary to curb the permission of everything, including *evil* in society.
7. *How come that without God everything would be permitted?*
   Leaders give rules to their societies, to those over whom they rule. But the Universe (as a society) has no leader except God. God gives rules to the universe as leaders make rules to their societies. Any society without rules would be in chaos, and so the Universe without God would have no rules and hence, chaos.
8. God can do anything, but he only does the good things.
9. *What makes you think contrary to the traditional Luo belief that every people (tribe) have their own God?*
   The Luo were mistaken in this belief. God is one for every person, tribe or race. There is one supreme God governing nature.
10. *Proof:* We have more *Kwe* (peace) and *Chanro* (uniformity) in the world than we have chaos: A goat, for example, brings forth a goat, not a hen. And a dog produces a dog, not a man. And this is a proof that there is one supermind governing nature and the world. *Chanro* (uniformity) is always the work of a mind. But chaos (*Kethruok* or *Nginjruok*) is often an accident arising from the absence of mind. At death, for example, the body rots *(Kethore)* because the mind abandons the body.

The Nigerian philosopher J. O. Sopido and his American colleague Barry Hallen both teach at the University of Ife in Nigeria. Sopido and Hallen maintain that many popular characterizations of "traditional African thought" as being uncritical and unreflective thinking come from the erroneous assumption that certain words and ideas are universal and cross-cultural. Most scholars of African culture, particularly anthropologists and ethnophilosophers, assume that

English words and concepts mean the same thing when found in African cultures. However, W. V. O. Quine, a contemporary Western philosopher, believes that it is impossible to accurately translate the abstract ideas of one language into another language—what Quine calls the *indeterminacy thesis of radical translation.* This creates a profound problem when Western-trained and English-speaking scholars try to represent and understand an alien belief system in another language. Sopido and Hallen test this claim by centering their research around discussions with Yoruba wise men called *onisegun* or "masters of medicine." With the help of the *onisegun,* Sopido and Hallen linguistically analyze (what they call conceptual analysis) three words and concepts integral to Yoruba thought systems: *aje* (witchcraft), *imo* (knowledge), and *igabago* (belief). Western-trained scholars commonly translate these African words with the meanings they hold in the English language. However, Sopido and Hallen's research reveals that *aje, imo, igabago* have something in common with "witchcraft," "knowledge," and "belief," but they are by no means equivalent; linguistic meanings are not universal; it is dangerous to assume that meanings in one language can be paradigms in another; and finally, conceptual systems of alien languages have implicit in them alternative moral, psychological, and metaphysical systems that are philosophically relevant in their own right. In the following reading, Sopido and Hallen summarize these findings and raise questions about some of the difficulties that such linguistic research and cross-cultural analysis with the *onisegun* (or anyone from another culture) inevitably brings.

Knowledge, Belief, and Witchcraft

BARRY HALLEN AND J. O. SOPIDO

At the very beginning we referred to the disrepute of African philosophy, and to the problematic between it and what is commonly

1

Barry Hallen and J. O. Sopido. *Knowledge, Belief, and Witchcraft: Analytical Experiments in African Philosophy.* London: Ethnographica, 1986.

referred to as traditional African culture. Africans themselves are understandably wary of attempts to codify inherited thought systems into static cultural ideologies to which the name "philosophy" is then appended. Attempts at "analysing" African conceptual and belief systems, again in the name of philosophy, have produced speculative abortions that in the end so discredited the field that further attempts were discouraged. Consequently there are any number of examples of what African philosophy in relation to traditional thought should not be, and few of what it should be, at least in our opinion.

Is this a book on or of African philosophy? The question may 2 seem redundant, but we think that it is not. In fact our answer to it must be carefully phrased: first in terms of methodology and then of content. In the broadest sense the methodology we are applying is a variety of conceptual analysis, which is certainly an acceptable approach as far as contemporary academic philosophy is concerned. Where we run into a problem with some of our colleagues in African studies and in philosophy generally is over the issue of who is performing or is entitled to perform the analyses.

Philosophy has its own tradition of being a *second-order* disci- 3 pline. This term too is given various definitions, but probably the most common is that the philosopher is a rather rare and also unique creature whose main task is to reflect upon ("analyse") and criticize things that most other people take for granted. A first-order discipline (let us take, for example, spiritual immortality) has empirical compatibility with other kinds of truths (scientific, for example). But the philosopher would not be expected, *qua* philosopher, to create a religion or to advise ordinary mortals on how to cope with their everyday problems.

The "problem" referred to above, that has arisen from our work 4 with the *onisegun* to date, arises from our supposed violation of this second-order convention in two respects. Firstly, in order to hold the discussions with them that we have had, we are doing fieldwork— going outside of academia and the university, into villages and people's homes, and in an embarrassingly empirical manner collecting information from them about what selected components of their conceptual system mean. This kind of first-order enterprise may be a task for the linguist or anthropologist, who are professionally trained for it. But it is not the sort of enterprise associated with philosophy or with the training one obtains from it as a discipline.

Secondly, our professional relationship with the *onisegun* is also 5 subject to challenge. If we relate to them as colleagues (and they to us), as philosophers in their own right, can this be justified in view of the fact that they have undergone no professional training in philosophy? And, if this cannot be justified, then precisely what sort of relationship do we bear to them? If their role is reduced to that of informants, then once again we seem to have got ourselves involved in the kind of first-order enterprise the professional, academic philosopher should not undertake.

We maintain that the evidence and arguments [comparing Yoruba   6
and English terms regarding knowledge] challenge this. The Yoruba do not in general *regard* oral tradition as knowledge, as is evidenced by their classifying it as *"igabago"* rather than *"imo."* The conditions or criteria they assign to it, and to second-hand information in general, indicate that it is regarded in a hypothetical and critical manner. Oral cultures, cultures that depend upon an oral *mode* for recording their beliefs, may express them in an apparently proverbial or unreasoned form due to considerations such as memorial economy. In other words, what an oral culture can afford to write down, and this may affect the manner in which information in the two cultures is recorded and expressed. But this need not imply that the intellectual attitudes maintained towards information in the two sorts of cultures are also different.

If a culture maintains its abstract meanings and beliefs in an oral   7
mode, and the academic philosopher decides to take an interest in them, there does not seem to be any other choice but for him to have face-to-face meetings with members of that culture. Exactly who would be the most appropriate members of that culture for him to meet is a question which we shall discuss later on. For the moment, surely this important if preliminary point may be acknowledged. Learning about oral cultures requires meeting with members of the cultures, for oral information comes out of mouths. Whether we went to meet the *onisegun* in their homes, or whether they came to meet with us in the university (would this too have been "fieldwork"?), was decided more out of considerations of diplomacy and mutual respect than of methodology (although meeting such people, relaxed and *in situ,* is somewhat easier).

We therefore argue that to refer to this kind of enterprise as "field-   8
work" is an unnecessary and misleading exaggeration. "Fieldwork" is a technical term better reserved for anthropology, to accounts and analyses arising from the likes of participant observation, and so forth. We prefer the term "collaborative analysis" to describe our own

approach, but before we will be in a position to explain why, we must first take up the issue of who it is that is competent *to* analyse.

The stereotype of the uncritical, unreflective, "closed" nature of   9
African systems of thought has proved extraordinarily resilient and resistant to criticism. One obvious reason for this is that most of the evidence available supports it. To a limited extent we would agree. However, on the basis of the evidence we have collected, we are arguing that (at least) not all of Yoruba society fits the stereotype. And that we have "discovered" this, leads us to suspect that our method-ological approach differs in some important respects from those of other academic and professional disciplines that have a similar inter-est. We also believe that further applications of our methodological approach, by philosophers, may lead to other interesting discoveries, not only about the Yoruba thought system but about those of other African ethnic groups as well.

Some of our colleagues in philosophy in Africa have already   10
arrived at an assessment of our approach on the basis of previous methodological and research publications arising from this same research project. This assessment differs in several important respects from our own understanding of what we are doing.

In this assessment our approach has been awarded the rather   11
unpalatable (euphoniously, at least) appellation of "philosophical sagacity." The most vigorous point of contention in the evaluation *of philosophical sagacity* stems from the following:

> It is one thing to show that there are men capable of philosophical dialogue in Africa and another to show that there are African philosophers in the sense of those who have engaged in organized systematic reflections on the thoughts, beliefs and practices of their people. [Bodunrin, "The Question of African Philosophy," p. 170]

This distinction, between the sage who is able to make *some* con-   12
tribution to philosophical discussion and the technical, analytic, aca-demic philosopher, coalesces with the following: "the philosopher's approach to this study [African traditional culture and beliefs] must be one of criticism, by which one does not mean negative appraisal, but rational, impartial and articulate appraisal whether positive or nega-tive" (Bodunrin, p. 173). And the ramification that: "showing why a people hold a particular belief is not sufficient to show that the belief is rational" (Bodunrin, p. 175).

We said earlier on that the best way to answer the question about   13
whether this is a book on African philosophy was to deal with it in
terms of methodology and content. The above discussion, however
incomplete, has concentrated upon methodology. We shall now make
the transition to discussing the *content* of our work with the *onisegun*
because this is a better ground upon which to base a reply to this
query about their philosophical capacities.

Let us first identify the level of analysis upon which we are work-   14
ing at present. Both Chapters 2 and 3 [comparing Yoruba and English
terms] demonstrate that deeply rooted assumptions about the universality of meanings ("knowledge," "belief," "witch") and the correlative
production of misrepresentative translations of Yoruba meanings said
to refer to the "same" things, have led to fundamentally false interpretations and analyses of Yoruba thought. In some cases these false
interpretations have themselves been universalized and said to be representative of African thought in general.

African philosophy, insofar as it may come to deal with the analy-   15
sis of African languages (or meanings) and evaluation of the beliefs of
African cultures, will not even be in a position to begin until such
things have been correctly understood and translated in a determinate
manner. Part of the power of our exposition derives from the fact that
it plays upon a dialectic between false and true meanings in translation; for example, the Yoruba being criticized for classifying certain
kinds of information as knowledge when in fact they do not.

What we are doing with the *onisegun,* therefore, is to begin the   16
process of understanding Yoruba meanings anew. No important
abstract meanings (we hope) are taken for granted because, as Quine
has pointed out, this is often how misrepresentation arises. The
detailed analyses of Yoruba meanings that constitute the heart of
Chapters 2 and 3 were performed by the *onisegun* as much or more
than by us. We feel this is amply demonstrated by their statements.
Discussions were "led" in the sense that we usually would select the
term we were interested in discussing and we would ask for clarifica-
tions of points that seemed obscure. But the *onisegun* with whom we
are dealing do not take kindly to being asked leading questions. *They*
are the authorities, and though they too respect us in our capacity as
university lecturers, in the discussions our role is that of the intellectual gadfly who persists in raising questions that do not often arise in
any society, and in reintroducing offshoots of them until our understanding and curiosity (as they see it) are satisfied.

We have never claimed that this role entitles them to be   17
acclaimed philosophers, in the professional, academic sense. In these
discussions we, as academic philosophers, also play a role, in that we
usually choose the topic, introduce it, pursue it, write it up in systematic form, and compare it with purported counterparts in other conceptual systems. But none of this could take place without the *analytic*
(as opposed to expository) contributions of the *onisegun*. . . .

When it comes to the question of criticism in the sense of either   18
the *onisegun* deliberately modifying or rejecting an element of the
conceptual system because they find it inadequate, or deliberately
creating and then comparing alternative concepts with a view to identifying the more satisfactory, there is only limited evidence of this kind
of thinking in the material we have presented.

As far as the first alternative is concerned, evidence of this is   19
found in those passages in which the *onisegun*, when explaining the
criteria governing the application of a certain term, clearly appreciate
the value of those criteria and the negative consequences of abandoning them. . . . And they are not simply rationalizing. With reference to the second alternative this was, from the outset, a task we had
assigned to ourselves. We hoped and have tried, once we had arrived
at a reasonably deliberate understanding of a selection of abstract
Yoruba meanings, to work out interesting comparisons with some of
their English-language counterparts.

To return to "philosophical sagacity." The terms "philosophy" and   20
"sage" are not, to our mind, compatible. The connotation of "sage" is
that of a wise man, but wise in the archaic ("traditional"?) sense of
being knowledgeable about his people's beliefs, and not particularly
or deliberately critical *of* them. If the philosopher's task is to
analyse/criticize, there is then an element of inconsistency in conjoin-
ing the two.

To return to "collaborative analysis." By the word "collaborative"   21
we mean to emphasize the fact that the *onisegun*, explicitly, deliberately, and without being "led," participate in the piecemeal analysis of
their conceptual and thought system. In the literature generally classi-
fied under the heading "African philosophy," one can go from the
extreme of the "sage" who undertakes the expression of an abstract
system of thought *entirely* on his own to that of the alien observer who
denies to an African people *any* significant powers of conceptual
analysis and undertakes the process entirely on his own. Our own
approach falls somewhere between the two. Both we and the *onise-*

gun participate in the process of analysis. They are men of keen intellect as well as of extraordinary practical skills. This is the basis upon which we work with them, and this is the sense in which we refer to them as our traditional colleagues.

We have still to come to terms with our original question about   22
the relationship between this book and African philosophy. As the title indicates we regard the entire enterprise as an experiment, open to modification or revision in terms of both methodology and content. There is a certain deliberate irony in using Quine's indeterminacy thesis as a translation factor, as the intellectual device that eventually enables us to argue for genuine Yoruba conceptual alternatives. For it is indeterminacy in translation that may be contained on the abstract level; the profound sensitivity it generates to the possibility of alternative meanings is invaluable to the academic engaged in cross-cultural studies.

For something has happened. A category of information that was   23
supposed to be "knowledge" no longer is. People who were supposed to be "witches" no longer are. From a cross-cultural point-of-view we therefore believe that this book introduces a new dimension in philosophy (not just into *African* philosophy) by demonstrating that the criteria governing the application of certain concepts in radically different language systems may be of genuine philosophical significance. That propositional attitudes may be culturally relative is a fairly radical claim. But that is our claim, and we think that further *cross-cultural* conceptual comparisons will provide stronger evidence of the diversity, the relativity of meanings, than of that familiar godsend, propositional universality.

Two final suggestions. If the Yoruba have proven to be so concep-   24
tually distinctive, there is reason to suspect that other African conceptual systems maintain their own distinctive criteria as well. In which case it is time to dispense with the term "African philosophy" when it is used to refer to some amorphous, pseudo-philosophical corpus of beliefs intellectually endemic to all African peoples. Secondly, we think it best to discontinue use of the "traditional" with reference to African systems of thought. Its use predisposes scholars to make certain assumptions that encourage misrepresentation of African meanings and attitudes.

Enough said. This phase of the experiment is at an end. There is   25
more work to be done.

NATIONAL-IDEOLOGICAL PHILOSOPHY

Perhaps Martinique-born Frantz Fanon's (1925–1961) most unique contribution to African nationalist-ideological literature is his sharp assessment of colonialism by wedding together revolutionary political theory and psychiatry. As a psychiatrist at a hospital in Algeria during the Algerian liberation struggle, Fanon discovered that certain psychological and sociopsychological problems faced by Africans could only be understood against the historical, economic, and cultural background of colonialism. Extending this thesis, the following reading is from the essay "Concerning Violence," included in the collection of essays *The Wretched of the Earth.* Fanon celebrates revolutionary violence on two levels. First, colonialism can only be destroyed through a bloody struggle between the colonizer and the colonized. Second, violence is a sort of metaphysical "cleansing force" which transforms oppressed, colonized peoples into real human beings with dignity and self-worth.

Concerning Violence

FRANTZ FANON

National liberation, national renaissance, the restoration of nation-   1
hood to the people, commonwealth: whatever may be the headings used or the new formulas introduced, decolonization is always a violent phenomenon. At whatever level we study it—relationships between individuals, new names for sports clubs, the human admixture at cocktail parties, in the police, on the directing boards of national or private banks—decolonization is quite simply the replacing of a certain "species" of men by another "species" of men. Without any period of transition, there is a total, complete, and absolute substitution. It is true that we could equally well stress the rise of a new nation, the setting up of a new State, its diplomatic rela-

Frantz Fanon. *The Wretched of the Earth.* Translated by Constance Farrington. New York: Grove Press, 1963.

tions, and its economic and political trends. But we have precisely chosen to speak of that kind of *tabula rasa* which characterizes at the outset all decolonisation. Its unusual importance is that it constitutes, from the very first day, the minimum demands of the colonised. To tell the truth, the proof of success lies in a whole social structure being changed from the bottom up. The extraordinary importance of this change is that it is willed, called for, demanded. The need for this change exists in its crude state, impetuous and compelling, in the consciousness and in the lives of the men and women who are colonised. But the possibility of this change is equally experienced in the form of a terrifying future in the consciousness of another "species" of men and women: the colonisers.

Decolonisation never takes place un-noticed, for it influences individuals and modifies them fundamentally. It transforms spectators crushed with their inessentiality into privileged actors, with the grandiose glare of history's floodlights upon them. It brings a natural rhythm into existence, introduced by new men, and with it a new language and a new humanity. Decolonisation is the veritable creation of new men. But this creation owes nothing of its legitimacy to any supernatural power; the "thing" which has been colonised becomes man during the same process by which it frees itself.   2

In decolonisation, there is therefore the need of a complete calling in question of the colonial situation. If we wish to describe it precisely, we might find it in the well-known words: "The last shall be first and the first last." Decolonisation is the putting into practice of this sentence. That is why, if we try to describe it, all decolonisation is successful.   3

The naked truth of decolonisation evokes for us the searing bullets and bloodstained knives which emanate from it. For if the last shall be first, this will only come to pass after a murderous and decisive struggle between the two protagonists. That affirmed intention to place the last at the head of things, and to make them climb at a pace (too quickly, some say) the well-known steps which characterise an organized society, can only triumph if we use all means to turn the scale, including, of course, that of violence.   4

You do not turn any society, however primitive it may be, upside-down with such a programme if you have not decided from the very beginning, that is to say from the actual formulation of that programme, to overcome all the obstacles that you will come across in so   5 doing. The native who decides to put the programme into practice, and to become its moving force, is ready for violence at all times. From birth it is clear to him that this narrow world, strewn with prohibitions, can only be called in question by absolute violence.

The colonial world is a world cut in two. The dividing line, the frontiers are shown by barracks and police stations. In the colonies it is the policeman and the soldier who are the official, instituted go-betweens, the spokesmen of the settler and his rule of oppression. . . . In the colonial countries . . . the policeman and the soldier, by their immediate presence and their frequent and direct action, maintain contact with the native and advise him by means of rifle-butts and napalm not to budge. It is obvious here that the agents of government speak the language of pure force. The intermediary does not lighten the oppression, nor seek to hide the domination; he shows them up and puts them into practice with the clear conscience of an upholder of the peace; yet he is the bringer of violence into the home and the mind of the native.   6

The violence which has ruled over the ordering of the colonial world, which has ceaselessly drummed the rhythm for the destruction of native social forms and broken up without reserve the systems of reference of the economy, the customs of dress and external life, that same violence will be claimed and taken over by the native at the moment when, deciding to embody history in his own person, he surges into the forbidden quarters. To wreck the colonial world is henceforward a mental picture of action which is very clear, very easy to understand and which may be assumed by each one of the individuals which constitute the colonised people. To break up the colonial world does not mean that after the frontiers have been abolished lines of communication will be set up between the two zones. The destruction of the colonial world is no more and no less than the abolition of one zone, its burial in the depths of the earth or its expulsion from the country.   7

    The natives' challenge to the colonial world is not a rational confrontation of points of view. It is not a treatise on the universal, but the untidy affirmation of an original idea propounded as an absolute. The colonial world is a Manichean world. It is not enough for the settler to delimit physically, that is to say with the help of the army and the police force, the place of the native. As if to show the totalitarian char-   8 acter of colonial exploitation the settler paints the native as a sort of quintessence of evil. Native society is not simply described as a society lacking in values. It is not enough for the colonist to affirm that those values have disappeared from, or still better never existed in, the colonial world. The native is declared insensible to ethics; he represents not only the absence of values, but also the negation of values. He is, let us dare to admit, the enemy of values, and in this sense he is the absolute evil. He is the corrosive element, destroying all that comes near him; he is the deforming element, disfiguring all that has to do with beauty or morality; he is the depository of maleficent powers, the unconscious and irretrievable instrument of blind forces. . . . All values, in fact, are irrevocably poisoned and diseased as soon as they are allowed in contact with the colonised race. The customs of the colonised people, their traditions, their myths—above all, their myths—are the very sign of that poverty of spirit and their constitutional depravity. That is why we must put the DDT which destroys parasites, the bearers of disease, on the same level as the Christian religion which wages war on embryonic heresies and instincts, and on evil as yet unborn. The recession of yellow fever and the advance of evangelisation form part of the same balance-sheet. But the triumphant *communiqués* from the missions are in fact a source of information concerning the implantation of foreign influences in the core of the colonised people. I speak of the Christian religion, and no one need be astonished. The Church in the colonies is the white people's Church, the foreigner's Church. She does not call the native to God's ways but to the ways of the white man, of the master, of the oppressor. And as we know, in this matter many are called but few chosen.

At times this Manicheism goes to its logical conclusion and dehumanises the native, or to speak plainly it turns him into an animal. In fact, the terms the settler uses when he mentions the native are zoological terms. He speaks of the yellow man's reptilian motions, of the stink of the native quarter, of breeding swarms, of foulness, of spawn, of gesticulations. When the settler seeks to describe the native fully in exact terms he constantly refers to the bestiary. The European rarely hits on a picturesque style; but the native, who knows what is in the mind of the settler, guesses at once what he is thinking of. . . . The native knows all this, and laughs to himself every time he spots an allusion to the animal world in the other's words. For he knows he is not an animal; and it is precisely at the moment he realises his

9

humanity that he begins to sharpen the weapons with which he will secure its victory.

Kwame Nkrumah (1909–1972) remains one of the most celebrated theorists and activists of the African independence struggle. From 1957 to 1966, Nkrumah was the leader of Ghana, the first independent African nation. Nkrumah wrote a political and philosophical analysis of the African revolution in *Consciencism*. In Chapter 3, Nkrumah defines his central theme of "philosophical consciencism"—by returning to the original, precolonial African consciousness, being, and personality, Africans can destroy colonialism and capitalism. African society consists of three heritages: that of precolonial, traditional African, of Islam, and of Euro-Christianity. Nkrumah believes that these heritages should be harmonized to fit into the "African personality," which embodies a group of humanist principles that underlie traditional African society. In the reading below, Nkrumah explains that socialism, not capitalism, is the only political and economic system that is natural to the African personality. Traditional Africa was a communal society—the land and means of production belonged to and benefited the entire community in which all individuals were equal and were not separated into exploiting and exploited classes. Therefore, socialism is simply a further development of traditional African communalist ideals of humanism and egalitarianism.

Consciencism

KWAME NKRUMAH

The need for subtle means of social cohesion lies in the fact that there is a large portion of life which is outside direct central intervention. In order that this portion of life should be filled with order, non-statutory methods are required. These non-statutory methods, by and large, are   1

Kwame Nkrumah. *Consciencism: Philosophy and Ideology for Decolonization and Development with Particular Reference to the African Revolution.* London: Heinemann Educational Books, 1964.

the subtle means of social cohesion. But different societies lay different emphases on these subtle means even if the range of conformity which they seek is the same. The emphasis which a particular society lays on a given means depends on the experience, social-economic circumstances and the philosophical foundation of that society.

In Africa, this kind of emphasis must take objective account of our   2
present situation at the return of political independence. From this point of view, there are three broad features to be distinguished here. African society has one segment which comprises our traditional way of life; it has a second segment which is filled by the presence of the Islamic tradition in Africa; it has a final segment which represents the infiltration of the Christian tradition and culture of Western Europe into Africa, using colonialism and neo-colonialism as its primary vehicles. These different segments are animated by competing ideologies. But since society implies a certain dynamic unity, there needs to emerge an ideology which, genuinely catering for the needs of all, will take the place of the competing ideologies, and so reflect the dynamic unity of society, and be the guide to society's continual progress.

The traditional face of Africa includes an attitude towards man   3
which can only be described, in its social manifestation, as being socialist. This arises from the fact that man is regarded in Africa as primarily a spiritual being, a being endowed originally with a certain inward dignity, integrity and value. It stands refreshingly opposed to the Christian idea of the original sin and degradation of man.

This idea of the original value of man imposes duties of a social-   4
ist kind upon us. Herein lies the theoretical basis of African communalism. This theoretical basis expressed itself on the social level in terms of institutions such as the clan, underlining the initial equality of all and the responsibility of many for one. In this social situation, it was impossible for classes of a Marxian kind to arise. By a Marxian kind of class, I mean one which has a place in horizontal social stratification. Here classes are related in such a way that there is a disproportion of economic and political power between them. In such a society there exist classes which are crushed, lacerated and ground down by the encumbrance of exploitation. One class sits upon the neck of another. In this sense, there were no classes in traditional African society.

In the traditional African society, no sectional interest could be   5
regarded as supreme; nor did legislative and executive power aid the

interests of any particular group. The welfare of the people was supreme.

But colonialism came and changed all this. First, there were the 6 necessities of the colonial administration. . . . For its success, the colonial administration needed a cadre of Africans, who, by being introduced to a certain minimum of European education, became infected with European ideals, which they tacitly accepted as being valid for African societies. Because these African instruments of the colonial administration were seen by all to be closely associated with the new sources of power, they acquired a certain prestige and rank to which they were not entitled by the demands of the harmonious development of their own society.

In addition to them, groups of merchants and traders, lawyers, 7 doctors, politicians and trade unionists emerged, who, armed with skills and levels of affluence which were gratifying to the colonial administration, initiated something parallel to the European middle class. There were also certain feudal-minded elements who became imbued with European ideals either through direct European education or through hobnobbing with the local colonial administration. They gave the impression that they could be relied upon implicitly as repositories of all those staid and conservative virtues indispensable to any exploiter administration. They, as it were, paid the registration fee for membership of a class which was now associated with social power and authority.

Such education as we were all given put before us right from our 8 infancy ideals of the metropolitan countries, ideals which could seldom be seen as representing the scheme, the harmony and progress of African society. The scale and type of economic activity, the idea of the accountability of the individual conscience introduced by the Christian religion, countless other silent influences, these have all made an indelible impression upon African society.

But neither economic nor political subjugation could be considered as being in tune with the traditional African egalitarian view of man and society. Colonialism had in any case to be done away with. The African Hercules has his club poised ready to smite any new head which the colonialist hydra may care to put out.

With true independence regained, however, a new harmony 10 needs to be forged, a harmony that will allow the combined presence of traditional Africa, Islamic Africa and Euro-Christian Africa, so that this presence is in tune with the original humanist principles underlying African society. Our society is not the old society, but a new society enlarged by Islamic and Euro-Christian influences. A new ideology which can solidify in a philosophical statement, but at the same time an ideology which will not abandon the original humanist principles of Africa.

Such a philosophical statement will be born out of the crisis of the 11 African conscience confronted with the three strands of present African society. Such a philosophical statement I propose to name *philosophical consciencism,* for it will give the theoretical basis for an ideology whose aim shall be to contain the African experience of Islamic and Euro-Christian presence as well as the experience of the traditional African society, and, by gestation, employ them for the harmonious growth and development of that society.

Slavery and feudalism represent social-political theories in which 12 the deployment of forces is not a problematic question. In both slavery and feudalism, workers, the people whose toil transforms nature for the development of society, are dissociated from any say in rule. By a vicious division of labour, one class of citizen toils and another reaps where it has not sown. In the slave society, as in the feudal society, that part of society whose labours transform nature is not the same as the part which is better fulfilled as a result of this transformation. If by their fruits we shall know them, they must first grow the fruits. In slave and feudal society, the fruit-eaters are not the fruit-growers. This is the cardinal factor in exploitation, that the section of a society whose labours transform nature is not the same as the section which is better fulfilled as a result of this transformation.

In every non-socialist society, there can be found two strata which 13 correspond to that of the oppressor and the oppressed, the exploiter and the exploited. In all such societies, the essential relation between the two strata is the same as that between masters and slaves, lords and serfs. In capitalism, which is only a social-political theory in which the important aspects of slavery and feudalism are refined, a stratified society is required for its proper functioning, a society is required in which the working class is oppressed by the ruling class; for, under capitalism, that portion of society whose labours transform nature and produce goods is not the portion of society which enjoys the fruits of this transformation and productivity. Nor is it the whole of society which is so enhanced.

This might indeed be termed a contradiction. It is a social contra- 14 diction in so far as it is contrary to genuine principles of social equity and social justice. It is also an economic contradiction in so far as it is contrary to a harmonious and unlimited economic development.

Capitalism is a development by refinement from feudalism, just as feudalism is a development by refinement from slavery. The essence of reform is to combine a continuity of fundamental principle, with a tactical change in the manner of expression of the fundamental principle. Reform is not a change in the thought, but one in its manner of expression, not a change in what is said but one in idiom. In capitalism, feudalism suffers, or rather enjoys reform, and the fundamental principle of feudalism merely strikes new levels of subtlety. In slavery, it is thought that exploitation, the alienation of the fruits of the labour of others, requires a certain degree of political and forcible subjection. In feudalism, it is thought that a lesser degree of the same kind of subjection is adequate to the same purpose. In capitalism, it is thought that a still lesser degree is adequate. In this way, psychological irritants to revolution are appeased, and exploitation finds a new lease of life, until the people should discover the *opposition* between reform and revolution. 15

In this way, capitalism continues with its characteristic pompous plans for niggardly reforms, while it coerces one section of a society somehow into making itself available to another section, which battens on it. That development which capitalism marks over slavery and feudalism consists as much in the methods by means of which labour is coerced as in the mode of production. Capitalism is but the gentleman's method of slavery. 16

Indeed, a standard ruse of capitalism today is to imitate some of the proposals of socialism, and turn its imitation to its own use. Running with the hare and hunting with the hounds is much more than a pastime to capitalism; it is the hub of a complete strategy. In socialism, we seek an increase in levels of production in order solely that the people, by whose exertions production is possible, shall raise their standard of living and attain a new consciousness and level of life. Capitalism does this too, but not for the same purpose. Increased productivity under capitalism does indeed lead to a rise in the standard of living; but when the proportion of distribution of value between exploited and exploiter is kept constant, then any increase in levels of production must mean a greater *quantity,* but not *proportion,* of value accruing to the exploited. Capitalism thus discovers a new way of seeming to implement reform, while really genuinely avoiding it. 17

If one seeks the social-political ancestor of socialism, one must go to   18
communalism. Socialism stands to communalism as capitalism stands
to slavery. In socialism, the principles underlying communalism are
given expression in modern circumstances. Thus, whereas communalism in an untechnical society can be *laissez faire,* in a technical
society where sophisticated means of production are at hand, if the
underlying principles of communalism are not given centralized and
correlated expression, class cleavages will arise, which are connected
with economic disparities, and thereby with political inequalities.
Socialism, therefore, can be and is the defence of the principles of
communalism in a modern setting. Socialism is a form of social organization which, guided by the principles underlying communism,
adopts procedures and measures made necessary by demographic
and technological developments.

These considerations throw great light on the bearing of revolu-   19
tion and reform on socialism. The passage from the ancestral line of
slavery via feudalism and capitalism to socialism can only lie through
revolution: it cannot lie through reform. For in reform, fundamental
principles are held constant and the details of their expression modified. In the words of Marx, it leaves the pillars of the building intact.
Indeed, sometimes, reform itself may be initiated by the necessities of
preserving identical fundamental principles. Reform is a tactic of self-
preservation.

Revolution is thus an indispensable avenue to socialism, where   20
the antecedent social-political structure is animated by principles
which are a negation of those of socialism, as in a capitalist structure
(and therefore also in a colonialist structure, for a colonialist structure
is essentially ancillary to capitalism). Indeed, I distinguish between
two colonialisms, between a domestic one, and an external one.
Capitalism at home is a domestic colonialism.

But from the ancestral line of communalism, the passage to   21
socialism lies in reform, because the underlying principles are the
same. But when this passage carries one through colonialism the
reform is revolutionary since the passage from colonialism to genuine
independence is an act of revolution. But because of the continuity of
communalism with socialism, in communalistic societies, socialism is
not a revolutionary creed, but a restatement in contemporary idiom of
the principles underlying communalism. The passage from a non-
communalistic society to socialism is a revolutionary one which is
guided by the principles underlying communism.

In my autobiography, I said that capitalism might prove too com- 22
plicated a system for a newly independent country. I wish to add to
this the fact that the presuppositions and purposes of capitalism are
contrary to those of African society. Capitalism would be a betrayal of
the personality and conscience of Africa.

GLOSSARY

aje: A Yoruba term that can be roughly translated as "witchcraft."

als-Struktur: German for "as-structure." According to Heidegger's concept of hermeneutics, interpretation makes explicit and manifests that
which is already understood. *Als* signifies the explicitness of something that is understood by being manifested. Thus, the *als-Struktur* is
the structure of something that has already been made explicit through
interpretation.

animism: The belief that a spiritual power, psychic force, or life force pervades all animate and inanimate things. Animism dominates many
African religions. Such power and force distributes itself in a cosmological hierarchy of a Supreme Being at the top followed by lesser
gods, dead ancestors, natural forces (the power in rivers, stones, etc.),
earthly kings and chiefs, and human beings.

Aristotle (384–322 B.C.E.):   An ancient Greek philosopher generally seen to
be one of the "founding fathers" of Western philosophy.

Chardin, Pierre Teilhard de (1881–1955):   A French Roman Catholic priest
who believed that all beings in the cosmos (particles to human beings)
have a spiritual energy.

consciencism: A concept systematized by Kwame Nkrumah aimed at
returning to precolonial consciousness and experience as a means of
undercutting the impacts of colonialism and capitalism.

Dasein: In the philosophy of Martin Heidegger, the term for "human
being" understood abstractly in its essential character of being present
in the world.

Descartes, René (1596–1650):   A French philosopher widely thought to be
the founder of modern Western philosophy. In his method of rational
inquiry, he found that the only indubitable fact about the world is that
he existed as a thinking and rational being, reflected in his *cogito, ergo
sum*—"I think, therefore I am."

Engels, Friedrich (1820–1885):   A colleague of Marx who helped develop
Marxism.

epistemology: The philosophy of knowledge.

ethnophilosophy: An approach that equates African philosophy with traditional tribal beliefs and worldviews, which are usually not expressed

explicitly through writing. This approach was frequently taken by missionaries. According to philosopher Paulin Hountondji, these churchmen were mostly concerned with understanding African culture as a monolithic system of beliefs to better civilize the native population.

hermeneutics: The theory and methodology of interpretation most associated with the twentieth-century European philosophers Paul Ricoeur (1912–), Martin Heidegger (1880–1976), and Hans-Georg Gadamer (1900–).

igabago: A Yoruba term that can be roughly translated as "belief."

imo: A Yoruba term that can be roughly translated as "knowledge."

indeterminacy thesis of radical translation: The claim asserted by W. V. O. Quine that it is impossible to translate the abstract concepts of one language into another.

Kant, Immanuel (1724–1802): Probably the most influential modern German philosopher. His idea of antinomies proved that a single idea could be simultaneously affirmed and denied.

logos: Greek for "word." It is frequently understood to mean reasoned speech, argument, explanation, or doctrine, taken to uncover the ultimate truths about the world.

Marx, Karl (1818–1883): A German social and economic theorist. His doctrine of Marxism predicted the overthrow of capitalism and the common ownership of the means of production in a classless society.

metaphysics: A branch of Western philosophy dealing with the nature of truth, reality, existence, and knowledge.

negritude: A term originally coined by the Martinique writer Aimé Césaire and systematically developed by Léopold Sédar Senghor into a complete theory about literature, politics, and culture. This theory is premised on the notion that there is a racial "essence" common to all Black people throughout the world.

onisegun: Yoruba "masters of medicine" or wise men.

ontology: A branch of Western philosophy dealing with the nature of being and essence.

Plato (ca. 427–347 B.C.E.): An ancient Greek philosopher.

propositional attitude: A concept used by Sopido and Hallen and borrowed from W. V. O. Quine. Words like "believe," "know," "doubt," "hope," and "want" are psychological attitudes that can be taken toward given propositions; when they do, they are propositional attitudes. For example, one can formulate sentences expressing these attitudes like, "I believe that he would die," or "I know that he has left."

ratio: Latin for "reason." This term is frequently used in connection with rationalism, the view that the mind can understand the truths about the world using human reason.

romanticism: An eighteenth- and nineteenth-century school in Western philosophy that rebelled against the rationalism and objectivity of the

Western philosophical tradition and celebrated, by contrast, inner imagination, spirituality, feelings, and emotions. Instead of manipulating and exploiting the Other, romanticism emphasized sensually experiencing the Other and erasing boundaries between the subject and the object.

sagacity: The wisdom and practice of sages or wise men in traditional African culture.

Socrates (469–399 B.C.E.):   An ancient Greek philosopher who drank poisonous hemlock after being condemned to death by the Athenian state for his controversial philosophical views.

Vorgriff, Vorhabe, Vorsicht: German for "preconception," "prior acquisition," and "prior view," respectively. The three foundations of interpretation, according to Heidegger. As Okere explains, "The *Vorgriff* . . . shows that the interpretation of the object is already prejudiced by the existing conceptual apparatus of the interpreter." "The *Vorhabe* . . . represents the entire heritage and tradition of the interpreter, a heritage which not only furnishes the material to be interpreted but the background of all interpretation." "The *Vorsicht* is the prior orientation which, generally in the form of a *Weltanschauung* or ideology, orients all our interpretation. The interpretation then either synchronizes the object to this view or otherwise locates, defines, and delimits it from the viewpoint of this pre-view."

Weltanschauung: German for "worldview."

FURTHER READINGS

W. E. ABRAHAM. *The Mind of Africa.* Chicago: University of Chicago Press, 1962.

LEO APOSTEL. *African Philosophy.* Belgium: Scientific Publishers, 1981.

KWAME ANTHONY APPIAH. *In My Father's House: Africa in the Philosophy of Culture.* New York: Oxford University Press, 1992.

P. O. BODUNRIN. *Philosophy in Africa.* Ile-Ife: University of Ife Press, 1985.

ALWIN DIEMER, ed. *Philosophy in the Present Situation of Africa.* Wiesbaden: Frantz Steiner Verlad, 1981.

FRANTZ FANON. *Black Skins, White Masks.* Translated by Charles Lam Markmann. New York: Grove Press, 1967.

GUTTORM FLØISTAD, ed. *Contemporary Philosophy*, vol. 5: *African Philosophy.* Dordrecht: Martinus Nijhoff, 1987.

SEGUN GBADEGESIN. *African Philosophy: Traditional Yoruba Philosophy and Contemporary African Realities.* New York: Peter Lang, 1991.

KWAME GYEKYE. *An Essay on African Philosophical Thought.* New York: Cambridge University Press, 1987.

LILYAN KESTELOOT. *Black Writers in French: A Literary History of Negritude.* Translated by Ellen Conroy Kennedy. Philadelphia: Temple University Press, 1974.

M. AKIN MAKINDE. *African Philosophy, Culture, and Traditional Medicine.* Athens: Ohio University Press, 1988.

JOHN S. MBITI. *African Religions and Philosophy.* Garden City, N.Y.: Doubleday, 1969.

EZEKIERL MPHAHLELE. *The African Image.* London: Faber and Faber, 1974.

V. Y. MUDIMBE. *The Invention of Africa: Gnosis, Philosophy and the Order of Knowledge.* Bloomington: Indiana University Press, 1988.

H. ODERA ORUKA. *Trends in Contemporary African Philosophy.* Nairobi, Kenya: Shirikon Publishers, 1990.

GEOFFREY PARRINDER. *African Traditional Religion.* London: Hutchinson's University Library, 1954.

LÉOPOLD SÉDAR SENGHOR. *Senghor: Prose and Poetry.* Edited and translated by John Reed and Clive Wake. London: Heinemann, 1965.

TSENAY SEREQUEBERHAN, ed. *African Philosophy: The Essential Readings.* New York: Paragon House, 1991.

KWASI WIREDU. *Philosophy and an African Culture.* New York: Cambridge University Press, 1980.

RICHARD A. WRIGHT, ed. *African Philosophy: An Introduction.* Lanham, Md.: University Press of America, 1984.

STUDY QUESTIONS

1. Is it possible for philosophical sagacity, professional philosophy, and national-ideological philosophy to use Western philosophical models to illuminate the contemporary African situation? What are the problems with this strategy, and can they be overcome?

2. Do the questions, "What is African philosophy?" and "Does African philosophy exist?" perpetuate the colonial mythology of African inferiority?

3. In what ways do ethnophilosophical ideas of race, history, and culture parallel racism in contemporary American society?

4. Ethnophilosophers believe that Black African culture is inherently traditional with its reliance on myths, folklore, and religion while Western culture is modern with its reliance on science, logic, and rationality. Are there elements of "traditionalism" underlying a supposedly "modern" Western society?

5. Would Fanon see the violence in Los Angeles in 1992 as morally, politically, and ethically justified? Think of the difference between a *revolt* and a *riot*.

6. According to Hountondji, African philosophy must be produced by Africans, with the geography of the philosopher defining what is and is not African philosophy. Is focusing on the geography of the author instead of the content of the author's work useful to the development of African philosophy?

7. African women are never represented in contemporary African philosophy, suggesting that African women did not philosophize, their work was substandard and not worth mentioning, or that African men denigrated work produced by women. How would a feminist reading of African philosophy transform the entire debate?

CHAPTER 9

"Western" Philosophy

ROBERT C. SOLOMON AND
KATHLEEN M. HIGGINS

In the sixth century B.C.E., about the same time that Confucius was active in China and the Buddha was beginning his adventures in India, the Greek philosopher Thales, his eyes on the heavens, fell in a well. This little but well-known anecdote suggests something significant about the nature of philosophy in the Western tradition. On the one hand, it is a tradition that is woven around charismatic personalities and brilliant eccentrics (although it should be commented that Thales also used his knowledge of the heavens to correctly predict the future of the olive market, making him something of a millionaire in his time). On the other hand, Western philosophy is the study of questions and ideas which have a life of their own, quite independent of the person or the personality who may have thought them up in the first place.

A few centuries after Thales had gotten Greek philosophy going, the notoriously brilliant "gadfly" Socrates was executed for "corrupting the minds of the youth" in Athens. Socrates taught, among other things, that virtue is the most valuable of all possessions, that the truth lies beyond the "shadows" of our everyday experience and it is the proper business of the philosopher to show us how little we really know. After his death, Socrates became *the* philosophical hero, the singular figure to whom all later thinkers would acknowledge their deference and their debt. And yet, Socrates did not try to set down his ideas in thematic order. What we know of him we know through the reports of others, and what we know is mainly his method—that is, his inquisitive conversation, those demanding dialogues in which he refutes one view, then another, his dialectic. (We shall see this term again, in the nineteenth-century philosophies of

Hegel and Marx.) And yet, between Thales and Socrates, the future of Western philosophy is already prefigured—in the search for ultimate reality and the evasiveness of all true knowledge.

Thales and Socrates are two definitive figures in the story of Western philosophy, which since ancient times has defined itself in terms of a few key figures, their books and ideas, particularly their ideas about the nature of reality and the possibility of knowledge. There is widespread agreement about the identity of at least a dozen of these figures, although there is considerable debate and dispute, of course, about the proper interpretation of their ideas. Knowledge and reality—in short, "truth"—play a central role in this story, but interwoven with those themes is always the Socratic concern for virtue and the right way to live, questions of faith and piety, personal and practical questions which all too often slip below the horizon of philosophical attention.

We therefore undertake this chapter with a sense of caution, for despite general agreement on the great figures of the tradition there is surprisingly little agreement on how that tradition, as a whole, should be viewed. Many Anglo-American and European philosophers today would still insist that philosophy is the search for truth and the foundations of knowledge, but others would reject that orientation with equal adamance and shift our attention to more spiritual and passionate and less scientific concerns. Some contemporary philosophers would insist that philosophy is primarily a sequence of arguments and counterarguments, and, looking back from such a perspective, Western philosophy does indeed appear to be a sequence of deliberations about logic and argument. But if we listen to other views, then philosophy becomes a series of visions, metaphors, figures of speech, personal confessions, rationalizations, moral advice, moral prejudices, or a search for the good life.

It has been said that Western philosophy is a continuous struggle to become scientific, and, accordingly, logic and the theory of knowledge play a central role. Others would say that the Western philosophical tradition is religious through and through, a search for God or an understanding of God or an expression of spirituality. Still others would insist that philosophy is ultimately the study (as well as the expression) of human nature, and some would add that it is thereby imminently practical, by its very nature embroiled in politics and social controversy. (Socrates is mentioned in virtually every one of these views.) In the end, it seems, philosophy is as philosophers do, and what they do is think and speculate about virtually everything.

As hard as it may be to reduce the voluminous debates of the past 2,500 years to twenty pages or so of brief exerpts, it is even more difficult to be evenhanded and do justice to all of the different perspectives and interpretations that these great works have inspired. This sensitivity to variations within and differing interpretations of the Western tradition should be borne in mind when reading all of the other traditions discussed in this book. From afar, and with little prior familiarity, they may seem available for easy summation or caricature. Indeed, Western philosophy has been reduced to caricature by many of its foreign critics (including professors in some of our own university departments). But from within and at close range, every philosophical tradition is equally laced with different approaches and differing interpretations, ranging from dogmatic orthodoxy and fundamentalism to the wholesale rejection or denial of the tradition from within. So, too, Western philosophy is not a single system of ideas, much less a single way of "doing" philosophy. But it is, whatever else it may be, a tradition, a tradition defined first and foremost by its most famous practitioners, their conflicts and concerns and their ideas. The best known, most influential, are:

Socrates	David Hume
Plato	Jean-Jacques Rousseau
Aristotle	Immanuel Kant
Augustine	G. W. F. Hegel
Aquinas	Karl Marx
René Descartes	Friedrich Nietzsche
John Locke	

The ultimate importance of more modern figures, needless to say, is much more in dispute. In the twentieth century, we should probably mention Martin Heidegger, Jean-Paul Sartre, Bertrand Russell, and Ludwig Wittgenstein, but their lasting influence is still an open historical question. Other scholars' lists of the great philosophers might vary somewhat from those mentioned here, but it is in terms of these figures and their concerns that the tradition is understood. How that tradition is to be understood, however, is subject to considerable debate.

That tradition itself, however, is always reinterpreting, reinventing, and challenging itself. More than occasionally, philosophers within that tradition reject it altogether. It is one of the peculiarities of the Western philosophical tradition, for example, that so many great philosophers have begun their greatest works by pointing out that virtually all of what their predecessors have said is just plain wrong. And many of these philosophers have, in turn, declared that they have finished with philosophy altogether, settled (or eliminated) the questions, gotten things right once and for all. And yet, there are always new philosophers, new critics, new ways of looking at things, and most of the great philosophers listed above, however "mistaken," remain at the center of the conversation.

In the attempt to summarize the entire Western tradition, it has been suggested that the whole of what we know as philosophy is but a footnote to Plato, or, just a bit more generous, an extension of the debate between Plato and Aristotle. Plato is speculative, suggestive, even poetic. His known works—all in dialogue form with Socrates as the main character—are as much drama as philosophy, and the ultimate ideas remain half-hidden, as if a great secret, glimpsed by the very few. Aristotle, on the other hand, is through and through a scientist, and although he may have written dialogues (now lost), what we know of his work is rather dry, clear and cautious, thoroughly analytic, and only rarely speculative. Of course, one can discern many arguments in Plato, and Aristotle has a few spectacular philosophical visions, but their differences in style and substance define two different temperaments that are interwoven throughout the Western tradition.

In Christian philosophy, Augustine follows Plato, and Aquinas follows Aristotle. In modern times, those philosophers who call themselves rationalists often look back to Plato in their appeal to reason as the faculty that can see beyond mere experience, and those who call themselves empiricists often resemble, even if they do not follow, Aristotle the scientist, the careful observer, suspicious of any idea that does not rest on the testimony of experience and common sense. The nineteenth-century German idealists and many twentieth-century European philosophers shared Plato's speculative sensibilities even if they rejected his philosophy, and twentieth-century analytic philosophy clearly follows Aristotle in its demand for precision, thoroughness, and clarity. Indeed, one might well look at philosophy as the conversation between those who are attracted to the

wild, sometimes woolly *vision* and those who insist rather on clear
and careful, even nit-picking *arguments.* But despite these influential
differences between Plato and Aristotle, it is essential that we
remember how much they are the same. After all, one was the
teacher of the other. In particular, they both applaud reason and
rationality, and they both insist on the truth above all.

A very different suggestion is this. We can view the Western tradition as the rise of Judeo-Christian philosophy from paganism and
mythology, and, in turn, as the rise of scientific philosophy from religious philosophy. Or we can distinguish these two threads—science
and religion—as themselves competing traditions that confront one
another from ancient times until today. The beginning of Western
philosophy is also the beginning of Western science, and a single-
minded defender of science and scientific philosophy might well
look at the millennium dominated by theology to the exclusion of
science as an eclipse of reason and a detour in the progress of philosophy. On the other hand, Greek science clearly had its origins in
Greek mythology and a devotee of religious philosophy might well
see the current fascination with science as a temporary eclipse of
spirituality and a detour as well. But if one wishes to trace the
Western tradition in philosophy according to the notion of
"progress"—rather than, say, as in China, as one set of ideas simply
occurring after another—one might choose to see the history of
(Western) philosophy either as the evolution of scientific thinking or
as the development of an increasingly refined sense of the spiritual.
Or, one can see both of these as part of the same process, together
defining the progress of the (Western) mind.

Both science and religion, however, tend to appeal to a profound
and presumably eternal truth that is independent of those who seek
them. That is, both science and religion tend to emphasize *transcendence* and *objectivity.* And we might note that what too easily tends
to get lost in both scientific and religious philosophy is the merely
personal, the subjective, the emotional and the social as well. In contrast to China (again) and most tribal philosophies, for example, the
importance of family plays at best a minor role in the Western tradition, and it is perhaps not beside the point to mention the fact that
almost all of the great philosophers on our list were bachelors. So,
too, community and cultural values remain clearly secondary to universal ideals and principles of human nature. But it is in the twin
notions of transcendence and objectivity, together with truth and

knowledge, that we will find the core of the Western tradition, the point to which the argument keeps returning, whether that truth is ultimately God or physics, even among those who take it as their main aim to attack the tradition and, with it, transcendence, objectivity, truth, and knowledge.

One last point, and this follows rather closely from the above. If the emphasis in Western philosophy is on truth and knowledge, then the ability of an individual to find out the truth is of paramount importance. But the way to the truth is not, in this tradition, any simple appeal to authority. The authorities sometimes get it wrong, and, indeed, whole societies may be mistaken about the nature of the truth. Thus the notion of *autonomy* becomes central to the tradition along with truth and knowledge, the ability of the individual to think and find out for him or herself. Thus Socrates flouted the wise men of Athens and finally got himself condemned by them, and Descartes initiated modern philosophy by sitting alone in his study, questioning everything that he ever learned before. Thus the importance of "great" individual figures and their books and private meditations on the ultimate truths. In the Western tradition, we find great hostility toward psychoanalysis and sociology and any attempt to "explain" a philosophy in terms of the personality or cultural context of the author. Such explanations undermine or eclipse the importance of the ideas themselves, which, if true, are not the possession of any individual or the property of any one society but true *as such*, for everyone everywhere and for all times.

In what follows, we have provided several short extracts rather than just one or two more substantial selections in order to give a sampling of the positions, arguments, styles, and concerns of the great philosophers. These should provide something to think and talk about, but they are by no means adequate texts for understanding the breadth and richness of these great thinkers, and the temptation to draw summary conclusions about the scope, style, and interests of Western philosophy should be avoided. There are certain recurrent problems, and a casual observer might well be impressed (or overly impressed) by the emphasis on logic, both as subject matter and as a mode of proceeding. Indeed, the most common criticism of Western philosophy from both within and without is the excessive trust in certain linear logical forms and, accordingly, an overly abstract conception of "rationality."

The brief survey that follows adopts a very conservative

approach, modeled on what is now considered the "standard" philosophy curriculum in most North American philosophy departments, but let us emphasize that it is by no means the only approach. The great philosophers of the past were typically at the forefront not only of philosophy but of science, religion, social theory, literature, and the arts as well, and their interests and writing reflect this breadth of interest. We will, however, limit ourselves to the questions of truth and knowledge, or, to give these areas their proper names, metaphysics and epistemology, with some attention to ethics, the study of how we should live and the right thing to do. Throughout the Middle Ages, in particular, religious questions will ultimately embrace both of these.

ANCIENT ("PAGAN") PHILOSOPHY

The Pre-Socratics

Before Socrates there was an explosion of philosophical activity in Greece. Most of it is lost to us, but its outlines are clear through remaining fragments and the commentary of later thinkers, especially Aristotle. The emergence of philosophy from the mythological tradition began in the sixth century B.C.E. with Thales. We have little direct evidence of Thales' philosophy, but according to Aristotle, he argued that "the earth rests on water." This might not sound particularly promising or profound to us, but, unlike its predecessors, it presented a "naturalistic," nonanthropomorphic account of the world in terms that we would call scientific. Moreover, the idea of a unified account of the world was distinctly different from the admittedly colorful but quite ad hoc stories of dozens of gods and goddesses and their exploits. It was Thales, accordingly, who is credited for initiating a radical new way of thinking in the Western world, a way of thinking that would give rise to science as well as philosophy.

A very different pre-Socratic philosopher was Pythagoras, best known today, perhaps, for his work in geometry, but a powerful and often mysterious influence in the ancient world. His studies of geometry were simply a small part of a grand worldview, one in which mathematics defined the basic order of the universe, a view very sympathetic to many physicists today. Pythagoras used his theory of proportions to explain, among other things, the nature of music and the movements of the stars, which he surmised made a great deal of noise (audible only to the gods) which he called "the music of the spheres." Pythagoras defended an account of the universe which did not focus on one of the material elements (such as water) but rather on the nonmaterial abstractions of mathematics.

The achievements of Thales and Pythagoras (and many other philosophers as well) were to sharpen the distinction between appearance and reality. This distinction had also been in play in archaic Greek mythology with its stories of gods and goddesses behind the scenes, of course; but the pre-Socratic philosophers were offering an account of a very different kind. This distinction took on further significance with Heraclitus, a philosopher who emphasized the changing nature of all things. It was he who insisted, famously, that one cannot step in the same river twice. (Actually, he said, "Upon those who step into the same rivers, different and again different waters flow.") He also insisted that the world was defined by opposites—health and disease, up and down, day and night, purity and pollution, man and god—but, nevertheless, he claimed that beneath the constant change and oppositions of the world of appearance was a permanent order and unity, a *logos*. The world was not just chaos, but profoundly ordered chaos. Other fragments from the notoriously obscure Heraclitus:

- Eyes and ears make bad witnesses if men cannot understand what they say.
- Though the *logos* is always so, men never understand it, neither before nor after they have heard it.
- Wisdom is one, knowing the thought by which it steers all things through all things.
- All things come to be in accordance with the *logos.*
- Listening not to me but to the *logos,* it is wise to agree that all things are one.
- The way up and the way back are the same.
- People do not understand how a thing can be in agreement by differing: harmony is opposing tensions, as in the bow and the lyre.
- War is father and kin of all.
- Nature loves concealment.

- The order which is common to all was not made by god or man, but it forever was, is, and will be an everlasting fire.*

Heraclitus's contemporary Parmenides further widened the distinction between appearance and reality with the suggestion that we could never know the real world, which does not change; we can only know the apparent world, the world of ordinary experience. This suggestion, that the world of our daily experience is in some sense an illusion, obviously set philosophers against common sense in a most dramatic way. But Parmenides, and his prize student Zeno, developed not only such exotic claims but also powerful arguments to prove what common sense could not comprehend. With Parmenides and Zeno, arguments and disputation moved to the center of Western philosophy. A new breed of philosopher, called Sophists, used these new techniques of argumentation to respond to Parmenides and, more significantly, to advance radical new ideas in religion and morality as well. These included the particularly radical idea that all human knowledge and values are relative, or as the Sophist Protagoras says, "man is the measure of all things," and the archaic but still problematic suggestion that all ideals are in fact nothing more than the ideals of those who rule, in other words, "might makes right." (This is the thesis of the Sophist Thrasymachus, reported in Plato's *Republic*.)

It was into this ferment of vigorous arguments, conflicting opinions, and the peculiar philosophical problem of appearance versus reality that Socrates made his own appearance, and after him, his student Plato.

Socrates

One philosopher above all best serves to exemplify the Western tradition, and that is Socrates. In many ways, he could be said to be in the same tradition as the Old Testament prophets, and he is often compared to Jesus. He presented his philosophy personally in the marketplace of Athens, exemplifying his own virtues and offending the authorities. Athens was the most democratic city-state in Greece, but nevertheless its jury condemned him to death. Ever since, he has exemplified the philosopher-as-hero, the ideal of a lone thinker defending lofty ideals and exemplifying them as well.

*Translation by Paul Woodruff.

Socrates did not write down his philosophy but instead employed it in conversations with his students and other philosophers who were his contemporaries. Nevertheless, we have ample documentation of his teachings in the writings of his student Plato and the contemporary historian Xenophon. Socrates defended a complex theory of the world, but at its core was a very special notion of *virtue*. The virtues represented what was best about a person, and foremost among these were the philosophical or intellectual virtues. Socrates might be said to have died for the sake of the virtues, for he claimed, in his own defense before the jury that condemned him, that he would rather die than give up the quest and the teaching of philosophy.

In the *Crito*, one of Plato's early dialogues, Socrates exemplifies his method and also provides us with a classic statement about the aims of philosophy, to tell us what to do, to dispassionately seek the truth, to think for ourselves and not be swayed by emotion or public opinion. In the following scene, Socrates' friend Crito has come to the prison to tell Socrates that his escape has been arranged. Socrates refuses to go. Here is his argument:

Crito

PLATO

S: It was said on every occasion by those who thought they 1 were speaking sensibly, as I have just now been speaking, that one should greatly value some people's opinions, but not others. Does that seem to you a sound statement?

You, as far as a human being can tell, are exempt from the likeli- 2 hood of dying tomorrow, so the present misfortune is not likely to lead you astray. Consider then, do you not think it a sound statement that one must not value all the opinions of men, but some and not others, nor the opinions of all men, but those of some and not of others? What do you say? Is this not well said?

C: It is. 3

Plato. *Crito*. In *The Trial and Death of Socrates*. Translated by G. M. A. Grube. Indianapolis: Hackett Publishing Company, 1975.

S: One should value the good opinions, and not the bad ones?   4

C: Yes.   5

S: The good opinions are those of wise men, the bad ones those   6
of foolish men?

C: Of course.   7

S: Come then, what of statements such as this: Should a man   8
professionally engaged in physical training pay attention to the praise
and blame and opinion of any man, or to those of one man only,
namely a doctor or trainer?

C: To those of one only. . . .   9

S: We should not then think so much of what the majority will   10
say about us, but what he will say who understands justice and injustice, the one, that is, and the truth itself. So that, in the first place, you
were wrong to believe that we should care for the opinion of the
many about what is just, beautiful, good, and their opposites. "But,"
someone might say "the many are able to put us to death."

C: That too is obvious, Socrates, and someone might well say so.   11

S: And, my admirable friend, that argument that we have gone   12
through remains, I think, as before. Examine the following statement
in turn as to whether it stays the same or not, that the most important
thing is not life, but the good life.

C: It stays the same. . . .   13

S: See whether the start of our enquiry is adequately stated, and   14
try to answer what I ask you in the way you think best.

C: I shall try.   15

S: Do we say that one must never in any way do wrong willing-   16
ly, or must one do wrong in one way and not in another? Is to do
wrong never good or admirable, as we have agreed in the past, or
have all these former agreements been washed out during the last few
days? Have we at our age failed to notice for some time that in our
serious discussions we were no different from children? Above all, is
the truth such as we used to say it was, whether the majority agree or
not, and whether we must still suffer worse things than we do now, or
will be treated more gently, that nonetheless, wrongdoing is in every
way harmful and shameful to the wrongdoer? Do we say so or not?

C: We do.   17

S: So one must never do wrong.   18

C: Certainly not.   19

S: Nor must one, when wronged, inflict wrong in return, as the majority believe, since one must never do wrong. 20

C: That seems to be the case. 21

S: Come now, should one injure anyone or not, Crito? 22

C: One must never do so. 23

S: Well then, if one is oneself injured, is it right, as the majority say, to inflict an injury in return, or is it not? 24

C: It is never right. . . . 25

S: Then I state the next point, or rather I ask you: when one has come to an agreement that is just with someone, should one fulfill it or cheat on it? 26

C: One should fulfill it. 27

S: See what follows from this: if we leave here without the city's permission, are we injuring people whom we should least injure? And are we sticking to a just agreement, or not? 28

C: I cannot answer your question, Socrates. I do not know. 29

S: Look at it this way. If, as we were planning to run away from here, or whatever one should call it, the laws and the state came and confronted us and asked: "Tell me, Socrates, what are you intending to do? Do you not by this action you are attempting intend to destroy us, the laws, and indeed the whole city, as far as you are concerned? Or do you think it possible for a city not to be destroyed if the verdicts of its courts have no force but are nullified and set at naught by private individuals?" What shall we answer to this and other such arguments? For many things could be said, especially by an orator on behalf of this law we are destroying, which orders that the judgments of the courts shall be carried out. Shall we say in answer, "The city wronged me, and its decision was not right." Shall we say that, or what? 30

C: Yes, by Zeus, Socrates, that is our answer. 31

Plato

Plato's philosophy was, first of all, a credible if extremely admiring account of Socrates, particularly Socrates' last days—his trial, imprisonment, and execution. (The *Crito* is one of these.) But Plato also defends a philosophy of his own, in particular, a theory about the difference between appearance and reality called the theory of the Forms. That theory is suggested in Plato's most famous work, the *Republic,* which among other things provided Plato's blueprint for the ideal society. In his later dialogues, Plato further develops and qualifies the theory of the Forms, but the basic idea pervades all of his work as well as the work of the many Neoplatonists who were to follow him for many centuries.

The theory of Forms is, in part, the culmination of the two centuries of philosophy that preceded Plato and the distinction between the changing world of everyday experience and the perfect, changeless world of which we can get only a glimpse. For Plato, these were literally two different worlds, our ordinary reality on the one hand and the superreality of the Forms on the other. Through reason, we get a glimpse of those eternal, perfect Forms. But the best-known illustration of Plato's two worlds appears not as a concrete example but rather as an allegory, the "Allegory of the Cave," from *The Republic.*

Republic

PLATO

Next, I said, compare the effect of education and the lack of it upon   1
our human nature to a situation like this: imagine men to be living in
an underground cave-like dwelling place, which has a way up to the
light along its whole width, but the entrance is a long way up. The
men have been there from childhood, with their neck and legs in fetters, so that they remain in the same place and can only see ahead of
them, as their bonds prevent them turning their heads. Light is provided by a fire burning some way behind and above them. Between the
fire and the prisoners, some way behind them and on a higher
ground, there is a path across the cave and along this a low wall has
been built, like the screen at a puppet show in front of the performers
who show their puppets above it.—I see it.

See then also men carrying along that wall, so that they overtop it,   2
all kinds of artifacts, statues of men, reproductions of other animals in

Plato. *Republic.* In *Plato's Republic.* Translated by G. M. A. Grube. Indianapolis: Hackett Publishing Company, 1974.

stone or wood fashioned in all sorts of ways, and, as is likely, some of the carriers are talking while others are silent.—This is a strange picture, and strange prisoners.

They are like us, I said. Do you think, in the first place, that such 3 men could see anything of themselves and each other except the shadows which the fire casts upon the wall of the cave in front of them?—How could they, if they have to keep their heads still throughout life?

And is not the same true of the objects carried along the wall?— 4 Quite.

If they could converse with one another, do you not think that 5 they would consider these shadows to be the real things?— Necessarily.

What if their prison had an echo which reached them from in 6 front of them? Whenever one of the carriers passing behind the wall spoke, would they not think that it was the shadow passing in front of them which was talking? Do you agree?—By Zeus I do.

Altogether then, I said, such men would believe the truth to be 7 nothing else than the shadows of the artifacts?—They must believe that.

Consider then what deliverance from their bonds and the curing 8 of their ignorance would be if something like this naturally happened to them. Whenever one of them was freed, had to stand up suddenly, turn his head, walk, and look up toward the light, doing all that would give him pain, the flash of the fire would make it impossible for him to see the objects of which he had earlier seen the shadows. What do you think he would say if he was told that what he saw then was foolishness, that he was now somewhat closer to reality and turned to things that existed more fully, that he saw more correctly? If one then pointed to each of the objects passing by, asked him what each was, and forced him to answer, do you not think he would be at a loss and believe that the things which he saw earlier were truer than the things now pointed out to him?—Much truer.

If one then compelled him to look at the fire itself, his eyes would 9 hurt, he would turn round and flee toward those things which he could see, and think that they were in fact clearer than those now shown to him.—Quite so.

And if one were to drag him thence by force up the rough and 10 steep path, and did not let him go before he was dragged into the sunlight, would he not be in physical pain and angry as he was dragged along? When he came into the light, with the sunlight filling his eyes, he would not be able to see a single one of the things which are now said to be true.—Not at once, certainly.

I think he would need time to get adjusted before he could see   11
things in the world above; at first he would see shadows most easily, then reflections of men and other things in water, then the things themselves. After this he would see objects in the sky and the sky itself more easily at night, the light of the stars and the moon more easily than the sun and the light of the sun during the day.—Of course.

Then, at last, he would be able to see the sun, not images of it in   12
water or in some alien place, but the sun itself in its own place, and be able to contemplate it.—That must be so.

After this he would reflect that it is the sun which provides the   13
seasons and the years, which governs everything in the visible world, and is also in some way the cause of those other things which he used to see.—Clearly that would be the next stage.

What then? As he reminds himself of his first dwelling place, of   14
the wisdom there and of his fellow prisoners, would he not reckon himself happy for the change, and pity them?—Surely.

And if the men below had praise and honours from each other,   15
and prizes for the man who saw most clearly the shadows that passed before them, and who could best remember which usually came earlier and which later, and which came together and thus could most ably prophesy the future, do you think our man would desire those rewards and envy those who were honoured and held power among the prisoners, or would he feel, as Homer put it, that he certainly wished to be "serf to another man without possessions upon the earth" and go through any suffering, rather than share their opinions and live as they do?—Quite so, he said, I think he would rather suffer anything.

Reflect on this too, I said. If this man went down into the cave   16
again and sat down in the same seat, would his eyes not be filled with darkness, coming suddenly out of the sunlight?—They certainly would.

And if he had to contend again with those who had remained   17
prisoners in recognizing those shadows while his sight was affected and his eyes had not settled down—and the time for this adjustment would not be short—would he not be ridiculed? Would it not be said that he had returned from his upward journey with his eyesight spoiled, and that it was not worthwhile even to attempt to travel

upward? As for the man who tried to free them and lead them upward, if they could somehow lay their hands on him and kill him, they would do so.—They certainly would.

Aristotle

As a student of Plato, Aristotle was particularly concerned with his teacher's theory of the Forms, which he rejected. There is no super-reality, insisted Aristotle, but only the individual things of this world, which he called by the specialized name *substances.* An individual human being, for instance, Socrates, is a substance. A horse, a tree, or a dog is a substance. To understand Socrates or a horse, a tree, or a dog, one need not get a glimpse of anything other than Socrates, a horse, a tree, or a dog. Perceiving the thing itself, one discovers its essence, those properties that make that thing what it is, those features that could not be otherwise. Part of the essence of Socrates, for example, is that he is a man; another is that he is a philosopher. Aristotle contrasts such essencial properties with merely "accidental" properties, those which are irrelevant to the true nature of a thing—such as Socrates' haircut. This down-to-earth notion of essence is central to Aristotle's philosophy, and it eliminates any need to talk in terms of Plato's mysterious Forms. The following excerpt is from Aristotle's *Metaphysics.*

Metaphysics
ARISTOTLE

The material is the cause of manufactured things, and fire and earth   1
and all such things are the causes of bodies, and the parts are causes
of the whole, and the hypotheses are causes of the conclusion, in the
sense that they are that out of which these respectively are made; but
of these some are cause as *substratum* (e.g. the parts), others as
essence (the whole, the synthesis, and the form). The semen, the

Aristotle. *Metaphysics.* Translated by W. D. Ross. London: Oxford University Press, 1927.

physician, the adviser, and in general the agent, are all *sources of change* or of rest. The remainder are causes as the *end* and the good of the other things; for that, for the sake of which other things are, is naturally the best and the end of the other things; let us take it as making no difference whether we call it good or apparent good.

These, then, are the causes, and this is the number of their kinds,   2 but the *varieties* of causes are many in number, though when summarized these also are comparatively few. Causes are spoken of in many senses, and even of those which are of the same kind some are causes in a prior and others in a posterior sense, e.g. both "the physician" and "the professional man" are causes of health, and "the ratio 2:1" and "number" are causes of the octave, and the classes that include any particular cause are always causes of the particular effect. Again, there are accidental causes and the classes which include these, e.g. while in one sense "the sculptor" causes the statue, in another sense "Polyclitus" causes it, because the sculptor happens to be Polyclitus; and the classes that include the accidental cause are also causes, e.g. "man"—or in general "animal"—is the cause of the statue, because Polyclitus is a man, and a man is an animal. Of accidental causes also some are more remote or nearer than others, as, for instance, if "the white" and "the musical" were called causes of the statue, and not only "Polyclitus" or "man." But besides all these varieties of causes, whether proper or accidental, some are called causes as being able to act, others as acting, e.g. the cause of the house's being built is the builder, or the builder when building.—The same variety of language will be found with regard to the effects of causes, e.g. a thing may be called the cause of this statue or of a statue or in general of an image, and of this bronze or of bronze or of matter in general; and similarly in the case of accidental effects. Again, both accidental and proper causes may be spoken of in combination, e.g. we may say not "Polyclitus" nor "the sculptor," but "Polyclitus the sculptor."

Aristotle wrote on virtually every topic, in science as well as philosophy, on theater and poetry and the nature of the soul. One of his most important works is in ethics, in which—as in his *Metaphysics*—he begins with a purposive, or *teleological*, view of human nature. People have purposes. They not only have immediate purposes—to catch that bus, to earn an A in the course or a promotion on the job, to get into law school—but an ultimate purpose, a purpose which, Aristotle tells us, is generally agreed to be happiness or, more accurately, "doing well." Aristotle's *Ethics*, accordingly, is the analysis of the true nature of happiness and its essential components, notably, reason and virtue.

Nicomachean Ethics

ARISTOTLE

Every craft and every investigation, and likewise every action and 1
decision, seems to aim at some good; hence the good has been well described as that at which everything aims.

However, there is an apparent difference among the ends aimed 2
at. For the end is sometimes an activity, sometimes a product beyond the activity; and when there is an end beyond the action, the product is by nature better than the activity.

Since there are many actions, crafts and sciences, the ends turn 3
out to be many as well; for health is the end of medicine, a boat of boatbuilding, victory of generalship, and wealth of household management.

But whenever any of these sciences are subordinate to some one 4
capacity—as e.g. bridlemaking and every other science producing equipment for horses are subordinate to horsemanship, while this and every action in warfare are in turn subordinate to generalship, and in the same way other sciences are subordinate to further ones—in each of these the end of the ruling science is more choiceworthy than all the ends subordinate to it, since it is the end for which those ends are also pursued. . . .

Suppose, then, that (a) there is some end of the things we pursue in 5
our actions which we wish for because of itself, and because of which we wish for the other things; and (b) we do not choose everything because of something else, since (c) if we do, it will go on without limit, making desire empty and futile; then clearly (d) this end will be the good, i.e. the best good.

Then surely knowledge of this good is also of great importance for 6
the conduct of our lives, and if, like archers, we have a target to aim

Aristotle. *Nicomachean Ethics*. Translated by Terence Irwin. Indianapolis: Hackett Publishing Company, 1985.

at, we are more likely to hit the right mark. If so, we should try to grasp, in outline at any rate, what the good is, and which science or capacity is concerned with it. . . .

Since every sort of knowledge and decision pursues some good, what   7
is that good which we say is the aim of political science? What [in
other words] is the highest of all the goods pursued in action?

As far as its name goes, most people virtually agree [about what   8
the good is], since both the many and the cultivated call it happiness,
and suppose that living well and doing well are the same as being
happy. But they disagree about what happiness is, and the many do
not give the same answer as the wise.

For the many think it is something obvious and evident, e.g. plea-   9
sure, wealth or honour, some thinking one thing, others another; and
indeed the same person keeps changing his mind, since in sickness he
thinks it is health, in poverty wealth. And when they are conscious of
their own ignorance, they admire anyone who speaks of something
grand and beyond them.

[Among the wise,] however, some used to think that besides these   10
many goods there is some other good that is something in itself, and
also causes all these goods to be goods. . . .

(a) We have found, then, that the human function is the soul's activity   11
that expresses reason [as itself having reason] or requires reason [as
obeying reason]. (b) Now the function of F, e.g. of a harpist, is the
same in kind, so we say, as the function of an excellent F, e.g. an
excellent harpist. (c) The same is true unconditionally in every case,
when we add to the function the superior achievement that expresses
the virtue; for a harpist's function, e.g. is to play the harp, and a good
harpist's is to do it well. (d) Now we take the human function to be a
certain kind of life, and take this life to be the soul's activity and
actions that express reason. (e) [Hence by (c) and (d)] the excellent
man's function is to do this finely and well. (f) Each function is completed well when its completion expresses the proper virtue. (g)
Therefore [by (d), (e) and (f)] the human good turns out to be the soul's
activity that expresses virtue.

And if there are more virtues than one, the good will express the   12
best and most complete virtue. Moreover, it will be in a complete life.
For one swallow does not make a spring, nor does one day; nor, similarly, does one day or a short time make us blessed and happy.

MEDIEVAL (CHRISTIAN) PHILOSOPHY

Since its inception, Christian thought has emphasized the inner life of the soul as opposed to external behavior and possessions. Reacting to the excesses of ritualistic practice in contemporary Judaism, the earliest Christians preached the importance of inner disposition, from which all external behavior should proceed. At first, Christians thought that Christ's second return was imminent. Little thought was given to establishing long-term policies, and ethical issues were largely settled on an ad hoc basis.

Soon, however, St. Paul, an educated man, introduced ideas more directly derived from Greek and Roman thought. In particular, he defended the idea of natural law, which was a common view among the Romans. According to this view, a human being could know moral precepts directly by means of reason. Paul used this claim to defend his acceptance of non-Jews into Christianity, arguing that although they lacked the benefit of Jewish scripture, Gentiles could carry out the moral law because it was enscribed in their hearts.

St. Augustine

Born in North Africa, St. Augustine (354–530) was the outstanding influence on the medieval Christian worldview. After a wild and dissipated youth, Augustine pledged his life to a quest for wisdom. Augustine's own behavior led him to ponder the reason for evil in human life. He first embraced the answer provided by the Manichaean sect (considered heretical both by orthodox Christianity and by the Zoroastrian religion from which it developed; see Chapter 5). The Manichaeans taught that the world is the battleground on which two gods, one good and one evil, struggle for control of the human soul. But Augustine found the Manichaean solution to the problem of evil unsatisfying. In Italy, he became acquainted with a number of Christian Neoplatonists, who considered Plato's thought to be compatible with the teachings of Christianity. In particular, the Neoplatonists admired Plato's distinction between the everyday world of appearance and a truer, spiritual world.

Embracing Christianity and Neoplatonism, Augustine developed Plato's distinction as the "city of man" versus "the city of God," the home of the person who accepts God's grace and lives a virtuous life. (Thus Augustine rejects the teleology of happiness and virtue in Aristotle.) Like Plato, Augustine respected reason, which he considered to be a share in God's own nature and a means of grasping (to some extent) the divine plan that structured the created world.

Augustine's concern for the problem of evil and the notion of original sin led him to write the West's first philosophical autobiography, *Confessions*. In the *Confessions*, Augustine tells the dramatic story of his spiritual life, beginning with his early days of sinfulness. Augustine addresses his story to God, whom he praises throughout.

Confessions

St. Augustine

Tell, I pray thee, O God, unto me thy suppliant: thou who art merci-   1
ful, tell me who am miserable, did my infancy succeed to any other age of mine that was dead before; or was that it which I past in my mother's belly? for something have I heard of that too, and myself have seen women with child. What passed before that age, O God my delight? Was I anywhere, or anybody? For I have none to tell me thus much: neither could my father and mother, nor the experience of others, nor yet mine own memory. Dost thou laugh at me for enquiring these things, who commandest to praise and to confess to thee for what I know? I confess unto thee, O Lord of heaven and earth, and I sing praises unto thee for my first being and infancy, which I have no memory of: and thou hast given leave to man, by others to conjecture of himself, and upon the credit of women to believe many things that concern himself. For even then had I life and being, and towards the end of mine infancy, I sought for some significations to express my meaning by unto others. Whence could such a living creature come, but from thee, O Lord? Or hath any man the skill to frame himself? Or is any vein of ours, by which being and life runs into us, derived from any original but thy workmanship, O Lord, to whom being and living

St. Augustine. *St. Augustine's Confessions.* Translated by William Watts. London: Macmillan Company, 1911.

are not several things, because both to be and to live in the highest degree, is of thy very essence? For thou art the highest, and thou art not changed; neither is this present day spent in thee; yet it is spent in thee, because even all these times are in thee; nor could have their ways of passing on, unless thou containedst them. And because thy years fail not, thy years are but this very day. And how many soever our days and our fathers' days have been, they have all passed through this one day of thine: from that day have they received their measures and manners of being; and those to come shall so also pass away, and so also receive their measures and manners of being. But thou art the same still; and all to-morrows and so forward, and all yesterdays and so backward, thou shalt make present in this day of thine: yea, and hast made present. What concerns it me, if any understand not this? let him rejoice notwithstanding and say: What is this? Let him so also rejoice, and rather love to find in not finding it out, than by finding it, not to find thee with it.

The Great Schism

Early Christianity was not characterized by a single style or practice. The early church was particularly effective in winning converts precisely because it assimilated into various local styles and practices. However, one effect of this openness was that church practice tended to recapitulate cultural differences, and this became especially pronounced in the case of the Latin and the Greek worlds. Eventually, the Eastern and the Western churches went their separate ways in what is called the Great Schism. The date usually given for the occurrence of the schism is 1054 C.E., but in fact the division was a gradual development, with roots in Constantine's declaration of Byzantium (also Constantinople and, currently, Istanbul) as the eastern capital of the Roman Empire in 330 C.E.

Many of the tensions that led to this break were political, although certain theological controversies were cited by the political adversaries involved. Ultimately, however, Western and Eastern Christianity were split by cultural differences. Most obviously, the two cultures spoke different languages. Religious style was also very different for the two churches. The Western church emphasized legalistic, codified belief and stressed the authority of the clergy, both for explicating doctrine and for conducting the liturgy. The Eastern church, which emphasized participation over belief, tolerated theological differences, underplayed clerical authority, and involved the whole community in liturgy, which incorporated many artistic forms.

These basic differences were exacerbated by the different fates of the Roman Empire in the West and in the East. Rome collapsed in, and the Western church became the sole surviving social or governmental structure. The Western church, therefore, had practical reason to assert its authority rather aggressively. The church was the sole preserver of high culture in the West, and it came to dominate educational institutions, which it preserved primarily for the training of the clergy. The Eastern empire, by contrast, continued to function until Constantinople fell to the Turks in 1453 C.E. While Rome was being invaded, Constantinople was becoming the most prosperous and urbane city in the Christian world.

The notion of "Western" thought as opposed to "Eastern" thought was originally understood in terms of this contrast between the cultures of the Latin and Greek worlds, which eventually became institutionally formalized in the Roman and Orthodox Christian churches. Although Christianity underwent many further fragmentations, this fundamental division of East and West remains a forceful distinction through modern times. It remains current in the recent cultural encounters that have resulted from the collapse of the Iron Curtain, formerly suspended between the communist East and democratic West.

Scholasticism

With St. Anselm of Canterbury (1033–1109), a new era in Christian thought in the West, known as Scholasticism, was begun. Scholasticism sought explanation of the way things are, which it pursued through the examination of conceptual puzzles. Although Scholasticism eventually seemed committed to logical analysis for its own sake, the movement began as an effort to illuminate the truths of religion. Anselm believed that Christian faith is a religious duty. Reason, he believed, could reinforce faith by demonstrating the necessity of the claims made by religious doctrines. The most famous of Anselm's proofs of this nature is the ontological proof for the existence of God. The basic argument is that reflection on the hierarchy of beings that are closer to or farther from perfection reveals the necessity of a most perfect being, or God.

Proslogion

ST. ANSELM

I do not endeavor, O Lord, to penetrate thy sublimity, for in no wise   1
do I compare my understanding with that; but I long to understand in
some degree thy truth, which my heart believes and loves. For I do not
seek to understand that I may believe, but I believe in order to under-
stand. For this also I believe,—that unless I believed, I should not
understand. . . .

CHAPTER III.

God cannot be conceived not to exist.—God is that, than which noth-   2
ing greater can be conceived.—That which can be conceived not to
exist is not God. And it assuredly exists so truly, that it cannot be conceived not to exist. For, it is possible to conceive of a being which
cannot be conceived not to exist; and this is greater than one which
can be conceived not to exist. Hence, if that, than which nothing
greater can be conceived, can be conceived not to exist, it is not that,
than which nothing greater can be conceived. But this is an irreconcilable contradiction. There is, then, so truly a being than which nothing greater can be conceived to exist, that it cannot even be
conceived not to exist; and this being thou art, O Lord, our God.

So truly, therefore, dost thou exist, O Lord, my God, that thou   3
canst not be conceived not to exist; and rightly. For, if a mind could
conceive of a being better than thee, the creature would rise above
the Creator; and this is most absurd. And, indeed, whatever else there
is, except thee alone, can be conceived not to exist. To thee alone,
therefore, it belongs to exist more truly than all other beings, and
hence in a higher degree than all others. For, whatever else exists does
not exist so truly, and hence in a less degree it belongs to it to exist.
Why, then, has the fool said in his heart, there is no God (Psalm xiv.
1), since it is so evident, to a rational mind, that thou dost exist in the
highest degree of all? Why, except that he is dull and a fool?

St. Anselm. *Proslogion.* In *Anselm's Basic Writings.* Translated by S. N. Deane. LaSalle,
Ill.: Open Court Publishing, 1962.

St. Thomas Aquinas

St. Thomas Aquinas (1224–1274), a Dominican priest, achieved a grand synthesis of Christian doctrine and Aristotelian philosophy. Like Aristotle, Aquinas was critical of Plato's view that there was a realm of Forms, separate from everyday reality. He, too, considered all things, including human beings, to have essential natures that make each the kind of thing it is. In the case of a human being, this essential nature was the soul. Because human beings all share an essential nature, they commonly possess certain capacities, including the ability to recognize right and wrong and the quest for eternal happiness in the company of God.

Like Anselm, Aquinas believed that reason was an important instrument for reinforcing faith by providing clarity and compelling assent to beliefs, as well as the means by which we come to know moral law. So convinced was Aquinas that our natural reasoning abilities could demonstrate the truths of faith that he offered five demonstrations of God's existence, each beginning with evident knowledge of the material world and employing the principle of causality to conclude that God must exist.

Summa Theologica

St. Thomas Aquinas

III. PRIMA VIA, THE ARGUMENT FROM CHANGE

122.   The first and most open way is presented by change or motion.   1
It is evident to our senses and certain that in the world some things are in motion.

Whatever is in motion is set in motion by another. For nothing is   2
in motion unless it be potential to that to which it is in motion; whereas a thing sets in motion inasmuch as it is actual, because to set in motion is naught else than to bring a thing from potentiality to actuality, and from potentiality a subject cannot be brought except by a being that is actual; actually hot makes potentially hot become actu-

St. Thomas Aquinas. *Summa Theologica*. In *Philosophical Texts*. Edited and translated by Thomas Gilby. London: Oxford University Press, 1951.

ally hot, as when fire changes and alters wood. Now for the same thing to be simultaneously and identically actual and potential is not possible, though it is possible under different respects; what is actually hot cannot simultaneously be potentially hot, though it may be potentially cold. It is impossible, therefore, for a thing both to exert and to suffer motion in the same respect and according to the same motion.

If that which sets in motion is itself in motion then it also must be   3
set in motion by another, and that in its turn by another again. But here we cannot proceed to infinity, otherwise there would be no first mover, and consequently no other mover, seeing that subsequent movers do not initiate motion unless they be moved by a former mover, as stick by hand.

Therefore we are bound to arrive at the first mover set in motion   4
by no other, and this everyone understands to be God.

Jewish Philosophy

Although the philosophy of the Middle Ages is often construed in terms of the history of the development of Christian theology, the fact is that there was a lively ongoing exchange of ideas between all three of the major "Western" religions, Judaism, Islam, and Christianity, especially in southern and eastern Europe and Asia Minor (Spain, Iran, and Iraq). In the Middle Ages, in particular, there was a rich tradition of thought that moved between Muslim and Jewish authors (see Chapters 4 and 5), and in late medieval philosophy there was a confluence of ideas between Christians and Jews. Jewish philosophy goes back many thousands of years, of course, to the Old Testament prophets and the most ancient texts of the Bible. The ancient philosopher Philo of Alexandria (fl. 20 B.C.–50 C.E.) attempted to couple the Jewish tradition with Greek philosophy, interpreting a Platonic conception of the *logos*, for example, as an accessible intermediary between God and his people.

What distinguished Jewish philosophy in the philosophical conversation of which they were always a part was the more or less continuous effort to interpret and remain faithful to the old traditions (cabala) and laws. As Jews became more assimilated into society, Jewish philosophy became less distinguishable as a phenomenon in its own right. When the Jews passed through periods of persecution and prejudice, Jewish philosophy would become more distinctive. Moses Maimonides (1135–1204) wrote his *Guide to the Perplexed* in the context of a rich exchange between Christians, Muslims, and Jews. Spinoza (1632–1677) wrote his epic *Ethics* in the wake of Descartes and modern philosophy, although Spinoza's other works more clearly display their medieval origins. Moses Mendelssohn (1729–1786) would contribute to ongoing debates in Germany in the (increasingly anti-Semitic) eighteenth century, and Martin Buber (1878–1965) would become one of the best-known existentialists in this century. For the most part, however, Jewish philosophers are participants in the ongoing debates of their times, and in Western philosophy today, the best-known Jewish philosophers are simply—philosophers.

The Reformation

Two centuries after Aquinas, Western Christianity split apart. The Reformation began with a number of specific protests against Catholic doctrine but ended up by dividing Europe. Martin Luther (1483–1546), a German monk, began the Protestant Reformation when he posted his ninety-five theses dissenting from Catholic doctrine on the door of Wittenberg's castle church in 1517. Luther was appalled by the common practice of giving money to the clergy in order to gain an "indulgence," which was believed to expiate punishment for already committed sins. Luther thought that the whole institution of indulgences rested on a faulty understanding of salvation. He denied that any action performed by a human being could earn that person salvation. Salvation stems from God's grace, according to Luther, not from our own efforts.

In articulating his doctrines, Luther made use of a distinction that had become fundamental in Western philosophy. Luther distinguished between the realm of the body, or the Flesh, and that of the soul, or Spirit. Human beings had a twofold nature, being both flesh and spirit; and these two aspects of our nature were always in conflict. Luther's emphasis on faith led him to emphasize the limitations of reason. He believed that reason could point to the idea that God must exist, but it could not show us what God was like. Luther distinguished between natural reason, which was an adequate instrument for dealing with human affairs on earth; presumptuous reason, which falsely purports to arbitrate truth in religious matters; and regenerate reason, which uses disciplined thought in understanding the word of God. Thus, reason could play a positive role in spiritual life, but only if it was kept properly subordinate to faith.

The Reformation had considerable influence on philosophy, especially in ethics. Kant's moral thought, for instance, was premised on the Lutheran notion that moral merit is a function of the inner person, not of external behavior; his influential moral theory claims that intention alone is the criterion of the moral value of an action. More generally, the Reformation also weakened respect for dogmatic authority and encouraged what would become the new emphasis on autonomy. In this respect, it paved the way for later critics of the philosophical tradition in the nineteenth and twentieth centuries.

MODERN PHILOSOPHY

Modern Western philosophy, like ancient Greek philosophy, begins with the rise in science. It is not that there had been no scientific thinking during the thousand years preceding the Renaissance in the thirteenth century, of course, but science had been clearly secondary and subservient to theology, and all theories of nature had to justify themselves in the court of religion. In the sixteenth century, Copernicus began to persuade a great many people that the earth was not the center of the universe, and a century later Galileo was censored by the church for advancing this teaching. (The church finally acknowledged that he was right—in 1992!) By the sixteenth century, however, science was in full swing and confrontations between the new science and the old theology became regular occurrences. Modern Western philosophy, accordingly, is in part the story of this confrontation and the ultimate emergence of science as the new court of appeal, in which now religion would have to defend itself (an exercise that sometimes goes by the name apologetics).

Descartes

The father of modern Western philosophy, appropriately, is a man who was born and raised into the Scholastic Jesuit tradition on the one hand and an accomplished scientist and mathematician on the other. His name was René Descartes, and the basic moves of his philosophy have defined much if not most philosophy ever since. His most important single move is one that we today take almost for granted, although against the background of the authority of the church it is radical indeed. It is his emphasis on the importance of intellectual autonomy, our ability to think for ourselves. His philosophy, accordingly, begins with the demand that each of us prove for ourselves the truth of what we believe. To this end, he invents a radical method, the method of doubt, in which he considers all of his beliefs suspicious until proven justified. Descartes's demonstration of these basic truths begins with his use of the mathematical method, the method of deduction, in which every principle must be derived, or "deduced," from prior principles which have already been established on the basis of other principles, or premises. Ultimately, all principles must be so derived from a fundamental set of definitions and axioms, that is, principles that simply spell out the meanings of the terms employed or are so obviously true that they are "self-evident." The key to Descartes's grand deduction, then, will be some axiom which will serve as a premise which is "self-evident," which cannot be doubted at all. That axiom, it turns out, is his famous claim, "I think, therefore I am."

The following excerpts are taken from Descartes's *Meditations* and his *Discourse on Method.*

Meditations on First Philosophy

René Descartes

MEDITATIONS ON FIRST PHILOSOPHY IN WHICH THE EXISTENCE OF GOD AND THE DISTINCTION OF THE SOUL FROM THE BODY ARE DEMONSTRATED

Meditation One: Concerning Those Things That Can Be Called into Doubt

Several years have now passed since I first realized how many were   1
the false opinions that in my youth I took to be true, and thus how doubtful were all the things that I subsequently built upon these opinions. From the time I became aware of this, I realized that for once I

René Descartes. *Discourse on Method and Meditations on First Philosophy.* Translated by Donald A. Cress. Indianapolis: Hackett Publishing Company, 1980.

had to raze everything in my life, down to the very bottom, so as to begin again from the first foundations, if I wanted to establish anything firm and lasting in the sciences. But the task seemed so enormous that I waited for a point in my life that was so ripe that no more suitable a time for laying hold of these disciplines would come to pass. For this reason, I have delayed so long that I would be at fault were I to waste on deliberation the time that is left for action. Therefore, now that I have freed my mind from all cares, and I have secured for myself some leisurely and carefree time, I withdraw in solitude. I will, in short, apply myself earnestly and openly to the general destruction of my former opinions.

Yet to this end it will not be necessary that I show that all my opinions are false, which perhaps I could never accomplish anyway. But because reason now persuades me that I should withhold my assent no less carefully from things which are not plainly certain and indubitable than I would to what is patently false, it will be sufficient justification for rejecting them all, if I find a reason for doubting even the least of them. Nor therefore need one survey each opinion one after the other, a task of endless proportion. Rather—because undermining the foundations will cause whatever has been built upon them to fall down of its own accord—I will at once attack those principles which supported everything that I once believed.

Whatever I had admitted until now as most true I took in either from the senses or through the senses; however, I noticed that they sometimes deceived me. And it is a mark of prudence never to trust wholly in those things which have once deceived us.

But perhaps, although the senses sometimes deceive us when it is a question of very small and distant things, still there are many other matters which one certainly cannot doubt, although they are derived from the very same senses: that I am sitting here before the fireplace wearing my dressing gown, that I feel this sheet of paper in my hands, and so on. But how could one deny that these hands and that my whole body exist? Unless perhaps I should compare myself to insane people whose brains are so impaired by a stubborn vapor from a black bile that they continually insist that they are kings when they are in utter poverty, or that they are wearing purple robes when they are naked, or that they have a head made of clay, or that they are gourds, or that they are made of glass. But they are all demented, and I would appear no less demented if I were to take their conduct as a model for myself.

All of this would be well and good, were I not a man who is 5
accustomed to sleeping at night, and to undergoing in my sleep the
very same things—or now and then even less likely ones—as do these
insane people when they are awake. How often has my evening
slumber persuaded me of such customary things as these: that I am
here, clothed in my dressing gown, seated at the fireplace, when in
fact I am lying undressed between the blankets! But right now I certainly am gazing upon this piece of paper with eyes wide awake. This
head which I am moving is not heavy with sleep. I extend this hand
consciously and deliberately and I feel it. These things would not be
so distinct for one who is asleep. But this all seems as if I do not recall
having been deceived by similar thoughts on other occasions in my
dreams. As I consider these cases more intently, I see so plainly that
there are no definite signs to distinguish being awake from being
asleep that I am quite astonished, and this astonishment almost con-
vinces me that I am sleeping.

Let us say, then, for the sake of argument, that we are sleeping and 6
that such particulars as these are not true: that we open our eyes,
move our heads, extend our hands. Perhaps we do not even have
these hands, or any such body at all. Nevertheless, it really must be
admitted that things seen in sleep are, as it were, like painted images,
which could have been produced only in the likeness of true things.
Therefore at least these general things (eyes, head, hands, the whole
body) are not imaginary things, but are true and exist. For indeed
when painters wish to represent sirens and satyrs by means of bizarre
and unusual forms, they surely cannot ascribe utterly new natures to
these creatures. Rather, they simply intermingle the members of various animals. And even if they concoct something so utterly novel that
its likes have never been seen before (being utterly fictitious and
false), certainly at the very minimum the colors from which the
painters compose the thing ought to be true. . . .

All the same, a certain opinion of long standing has been fixed in my 7
mind, namely that there exists a God who is able to do anything and
by whom I, such as I am, have been created. How do I know that he
did not bring it about that there be no earth at all, no heavens, no
extended thing, no figure, no size, no place, and yet all these things
should seem to me to exist precisely as they appear to do now?
Moreover—as I judge that others sometimes make mistakes in matters
that they believe they know most perfectly—how do I know that I am

not deceived every time I add two and three or count the sides of a square or perform an even simpler operation, if such can be imagined? But perhaps God has not willed that I be thus deceived, for it is said that he is supremely good. Nonetheless, if it were repugnant to his goodness that he should have created me such that I be deceived all the time, it would seem, from this same consideration, to be foreign to him to permit me to be deceived occasionally. But we cannot make this last assertion.

Perhaps there are some who would rather deny such a powerful 8 God, than believe that all other matters are uncertain. Let us not put these people off just yet; rather, let us grant that everything said here about God is fictitious. Now they suppose that I came to be what I am either by fate or by chance or by a continuous series of events or by some other way. But because being deceived and being mistaken seem to be imperfections, the less powerful they take the author of my being to be, the more probable it will be that I would be so imperfect as to be deceived perpetually. I have nothing to say in response to these arguments. At length I am forced to admit that there is nothing, among the things I once believed to be true, which it is not permissible to doubt—not for reasons of frivolity or a lack of forethought, but because of valid and considered arguments. Thus I must carefully withhold assent no less from these things than from the patently false, if I wish to find anything certain.

Discourse on Method
RENÉ DESCARTES

I do not know whether I ought to tell you about the first meditations I 1 made there; for they were so metaphysical and so out of the ordinary, that perhaps they would not be to everyone's liking. Nevertheless, so that one might be able to judge whether the foundations I have laid are sufficiently firm, I am in some sense forced to speak. For a long time I have noticed that in moral matters one must sometimes follow

René Descartes. *Discourse on Method and Meditations on First Philosophy.* Translated by Donald A. Cress. Indianapolis: Hackett Publishing Company, 1980.

opinions that one knows are quite uncertain, just as if they were indubitable, as has been said above; but since I desired to attend only to the search for truth, I thought it necessary that I do exactly the opposite, and that I reject as absolutely false everything in which I could imagine the least doubt, so as to see whether, after this process, anything in my set of beliefs remains that is entirely indubitable. Thus, since our senses sometimes deceive us, I decided to suppose that nothing was exactly as our senses would have us imagine. And since there are men who err in reasoning, even in the simplest matters in geometry, and commit paralogisms, judging that I was just as prone to err as the next man, I rejected as false all the reasonings that I had previously taken for demonstrations. And finally, taking into account the fact that the same thoughts we have when we are awake can also come to us when we are asleep, without any of the latter thoughts being true, I resolved to pretend that everything that had ever entered my mind was no more true than the illusions of my dreams. But immediately afterward I noticed that, during the time I wanted thus to think that everything was false, it was necessary that I, who thought thus, be something. And noticing that this truth—*I think, therefore I am*—was so firm and so certain that the most extravagant suppositions of the sceptics were unable to shake it, I judged that I could accept it without scruple as the first principle of the philosophy I was seeking.

Then, examining with attention what I was, and seeing that I   2 could pretend that I had no body and that there was no world nor any place where I was, but that I could not pretend, on that account, that I did not exist; and that, on the contrary, from the very fact that I thought about doubting the truth of other things, it followed very evidently and very certainly that I existed. On the other hand, had I simply stopped thinking, even if all the rest of what I have ever imagined were true, I would have no reason to believe that I existed, from this I knew that I was a substance the whole essence or nature of which was merely to think, and which, in order to exist, needed no place and depended on no material thing. Thus this "I," that is, a soul through which I am what I am, is entirely distinct from the body, and is even easier to know than the body, and even if there were no body, the soul would not cease to be all that it is.

After this, I considered in a general way what is needed for a   3 proposition to be true and certain; for since I had just found a proposition that I knew was true, I thought I ought also know in what this certitude consists. And having noticed that there is nothing in all of this—*I think, therefore I am*—that assures me that I am uttering the truth, except that I see very clearly that, in order to think one must exist, I judged that I could take as a general rule that the things we conceive very clearly and very distinctly are all true, but that there remains some difficulty in properly discerning which are the ones that we distinctly conceive.

Empiricism

In England, John Locke reacted critically to Descartes's uncritical confidence in reason; he suggested that instead of abstract reason and speculation, we should place our confidence in experience, in our ability to learn and know about the world through our senses. As he writes in his "Essay Concerning Human Understanding,"

> The knowledge of our own being we have by intuition. The existence of God, reason clearly makes known to us. The knowledge of the existence of any other thing we can have only by sensation. . . . For the having the idea of anything in our mind, no more proves the existence of that thing, than the picture of a man evidences his being in the world, or the visions of a dream make thereby a true history.

Locke's "empiricism" (from the Greek word for "experience") is soon taken up by the Scotch philosopher David Hume.

Hume was an enthusiastic and thoroughgoing empiricist, and he was also one of the great defenders of the Enlightenment, a bold new confidence in the powers of human reason. But Hume brought empiricism and the new emphasis on autonomy to a terrifying conclusion, an uncompromising scepticism. Hume turned what began as a celebration of the powers of human reason into a demonstration (using reason, of course) that reason was incapable of providing even the most rudimentary justification for the most obvious principles of common sense and science, such as the very existence of the "external" world. In morals, too, Hume defended the shocking thesis that, quite against the rule of reason in ethics, "reason is and ought to be the slave of the passions." Thus the Western rational tradition finds itself in an odd situation, to say the least: unwilling to give up its insistence on autonomy and the powers of reason and yet incapable of defending itself in the most basic terms.

Treatise of Human Nature

David Hume

All reasonings may be divided into two kinds, namely, demonstrative   1
reasoning, or that concerning relations of ideas, and moral reasoning,
or that concerning matter of fact and existence. That there are no
demonstrative arguments in the case seems evident; since it implies
no contradiction that the course of nature may change, and that an
object, seemingly like those which we have experienced, may be
attended with different or contrary effects. May I not clearly and distinctly conceive that a body, falling from the clouds, and which, in all
other respects, resembles snow, has yet the taste of salt or feeling of
fire? Is there any more intelligible proposition than to affirm, that all
the trees will flourish in December and January, and decay in May
and June? Now whatever is intelligible, and can be distinctly conceived, implies no contradiction, and can never be proved false by
any demonstrative argument or abstract reasoning *a priori.*

If we be, therefore, engaged by arguments to put trust in past   2
experience, and make it the standard of our future judgement, these
arguments must be probable only, or such as regard matter of fact and
real existence, according to the division above mentioned. But that
there is no argument of this kind, must appear, if our explication of
that species of reasoning be admitted as solid and satisfactory. We
have said that all arguments concerning existence are founded on the
relation of cause and effect; that our knowledge of that relation is
derived entirely from experience; and that all our experimental conclusions proceed upon the supposition that the future will be conformable to the past. To endeavour, therefore, the proof of this last
supposition by probable arguments, or arguments regarding existence,
must be evidently going in a circle, and taking that for granted, which
is the very point in question.

Rationalism

It was this intolerable conclusion that awakened one of the greatest
philosophers of modern times "from his dogmatic slumbers." This
was Immanuel Kant (1724–1804), who answered Hume's skepticism
and all of modern philosophy by denying that ancient underlying

distinction between appearance and reality and, with it, the underlying idea that our knowledge of the true world was somehow
inferred from experience or discovered by way of reason. What Kant
suggested, in a phrase, was the idea that we "constitute" reality
through certain necessary (a priori) principles. Thus it is not a question of access to a transcendent reality but a matter of recognition of
our own transcendental role in knowing. And in ethics, too, Kant
suggests that there are a priori principles, which he calls "categorical imperatives," which dictate the duties of morality just as surely
as the human mind dictates the necessary laws of knowledge.

Prolegomena to Any Future Metaphysics That Will Be Able to Come Forward as Science

IMMANUEL KANT

I openly confess that my remembering David Hume was the very   1
thing which many years ago first interrupted my dogmatic slumber
and gave my investigations in the field of speculative philosophy a
quite new direction. I was far from following him in the conclusions
to which he arrived by considering, not the whole of his problem, but
a part, which by itself can give us no information. If we start from a
well-founded, but undeveloped, thought which another has
bequeathed to us, we may well hope by continued reflection to
advance further than the acute man to whom we owe the first spark of
light.

So I tried first whether Hume's objection could not be put into a   2
general form, and soon found that the concept of the connection of
cause and effect was by no means the only concept by which the
understanding thinks the connection of things *a priori,* but rather that
metaphysics consists altogether of such concepts. I sought to ascertain
their number; and when I had satisfactorily succeeded in this by starting from a single principle, I proceeded to the deduction of these con-

Immanuel Kant. *Prolegomena to Any Future Metaphysics That Will Be Able to Come Forward as Science.* Translated by James W. Ellington. Indianapolis: Hackett Publishing Company, 1977.

cepts, which I was now certain were not derived from experience, as
Hume had tried, but sprang from the pure understanding. This deduction (which seemed impossible to my acute predecessor and had
never even occurred to any one else, though no one had hesitated to
use the concepts without investigating the basis of their objective
validity) was the most difficult task ever undertaken in the service of
metaphysics; and the worst was that metaphysics, such as it then
existed, could not assist me in the least because this deduction alone
can render metaphysics possible. But as soon as I had succeeded in
solving Hume's problem, not merely in a particular case, but with
respect to the whole faculty of pure reason, I could proceed safely,
though slowly, to determine the whole sphere of pure reason completely and from universal principles, in its boundaries as well as in its
contents. This was required for metaphysics in order to construct its
system according to a sure plan.

Grounding for the Metaphysics of Morals

Immanuel Kant

There is no possibility of thinking of anything at all in the world, or   1
even out of it, which can be regarded as good without qualification,
except a *good will*. Intelligence, wit, judgment, and whatever talents
of the mind one might want to name are doubtless in many respects
good and desirable, as are such qualities of temperament as courage,
resolution, perseverance. But they can also become extremely bad
and harmful if the will, which is to make use of these gifts of nature
and which in its special constitution is called character, is not good.
The same holds with gifts of fortune; power, riches, honor, even
health, and that complete well-being and contentment with one's
condition which is called happiness make for pride and often hereby
even arrogance, unless there is a good will to correct their influence
on the mind and herewith also to rectify the whole principle of action
and make it universally conformable to its end. The sight of a being
who is not graced by any touch of a pure and good will but who yet

Immanual Kant. *Grounding for the Metaphysics of Morals.* Translated by James W.
Ellington. Indianapolis: Hackett Publishing Company, 1981.

enjoys an uninterrupted prosperity can never delight a rational and impartial spectator. Thus a good will seems to constitute the indispensable condition of being even worthy of happiness. . . .

The categorical imperative would be one which represented an action as objectively necessary in itself, without reference to another end. 2

Every practical law represents a possible action as good and hence as necessary for a subject who is practically determinable by reason; therefore all imperatives are formulas for determining an action which is necessary according to the principle of a will that is good in some way. Now if the action would be good merely as a means to something else, so is the imperative hypothetical. But if the action is represented as good in itself, and hence as necessary in a will which of itself conforms to reason as the principle of the will, then the imperative is categorical. 3

Social Philosophy, Hobbes, and Rousseau

Along with its fascination with the possibility of knowledge, modern philosophy in the West has also indicated an obsession with the nature of society and, accordingly, human nature. This concern has emerged in a two-part myth, which can be traced back to ancient times. The first part of the myth is an attempt to discover what people are really like, before their "socialization" and prior to their membership in society. It is often called "the state of nature." (Perhaps the primary version of this thesis is the account of the Fall in Genesis and the Biblical account of human nature as essentially sinful, prideful, and disobedient.) The second part of the myth is the origin of society itself, and the dominant theory of this origin rests on the idea that society exists and governments are legitimate only because of mutual agreement, or what is called "the social contract." This two-part myth was defended by Locke and after him by Hume and Kant. But before was a particularly fascinating philosopher named Thomas Hobbes (1588–1679). Hobbes surmised that the state of nature was a "war of all against all," and our lives, accordingly, were "nasty, brutish, and short."

Recognizing the high price of our brutal and unbridled competition, we banded together to form a society, agreeing, in effect, to surrender much of our power to hurt one another and hand it over to a sovereign, who would thenceforth keep us in check. Society, in other words, is a compromise, a "social contract" in which we sacrifice a dubious and dangerous freedom for the benefits of security and cooperation.

Leviathan

Thomas Hobbes

Nature hath made men so equal, in the faculties of body, and mind; as that though there be found one man sometimes manifestly stronger in body, or of quicker mind than another; yet when all is reckoned together, the difference between man, and man, is not so considerable, as that one man can thereupon claim to himself any benefit, to which another may not pretend, as well as he. For as to the strength of body, the weakest has strength enough to kill the strongest, either by secret machination, or by confederacy with others, that are in the same danger with himself. . . .   1

For such is the nature of men, that howsoever they may acknowledge many others to be more witty, or more eloquent, or more learned; yet they will hardly believe there be many so wise as themselves: For they see their own wit at hand, and other men's at a distance. But this proveth rather that men are in that point equal, than unequal. For there is not ordinarily a greater sign of the equal distribution of any thing, than that every man is contented with his share. . . .   2

Hereby it is manifest, that during the time men live without a common power to keep them all in awe, they are in that condition which is called war; and such a war, as is of every man, against every man. For WAR, consisteth not in battle only, or the act of fighting; but in a tract of time, wherein the will to contend by battle is sufficiently known. . . .   3

And consequently it is a precept, or general rule of reason, *that every man, ought to endeavour peace, as far as he has hope of obtaining it; and when he cannot obtain it, that he may seek, and use, all helps, and advantages of war.* . . .   4

From this fundamental law of nature, by which men are commanded to endeavour peace, is derived this second law; *that a man*   5

Thomas Hobbes. *Leviathan.* In *Classics of Moral and Political Theory.* Edited by Michael L. Morgan. Indianapolis: Hackett Publishing Company, 1992.

be willing, when others are so too, as farforth, as for peace, and defence of himself he shall think it necessary, to lay down this right to all things; and be contented with so much liberty against other men, as he would allow other men against himself. For as long as every man holdeth this right, of doing any thing he liketh; so long are all men in the condition of war. But if other men will not lay down their right, as well as he; then there is no reason for any one, to divest himself of his: for that were to expose himself to prey, (which no man is bound to) rather than to dispose himself to peace. This is that law of the Gospel; *whatsoever you require that others should do to you, that do ye to them.*

Rousseau, in his early essays, challenged the alleged benefits of "civilization" and defended life in the state of nature as quite pleasant, much to the shock of self-satisfied Europe. In such books as *Emile* and *The Social Contract* he elaborated his theory of human nature as "basically good" and his conception of human society in which we do not so much band together out of mutual security (as Hobbes had suggested) as we come together to realize our "higher" rational natures, as "citizen" and as participants in "the General Will" of society. Happy as it might have been, the state of nature was no place to cultivate and exercise the human virtues. In society we can do so, but without necessarily sacrificing the blessings of the state of nature. In the ideal society, as in the state of nature, we remain free and independent, for we impose the law on ourselves. Thus the central Western ideal of individual autonomy is rendered compatible with the problematic question of the legitimacy of the state, and the ideal of the natural goodness of humanity replaces the age-old notion of "original" human sin.

On the Social Contract

JEAN-JACQUES ROUSSEAU

Man is born free, and everywhere he is in chains. He who believes himself the master of others does not escape being more of a slave

Jean-Jacques Rousseau. *On the Social Contract.* In *The Basic Political Writings.* Translated by Donald A. Cress. Indianapolis: Hackett Publishing Company, 1987.

than they. How did this change take place? I have no idea. What can render it legitimate? I believe I can answer this question.

Were I to consider only force and the effect that flows from it, I   2
would say that so long as a people is constrained to obey and does obey, it does well. As soon as it can shake off the yoke and does shake it off, it does even better. For by recovering its liberty by means of the same right that stole it, either the populace is justified in getting it back or else those who took it away were not justified in their actions. But the social order is a sacred right which serves as a foundation for all other rights. Nevertheless, this right does not come from nature. It is therefore founded upon convention. . . .

OF THE FIRST SOCIETIES

The most ancient of all societies and the only natural one, is that of   3
the family. Even so children remain bound to their father only so long as they need him to take care of them. As soon as the need ceases, the natural bond is dissolved. Once the children are freed from the obedience they owed the father and their father is freed from the care he owed his children, all return equally to independence. If they continue to remain united, this no longer takes place naturally but voluntarily, and the family maintains itself only by means of convention.

This common liberty is one consequence of the nature of man. Its   4
first law is to see to his maintenance; its first concerns are those he owes himself; and, as soon as he reaches the age of reason, since he alone is the judge of the proper means of taking care of himself, he thereby becomes his own master. . . .

ON THE SOCIAL COMPACT

I suppose that men have reached the point where obstacles that are   5
harmful to their maintenance in the state of nature gain the upper hand by their resistance to the forces that each individual can bring to bear to maintain himself in that state. Such being the case, that original state cannot subsist any longer, and the human race would perish if it did not alter its mode of existence.

For since men cannot engender new forces, but merely unite and   6
direct existing ones, they have no other means of maintaining them-

selves but to form by aggregation a sum of forces that could gain the upper hand over the resistance, so that their forces are directed by means of a single moving power and made to act in concert.

This sum of forces cannot come into being without the coopera- 7
tion of many. But since each man's force and liberty are the primary instruments of his maintenance, how is he going to engage them without hurting himself and without neglecting the care that he owes himself?

Thus, in order for the social compact to avoid being an empty formu- 8
la, it tacitly entails the commitment—which alone can give force to the others—that whoever refuses to obey the general will will be forced to do so by the entire body. This means merely that he will be forced to be free. For this is the sort of condition that, by giving each citizen to the homeland, guarantees him against all personal dependence—a condition that produces the skill and the performance of the political machine, and which alone bestows legitimacy upon civil commitments. Without it such commitments would be absurd, tyrannical and subject to the worst abuses.

THE NINETEENTH AND TWENTIETH CENTURIES

G. W. F. Hegel (1770–1831) was a follower of Kant and a "German idealist," who added a dimension to the enterprise of philosophy, namely, its history. To be sure, other philosophers had generously or critically referred to their predecessors, but the idea of a true history of philosophy, that is, the idea of philosophy as a progression—as progress—that was an exciting idea whose time had come. Hegel's main idea was that there is a "worldspirit" which was about to come to full self-realization, and as humanity was about to enter into this new era, philosophy too was about to achieve its final goal, an all-embracing comprehension which would include a breakdown of the old appearance-reality distinction. Thus Hegel introduces, on the basis of a Kantian foundation, the radical conception of a "spirit" that encompasses all of us, all nations and all of nature too. It was, in some ways, a self-conscious return to the most speculative mythology of the ancient Greeks, before philosophy, but it was also an attempt to deny the various distinctions and warring camps that had defined philosophy for the past two and a half millennia. All such distinctions must be seen in the larger context of world spirit, as local scuffles and disagreements rather than as definitive contrasts. Thus secularism and monotheism, science and spirit, reason and passion, individual and community—all find their place, as concepts that may be useful in certain contexts and may conflict in certain instructive ways. This conflict and resolution, this movement from more simplistic to more complex and all-encompassing ideas, is called "dialectic." Hegel's philosophy is sometimes stated in the arrogant language of "the absolute," but it is in fact a sort of grand philosophical humility, the awareness that we are all part of a dialectic much greater than ourselves, and our individual contributions to knowledge and the truth can never be definitive but will always be partial and one-sided.

The Phenomenology of Spirit
G. W. F. HEGEL

Now, because it has only phenomenal knowledge for its object, this   1
exposition seems not to be Science, free and self-moving in its own peculiar shape; yet from this standpoint it can be regarded as the path of the natural consciousness which presses forward to true knowledge; or as the way of the Soul which journeys through the series of its own configurations as though they were the stations appointed for it by its own nature, so that it may purify itself for the life of the Spirit, and achieve finally, through a completed experience of itself, the awareness of what it really is in itself.

Natural consciousness will show itself to be only the Notion of   2
knowledge, or in other words, not to be real knowledge. But since it directly takes itself to be real knowledge, this path has a negative significance for it, and what is in fact the realization of the Notion, counts for it rather as the loss of its own self; for it does lose its truth on this path. The road can therefore be regarded as the pathway of *doubt,* or more precisely as the way of despair. For what happens on it is not what is ordinarily understood when the word "doubt" is used:

G. W. F. Hegel. *The Phenomenology of Spirit.* Translated by A. N. Miller. Oxford: Oxford University Press, 1977.

shilly-shallying about this or that presumed truth, followed by a return to that truth again, after the doubt has been appropriately dispelled— so that at the end of the process the matter is taken to be what it was in the first place. On the contrary, this path is the conscious insight into the untruth of phenomenal knowledge, for which the supreme reality is what is in truth only the unrealized Notion. Therefore this thoroughgoing scepticism is also not the scepticism with which an earnest zeal for truth and Science fancies it has prepared and equipped itself in their service: the *resolve,* in Science, not to give oneself over to the thoughts of others, upon mere authority, but to examine everything for oneself and follow only one's own conviction, or better still, to produce everything oneself, and accept only one's own deed as what is true.

The series of configurations which consciousness goes through   3 along this road is, in reality, the detailed history of the *education* of consciousness itself to the standpoint of Science. That zealous resolve represents this education simplistically as something directly over and done with in the making of the resolution, but the way of the Soul is the actual fulfilment of the resolution, in contrast to the untruth of that view.

The necessary progression and interconnection of the forms of the   4 unreal consciousness will by itself bring to pass the *completion* of the series. To make this more intelligible, it may be remarked, in a pre- liminary and general way, that the exposition of the untrue conscious- ness in its untruth is not a merely *negative* procedure. The natural consciousness itself normally takes this one-sided view of it; and a knowledge which makes this one-sidedness its very essence is itself one of the patterns of incomplete consciousness which occurs on the road itself, and will manifest itself in due course. . . . The result is con- ceived as it is in truth, namely, as a *determinate* negation, a new form has thereby immediately arisen, and in the negation the transition is made through which the progress through the complete series of forms comes about of itself.

After Hegel's death in 1831, his philosophy provided inspiration for a new generation of politically rebellious students, who saw in Hegel's "dialectic" a way of understanding history and political conflict. The most famous of these was Karl Marx (1818–1883), who converted Hegel's dialectic of ideas into a theory about the power of economics. In place of worldspirit were the forces of production, and in place of competing ideas there were competing socioeconomic classes. History has always consisted of class conflict, the haves against the have-nots, Marx tells us, from the masters and slaves of the ancient world and the manor lords and their serfs of feudal times to the entrepreneurs and their workers, the proletariat, in the modern industrial age. But just as Hegel had shown how a way of thinking or a way of life can fail because of its own internal contradictions, Marx argues that the capitalist way of life, which pits a few wealthy industrialists against a mass of exploited subsistence workers, will collapse of its own internal contradictions. Ideally, Marx predicts, this will finally result in a classless society, in which work and its rewards will be equitably shared, no one will be exploited, and no one will suffer the deprivations of poverty. Marx's utopian vision would become one of the most powerful ideologies in the world, even surviving the worldwide collapse of communism in the 1990s.

Although Hegel had pervasive influence on the generation that succeeded him, he was not universally admired. Søren Kierkegaard (1813–1855), a Danish theologian and philosopher, rejected Hegel's philosophy because it analyzed history as progressing toward an increasingly rational condition and because it emphasized the universal dimension of human experience over individual experience. Kierkegaard saw these emphases as harmful to religious faith.

A Lutheran, Kierkegaard believed that religion was essentially a matter of the inner human being. He was convinced that Hegel's emphasis on world historical events reinforced his contemporaries' tendency to attend to external practices, such as attending church on Sunday, while ignoring their inner life. But genuine religion, according to Kierkegaard, is a matter of passionate inwardness and commitment to a faith that transcends reason. While Hegel sees humanity's primary purpose as a collective progress toward a fully rational understanding and appropriation of reality, Kierkegaard sees humanity's ultimate purpose as the individual's "leap" beyond rational categories to faith and a dynamic, personal relationship with God.

Toward the end of the nineteenth century, the German philosopher Friedrich Nietzsche (1844–1900) completed what might be seen as a long progression of attempts to gain access to a transcendent world by denying, in the most vituperative terms, the very idea of such a world, a reality behind the appearances, a world that is other than—better than—this one. Nietzsche's attacks on the "otherworldly" had their most obvious target in the Judeo-Christian tradition, with the idea of an all-powerful benign deity behind the scenes, but his indictment reaches back to Plato ("Christianity is Platonism for the masses") and encompasses just about the entire Western tradition in philosophy. He rejected the very idea of "truth," insisting that what is important is only the usefulness of our beliefs and the quality of the lives we live with them, and he resisted the very notion of "morality," insisting that many if not most of the prohibitions of Judeo-Christian (and Kantian) ethics were in fact "leveling" devices intended to protect the weak and mediocre and put the talented and stronger spirits in society at a disadvantage. The following excerpt is from Nietzsche's mock-Biblical epic, *Thus Spoke Zarathustra*.

Thus Spoke Zarathustra

FRIEDRICH NIETZSCHE

ZARATHUSTRA'S PROLOGUE

1

When Zarathustra was thirty years old he left his home and the lake of   1
his home and went into the mountains. Here he enjoyed his spirit and his solitude, and for ten years did not tire of it. But at last a change came over his heart, and one morning he rose with the dawn, stepped before the sun, and spoke to it thus:

"You great star, what would your happiness be had you not those   2
for whom you shine?

"For ten years you have climbed to my cave: you would have   3
tired of your light and of the journey had it not been for me and my eagle and my serpent.

"But we waited for you every morning, took your overflow from   4
you, and blessed you for it.

"Behold, I am weary of my wisdom, like a bee that has gathered   5
too much honey; I need hands outstretched to receive it.

Friedrich Nietzsche. *Thus Spoke Zarathustra*. In *The Portable Nietzsche*. Translated and edited by Walter Kaufmann. New York: Viking, 1968.

"I would give away and distribute, until the wise among men find 6
joy once again in their folly, and the poor in their riches.

"For that I must descend to the depths, as you do in the evening 7
when you go behind the sea and still bring light to the underworld,
you overrich star.

"Like you, I must *go under*—go down, as is said by man, to whom 8
I want to descend.

"So bless me then, you quiet eye that can look even upon an all- 9
too-great happiness without envy!

"Bless the cup that wants to overflow, that the water may flow 10
from it golden and carry everywhere the reflection of your delight.

"Behold, this cup wants to become empty again, and Zarathustra 11
wants to become man again."

Thus Zarathustra began to go under. 12

2

Zarathustra descended alone from the mountains, encountering no 13
one. But when he came into the forest, all at once there stood before
him an old man who had left his holy cottage to look for roots in the
woods. And thus spoke the old man to Zarathustra:

"No stranger to me is this wanderer: many years ago he passed 14
this way. Zarathustra he was called, but he has changed. At that time
you carried your ashes to the mountains; would you now carry your
fire into the valleys? Do you not fear to be punished as an arsonist?

"Yes, I recognize Zarathustra. His eyes are pure, and around his 15
mouth there hides no disgust. Does he not walk like a dancer?

"Zarathustra has changed, Zarathustra has become a child, 16
Zarathustra is an awakened one; what do you now want among the
sleepers? You lived in your solitude as in the sea, and the sea carried
you. Alas, would you now climb ashore? Alas, would you again drag
your own body?"

Zarathustra answered: "I love man." 17

"Why," asked the saint, "did I go into the forest and the desert? 18
Was it not because I loved man all-too-much? Now I love God; man
I love not. Man is for me too imperfect a thing. Love of man would kill
me."

Zarathustra answered: "Did I speak of love? I bring men a gift." 19

"Give them nothing!" said the saint. "Rather, take part of their 20
load and help them to bear it—that will be best for them, if only it
does you good! And if you want to give them something, give no
more than alms, and let them beg for that!"

"No," answered Zarathustra. "I give no alms. For that I am not   21
poor enough."

The saint laughed at Zarathustra and spoke thus: "Then see to it   22
that they accept your treasures. They are suspicious of hermits and do
not believe that we come with gifts. Our steps sound too lonely
through the streets. And what if at night, in their beds, they hear a man
walk by long before the sun has risen—they probably ask themselves,
Where is the thief going?

"Do not go to man. Stay in the forest! Go rather even to the ani-   23
mals! Why do you not want to be as I am—a bear among bears, a bird
among birds?"

"And what is the saint doing in the forest?" asked Zarathustra.   24

The saint answered: "I make songs and sing them; and when I   25
make songs, I laugh, cry, and hum: thus I praise God. With singing,
crying, laughing, and humming, I praise the god who is my god. But
what do you bring us as a gift?"

When Zarathustra had heard these words he bade the saint   26
farewell and said: "What could I have to give you? But let me go
quickly lest I take something from you!" And thus they separated, the
old one and the man, laughing as two boys laugh.

But when Zarathustra was alone he spoke thus to his heart: 27
"Could it be possible? This old saint in the forest has not yet heard
anything of this, that *God is dead!*"

With Nietzsche, we enter into the tumultuous twentieth century,
where the philosophy becomes alternatively as arrogant and confused as that century itself, with two world wars, the global conflict
between communism and capitalism, the explosion of nationalism,
the proliferation of both deadly and life-saving technologies. In the
United States, the philosophy of *pragmatism* attempts to elaborate
the new world "experience" through the philosophies of William
James and John Dewey, but it never succeeds in making an impact
in the already established philosophical world of Europe.
(Philosophically, the United States has long been a Third World
country, identifying too wholeheartedly with British and European
thinkers but rarely contributing anything radically new of its own.)
Meanwhile, both empiricism and rationalism make new appearances as Anglo-American philosophy becomes obsessed with
questions of logic and language, so-called analytic philosophy.
European philosophy, meanwhile, struggles to come to grips with
two terrible wars and the Holocaust. Early in the century, European

philosophers were inspired by a new version of Cartesian philosophy, formulated by Edmund Husserl and called phenomenology. Following its Cartesian predecessor, phenomenology took as its object of study "the essential structures of consciousness." One of Husserl's students, Martin Heidegger, turned phenomenology toward the study of human existence, and, with its entry into France just before World War II, phenomenology became existentialism in the hands of Jean-Paul Sartre. Existentialism brings to a head the heavy emphasis on individualism, individual rights, and individual freedom and responsibility that has been developing in Western philosophy since the Greeks. Writing within the existentialist movement, Simone de Beauvoir analyzed the status of women, which nineteenth-century feminists had earlier deplored in existential terms. Beauvoir suggested that women's identities were shaped to gravitate toward subordinate roles, thereby launching feminist theory as a new dimension in Western philosophy. As the century comes to a close and individualism threatens to divide philosophy and politics even more, a postmodern movement now talks about the fragmentation of the West and its philosophical claims and ambitions. But with this, there is now also room for a renewed appreciation for the wisdom of other peoples who had so far been left out of account. That is where we are now, and what will follow, what philosophy is and will be, is a question that is as open as our minds can be.

FURTHER READINGS

REGINALD E. ALLEN, ed. *Greek Philosophy: Thales to Aristotle.* New York: The Free Press, 1966.

LEWIS WHITE BECK, ed. *Eighteenth-Century Philosophy.* New York: The Free Press, 1966.

FREDERICK COPELSTON. *The History of Philosophy,* 9 vols., rev. ed. Westminster, Md.: The Newman Press, 1946–1974.

BRIAN P. COPENHAVER. *Renaissance Philosophy.* New York: Oxford University Press, 1992.

PATRICK GARDINER, ed. *Nineteenth-Century Philosophy: Hegel to Nietzsche.* New York: The Free Press, 1969.

G. H. R. PARKINSON and S. G. SHANKER, eds. *Routledge History of Philosophy,* 10 vols. London: Routledge, 1993f.

RICHARD H. POPKIN, ed. *The Philosophy of the Sixteenth and Seventeenth Centuries.* New York: The Free Press, 1966.

Jason L. Saunders, ed. *Greek and Roman Philosophy after Aristotle.* New York: The Free Press, 1966.

John Skorupski. *English-Language Philosophy, 1750 to 1945.* New York: Oxford University Press, 1993.

Robert C. Solomon. *Continental Philosophy since 1750: The Rise and Fall of the Self.* New York: Oxford University Press, 1988.

Morris Weitz, ed. *Twentieth-Century Philosophy: The Analytic Tradition.* New York: The Free Press, 1966.

Father Allan B. Wolter, ed. *Medieval Philosophy: St. Augustine to Ockham.* New York: The Free Press, 1969.

R. S. Woolhouse. *The Empiricists.* New York: Oxford University Press, 1988.

STUDY QUESTIONS

1. Do you recognize any characteristics that seem applicable to the Western philosophical tradition as a whole? How would you compare these to characteristics of other philosophical traditions?

2. Do you notice any similarities between any of the figures discussed in this chapter and any considered in other chapters? If so, what are these similarities? How do the figures differ?

3. What relationship does religion have to the various stages of Western philosophical thought? What relationship does science have to these stages? Do you notice any correlations? How do these relationships compare to those of religion and science in connection with other philosophical traditions?

A Note on the Contributors

Roger Ames is professor of philosophy at the University of Hawaii in Honolulu, editor of the journal *Philosophy East and West*, translator of *Sun Tzu, The Art of Warfare*, author of *The Art of Rulership*, and coauthor, with David Hall, of *Thinking Through Confucius*.

J. Baird Callicott and **Thomas W. Overholt** are both professors of philosophy at the University of Wisconsin at Stevens Point and the authors of *Clothed-in-Fur and Other Tales*.

David Hall is professor of philosophy at the University of Texas at El Paso, coauthor, with Roger Ames, of *Thinking Through Confucius*, and the author of a novel, *The Diasporian Eye*.

Kathleen M. Higgins is associate professor of philosophy at the University of Texas at Austin and the author of *Nietzsche's Zarathustra* and *The Music of Our Lives*.

Janet McCracken is assistant professor of philosophy at Lake Forest College and the author of a study of Persian philosophy.

Eric L. Ormsby is a professor at McGill University, a member of the Institute of Islamic Studies and director of the McClennen Library in Montreal, and the author of several books on Arabic and Islamic philosophy.

Graham Parkes is professor of philosophy at the University of Hawaii in Honolulu and the author of *Nietzsche and the Asian Tradition*.

Steven Phillips is associate professor of philosophy at the University of Texas at Austin, an internationally known Sanskrit scholar, and the author of *Aurobindo*.

Homayoon Sepasi-Tehrani is in the graduate program at St. John's College at Annapolis, Maryland, and is the author of a study of Persian philosophy.

Robert C. Solomon is Quincy Lee Centennial Professor of Philosophy at the University of Texas at Austin and the author of many books and textbooks in philosophy, including *From Rationalism to Existentialism, The Passions, Up the University* (with Jon Solomon), and *Morality and the Good Life* (also published by McGraw-Hill).

Jacqueline Trimier has recently completed her studies as a Marshall Scholar at the University of Warwick. She is currently teaching for the British Overseas Development Administration in Nguru, Nigeria. She is the author of a study of "authenticity" in African philosophy.

Jorge Valadez is an assistant professor of philosophy at Marquette University and the author of a study of pre-Columbian and modern philosophy in Latin America.

Index

344